DATE DUE			

American Sociology

AMERICAN SOCIOLOGY

**Worldly Rejections of Religion
and Their Directions**

**ARTHUR J. VIDICH AND
STANFORD M. LYMAN**

Yale University Press
New Haven and London

Designed by Nancy Ovedovitz and set in Baskerville type by The Composing Room of Michigan, Inc. Printed in the United States of America by Book-Crafters, Inc., Chelsea, Michigan.

Library of Congress Cataloging in Publication Data

Vidich, Arthur J.
  American sociology.
  Bibliography: p.
  Includes index.
  1. Sociology, Christian—United States. I. Lyman, Stanford M.
II. Title.
BR517.V47 1985   301'.0973   84-2268
ISBN 0–300–03037–1 (cloth)
ISBN 0–300–04041–5 (pbk.)

The paper in this book meets the guidelines for permanence and durability of the Committee on Production Guidelines for Book Longevity of the Council on Library Resources.

10   9   8   7   6   5   4   3   2

"Let the dead poets make way for others. Then we might even come to see that it is our veneration for what has already been created . . . that petrifies us. . . ." Mad Artaud carried the anxiety of influence into a region where influence and its counter-movement, misprision, could not be distinguished. If late-comer poets are to avoid following him there, they need to know that the dead poets will not consent to make way for others. But it is more important that new poets possess a richer knowing. The precursors flood us, and our imaginations can die by drowning in them, but no imaginative life is possible if such inundation is wholly evaded.

—Bloom, 1973, 154

CONTENTS

PREFACE

From the beginning social thought in the United States had its roots in Christian religion, especially Protestantism. The emergence of secular social thought out of Protestant theology may thus be regarded as a transmission of religious values into civil society. Protestant thought fosters a secular attitude toward the world—in Weber's terms, it is inner-worldly rather than other-worldly. It is guided by a mission—that of establishing the Kingdom of God on earth. Nearly all of the major proponents of American sociological thought have hoped that sociology would contribute to forming a better world, even a utopia. Frequently they thought of their science as an instrument that would help carry forward the Christian religious promise.

This book is neither a history nor an exegesis but is concerned with establishing the links between the religious roots of nineteenth-century thought and the central concepts of contemporary American sociology. Its subtitle, "Worldly Rejections of Religion and Their Directions," points to the intellectual and moral problems that the social sciences confront when their concepts are transvalued from religious into secular terms.

We analyze the religious underpinnings of the ideas of Henry Hughes, Lester F. Ward, William Graham Sumner, Edward Cummings, Albion W. Small, Thomas Nixon Carver, Franklin H. Giddings, E. A. Ross, Frederick J. Teggart, Robert E. Park, William F. Ogburn, Luther Lee Bernard, George A. Lundberg, Talcott Parsons, George Homans, Herbert Blumer, Robert Merton, and Erving Goffman. The theories and problems addressed by these thinkers, spanning more than a hundred years, embrace American social thought before it came to be located in universities. Accordingly, we focus on the preacademic sociologists—Henry Hughes and Lester F. Ward—and on the institutions of higher learning from which sociology was disseminated—Yale, Harvard, Columbia, the University of Chicago, the University of Wisconsin, Stanford University, and the University of California at Berkeley. Our major purpose is to provide contemporary sociology with an understanding of that part of its religious past that continues to affect its intellectual perspectives.

It is impossible to isolate the ideas of American sociologists from those of American philosophers and selected European social scientists. In the nineteenth and early twentieth centuries, the social sciences were not specialized in their present form; sociology, psychology, political science, anthropology, and economics had not been separated from philosophy and were not professionalized. Earlier students of society did not confine their perspective within a single discipline: they attempted to comprehend society as a whole. In carrying out our analysis, therefore, we found it necessary to consider the works of Josiah Royce, William James, George Herbert Mead, Francis G. Peabody, Louis Agassiz, Richard Clarke Cabot, Hugo Munsterberg, Joseph Le Conte, Thorstein Veblen, Richard T. Ely, John R. Commons, Selig Perlman, John B. Watson, Frank Taussig and such European thinkers as Comte, Marx, Weber, Simmel, Durkheim, Le Bon, and Tarde.

We believe that sociologists cannot return to the proper study of society unless they understand the philosophical and historical origins of their own past. A science that forgets its past cannot learn the wisdom of precursors and suffers the hubris of vanity.

Daria Cverna-Martin has collaborated with us in all stages of our research and writing. Her administrative and editorial contributions were vital.

We wish to thank Michael W. Hughey and Joseph Bensman for criticisms, comments, and editorial suggestions. Hughey, our former student, read the manuscript in several drafts and helped us to sharpen the analysis at a number of critical points. Bensman read earlier drafts and made helpful suggestions for revision and reorganization. Herbert Hill's critical reading led us to reassess our materials on the relation of labor problems to American sociology. Marvin B. Scott helped us to clarify our presentation of social psychology.

While we were completing the final draft, Jack Davis introduced us to the work of M. H. Abrams as presented in *Natural Supernaturalism* (1971). Abrams's analysis of the Romantic poetry of Milton, Wordsworth, Blake, and Keats and of the philosophies of Hegel, Marx, and Nietzsche points to the elective affinities connecting Christianity with poetry, metaphysics, and sociology.

We wish to thank the Graduate Faculty of the New School for Social Research for its generous support of this project. The Staff Seminar of the Department of Sociology at the New School for Social Research read and criticized portions of the manuscript. Wolfgang Schluchter, Guy Oakes, and Andrew Arato generously provided us with constructive criticisms and commentary. We thank them and the other participants in the seminar—Paul Cantrell, José Casanova, Jeffrey Goldfarb, Ernest Kilker, Ira L. Mandelker, Ahmad Sadri, and Mahmoud Sadri—for their reactions.

We gratefully acknowledge the research assistance of Gary Biester, Ann Bowler, Tony Carnes, Cecil Greek, Brian Hamilton, Harry Hunkele, Kathy Keller, Gary Kriss, Derrick Norman, Reuben Norman, Linnea

Osth, and Philip Yanowitch, and the work-study program at the New School for Social Research, which made possible their participation on this project.

Ronald T. Takaki provided Stanford M. Lyman with microfilm copies of the *Diary of Henry Hughes* and newspaper accounts of Hughes's antebellum lectures. Two unpublished dissertations—"Reconciling Industrial Conflict and Democracy: The Pittsburgh Survey and the Growth of Social Research in the United States," by Steven R. Cohen, and "Sociology in America: A Study of Its Institutional Development Until 1900," by J. Graham Morgan—were kindly loaned to us by their authors. Herbert Blumer aided us in gathering some of his difficult-to-acquire papers that originally appeared in European and Latin American publications.

We wish to thank Gladys Topkis, senior editor at Yale University Press, for editorial advice and for the care and attention she gave to the final production of our book, and Anne Lunt for the depth of understanding that she brought to copyediting our manuscript.

Mary Rudolph Vidich facilitated our project with generosity, understanding, and endless patience.

Portions of the argument have appeared in different form in Stanford M. Lyman and Arthur J. Vidich, "Prodigious Fathers, Prodigal Sons," *Qualitative Sociology* 2 (January 1980): 99–112; Arthur J. Vidich and Stanford M. Lyman, "Secular Evangelism at the University of Wisconsin," *Social Research* 49 (Winter 1983): 1047–72; Stanford M. Lyman, "The Rise and Decline of the Functionalist Positivist Paradigm: A Chapter in the History of American Sociology," *Hyoron Shakaikagaku* [Social Science Review] *of Doshisha University* 30 (March 1982): 4–19; Stanford M. Lyman, "Interactionism and the Study of Race Relations at the Macrosociological Level: The Contributions of Herbert Blumer," Tenth World Congress of Sociology, Mexico City, August 1982; Stanford M. Lyman, "De la Ciudad Sociologia Urbana," *I Cursos de Verano en San Sebastian*, San Sebastian, Spain, 24 August 1982; and Arthur J. Vidich, "Estado Actual de la Sociologia Norteamericana," Fourth Colombian National Congress of Sociology, Cali, August 1982.

New York, 1985   Arthur J. Vidich
                                                         Stanford M. Lyman

POSITIVISM AND PROTESTANTISM IN AMERICAN SOCIOLOGY

The Puritanism reconstituted as the Social Gospel in New England, New York, and Chicago and the antebellum southern Presbyterian theism that survived the Civil War provided images of a society that would be guided on its path to redemption by social science. Because religion for them was an inspirational *resource*, the first American sociologists, unlike their counterparts in Europe, did not regard spiritual guidance or theodicy—a justification of the ways of God to man in the face of evil and misfortune— as topics for investigation. But in the early decades of the twentieth century, American sociology began to separate itself from its most visible religious orientations. Substituting sociodicy—a vindication of the ways of society to man—for the theodicy that had originally inspired them, American sociologists retained the original spirit of Protestant world salvation. They substituted a language of science for the rhetoric of religion.

From 1854, when the first works in sociology appeared in the United States, until the outbreak of World War I, sociology was a moral and intellectual response to the problems of American life and thought, institutions, and creeds. A decade before the outbreak of the Civil War, the impact of the first phase of America's industrial revolution had profoundly affected the relationship between the North and South and accented the contrast between the industrial, "free" labor system of the North and the agricultural slave order of the South. As the two sections diverged, each felt increasing pressure to find ideological justification for its own form of social order and practical solutions for its particular social problems. Both northern Puritanism, which had not yet developed a doctrinal position on the labor question, and southern Protestantism, which had persuaded itself of the theological legitimacy of slavery, were questioned and debated. The great nineteenth-century religious revival movements had addressed issues raised by the fundamental social changes in American society wrought by its industrial revolution. American Protestantism in all its variations was called upon to come to terms with new forms of social and economic inequality, with a new leadership recruited from military and business institutions, and with the shift from an agricultural to an increasingly entrepreneurial and plutocratic base.

Rapid changes in America's social structure had brought new social problems: vast numbers of unacculturated immigrants from Europe and Asia; black slaves and, after 1865, free blacks; an indigenous population of tribally organized aborigines whose lands were being steadily expropriated and whose very peoplehood was being threatened; an increasing number of poverty-stricken urban dwellers whose social needs, economic condition, cultural advancement, and political outlook had been left to the blind forces of history and laissez-faire; and a congeries of movements aiming at human emancipation through communal societies, feminism, the struggle of classes or of races, genetic controls, eugenic engineering, or the rationalization of charity, reform, or progress. Implicit in the definition of all these problems were the Protestant hope and expectation that they could be solved by secular means. The emergence of modern industry contained the promise of a heavenly kingdom on earth.

America's structural transformation was not the only source for the particular form and outlook that American sociology took. A heritage of European philosophical and historical thought, a religious doctrine stemming from the Reformation and its effects on the social and moral outlook of Europe and America, and the rising mode of discourse and investigation called science also affected the form and catalyzed the growth of the new discipline. Europe's great social transformations following the collapse of feudalism and the beginnings of modern science and industrialization inspired intellectual movements that proclaimed the possibility of a scientifically managed society. Such French social thinkers as Babeuf, St. Simon, and Comte had elaborated theories of a secularly organized utopian world. The works of Comte, who gave sociology its name, were read by many American social thinkers and influenced the formation of America's ideas of a society redeemed by religiously inspired social technocrats.

PROTESTANTISM AND COMTEANISM

A Comtean American sociology first developed outside of the academy. It proclaimed that society in general and American society in particular could be rescued from contemporary social evils; that a societal utopia could be created if only this new science were given a place of honor and authority in policy making, and put to use in social reconstruction. Comte's thought elicited a response not only from northern Protestant theologians grappling with the problems of the deepening secularization of Puritan civilization but also from southern social thinkers who hoped to preserve, expand, and improve upon the slave system.[1]

Even before Harriet Martineau's translation made it available in English, at least the main parts of Comte's work were widely discussed and debated by such leading Protestant intellectuals as William Ellery Channing, Theodore Parker, George Ripley, Orestes Brownson, James Walker, Thomas Hill, Robert Turnbull, and Joseph Henry Allen (Hawkins, 1936, 14–25). Most of these theologians were repelled by Comte's nescience, his exaltation of science in general and the "Positive Philosophy" in particular, and his proclamation of a new religion of humanity. Thomas Hill was grateful that John Stuart Mill, who had summarized Comte's *Cours* in *A System of Logic*, had not succumbed to the French philosopher's godlessness; Robert Turnbull confused positivism with materialism and, excoriating the latter, failed to perceive that Comte's work was founded on idealist principles. Joseph Henry Allen was more judicious, admiring the fact that in Comte's search for a "way to answer the whole great problem that weighs upon the mind and destiny of Europe. . . . there is an apparent good faith, a strong sense of morality, a humanity amounting at times to tenderness, a force of conviction that, though he may not be heard now, he is yet saying what men must some time . . . be inevitably compelled to accept and apply." Lamenting Comte's endorsement of a break with the theological state of mind and an absolute assertion of the Positive or scientific mentality, Allen perceived therein "what we must regard as a most unfortunate feature, if not a radical vice and fallacy, of his work." He admonished both Comte and his readers to restrict science narrowly: "In its processes, science must deal with facts strictly as if there were nothing beyond. Science and its laws merely confirm believers in their religious conceptions, in their idea of God." Allen had no quarrel with Comte's desire to discard theology as a basis for social reconstruction, however. In the United States, he believed, the Constitution had already done the same thing without undermining the people's faith.

Ultimately, meliorist northern Protestants made their peace with Comtean Positivism, rejecting its agnosticism and its secular religion of humanity but adopting its scientific outlook. They perceived the new discipline of sociology as both a social science and a source of moral regeneration and accepted Comte's view that the state, advised by Positive social physicians, might become the agency of social regeneration.

Their acceptance of Comte rested in part on the ideological affinities between the Protestant and Positivist vocations: laboring for the perfection of society. For the Protestants, especially the New England Calvinists, all callings had to serve some public good. What better good than to discover the laws of social development, laws that could then be utilized to speed progress toward the good society, the social equivalent of the Holy Commonwealth?[2] The Positivist promise of progress was thought to restate the Protestant prophecy in secular terms. The appeal of Positivism to Protestants was in its description of how ministers of the Gospel might diligently live up to the demands of their calling. Successfully adapted to Protestant doctrine, whose claim to authoritative moral guidance had been eroded by the rise of business ethics, Positivism might reinstate the legitimacy of religious authority over public affairs.[3]

In the South, Comte's system of positive polity and new social science found its first sociological expression in works that are usually regarded as apologia for slavery: Henry Hughes's *Treatise on Sociology* (1854), the first American work to use the term *sociology*, and George Fitzhugh's *Sociology for the South* (1854).[4] The American South's sociologists have been not only expunged from the record of American sociology but also denied recognition for their contributions to the basic conceptual scheme of the discipline, positivism and social systems theory. Yet Hughes's work was the first American sociological treatise elaborating the idea of society as a *social system*, and Fitzhugh provided a striking comparative analysis of the political economy of slave and free labor. George Frederick Holmes developed the first Aristotelian justification of American slavery and in the years following the Civil War turned against Comte and laid a basis for a general science of society. With the abolition of slavery, Joseph Le Conte brought his unique synthesis of Comte, Agassiz, and Darwin to the University of California, where he espoused sociology as a natural science and provided both vindication for slavery in evolutionary terms and justification for a free labor market within a racial hierarchy.

Although American positivism has some of its roots in Europe—not only in the works of St. Simon and Comte but also in the later contributions of the Vienna School—its ethos, and especially its methods and adaptation to public policy and to American business, are much more technical and antitheoretical than those of its European forebears. The positivism of American sociology owes much of its outlook to Puritan practicality and to the Puritan impulse to engineer the perfection of American society and the world. Fundamentally it reflected the idea that rational Christians could find rational solutions to social and political problems. This notion helped merge America's special variant of the Protestant ethic with technocentric positivism and the optimistic spirit inherited from the French Enlightenment.

American sociology developed its theories and techniques of research in response to the major issues of American society—slavery and the organization of labor, industrialization and its social and moral effects, race relations in an increasingly pluralized society, urban problems, social disorganization, the rise of mass society and culture, and personal anxieties. As the several strands of sociology developed their intellectual and public-spirited trajectories, represented in such universities as Harvard, Columbia, Chicago, Wisconsin, and California, they began to intertwine, despite sometimes serious disagreements over perspective, method, technique, and ultimate vision. By the third decade of the twentieth century an antimetaphysical Comteanism was combined with statistical technique to shape a specifically American positivism which, activated as social technocracy, promised to deliver America from the problems that had been addressed by the old Social Gospel and the Presbyterian theodicy. It would later make common cause with social system theory to forge a new secular social-scientific orthodoxy. It left in its wake several heterodoxies, comprised of rival schools of thought and the sociological visions of independent scholars. The rise and legitimation of that orthodoxy as well as the spirit of the heterodoxies constitute the several directions taken by modern American sociology's worldly rejections of religion.

NOTES

1. Comte's *Cours de philosophie positive* appeared in six successive volumes published in 1830, 1835, 1838, 1939, 1841, and 1842. A free translation and condensation by Harriet Martineau, published in 1853, had an immense effect on social-scientific developments in America and Europe and was eventually retranslated into French.

2. Like many other Protestant conceptions, the requirement of warrantable callings continued to have an effect on American social life in areas other than social thought—well after its religious content had faded. For a reference to warrantability in its religious context, see John Cotton, "Christian Calling," in Perry Miller, 1956, 172–82.

3. Without marking its significance for the development of the American sociological perspective, many observers of the American social sciences have noted the close affinity between sociology and Protestant ministers, particularly the tendency of ministers and ministers' sons to enter the sociological profession in the decades after the Civil War. There was another drift of ministers into the profession after World War II, when the American social system began to hold out the promise of secular salvation for the whole world. In those decades, Protestant ministers were joined by Catholic priests whose desire for secular solutions was matched by their disenchantment with the other-worldliness of Catholic theology; the Comtean revolt against Catholic theology reached America after a delay of more than 120 years.

4. Most of Comte's other American admirers opposed slavery. Harriet Martineau (1802–76) was among the most perceptive analysts and powerful opponents of slavery and racial caste in the United States. (See Martineau, [1837] 1962, 122–25, 182–237, 259–63, 355–57.) Julia Ward Howe (1819–1910), who fell under the spell of Comte's Positive philosophy after 1851, was a leading American abolitionist. (See Howe, [1899] 1969, 210–11, 307.) John William Wallace (1815–84), brother of Horace Binney Wallace (1817–52), Comte's principal disciple in America and his American benefactor (from Bernard and Bernard, [1943] 1965, 177–91), was a less forceful critic of slavery, opposing its expansion into the new states but fearful of the consequences of an immediate emancipation. (See Hawkins, 1936, 48–62.)

PART I

Religion, Inequality, and the Management of Civil Society

CHAPTER 1

Protestantism, Slavery, and the Social System: Henry Hughes

In 1854, a twenty-five-year-old lawyer from Port Gibson, Mississippi, Henry Hughes (1829–62), published the first full-length monograph employing Comte's language and system—*A Treatise on Sociology, Theoretical and Practical*. Since its rediscovery by L. L. Bernard, the twentieth-century champion of Comteanism, it has been hailed as a "fairly successful attempt at the treatment of the Sociology of Economic Relations" (Bernard, 1936a), praised as a forerunner of the social philosophy of the New Deal (H. G. and W. L. Duncan, 1937), and excoriated as an example of the vision of a "Marx of the Master Class" (Takaki, 1979, 128–36). It has not, however, been examined in relation to the development of American sociology as a discipline. Hughes's *Treatise* is, in fact, valuable for understanding the shape and direction American sociology has taken and for comprehending its penchant for combining social reconstruction with system building, for perceiving America as an already near-perfected utopia, for regarding the race question as solvable within the framework of existing social organization and ideology, and for placing a particular national or local problem in the context of a general, comprehensive theory of society.

Hughes had studied the works of Charles Fourier and John Stuart Mill, had tried to see Comte in Paris, and been deeply influenced by his *Cours*. Comte's views on slavery and race probably impressed Hughes. In 1822 Comte had pointed out: "Slavery, which is now a monstrosity, was certainly at its origin an admirable institution, designed to prevent the strong from destroying the weak, constituting an unavoidable transition in the general development of civilization."[1] On the basis of the French social scientist's approach, Hughes revised his *Treatise* into a work of theoretical and practical sociology. He followed Comte in asserting the importance of enlisting an intellectual elite of social scientists, an aristocracy engaged in societal guidance, contrasting a society so guided with one left to flounder in a free market in industry and labor. Thus Hughes placed his work squarely in the middle of the ideological conflict between North and South.

Hughes's treatise contains all the fundamental issues of modern sociology, addressed to the contrast between the two social orders then existing in the United States. Sociology was then as now poised between two poles of thought, asserting the primacy of either individual liberty or social security, either democratic government of scientifically guided management, either rule by an aristocracy of talent or compromise through a plurality of interests, either an absolute standard of justice or the chaos generated by recognizing the relativity of values.

Hughes perceived the structure of American society as organized around two opposed ideas—that of laissez-faire or "free sovereign" society and that of "warranteeism," or an "ordered sovereignty." Laissez-faire, found in the North, was characterized by liberal principles and practices, including a formally free market in labor and personal—but not societal—responsibility for subsistence and economic security. It implied no public obligation to work or to supervise in the societal interest; no caste restrictions on human association. It was indifferent toward the regulation, even the attainment, of progress. A liberal, laissez-faire, democratic, and haphazardly directed society was clearly both immoral and unscientific. "Warranteeism," in the South, found its quintessential expression in slavery—a misnomer, Hughes insisted. Warranteeism was not "an obligation to labor for the benefit of the master without the contract or consent of the servant" but rather "a public obligation of the warrantor and the warrantee, to labor and do other civil duties, for the reciprocal benefit of (1) the State, (2) the Warrantee, and (3) the Warrantor" (Hughes, 1854, 166–67). Hughes saw warranteeism as the social and political expression of a scientific sociology. The science of societary organization, invented by Comte and developed by himself, had already discovered and directed what should be the proper mode and aim of every form of human association. A model for the properly guided societal system already existed in the institutions and codes of the plantation South. A union of scientific knowledge, true concern for progress, and morally ordained societal guidance would arise when sociology was recognized as the first salutary science and warranteeism as its political, economic, and cultural praxis.

Protestant, especially Calvinist, thought also emphasizes "warrantable" callings that contribute to the public good. Southern ideologues were hard pressed to justify slavery within the framework of Christian doctrine; the role of the slavemaster could not easily be defended as warrantable. Yet if a link was made between a societal system and its function in fulfilling the work of God, then all members of society—warrantees and warrantors, slaves and masters, men and women—could be thought of as engaged in ethically warrantable callings. By his casuistic shift of the warrantable calling from an individual responsibility to a societal teleology, Hughes was able to ground his theory of the social system in both an acceptable religious and a rational scientific rhetoric.

SOCIETY AS A SOCIAL SYSTEM

Hughes's idea of a social system bears considerable resemblance to that of Talcott Parsons. For both Hughes and Parsons, the organic whole that is said to characterize society arises from the fact of human "gregation" (to use Hughes's term) but is organized as a union of subsystems (as Parsons put it) that act teleologically to accomplish societal ends. Hughes's distinction of two principal systems, the political and the economic, and five subsystems—the hygienic, the philosophic, the esthetic, the ethical, and the religious—embraces no more activity than Parsons's smaller set (Hughes, 1854, 62). Whereas for Parsons the idea of the social system has been so abstracted from reality that it is morally eviscerated, for Hughes it was a definite moral order, under a specific moral obligation. Parsons's system achieves its *telos* in the ever-renewed morally neutral state of equilibrium; whatever moral form is realized in any particular social system springs from the evolution of its founding principles. Hughes's system is closer to Comte's, combining (or confusing, as Bernard would contend in 1936) moral, purposeful, and obligatory norms with an empirically grounded science. Each of these ideas of a social system reflects the American society of its time. Parsons's system, with its specification of the rights and duties of social roles and with the elimination of individual affectivity, embodies a godless, market-oriented, bureaucratized society. Potentially immortal, it functions to perpetuate itself and achieves an ordered universe by postulation of a common set of core values. A slave system could be upheld only by force and a military caste, whereas a bureaucratic system might be upheld by administrators and intellectuals who provide meaning and motivation for the masses. It was Parsons's system that guided the large-scale organizations of government and business begun during the New Deal and continued during World War II and the Cold War. In each case, however, the thrust of the theory is to supply an architectonic for a total social order.

Society has two ultimate ends, according to Hughes: "The first end of society is the existence of all. Its second end is the progress of all" (47). Existence becomes "the subsistence of every member of society"; societal philanthropy includes an obligation to guarantee "the subsistence of every class; or a comfortable livelihood for everybody" (140). The mechanism is a state-controlled political economy, harnessing public obligation to societal progress. But such a system could function only if all were morally committed to work. Therefore, Hughes stressed the value of work as an essential part of political economy.

THE MORAL BASIS OF POLITICAL ECONOMY

Hughes's conception of political economy embraces four classes of producers: capitalists, or "mentalists"; skilled workers, or "mental-manualists"; unskilled white laborers, or "manualists"; and Negro slaves. When organized according to the scientific principles of warranteeism, these groups will function harmoniously not only for the public good but also for social progress (see H. G. and W. L. Duncan, 1937). Under the laissez-faire economy in the North, however, the producer units consisted of classes in conflict with one another, and class conflicts undermine social order and impede societal advancement. "In such a society," wrote Bernard (1936a), "unemployment, idleness, unfair wages, strikes, riots, exploitation of labor by capital, and the worst forms of want and vice are bound to prevail and persist." However, under warranteeism, the state would reorganize society so as to guide political economy toward universal productive labor, insured subsistence, and ultimate progress. The state would in turn be powered and guided by masters of rationality, and these men of reason would guide social legislation in accordance with natural law. "Such gregation is the means of existence: reason discovers and realizes it and reason prescribes or promulgates the law of Nature" (Hughes, 1854, 196). Moreover, warranteeism institutionalizes the moral and social obligations of each individual to labor according to his mental or manual talent through the enforcement power of the state. As such, it does away with that misconception of free will that justifies liberal ideology and laissez-faire social practice.

The proper form and harmony of the obligatory human association are to be assured by the powers of the state. However, since "the economic system is the organ of subsistence; the political system, the organ of security" (47), the state must be formed through the combination of these two systems. That combination will in turn coordinate the other five systems into a harmonious, progressive, federated whole.

Aside from the authority of the state, compliance is to be obtained by an ethic of labor. Hughes's peroration on the duty of work is not only one version of the "producer ethic" that swept over American thought about labor in the nineteenth century (see Saxton, 1971) but also in effect a restatement of the Calvinist ethic. However, this time it is transformed into a state-supported doctrine buttressing the "warranted" relationship that is supposed to obtain between capital and labor, master and servant, men and women, state and subject:

> Labor, whether of mind or body, is a duty. We are morally obliged to contribute to the subsistence and the progress of society. The obligation is universal. To consume, and not to produce either directly or remotely, is wrong. Idleness is a crime. It is unjust. Every class of society has its economic duty. If it does not do it; if it positively or negatively violates its duty; that is criminal. [Hughes, 1854, 95]

According to Protestant doctrine, good works included both charitable efforts and a warrantable calling. The linking of the work ethic and productivity in a slave system required some theological modifications, which Hughes introduced by universalizing in the interest of profane societal maintenance the once sacred obligation to work. In his words, "Production is a societary obligation."

One of the limitations of Calvinist theology was that it lacked a theodicy for sex, class, or racial inequalities other than to hold that the poor were dutybound to be ever faithful. Hence, the application of Puritan theodicy to American sex, class, and racial codes has been fraught with ambivalence. Hughes was the first sociological thinker to attempt to redress this deficiency by constructing a system that would distribute social rewards according to the merit and status of social tasks and their overall value to the system. In short, he invented his own variety of structural-functionalism. The arbiter of the social system was no longer God but the state.

Hughes's version of the morally ordained producer ethic is, in turn, related to a systemic understanding of political economy linking production, distribution, exchange, and consumption.

> Consumption is the immediate means of subsistence; production, the ultimate. Distribution is intermediate. The perfection of any one of these is the perfection of all. There cannot be perfect production without perfect distribution; nor perfect consumption without both. For distribution and consumption are not ends only of production; they are means of it. [119]

The perfection of production, distribution, and consumption depends upon the incentives and volitions of men, conceived as motives. As in the social system Parsons envisioned a century later, so in Hughes's human motivation must be socialized: "Unless the motives . . . are perfect, the product never can be. Men will not work without they have a good inducement. The better they are induced, the better they produce." The socialization of human motivation arises out of "ordering" human wants and interests. "Desire and fear are the springs of human action. By ordering these, men are ordered. By these they are associated, adapted, and regulated" (55). Ultimately Hughes postulated a social psychology that rested on aspirations for personal betterment, fears of downward mobility, general human affections, moral duties, and brutal coercion. Groups that were committed to the system were motivated differently from those not so committed, he thought. Thus he confronted the problem of how to deal with those elements in society that did not measure up to its postulated moral and ethical standards.

Desires, affections, and duties were of a "higher" character, Hughes believed, and their social control was preferable to the manipulation of fears. However, the "higher" elements were more likely to be found within the capitalist and "mental" and the mental-manual (i.e., skilled-labor) groups than in unskilled workers and slaves. Capitalist, "mentalist," and skilled-labor classes, industrious out of their own self-interest, can be relied upon to do their duty, but unskilled workers and slaves, whose self-interest does not coincide with social interests, cannot.

What means would society employ to train these groups to accept its moral and ethical standards? Under Calvinist Puritanism, there was always the hope that the unregenerate could still be saved if they showed signs of industriousness and efforts toward self-improvement. For the worthy poor, charity might lead to personal and social regeneration if they used it wisely, displaying thrift, industriousness, and moral purity. But the unworthy poor, who refused to accept the Holy Commonwealth's terms of participation, were cast out of the community and could be mercilessly exploited on the grounds of their moral unworthiness. For them, compulsion and motivation through fear would be required: "The fear of want or worse condition may be the implement of production" and, more concretely, "the fear of adequate punishment is a certain spring: it warrants action." Fear is a wonderful goad: "It is universal, adaptable, and regular" (90). Recalcitrant Negro slaves, Hughes proposed, might be branded "like beeves." Combining an authoritarian mechanism for social control with utilitarian motivational theory, Hughes anticipated the nonstatist and far more benevolent (though no less comprehensive) social psychologies that linked moral character to societal structure in the works of Talcott Parsons. And Hughes proposed what was in effect an experiment to test his thesis and to perfect the utopian slavocracy that warranteeism promised: a reopening of the African slave trade—forbidden since 1808 by the Constitution—and the recruitment of a new body of Negroes to be socialized according to his proposed methods of indoctrination in the ethics of production. Legally classified as "voluntary workers," these Negroes would at first be indentured, as "cotton pickers and Christians"; later, they would become ordinary slaves.[2] However, Hughes denied that the labor system of the South was or ever would be true slavery. "Property in man," he wrote, "is absurd. Men cannot be owned. In warranteeism, what is owned is the labor-obligation, not the obligee. The obligee is a man" (167–68). Slave and master are equally necessary to the system, but the participation of the slave, in contrast to that of the slavemaster, who is God's steward, is measured by work and industriousness.

Hughes's sociology of women and the family was also linked to his conception of a higher service to God, but unlike slaves, women were closer to God than their worldly masters were.[3] They were naturally "subsovereign" to men, outfitted by nature to bear and nurture children, given to greater fatness in order to be both beautiful and domesticated, and closer to God because, like Him, they were "intuitive." The alleged "marriage evil," Hughes insisted, was a product of faulty connubial relations—apathy, antipathy, infidelity—which could be remedied if marriage were founded on a proper basis. That basis is love, and love must take precedence over such infernalizing passions as lust, avarice, and ambition.

Women, Hughes argued (forgetting about the female field slaves in the South and mill workers in the North), have been given their deserved status by nature: "they have not physical power to be anything other than home folk." Women have fewer rights than duties. Their principal duty is to provide inspiration to men. The movement for "Women's Rights . . . is an unnatural condition of things; making woman mortal instead of divine, which God intended she should be." In contrast to slaves, whose subordination was justified by their obligation to work, that of women rested on their proximity to the Deity.

Hughes's romantic but religious anthroposociology allotted women an awesome but restricted place in the social system: "The love of the beautiful is a divine aspiration; wherefore it is woman's duty to render herself attractive; in doing which a Woman's Rights convention is less effective than a milliner's shop. The complexity of female nature is what ennobles her. If women were she-politicians, a nightingale should supplant the eagle in our national banner." By sharing God's divinity, women were removed from the world, leaving its management to the husband-slavemaster.[4]

TOWARD THE SECULARIZATION OF SOCIOLOGY

Hughes's political economy was founded on the sociological concept of gregarious human association; a concept similar to that of interaction or social relations that in modern sociology stresses the social impulse, complementarity, reciprocation, and exchange. But for Hughes, human association was not based on freedom but commanded by God.[5] Thus, departing from Comte's secular religion of humanity, he linked his conception of an ordered social world to God's will. His *Treatise* fore-shadowed the amalgamation of sociology, Social Gospel, and social reform that occurred in America after 1865. However, Hughes's image of the reconstruction of society went far beyond mere social reform. It rejected the contractual theory of the state and reconceived free will itself, arguing that all humans had a sacred duty to associate harmoniously for the common good.

> It is a duty or law of God. And the will is not free to do or not to do a duty. There is no choice. Duty is without alternative. Society substantially, is therefore, not from contract or agreement. The substance of society is perfunctory—every individual is under an obligation to associate for the existence and progress of himself and others. [Hughes, 1854, 176]

In Hughes's image of society, each individual has a duty to perform according to his or her status and role, and all are functionally interrelated. Society does not allow for dissociation, and all of its members contribute to the perfectibility of God's world. Hence, Hughes's concept of "duty" is strikingly similar to Parsons's, with the difference that Parsons sees duty as a social role whereas Hughes perceives it as obedience to the law of God. By the same token, where for Parsons the social system is legitimated by its inherent tendency to equilibrium, for Hughes the legitimacy of the system is located in the divine: "When these and more than these, shall be the fulfillment of Warranteeism; then shall this Federation and the World, praise the power, wisdom and goodness of a system, which may well be deemed divine; then shall Experience aid Philosophy, and VINDICATE THE WAYS OF GOD, TO MAN" (292). Choosing to speak for God and to propound a societal system that would vindicate His ways to man, Hughes attempted to formulate images of society and of the world that would be consistent with a far more "this-worldly" Protestant orientation.

The Civil War not only killed Henry Hughes, in 1862, but also put an end to his dream of a benevolent, totally institutionalized slavocracy in the United States. In 1855, Hughes and three other American Comteans—George Fitzhugh (1806–81), George Frederick Holmes (1820–97), and Stephen Pearl Andrews (1812–86)—made an unsuccessful attempt to formulate a common disciplinary perspective (see Wish [1943] 1962; 1941; 1941a; Genovese, 1969, 118–244; Hawkins, 1936, 63–142; M. B. Stern, 1968). Although Holmes, Andrews, and Fitzhugh would contribute to social science in the postwar years, their effort in fact adumbrated the death of the kind of sociology that had begun to develop in the antebellum period.

Andrews, dedicated to abolition, the preservation of individualism, and the advancement of scientifically guided cooperativism, eventually produced *The Basic Outline of Universology* (1872), a work that, not unlike Comte's *Cours*, attempted to synthesize all natural and social-scientific knowledge and advocated a "pantarchy," a benevolently directed society of mutually tolerating individuals. But his theoretical and practical science met with widespread derision and inspired only local, short-lived communal experiments (Wish, 1941a, 482).

Holmes, like his three colleagues, believed that he was living at a moment of great social stress, intellectual confusion, and moral chaos and exhorted his fellow intellectuals to develop "a more profound study of the laws and mechanisms of communities, [by means of which] we must probe the wounds of society and discover medicaments" (Holmes, 1849, 78). Convinced that Comte's religion of humanity was heretical and that Spencer's *Social Statics* was a throwback to anarchism, he also rejected all socially conscious movements aimed at abolition, women's rights, free love, Fourierism, and Proudhonism. He advocated the establishment of a scientifically viable community under the guidance of "some controlling authority extrinsic to the individual conscience of its members" (Holmes, 1857). As the author of the first college textbook in sociology (1883), he sought to produce a social science that would not depart from Christian, Aristotelian, and capitalist principles.

Fitzhugh opposed the postwar reconstruction of the South, which he regarded as a program for racial amalgamation. But by 1872 he had accommodated himself to what he perceived, with approval, as the feudal aspects of growing monopoly capitalism in America.

Except for Holmes, who held a professorship in "historical science" and literature at the University of Virginia from 1857 until his death, and Joseph Le Conte—whose work is examined in part 5—the antebellum sociologists were not academics. Since they were antagonists in the slavery controversy, their respective systems reflected a considerable bias and a contemporaneity that did not permit much further intellectual development in the postwar years. What survives of their contributions are the centrality of race and labor in American social scientific thought, the penchant for system building that they had derived from Comte, and a scientific ambivalence about, as well as a moral resource in, religion.

NOTES

1. Comte couched his views on slavery and race within his larger conception of historical development. According to Comte, the social science of societal development had to recognize that just as in biology "we can hardly imagine a completely new organism free from all incompatibilities," so in "sociology the difficulty is even greater; there the freest dreams have ever fallen short of actual changes, the most striking instance being that of slavery." His views on the hierarchy of the races and the distinctions among them were also pronounced. He was persuaded that race was first among the "chief causes of social variation," and that

the "future progress of social regeneration . . . originates in France, . . . is limited at first to the great family of Western nations," and "will afterwards extend, in accordance with definite laws, to the rest of the white race, and finally to the other two great races of man." Comte's proposed method of diachronic study, the single social series, required that the investigation be restricted to "the development of the most advanced nations" and confined to "the vanguard of the human race, . . . the greater part of the white race, or the European nations—even restricting ourselves, at least in regard to modern times, to the nations of Western Europe." He put the fundamental question—"the most important sociological inquiry that presents itself"—thus: "Why is Europe the scene, and why is the white race the agent, of the highest civilization?" (*The Positive Philosophy of Auguste Comte*, freely translated and condensed by Harriet Martineau, 1875, 2:151, 154). This question could be used both to justify slavery ideologically and to give the Christian mission a special role in ordering the fabric of society as a whole.

2. This appears to be a matter of controversy among Hughes's biographers. Takaki (1979, 178) quotes Hughes's letter to the Jackson *Semi-Weekly Mississippian* of January 12, 1858: "Some have asked what shall be done with the African negroes after their term of service has expired. It is answered that the State has the right and power to fix their status. I propose that they shall be elevated into slavery." Duncan and Duncan (1937, 245–46) assert that the Africans would have either become free wage-laborers in America or been voluntarily repatriated to Africa. They further cite Malcolm Guess (1930, 60) to the effect that the Negroes were to become "a special group whose social bounds were to be limited to those of a progressive agricultural society. While denied the right of the ballot they were to be warranted the first end of society and in time all other ends of progress."

3. Hughes's contribution to the sociology of women, marriage, and the family survives in his diary and in the newspaper reports summarizing his public lectures. In his diary Hughes recorded his growing recognition of the issue of sex, love, marriage, and the place of women in society. In February, 1852, he had begun reading Fourier's *Passions of the Human Soul,* which was to have a profound effect on him. Troubled by bouts of debilitating illness and doubts about God's love and very existence, alternatively elated and depressed by his megalomaniacal desires for power and success, Hughes recorded on March 14, 1852: "Continued reading Fourier . . . The Social Problem: Shall I solve it?" Eventually Hughes came to his own pseudoanthropological justification for supporting the continued subjugation of women, their relegation to hearth and housework, and their elevation to the pedestal: "Woman, dear, dearest woman," he wrote in his diary on January 20, 1850, "if the exertions of the loving aspirant can accomplish it, you shall be advanced towards, shall attain, your deserved dignity." Yet both his own sexual doubts and, significantly, the religiously justified challenge to monogamous marriage evoked by the new Mormonism continued to trouble him. On May 31, 1851, Hughes exclaimed, "My brother-in-law, whom I so much—so much love—for man can love man—and I will test socially the dear fact!" Eight months later, on January 11, 1852, he inquired, "What of marriage? Shall it be for life? What of polygamy? Is it sin? Can many be loved?" By June 27 of that year he reported, "I have begun to study the politics and sociology of marriage." On September 26, he put the question squarely to the new Comtean science that he would develop: "What is the province of Woman? That is the most difficult question in Sociology." Less than three months later he asked, "What of marriage civil and religious? What is best?" By January 1853 Hughes anxiously queried, "Are the women of civilization slaves? Are they dependents? Can they be independents, without the elements of courage? . . . What of fascination?" "Do we want a new Jesus?" asked Hughes in reference to the raging debate over Mormonism in May 1853. "Mormonism will succeed on account of its social organization," he predicted on May 1, but that "Mormonism is not civilization" he was sure, for "monogamy is the essence of civilization." (The foregoing is taken from the *Diary of Henry Hughes of Port Gibson, Mississippi, January 1, 1848–May 1, 1853,* the *Port Gibson Herald and Correspondent,* 11 April 1858, and the *New Orleans Delta,* 16 April 1858.)

4. The political economy of sex in the southern slave system posed a number of vexing problems for the theoreticians of that system. The most vexing was that of heterosexual relations between the races. The elevation of white women to divine status tended to make them less accessible to white men, leaving them with less sexual recourse within their own race. The establishment of this sexual distance between white men and white women enhanced the sexual value of black women for white men and black men for white women and contributed to the frequency of sexual intermixing (as evidenced by the phenotypic characteristics of blacks/whites in the United States). This, however, has rarely been officially recognized in the public life of the society. Instead, public mores and official policy recognized only blacks and whites, a kind of color blindness that can be explained only by a theory of the social determination of color perception. The sexual economy of the South was first portrayed by John Dollard in *Caste and Class in a Southern Town* (1957), in which he analyzes the structure of intercaste sexual relations and the gains and losses involved for the sexes and races.

5. Hughes confided occasional doubts about the existence of God to his diary. For a psycho-historical interpretation of Hughes, emphasizing his close paternal relations with elderly male slaves who served as father substitutes, his difficulties with women and sex, his religious doubts, his inordinate personal and political ambitions, and his "crisis of identity," see Takaki (1971, 86–102).

CHAPTER 2

A Sociological Rejection of Religion: Lester Ward

The defeat of the South in the Civil War was also a defeat for a sociology inspired by the South's agrarian philosophy and plantation social structure. American sociology would thereafter develop primarily in the North. Although northern sociologists were, like Hughes, greatly influenced by Comte, they addressed his positivist perspective to the problems arising out of an emergent capitalist, industrial order and adapted it to the secularized values of the new society—values that threatened the verities of New England Puritanism and provided a new challenge for northern Protestantism.

In sharp contrast to Hughes, as well as to his own social-scientific contemporaries, Lester Ward (1841–1913) rejected religion and accepted a nonreligious interpretation of society. Yet, ironically, Ward introduced a sociodicy and an inner-worldly eschatology into his sociology. Precisely because of his vigorously atheistic outlook, he postulated a major role for sociology in the political administration of society.

WARD'S CONFRONTATION WITH RELIGION

Ward believed he had overcome the weakness in Comte's thought—his inability to separate his science from religion—through his enunciation of "monism," or the principle of unity and continuity in all of nature (Chugerman, 1939, 244–57). Ward was not a dialectical thinker. Derived from the ideas of the ancient Greek philosophers and from Spinoza, Ward's monism insisted on *the oneness of matter and spirit.* A dedicated evolutionist, Ward opposed all contemporary religions—especially Christianity—as anachronistic obstacles to human progress. He replaced them with his own faith in man's ever-enlarging control over his own destiny through reason, knowledge, and intellect. Because of Christianity's promise of immortality in extraterrestrial spiritual bliss, "life is despised and death courted." Religious asceticism produces "a complete indifference to natural phenomena" (Ward, 1883, 2:299), encouraging inhumanity in such forms as self-inflicted humiliation, starvation, and flagellation, as well as a disinclination to relieve—or even care about—the sufferings of others. Among nineteenth-century American sociologists, Ward stood alone in his derogation of all religions as "derivative and distorted cults," opiates of the people, and barriers to progress (Stern, 1935, 171, 202, 218, 251–53, 274–76).

Comte's "religion of humanity" was distasteful to Ward, who looked to the continued advancement of knowledge to transform all religious institutions "to a new and useful purpose." "The day will come," he predicted, "when every church spire will loom up as a center of education," when religious proscriptions on the dissemination of knowledge would be overthrown and "every bit of knowledge shall be offered to all." Churches may then be called "Halls of Science" (Chugerman, 1939, 246). Education rather than religion or revolution was to save America.

Ultimately, Ward predicted, religion and ethics would disappear altogether as constraints on human conduct:

> It might easily be shown, that, just as reason, even in early man, rendered instinct unnecessary, so further intellectual development and wider knowledge and wisdom will ultimately dispense with both religion and ethics as restraints to unsafe conduct, and we may conceive of the final disappearance of all restrictive laws and of government as a controlling agency. [1903, 135]

The time for the final disappearance of religion was not yet at hand, but its retreat before the forces of intellect and science was everywhere to be seen. Science would become the basis of a new social order:

> Within the historic period, the territory once belonging to the gods, which has been contested and reclaimed by science, embraces the entire fields of astronomy, physics, chemistry, and geology. That of biology has now fairly passed out of theological supremacy, while those of moral and social phenomena are at present time the battleground between science and religion. [1883, 269]

Sociology was one terrain on which the struggle between science and religion was being fought, and Ward threw himself squarely into the battle. His championing of the scientific cause led him to exclude from sociology all those reformist and eleemosynary activities that had been inspired by the Social Gospel. He provided an inventory of what he considered to be a pseudosociology:

> It is the housing of the poor, charity work generally, slumming, reform work in the neglected quarters of cities, settlement work, etc. Sometimes it gets

beyond the tenement house and sweating system and deals with consumers' leagues and cooperative stores. It includes such municipal reforms as public baths and lavatories, and the placing of public parks, gardens, and art galleries within the reach of the less well-to-do classes. [1902, 477]

"Good works" and social activism are "not science at all, and therefore . . . cannot be sociology at all" (477–78). Nevertheless, philanthropy was to be recognized as "social work, often of a higher order, and for the most part very useful" (478). But such activities proceeded from a prescientific perspective and prescribed only a piecemeal resolution of the Social Question. Meliorism would and should supplant the well-meant but anachronistic endeavors of the religiously inspired lovers of humanity, but it would eventually be replaced by scientific praxis. Ward stated: "Applied psychology aims at the complete social transformation which will follow the assimilation of discovered truth" (1906, 85).

There can be little doubt that Ward's uncompromising opposition to religion made his work less acceptable to many American sociologists. In his day the major institutions of higher learning were denominational colleges and universities, and most sociologists were former or would-be ministers. The citadels of learning—whether trade schools, colleges, graduate centers, or state university systems—had not yet become the centers of instruction, research, and culture that we know today. Before America became an urban society and before mass religion was beamed to consumers electronically, the community church stood dominant over public life. By the middle of the twentieth century, however, sociology had created an autonomous image, and both its origins in and its confrontations with religion were all but forgotten. Religious activity had also become much more formal and narrowly restricted, largely secularized and social in its orientations. In a period of fifty-two years—let us say between the publication of Ward's *Pure Sociology* in 1903 and that of Will Herberg's *Protestant, Catholic, Jew* in 1955—sociology had become professionalized and thoroughly secularized, and religion had become an undifferentiated consumer item.

It was in Ward's work more than in that of any other sociologist that the answers formerly provided by theodicy were transformed into sociodicy. In dismissing religion as archaic and irrelevant to the modern world, he was the first American sociologist to commit himself to a completely secular vision of the world and its operations.

A self-educated man of the midwestern frontier, Ward was less committed to the values of eastern Puritanism and more receptive to the secular dimensions of Darwinian evolutionism that swept through America during his lifetime. When the certainties and comforts of a religious world view are rejected, the secular thinker has little choice but to seek comprehension and understanding on other grounds. Indeed, precisely because Ward rejected religion, he was forced to deal with the same problems and questions that would be taken for granted by a self-avowed religious thinker. In Ward's work, religious issues are transvalued into sociological problems.

WARD'S TRANSVALUATION OF THEODICY

Man's Role in Evolution and History

Like other thinkers of this era, Ward found in the new theory of evolution the solution to the problems he set for himself. But the new biology threatened to reduce man's importance in the cosmological hierarchy and to minimize his ability to control his destiny. "Progressive development," in Darwin's perspective, was produced by natural selection (Darwin n.d. a, 160).

And in species, at any rate, progressive development was synonymous with "the degree to which the parts have been specialized or differentiated; and natural selection tends towards this end, inasmuch as the parts are thus enabled to perform their functions efficiently" (160). What Ward did with such concepts as these was truly prodigious: he accepted the general principles of evolution but argued that their outcome in man was the production of mind.[1] Mind, in turn, was unique in that it was "immaterial" and an "attribute." For Ward, the phenomenon of mind, and its attendant capacity for reason, was so remarkable that it called for the constitution of a new science (which in 1894 he supposed would be psychology). And more important, it assured man's power to shape his own society. "Mind," he observed in 1894, "has wrought mighty changes in the past and is destined to work still mightier ones in the future" (207).

Ward asserted in 1892: "The history of man, if it should ever be written, would be an account of what man has done" (1892 [1906], 97). He thus seemed to agree with Marx that man makes his own history, but unlike Marx, Ward believed that scientific man could make history as he chose, unconstrained by property, class, and false consciousness. Like the Enlightenment *philosophes*, Ward believed that reason, science, and education could accomplish the task. Human or social phenomena are produced by "psychic forces": "Man is the instrument through which these forces operate, and the immediate cause of the phenomena is human action" (97). Human action, in turn, is social in character because "man has been a social being during the greater part of his history, and [because] the principal results of his activities have been brought about by some form of cooperation" (97). The new study of history thus becomes the study of the "laws and principles of such action" and belongs "to social science, or sociology," which "rests directly upon psychology, and especially upon subjective psychology" (97).

Ward refused to concede "that civilization can only be achieved through the action of the individual, unconscious of the end, doing that which will conduce to the end" (98). Like Marx, he held out hope that society would become a conscious agent able to make social improvements its first priority.

Yet, despite Ward's wholesale appropriation of what was once God's into sociology, the values underlying his worldly perspective retained a remarkable similarity to those of the Protestant ethic. Thinly disguised Protestant values continued to inform his work—hard work, intellectual practicality, rationality, individual and social uplift, self-help, full utilization of the mind, and complex standards as measures for admission into the elect. Inequalities of race, class, gender, and intelligence he regarded as barriers to the realization of the brotherhood of man, a powerful theme in Christian thought.

Among the earlier Protestant sects, regeneration not only was a religious matter but also bestowed upon the chosen the right to vote and to hold office. It meant acceptance into the community, equality of status, respectability, and civic standing. The sense of mission so characteristic of one aspect of the early sectarian view of America filtered back into Ward's sociology, which allowed for the regeneration of races, ethnics, and women within an evolutionary process that would also reconstitute the "national" community.

The missionary elements in Ward's sociology extended to a simple faith in the superiority of the institutions of Western society. He retained his faith in conjugal love and the monogamous family. For Ward, like many social scientists after him, the world could be saved if Western civilization were taken as a model for the future and used as an example for social-policy decisions in the present. His evolutionism, with its telic dimension, owes much more to Hegel than to Darwin, who regarded biological evolution as nonteleological. Ward accepted evolutionism with important reservations, especially as Darwin's open-ended theory went beyond his own postulation of progress toward sociocracy.

Ward distinguished between natural and artificial evolutionary forces. The latter were central to the drive for social amelioration since "art is the natural product of the inventive faculty, which is only a form of intuitive perception or intuitive reason, and belongs to the main trunk of the intellect." The products of the intellect are therefore artful accomplishments. Further, the "simple truth is that everything that is done at the behest of the intellectual faculty is *per se* and of necessity purely artificial in the only sense that the word has" (286). Progress, Ward insisted, should be rigidly defined: "As the only final end of human effort is human

happiness, so there can be no true progress except toward that end."
Civilization itself, however, is not synonymous with progress. "Civilization is the product of many men at work with their inventive brains, each
seeking to compel the forces of nature to do something for himself." The
fundamental problem for a praxeological sociology, Ward believed, was
"that of identifying civilization with progress, of making society at large
the beneficiary of the products of art, skill, industry, and labor" (287).

By treating mind as a product of natural evolution, Ward sought to
overcome the accusation that meliorism was merely a branch of ethical
idealism or that it had to do exclusively with morals. Problems such as
injustice and inequality, he asserted, "have nothing to do with ethics.
They are not moral questions, although upon their solution more than
upon anything else depends the moral progress of the world." They are
"purely social problems and can only be properly considered in the dry
light of science" (290).

Both Ward and Marx believed that a science of society could resolve
issues of ethics, morality, and social injustice.[2] But in contrast to Marx,
who put his faith in the proletarians who would emerge as the final actors
on the last stage of history, Ward placed his faith in knowledge and in an
intelligentsia that would directly manage society. This intelligentsia,
weighing social problems "in the dry light of science," would coordinate
and direct the progress of society. Under its guidance, civilization would
be identified with social progress.

Ward was among the first American social philosophers to assign a
central role to the university as the intellectual and cultural substitute for
the church (an idea that in Ward's day was given substance by Harvard's
Hugo Munsterberg and has more recently been revived and elaborated
by that same university's Daniel Bell [1973]). Ward also saw that societal
management would require the services of civil servants and administrators, and in this respect he anticipated the idea of the technocratic classes
later described by Thorstein Veblen ([1921] 1965), James Burnham
(1941), John Kenneth Galbraith (1958), and more recently, George
Konrád and Ivan Szelényi (1979).

THE PROBLEM OF SOCIAL INEQUALITY

Ward's rejection of all religious theodicies forced him to reopen the question of class, racial, and gender inequality in entirely new terms. For him,
all human suffering was caused either by incomplete development or by
failed application of human resources. In his studies he focused on three
human groups and the special character of their socially redeemable
suffering: the proletarianized classes; the nonwhite races; and women.
Ward's discussions of each of these groups are not always fully developed

and are scattered throughout his writings, but to him the problems they posed constituted the primary focus for the relief of human suffering and the social progress that a just society would ensure.

Class Inequalities

Ward, like Marx, envisaged a dual class system composed of an exploiting and an exploited class. "Thus far," he wrote in 1903, ". . . it has always been a special class that has been able to obtain the means . . . fully to nourish the body. That class had always been superior physically to the much larger class that has always been inadequately nourished. Adequate protection from the elements in the way of houses, clothes, and fires, tends in the same direction, while improper exposure dwarfs and deforms both body and mind" (288–89). The natural drives for food and shelter led to the social appropriation of property, but labor itself was something instilled into man only by centuries of subordination, beginning in slavery and transposing itself through much struggle into the modern situation of the industrial and leisure classes (266–80).

Equally important in the formation and maintenance of classes is the social distribution of knowledge and the opportunity to use it. Ward denied that great men were naturally entitled to eminence. "Great men . . . are the mentally endowed who have had a chance to use their talents," but there "is reason to believe that this is only a small percentage of those who possess talents" (1906, 133). Knowledge, the central ingredient for all achievement, "has to be acquired anew by every member of society" (1903, 34). However, the development of social differentiation served also to limit the acquisition and spread of knowledge and its social applications. The members of modern industrial societies are thus classifiable not only into laboring and leisurely classes but also concomitantly into the intelligent and the ignorant. "In even the most advanced societies," Ward observed, "the latter always exceed the former numerically, usually constituting at least three fourths or four fifths of the population" (1906, 91). Finally, knowledge and the opportunity to use it are the basis for the formation of the ruling classes: "The control of society is also entirely in the hands of the intelligent few, and the ignorant mass can only submit to whatever regulations their superiors choose to impose." Social inequity, then, is a problem not only of the scramble to obtain material goods but also of the acquisition, distribution, and social usages of knowledge.

Solving the problem of class inequalities depended on dissolving the intellectual stratification system. This was especially important in democratic societies because the ruling class could easily manipulate the ignorant masses. The "intelligent classes of modern society know enough of human nature to see how the uninformed class can be utilized in promoting their interests" (92–93). Kept down by the requirements of mindless labor, members of the underclass are rendered almost helpless: "Compulsory exertion in the form of excessive and protracted labor blunts and stunts all the faculties and tends to produce a more or less deformed, stiffened, and distorted race of men" (1903, 289).

Unlike the Marxists, Ward did not rely on class revolution as the solution to the Social Question. "There is too much truth in the dictum that intelligence will rule," he observed (1906, 98). Precisely because inequality "of intelligence necessarily results in the cleavage of society into an exploiting and an exploited class," Ward concluded that if "there is no way of equalizing intelligence, social reform in this direction seems out of the question." Reasserting in a secular form the Puritan commitment to the practical worth of knowledge, he committed himself to education as the ultimate solution to economic inequalities. In the older civic covenant established by the Puritans, social acceptance and civic membership had been determined by a demonstration of faith. By upgrading the intelligence of the entire population, Ward hoped to establish intelligence as a new criterion. Thus Ward changed the foundations of the original Holy Commonwealth into a secular vision of a brotherhood of the educated, replacing a covenant of faith with a covenant of knowledge.

However, Ward's covenant of knowledge, like tests of faith, later came to be used to differentiate levels of inner-worldly election. The inscrutable will of God was replaced by the IQ test and the examinations produced by the Educational Testing Service at Princeton, New Jersey. The unregenerate become those hopeless cases incapable of learning. For them, there are special communities of the retarded. Doctors and experts in "special education" minister to their minds—but not to their souls—and institutes of learning attempt to discover methods to regenerate the more fortunate among them. When all else fails, theories of socio-biological inadequacy—far more conservative than those advocated by Ward—supply new scientifically based explanations that help to sustain credence in the new sociodicy. Under this sociodicy, social differentiation is accepted within a framework of scientifically legitimated stratified intelligence.

Racial Inequality

Ambivalence about the contending scientific theories of race and the opposed policies that flowed from them permeates Ward's work. In his opinion, the very origin of races was a problematic feature of evolutionary theory. Ward conceded a capacity for high intellectual development within each race, but he was guarded about the intelligence that would be generated by racial amalgamation. Convinced that the ultimate outcome of social evolution would be a raceless, classless cosmopolis, he resolved his doubts with an optimistic assurance that racial equality was achievable.

Ward attempted to ground his sociology of race in a new theory of origins based on biology and evolution. He was aware that Darwin's monogenetic perspective had already won the day in respectable scientific circles, but his leaning toward a polyphyletic theory of race led him to postulate a pluralistic development of racial intelligence. The "true nature of the development of the advanced races" was represented by the various kinds and degrees of racial intelligence. Although Ward enunciated more than once his belief that progress occurred through the merger of cultures, he recognized that the relations between culturally distinctive races were fraught with conflict and prejudice.[3] Lamentable as such conflict was, he regarded it as inherent in the progressive evolutionary development he called *social karyokinesis*. "Thus far there has been only one way by which society has been formed, and that is through social assimilation by conquest, struggle, caste, inequality, resignation, concession, compromise, equilibration, and finally interaction, cooperation, miscegenation, coalescence, unification, consolidation, and solidarization" (1906, 215). The presence of various kinds and degrees of racial intelligence augured further developments in the process. Thus, Ward managed to link a theory of racial equality with the justification and legitimation of conquest. The expansion of Western industrial civilization, despite its more immediate negative effects, would eventually lead to equality among the world's races.

Social assimilation, which was the ultimate outcome of social karyokinesis, could be schematized in seven consecutive steps: (1) subjugation of one race by another; (2) development of caste relationships; (3) mitigation of caste, leaving a residue of individual, social, and political inequality; (4) substitution of law and the principles of legal rights for rule by force; (5) establishment of the state composed of stratified classes, each with its own distinctive rights and duties; (6) cementing of the heterogeneous elements into a more or less homogeneous people; (7) development of a sentiment of patriotism and the formation of a nation (205). "Races, states, peoples, nations are always forming, always aggressing, always clashing and clinching, and struggling for the mastery, and the long, painful, wasteful, but always fruitful gestation [that] must be renewed and repeated again and again." Ward underscored the fact that the units undergoing transformation might have different histories of culture contact. "For example, the conquering race may have resulted from a third or fourth assimilation, while the conquered race may only represent a second assimilation, and have therefore acquired an inferior degree of social efficiency" (213). In this sociodicy, mankind would eventually come together on equal terms, but this promise of racial equality would be realized only as a result of a long and bloody biohistorical process.

Ward applied his theory to such differing instances of the assimilation process as those occurring in Great Britain, Ireland, France, Germany, and Austria, as well as to the racial situation in the United States. He believed that the "inhabitants of southern, central, and western Europe, called Aryan or Indo-Germanic, . . . have led the civilization of the world ever since there were any records" (238). Every "assimilation is a fresh cross fertilization of cultures and renders the resulting social unit more and more stable and solid" (214). Since the Aryans "are and have been throughout all this time the repository of the highest culture . . . have the largest amount of social efficiency . . . have achieved the most, and . . . represent the longest uninterrupted inheritance and transmission of human achievement" (238), their amalgamation with other peoples could have a positive effect on world civilization. But though "all cultures are supposed to be assimilable . . . there are some races whose culture differs so widely from that of others that they seem to form an exception to this law" (237). In the matter of intelligence, Ward pointed out that the "assimilation of an alien civilization . . . cannot be accomplished in a single generation. . . . Indeed, nothing short of the practical absorption of a race into another during a long series of generations, during which all primitive influences and tendencies are definitively eliminated, can be expected fully to prepare such a race for a comparison of its intellectual capacities with those of civilized races" (1903, 109).

Nonwhite immigrants to America would have to demonstrate intelligence equal to that of the evolutionary front-runners. However, it was on just this issue that Ward had doubts. "What then, can be said . . . of the other races of men lying outside of this great current of culture, chiefly of a different color from the other—yellow, red, black, or some shade between these—and who have not to any marked degree received the social heritage of achievement which constitutes western civilization?" He was certain that "within each such race, for there are many, intellectual equality . . . can be safely affirmed, but the question is whether it can also be posited as between the colored races and the white races" (107). Ward criticized the sociologists—Comte, Quatrefages, and his own contemporary Franklin H. Giddings—who held that the nonwhite races were inherently inferior in intelligence or in innate ability, but he sidestepped a definitive answer in a carefully worded conclusion:

> It is not therefore proved that intellectual equality, which can be safely predicated of all classes in the white race, in the yellow race, or in the black race, each taken by itself, cannot also be predicated of all races taken together, and it is still more clear that there is no race and no class of human beings who are incapable of assimilating the social achievement of mankind and of profitably employing the social heritage. [110]

Ward's theory substitutes theology's promise of a racial utopia in the afterlife with a racial utopia to be achieved in this world, the ultimate and inevitable universal brotherhood of man. He depicts the homogeneous group that would finally emerge: "The final great united world-race will be comparable to a composite photograph in which certain strong faces dominate the group, but in which may also be detected the softening influence of faces characterized by those refining moral qualities which reflect the soul rather than the intellect" (108).

Inequalities of Sex and Gender

Ward's explanation for the unwarranted triumph of androcracy—the supremacy of males over females—is a distinctive contribution to the study of marriage and familial institutions. He unhesitatingly attempted to supply a substitute for the ideas in the sacred books and customs of Christianity about sex and gender. He began with his own version of human origins in which not God but nature and evolution played the key roles in the differentiations of gender. Ward regarded the inherent superiority of the female as a proven fact. "According to the normal processes of evolution, the female is the principal sex and constitutes the main trunk of development, she alone continuing the race" (1892, 87). Over a long period of human history, a male-dominated society had forced women either to become chattel-slave wives or to fail utterly in life, not only restricting their opportunities but actually retarding their evolutionary development.

The rise of masculine authority is a by-product of evolution's most important development—the emergence of rationality and its unequal distribution between the sexes. Borrowing from the ethnological researches of Bachhofen, McLennan, and Morgan, Ward asserted that gynaecocracy—matriarchy, mother-right, the metronymic family, amazonism—was the original form of human group association. The power of the female during this remote but long-lasting period derived from the fact that human intelligence had not yet grasped the relationship between intercourse and reproduction (340), and the natural principle of female aesthetic selection prevailed in the choice of male sex partners. "The voice of nature speaking to the male in the form of an intense appetitive interest, says to him: fecundate! the order to the male is: cross the strains! that to the female is: choose the best!" (325). The process of mate selection includes the female's "idea of male beauty" as well as "such moral qualities as courage, persistence, and powers of persuasion." Natural selection and the Lamarckean principle operated, in turn, such that males began to develop "certain mental qualities . . . especially cunning in outwitting, circumventing, and thereby overcoming rivals." Through this formulation Ward explained how the biological superiority of women had unwittingly facilitated masculine hegemony.

The male strong man who overwhelms the female by brute strength appears at a later stage of human evolution and constitutes an obstacle to equality of the sexes. It was the development of the male brain through the concomitant processes of female sexual selection that "brought about the great change, and . . . constituted man a being apart from the rest of creation." The masculine regime permitted man to exercise most power-fully "his egoistic reason, unfettered by any such sentiment as sympathy, and therefore wholly devoid of moral conceptions of any kind," and to employ his cunning and brute strength to strike down the "aegis and palladium of the female sex"—her "power of choice." This reversal had been accomplished quite early in the development of human institutional life, and thereafter "for the mother of mankind all was lost."

Precisely because female domination had rested on woman's singular role in parturition, Ward insisted, a change to male rule could occur only after man's discovery of his own role in the process of procreation. Primi-tive man at first had no idea of the relationship between mating and conception. When such an idea did emerge, it found unique expression in the *couvade,* in which a man appears to suffer the pregnancy "sickness" and thereby establishes "by a fiction the fact of paternity or joint action with the mother in bringing the child into existence" (344). The idea of fatherhood led first to man's elevation to a position of equality with the mother in authority over their children, and then—after a comparison of brute strength between the male and the female—to the exercise of a more generalized masculine power "which at that stage meant simply [his greater] physical strength." The "natural sequel" to all of this was the "patriarchate or patriarchal system, in which the man assumed complete supremacy."

The patriarchal image of the Christian God defined the religious role of women in both the Catholic and Protestant churches. Puritanism, with its conception of the relation of the individual to *his* God, left aside the relationship between the female and *her* God. The Puritan woman in America remained religiously disenfranchised. Men spoke for her to God and appropriated to themselves all official churchly roles. This religiously appropriated authority was gradually transferred to secular roles in the arts, the professions, politics, and business. By defining the relations between the sexes in secular evolutionary terms, Ward inverted religion's justification of male dominance, claiming that women had been deprived of their original role as the superior sex.

As in all of his discussions of social problems, Ward was optimistic about the future status of women. The outcome of social and sexual evolution would be the *gynandrocratic* stage "in which both man and woman shall be free to rule themselves" (377). The future heralded a new emergent form in which sexual altruism would prevail, equality would become a fact of everyday life, and—perhaps most important—women would become

economically independent. Economic emancipation would liberate wom-
en from prostitution as well as bad marriages and "could scarcely fail to
produce a profound revolution in marriage institutions" (358n). But economic equality was more in the nature of a precondition than a solution,
for ultimately each party to the sexual relationship would have to become
altruistic before equality could prevail.

Among the phylogenetic forces bringing civilization closer to gy-
nandrocracy were two branches of the instinct of "natural love"—its "romantic" and "conjugal" forms. Romantic love "is mutual," the result of
simultaneous sexual selection by a man and a woman, and finds its "most
striking characteristic . . . in the phenomenon called 'falling in love'"
(396). The most important aspect of falling in love was not a part of either
partner's intention: "When a man and a woman fall in love it means that
the man has qualities that are wanting in the woman which she covets and
wishes to transmit to her offspring, and also that the woman has qualities
not possessed by the man, but which he regards as better than his own and
desires to hand on to posterity." The effect of these unconscious desires,
"often appearing absurd or ridiculous to disinterested spectators," is to
"work in the direction of righting up the race and bringing about an ideal
mean." Linking romantic love to biological selection in effect dissolved
the covenanted community of the Holy Commonwealth which had spec-
ified the character of sex roles and replaced it by the naturally guided
social interaction of two individuals.

Ever since the end of the feudal era, Ward believed, among women of
all social ranks there had arisen a demand for "support and the comforts
of life, luxuries where possible, and more and more leisure and accom-
plishment." Women demanded "a home, social position, ease, and economic freedom." A woman selects a husband on the basis of his "industry,
thrift, virtue, honesty, and intelligence"—that is, on the basis of his possession of those virtues that are likely to satisfy her economic aspirations.
However, once possession of the loved one was consummated, Ward
asserted, the fire of passion was extinguished. Fortunately, he pointed
out, there had emerged only since the Middle Ages, and solely among
Aryans, a quite different sentiment—*conjugal love*—which, though
hedged about with difficulties and contradictions, could cement the relationship first kindled by romance. Conjugal love is inextricably connected
to monogamy, to the elevation of women above the status of chattel, and
to the establishment of the family. The attachment of the husband to his
family "is sufficiently intense to cause sustained effort, and instead of
being only an episode of a few months' or at most years' duration, it is
permanent, and continues from the date of the marriage until death to
impel to deeds, if not of glory and renown, at least of usefulness and social
value" (412). For Ward, the binding nature of the conjugal relationship,

based on an act of choice, provided the basis for stable marriages; it also heralded the eventual salvation of women as the equals of men.

Ward was convinced that his great engine of human achievement and social progress, conjugal love, was moving down the track of history toward ultimate equality in sexual and marital relations. Each conjugal relationship consisted of a renewal of the sacrament of sex, Ward seemed to suggest, and the biological authority of this sacrament was the foundation for the redemption of mankind. Social evolution of the various stages and degrees of love would lead to an ubiquitous conjugal monogamy.

SOCIOCRACY AND BUREAUCRATIC SOCIETY

Ward synthesized the idea of evolutionary progress evoked in Darwin's work with his own version of Comte's "Plan of the Scientific Operations Necessary for Reorganizing Society" (1822). The link between evolution and social advance was intelligence. Intelligence had itself evolved—here Ward broadly adapted Comte's perspective—in such a way that scientific knowledge was the highest intellectual form yet attained. Ward placed his greatest faith in scientific knowledge and looked to the science of society to solve social problems. For him, the future of society, its progress and steady improvement, lay in the evolutionary tendency toward *sociocracy*. Ward's innovative employment of nineteenth-century evolutionary theory harnessed the natural forces discovered by science to the inventive capacity of man and the social institutions he could create. The result was a "collective telesis" in which institutions—especially governments—actively engaged in the reconstruction and reorganization of society.

Ward's sociocracy envisions the translation of all social and political issues into techno-scientific problems whose solutions can be discovered by means of hypothesis, induction, experiment, and cost accounting. In the early phases, however, and for "a long time to come, social action must be chiefly negative and be confined to the removal of evils that exist." Ward anticipated a large-scale transformation of social institutions that would clear away the historically accumulated social debris, after which "a positive stage will ultimately be reached in which society will consider and adopt measures for its own advancement" (1892, 328–29). At this stage, scientists will govern society.

Bureaucratic scientism would substitute for the perennial and inefficient debates of a legislature. In a sociocracy, legislative votes would "become a merely formal way of putting the final sanction of society on decisions that have been carefully worked out in what may be called the sociological laboratory." The legislation itself would "consist in a series of exhaustive experiments on the part of true scientific sociologists and sociological inventors working on the problems of social physics from the

practical point of view." Positive scientific legislation, produced by sociologists conducting practical experiments, and passed quickly and easily
by intelligent and melioristic—and docile—legislatures, would provide
nothing less than the scientific "organization of human happiness" (1903,
338–39).

Ward's sociocracy was a product of a peculiar optimism about the capacity of applied science to overcome the problems of industrial society
and the Protestant meliorism that he himself opposed. Its authority parallels that of the colonial Puritan divines who claimed the right to guide the
earlier New England communities. This role no doubt appealed to the
first generation of American sociologists, many themselves recent occu-
pants of the pulpit, who were accustomed to believing they were right
about their interpretation of American society and the means for its
salvation. In their new status as a secular and scientific priesthood Protestant Social Gospel intellectuals could provide a new form of societal guidance for the industrial world. Ironically, Ward's atheistic sociology provided grounds for the resurrection of appropriately disguised Protestant
authority.

The grand features of Ward's melioristic sociology could not survive
the pessimism about unlimited social progress that set in after the outbreak of World War I. However, sociologists did not give up their desire
to effect social reforms through the application of social science to policy
formulation. Since Ward's day, the ideology of scientific governance has
become a mainstay of social scientific claims to participate in the formation of public policy. Indeed, the positive social scientific activity that
Ward imagined foreshadowed the proposals for governmental cooperation with and subsidy of sociology made in the 1930s and 1940s by
Lundberg, Ogburn, and others.

The positivism that followed Ward and wedded itself to government
and public subsidy, though grounded in Ward's work, lost his sense of
detachment and objectivity toward its subject matter. Ward had supposed
that "science is ill-adapted to the competitive and feverish methods and
sentiments that obtain in nearly all departments of [American] private
life." The new post-Wardian positivism accepted both the competitive
spirit and the demand for quick results that characterize government-
sponsored research, even when this necessitated reducing the scope of
the problem to be investigated. Ward had insisted that science must not be
forced into "degenerating into charlatanism" and that it "must be independent." He imagined that for an independent, honest, and unhurried
social science, "the service of the state is admirably adapted" (1906,
583–84), but he had hoped that his scientist would be exempted from the
petty politics of government and the "politics" of his own profession.
Ward projected his own disinterested scientific utopianism onto his fellow

practitioners and failed either to see or to anticipate the bureaucratization and politicization of science itself.

SOCIOLOGY AS SECULAR ESCHATOLOGY

Ward replaced God with science. The theodicies of class, race, sex, and gender could be rewritten to conform to the new secular science of society. It was assumed that the fulfillment of the promise of science would be also the fulfillment of a secular eschatology—perfectability on this planet. Unlike his contemporary and antagonist, William Graham Sumner, Ward was prepared to apply his findings to the task of reconstructing the world, remaking its politics in the image of the technocratic administrative state.

NOTES

1. Darwin seems to have reached a similar conclusion. See *Metaphysics, Materialism and the Evolution of Mind: Early Writings of Charles Darwin,* transcribed and annotated by Paul H. Barrett (1980).

2. Ward regarded a professedly serious sociologist who took sides in "current events and the popular or burning questions of the hour" as one who "abandons his science and becomes a politician." He hinted that both Spencer and Marx belonged in this category. He characterized politics as "art and not science." Political movements and ideologies are objects for study, not for a sociologist's participation. "Misarchism, anarchism and socialism are programs of political action, negative or positive, and belong to the social art. They are not scientific theories or principles and do not belong to social science." The true sociologist "observes them all, as he does all social phenomena, but they only constitute data for his science. All that he objects to is that any of these things be called sociology" (1906, 10–11).

3. Ward's "philosophy of rape" seems to justify the lynching of Negroes in the South. White women were naturally attracted to "crossing the strain" through black males; the latter sought to "improve" their own race by mating with whites; and white males exercised a proprietary interest in protecting the females of their own race by killing the black predator [1903, 1907], (1970, 359–60).

CHAPTER 3

Capitalism and Calvinism: William Graham Sumner

William Graham Sumner (1840–1910), drawing primarily on Spencer and Darwin and on the Puritan aspect of his Protestant heritage, produced a sociology that emphasized the doctrines of individualism and self-reliance. Sumner's vision of the social world bears no resemblance to that of Lester Ward or Auguste Comte.

Sumner responded selectively to the main lines of European thought in his day, but in several important ways his outlook parallels those of Darwin, Marx, and Weber. He rejected Darwin's open-ended evolutionism and developed a materialistic theory of history similar in some respects to that of Marx. He understood that social world views in the United States were undergoing a major change and, like Weber, saw the secularization of the Protestant ethic as a major turning point in world history. Sumner offered no promise of either secular or sacred redemption.

Icily dissecting the dissolution of America's once paramount Puritan ethic, Sumner analyzed social and cultural change *without* the perspective of a determining, unilinear, and inevitable evolutionary trajectory.[1] Both the character and the quality of what he called mores and folkways had shifted, in accordance with the vicissitudes of "social power," toward a culture based on the primacy of material wealth.

Emergent American capitalism had not yet developed a value system consistent with its institutional framework. "In modern times, movable capital has been immensely developed, . . . has disputed and largely defeated the social power of land property [and] . . . has become the social power" (Sumner, 1906, 162). Immense quantities of movable capital and its corollary elements—"opportunities in commerce and industry offered to men of talent, . . . immense aid of science to industry, . . . opening of new continents and the peopling of them by the poorest and worst in Europe"—undermined the old mores.

The moral duties to work and be frugal, to be thankful for God's providence but suspicious of prosperity, and to be ever on guard against the vices of extravagance, idleness, and sloth had given way by Sumner's day to what he regarded as unbridled plutocracy, conspicuous consumption, an unwarranted sense of optimism, and a widespread but misguided belief in progress.

The idea of progress "drew from millennialism its sense of the irreversible secular trend of the historical process, and from the moralism of the cyclical theory the assumption that the role of the individual in history is a purposive and creative one" (Persons, 1968, 63). Sumner's reading of history rejected such optimistic assumptions.[2] The individualism of his own era, having found its mode of expression in what he called "the cult of success," could not hold out a promise of moral or social progress:

> This deep depravation of all social interests by the elevation of success to a motive which justified itself has the character of an experiment. Amongst ourselves now, in politics, finance, and industry, we see the man-who-can-do-things elevated to a social hero whose success overrides all other considerations. Where that code is adopted it calls for arbitrary definitions, false conventions, and untruthful character. ([1906] 1940, 652)

His own attitude toward these emerging values was uncomfortably ambivalent. Although he opposed them as morally derelict and scientifically unsound, he knew that the emergence of the new values could not be halted.

> The philosophical drift in the mores of our time is towards state regulation, militarism, imperialism, towards petting and flattering the poor and laboring classes, and in favor of whatever is altruistic and humanitarian. . . . We have no grounds for confidence in these ruling tendencies of our time. [98]

This drift, Sumner lamented, suggested the unfortunate triumph of metaphysical pathos over social scientific reason. These tendencies "are only the present phases in the endless shifting of our philosophical generalizations," generalizations that were not applicable to a chaotic age in which America was struggling for some kind of societal stability and moral understanding. Instead of these, "it is only proposed, by the application of social policy [by our leaders], to subject society to another set of arbitrary interferences, like the civil war dictated by a new set of dogmatic prepossessions that would only be a continuation of old methods and errors."

According to Sumner, America's basic cultural values, more or less established before 1861, had crumbled in the aftermath of the Civil War. He believed that he was living in the final phase of a transition of a not-yet-

formulated set of custom controls. A remnant of Puritanism's more positive character had survived, finding expression in Comstock's sumptuary
laws and in the basic American temperament. The new mores would
benefit a little in their formative period from the potency remaining in
the Puritan ethos. It had already had an effect on the peoples new to
America, and indeed on world civilization:

> The mores of New England . . . still show deep traces of the Puritan temper
> and world philosophy. Perhaps nowhere else in the world can so strong an
> illustration be seen both of the persistency of the spirit of the mores and of
> their variability and adaptability. The mores of New England have extended
> to a large immigrant population and have won large control over them. They
> have also been carried to the new states by immigrants, and their perpetua-
> tion there is an often-noticed phenomenon. The extravagances in doctrine
> and behavior of the seventeenth-century Puritans have been thrown off and
> their code of morals has been shorn of its angularity, but their life policy and
> standards have become to a very large extent those of the civilized world.
> ([1906] 1940, 85–86)

It would be incorrect to attribute to Sumner a full-scale commitment to
fundamental Puritan values (see Heyl and Heyl, 1976). On the contrary,
he argued that "the mores made by an age for itself . . . are good and
right for that age, but it follows that they can suit another age only to a
very limited extent" (Sumner [1906] 1940, 94). The English Puritans of
the seventeenth century, eager to transform the mores of their era, "emigrated to uninhabited territory in order to make a society in which their
ideal mores should be realized." Having landed in New England, they
"tried to build a society on the Bible, especially the books of Moses. The
attempt was in every way a failure." Not only were the biblical prescrip-
tions "ill-adapted to the seventeenth-century facts," they also came into
conflict with those of other sectarian groups—most notably the Quakers—who had emigrated to North America for the same purpose. In New
England the Quakers, "who went to the greatest extreme in adopting
dress, language, manners, etc., which should be different from the current usages," attempted to establish "states of mind and traits of social
character which they had selected as good, and their ritual was devised to
that end (humility, simplicity, peacefulness, friendliness, truth)." As
Sumner perceived it, both the original Puritan and Quaker experiments
had already been undermined by the forces of history and social change.
Speaking in 1906 of the religious doctrines of the Quakers, he observed:
"They are now being overpowered and absorbed by the mores of the
society which surrounds them. The same is true of Shakers, Moravians,
and other sects of dissenters from the mores of the time and place" (94,
96–97). Grappling with the fundamental problem of the relationship
between ideology and social structure and the effects of social processes

upon it, Sumner was caught in a historical moment between memories and dreams: "The mores which once were are a memory. Those which anyone thinks ought to be are a dream" (78).

Sumner attempted to comprehend directly the social and historical realities of his age. In the course of his life he wrote innumerable essays responding to almost every major social issue: "The Conflict of Plutocracy and Democracy," "The Influence of Commercial Crises on Opinions about Economic Doctrines," "What the 'Social Question' Is," "The Absurd Effort to Make Over the World," "The Bequests of the Nineteenth Century to the Twentieth," "What is Free Trade?" He also developed theories of American culture, social change, ideology, history, and the role of sociology in society.

Sumner's sociology, usually regarded as exemplary of American Spencerianism (see Barnes, 1948a, 155–72), in fact transcended its period at the very moment that it interpreted the epoch. It opposed the evolutionary illusions of the age, stood apart from the drive toward professionalization, and laid the groundwork for a comparative cultural history of consciousness and conduct that has yet to be recognized for its intellectual potential. Critics have neglected the total value of Sumner's work in their attempts to relegate his legacy to that of either a conservative social Darwinist, (Hofstadter, 1955, 51–66), an uncompromising opponent of social reform (Schwendinger and Schwendinger, 1974), or a contributor of once interesting but no longer relevant concepts.[3] Few disciples or critics have recognized that he was less concerned with developing an abstract conceptualization of society than with confronting its empirical and historical reality. He examined that reality within a framework of material and ideal values bearing a remarkable resemblance to those discussed by Weber and Marx. Sumner wrote with the passion and commitment of a man who saw vast, abrupt changes that had affected both the fundamental character of civilization and his own intellectual orientation to it.

For Sumner, a period of social convulsion like that following the Civil War required a transition from one set of custom controls to another. He did not believe that such controls could be legislated—he perceived more clearly than most thinkers of his day how limited was the power of ideals in giving new directions to society. Later sociologists, by focusing on "mores and folkways" in the abstract, separated Sumner's ideas from the specific problem he had investigated and, even more unfortunately, lost sight of their specific American content.

Sumner witnessed the triumph of industrial over landed capital in a society where European feudalism had never existed, and he documented the transformation of religion's social values into secular and especially economic ideologies of plutocracy and socialism. These religious values now lacked the strength either to confront or to resist the new materialism of American business. By the same token the newer materialism had begun to shape the character of America's major social institutions.

STATE AND CIVIL SOCIETY

Sumner attempted to come to terms with the problem of a new sociodicy for America at the very moment when there were no mores upon which such a sociodicy might be built. A fixed set of mores is, according to Sumner, "the ways of doing things which are current in a society to satisfy human needs and desires, together with the faiths, notions, codes, and standards of well living which inhere in those ways, having a genetic connection with them" ([1906] 1940, 59). Such mores, he observed, are never far removed from naked or veiled force, which has played a major part in their institutionalization. Although coercive force might be "screened by different devices," it "is always present, and brutal, cruel force has entered largely into the development of all our mores, even those which we think most noble and excellent" (65). Although the mores of the North and South had "become similar and the sectional dislike has disappeared" since the end of the Civil War (111), there remained what Sumner regarded as "the great problem of societal organization" (266)— how the mutual service of one part of mankind to another might be organized properly. For Sumner ([1890] 1969, 1:435–41) the modern "social question"—that is, the inherent conflicts of interest between socioeconomic groups in the "higher forms of civilization"—had for five hundred years turned on the antagonism of classes. The current class struggle, he believed, is over the question of "whether some one class is getting its share of the fruits of the common victory" ([1890] 1969, 1:438) over feudalism. Unlike Marx, however, Sumner did not believe that the class struggle could ultimately be resolved through a proletarian victory. And certainly he had no faith in a final utopian solution; for him the struggle was never ending.

However, Sumner explained, the form of the modern class struggle is dictated by the emancipation of men from ascriptively based associations and, more significantly, by the emancipation and increase in capital. "If there had not been an immense enhancement of luxury, culture, and power, the classes and the masses would never have come into antagonisms. . ." ([1890] 1969, 1:439) But the demands of the dispossessed elements are at least partly false; if "it were true that a part of those who have won the social and industrial victories had been deprived of their share in the fruits thereof, then they would have no hope of compelling any attention to their complaints, for they would have no force at their disposal." ([1890] 1969, 1:439) Capital, as a powerful social force, was now available to labor as a weapon in its own struggle against capitalists.

Democracy . . . sets the power of numbers against the power of "money," but democracy, the power of the masses, is the greatest proof of the power of capital, for democracy cannot exist in any society unless the physical conditions of social power are present there in abundance, and in such general distribution, that all the mass of the population is maintained up to the level below which they cannot perform the operations which democracy assumes that they can and will perform. ([1890] 1969, 1:440)

The current state of capitalist development is both the cause and the condition of social unrest, Sumner noted; it "maintains a number of men on a level where they can struggle to get all the material welfare which the labor market really holds for them, and where they can be democrats and win both full civil rights and a share, perhaps a predominant share, in political power." ([1890] 1969, 1:440)

Public welfare or other political solutions to problems of social and economic inequality could never be an adequate substitute for the eroded Puritan theodicy, Sumner believed. He rejected sentiment or "do-good-ism" as the foundation for a new moral community. Recovery from the collapse of Puritan values and the world they had sustained could be accomplished only by the emergence of new mores and folkways within the framework of competitive struggles between labor and capital, the classes and other interest groups. Yet, espousing the Puritan value of individualism—every man and woman in a personal relationship with God—Sumner denied that the state could act as a surrogate for upholding the utopian ideal of a Kingdom of Heaven on earth.

Sumner's championship of laissez-faire was based on his distrust of political power and governmental institutions and his certainty about the primacy of capital as a social and political force.

It is impossible to stir a step in any direction which has been selected without capital: we cannot subsist men, i.e., laborers, without it; we cannot sustain study or science without it; we cannot recruit the wasted energies of the race without it; we cannot win leisure for deliberation without it; we cannot, therefore, undertake greater tasks, that is, make progress, without it. ([1890] 1969, 1:435)

Sumner regarded government as either inadequate or utterly corrupt. He placed little faith in the efficacy or consequences of such legislation as antitrust laws and regulation of interstate commerce. More significant, he feared the growth of government itself. However, he did not claim that laissez-faire allowed "the unrestrained action of nature" nor did he oppose all forms of rational control or institutional guidance.

The wartime collapse of customs and values had produced a moral chaos that extended into the postwar period and threatened the legitimacy of government itself. At first Sumner thought that the Civil War had strengthened the fundamental ethics that had originally inspired the

Founding Fathers: "The rights of conscience, the equality of all men before the law, the separation of church and state, religious toleration, freedom of speech and of the press, [and] popular election, are vital traditions of the American people . . . [that] are not brought in question; they form the stock of firm and universal convictions on which our national life is based." (1969, 1:89–90) Within the next quarter-century, however, the failure of Reconstruction, deteriorating relations between the races,[4] revelations of vast corruption in the federal government, the aggressive imperialism embarked upon in the 1890s, and the panaceas proposed by both the new men of power and the advocates of social reform gradually convinced him that the nation was mired in cultural and political chaos.

"So long as a nation has not lost faith in itself it is possible for it to remodel its institutions," Sumner wrote in 1887. (1969, 2:143) But it was precisely such a loss of faith—a breakdown of its once cherished customs, beliefs, and values—that had occurred in the United States. In the Spanish-American War a once noble dream of an isolated, parsimonious, democratic republic had become a nightmare of misguided patriotism by people who felt "that the United States never was a great nation until in a petty months' campaign it knocked to pieces a poor, decrepit, bankrupt old state like Spain" ([1899] 1969, 2:303). Imperialism, as well as federal regulation, indicated that the American government had become a cockpit for contending private interests and did not serve any useful public purpose. Sumner found numerous examples in the policy wrangles of regulatory agencies: "The interstate commerce law was thought to be a great gain when it was passed. It was planned to satisfy certain views and to override and destroy certain usages. The assailed interests defended themselves and sought escape" ([1933] 1969, 1:215). But his general point was that while the "great social organization all the time tends to promote a great political organization" (1969, 2:331), the "forces of discord and divergent interest" tend to paralyze action and promote corruption.

> Can the state find anywhere power to repel all the special interests and keep uppermost the one general interest or the welfare of all? Will the state itself degenerate into the instrument of an attack on property, and will it cripple wealth-making or will the wealth-making interests, threatened by the state, rise up to master it, corrupt it, and use it? This is . . . the antagonism of democracy and plutocracy. [(1933) 1969, 1:215]

Sumner saw democracy as threatened by the new, powerful political interests, including those of plutocrats, professional politicians, and government bureaucrats. Prior to the Civil War, the "United States, starting on a new continent, with full chance to select the old-world traditions which they would adopt, [had] become the representatives and champions in modern times of all the principles of individualism and personal liberty" ([1887] 1969, 2:142). Contrary to the position enunciated more than a half-century later by Lipset (1963) and Parsons (1966), Sumner did not believe that a balanced continuity of these principles had survived the war. It had "caused an immense destruction of capital and left a large territory with millions of inhabitants almost entirely ruined in its industry, with its labor system exposed to the necessity of an entire reformation" (1969, 2, 54). The war had arisen out of the fact that "the first condition of the Union; *viz.*, that all the states' members of it should be on the same plane of civilization and political development; that they should all hold the same ideas, traditions, and political creed; that their social standards and ideals should be such as to maintain cordial sympathy between them . . . was imperfectly fulfilled" ([1899] 1969, 2:280).

In the wake of the war a little noticed but "great change" came about in the federal system, *a centralization of authority* and *higher organization* that "means a movement away from liberty, . . . attended by irritation until men became habituated to the constraint of the organization and realize its benefits" (1969, 2:331). In his expression "the constraint of the organization," Sumner raised the issue of legitimacy and of bureaucratization in American government. Bureaucratization and centralization were founded on false and improvident principles, among them the erroneous assumption that the outcome of the Civil War had settled once and for all the question of the indissolubility, the legitimacy, of the Union. The fact is, "the union . . . will be threatened again and again whenever there is a well-defined group which believes its interests jeopardized inside the Union and under the dominion of those who control the Union" (1969, 2:348). Large-scale organization intensified the struggles between competitive groups because it made the fruits of victory so much greater: these trends would make possible the political domination of all social and economic institutions—indeed, of all civil life.

The modern industrial system, Sumner argued, tended toward the subversion of all the older sources of community among men, not merely the federation that made for the United States, but also friendship,[5] kinship, and the religious basis for group solidarity. "The men, or groups of men, are dissevered from one another, their interests are often antagonistic, and the changes which occur take the form of conflicts of interest." Precisely because of these conflicts of interest and the new combinations they generate, Sumner ridiculed the popular nostrum that "consists in rehabilitating the old and decaying superstition of government." The "poetical and fanciful attributes" ascribed to the state are chimerical, because "it appears that the state is only a group of men with human interests, passions, and desires, or, worse yet, the state is . . . an obscure clerk hidden in some corner of a governmental bureau. . . ." (1969, 2:62–63) "When the old-fashioned theories of State interference are applied to the new democratic State, they turn out to be a device for setting separate interests in a struggle against each other inside the society." ([1887] 1969, 2:145) Such a struggle would insure neither fairness, justice, nor equity, because, contrary to certain metaphysical doctrines, the state is not "an ethical person." That dogma is but "the latest form of political mysticism" ([1887] 1969, 2:144–45).[6]

A society divided by conflicting interests encourages each of the interests to capture control of the state. Sumner pointed to the "*naiveté* [of] the advocate of interference . . . [who supposes] that he and his associates will have the administration of their legislative device in their own hands and will be sure of guiding it for their purposes only." ([1888] 1969, 2:217) Not only would "the device, when once set up, . . . become the prize of a struggle," but it would also "serve one set of purposes as well as another." The conflict of interests, he urged, produces an unedifying contest for power which draws in "the politicians, editors, economists, *litterateurs*, lawyers, labor agitators, and countless others who . . . join in the struggle, taking sides with the principal parties, or hovering around the strife for what may turn up in it" ([1888] 1969, 2:217–18). Sumner opposed legislation of a socially ameliorative character, which would engender both corrupting competition for control and vicious counterreactions by the once unregulated concerns:

> When once the fatal step is taken of invoking legislation . . . the questions are: Who will get this legislative power? Which interest or coalition of interests (such as passed the bill) will get this, the decisive position in the battle, under its control? . . . The majority interest, by numbers, seizes the power of the state and proceeds to realize its own interest against all others in the most ruthless fashion. That capital [which Sumner supposed was *not* the majority interest] has means of defense is unquestionable; that it will defend itself is certain; that it cannot defend itself without resorting to all the vices of plutocracy seems inevitable. [(1888) 1969, 2, 218–19]

Faced with an inexorable class struggle, deepening racial conflicts, and the ever-enlarging danger of plutocracy through concentration and attempted regulation of industrial capital, Sumner favored only legislation that would break down obstacles to individual participation in the competition and encourage social advance indirectly. Legislative experiments in social amelioration were doomed "for it is not possible to experiment with a society and just drop the experiment whenever we choose" (1969, 2, 473). Among indirect efforts Sumner looked favorably on such examples as:

1. The social consequences of technological advances: "An improvement in surgical instruments or in anaesthetics really does more for those who are not well off than all the declamations of the orators and pious wishes of the reformers."

2. The gains to be made by eliminating political corruption: "Civil service reform would be a greater gain to the laborers than innumerable factory acts and eight-hour laws."
3. The positive functions of unprotected international competition: "Free trade would be a greater blessing to 'the poor man' than all the devices of all the friends of humanity if they could be realized."
4. Appropriate currency reform: "If the economists could satisfactorily solve the problem of the regulation of paper currency, they would do more for the wages class than could be accomplished by all the artificial doctrines about wages which they seem to feel bound to encourage."
5. The federal regulation of banking: "If we could get firm and good laws passed for the management of savings-banks, then refrain from the amendments by which those laws are gradually broken down, we should do more for the non-capitalist class than by volumes of laws against 'corporations' and the 'excessive power of capital'" (Sumner, 1883, 160–62).

Most of Sumner's attitudes toward social improvement paralleled those of Herbert Spencer. Hoping to increase the emancipation of men and women so that they might have greater opportunity to participate in the "struggle for existence," he saw the role of the state as that of an obstacle remover. Nature, working through predominant social forces and through the crescive social institutions fostered by new values, would do the rest. "Acts of legislation come out of the mores" ([1906] 1940, 55). Legislation could not effectively leap ahead of the development of new values. In the face of the growth of the centralized, bureaucratic state, Sumner remained the competitive individualist, a hardheaded, pessimistic realist. His ideology of laissez-faire was later to be stripped of its concern for civil liberties and civilized procedures and adopted by the very political and economic interests against whom it was aimed.

SOCIETY WITHOUT GOD

To understand Sumner's position we must recognize the essentially materialist perspective that dominated his thought, specifically his belief in a universal "struggle for existence." But he did not, except for the primordial hordes, associate that struggle with strictly natural processes. Rather, in civilized societies, and especially in the postfeudal epoch, he perceived it in terms of the competition for capital, or for that which produces capital: land and labor. However, while Sumner credited his own era with ushering in the age of "the great masters of industry" (1889), he also regarded industrialization as having something of the character of a "natural" social force, one that must be recognized and could be adjusted to, but neither obliterated, turned back on itself, nor halted altogether. Industrialization had been made possible by the harnessing of steam power to machine production, improvements in the capacity to send goods and information on land and water, the centralization of mass markets through advertising techniques and technology, and advances in communication by telegraph and telephone. The "whole industry and commerce of the world had been built up into a great system in which organization has become essential and in which it has been carried forward and is being carried forward every day to new developments." (1969, 2, 45–46) Both social scientists and the public needed to recognize that this "system of industry is built upon the constancy of certain conditions of human existence, upon the certainty of the economic forces which thence arise, and upon the fact that those forces act with perfect regularity under changeless laws" (1969, 2, 45–6). Hence, he lashed out at "absurd legislation, charitable philanthropy, or activated sentimentality" (1969, 1, 99–106). The forces of industrialism constituted both an irremediable social fact and an inexorable social process. Under the modern revolution of capitalism, the mores governing society were no longer the displaced (and obsolete) values of covenant-oriented Puritanism but rather a new set of rules, not yet fully defined.

Sumner himself was caught between the older Puritan values of self-sufficiency, hard work, and individualism and the newly emergent institutions that challenged those values. As one of the last of the truly inner-directed Protestant sociologists, it was his moral duty to state his convictions openly, no matter how unacceptable they might be to public and civic opinion, and this gives his work the flavor of a jeremiad. He spoke as if from the pulpit, presenting his "sermon" as an observer of a society in process of abandoning the values on which it had been built. His analysis is in some ways comparable to that of Thorstein Veblen (1857–1929), who was one of his students, though Veblen saw earlier than he the debasement of laissez-faire. But in contrast to Veblen, who relied on irony for his sting, Sumner used a radical individualism to confront liberal and pluralistic ideologies that came into prominence during his lifetime. His rejection of any ideological or practical effort to reconstitute the Puritan covenant made him a thoroughly secular thinker. Modern society had expelled God and theodicy; each individual was left alone to come to terms with society as well as wit and worth would allow. The Puritan had faced God in a one-to-one relationship but could never be certain of achieving a state of grace; so also the individual in Sumner's vision of a secular society faced life without benefit of church or state and could not be certain of success or survival. Charity, philanthropy, and governmental protection of the weak undermined the moral fiber of the individual and placed hindrances in the way of a state of social grace. Sumner in effect replaced the inscrutable, unrelenting Calvinist god with equally inscrutable, unrelenting economic laws; but unlike Ward, who did much the same thing, he made no effort to supply a secular sociodicy as a source for hope in either planned control of these inexorable laws or science as mode of salvation.

The equation of God with society was a central feature of the work of Sumner's French contemporary Emile Durkheim. Durkheim, however, hoped to rescue the mythic power of religion for use in cementing a fractured civil society. Sumner's deification of society flowed from an entirely different source: the logic of secularization inherent in the intellectual and social history of Calvinism and capitalism. Like Calvin's omniscient and omnipotent god, Sumner's society is lacking in both love and compassion and is always severe in its demands. Parsons, whose heritage combined Durkheimianism with Calvinism, worked from a considerably mellowed, more loving and compassionate conception of God. The years between Sumner and Parsons have taken much of the harshness off the original Puritan conception.[7] Sumner's transvalued version of hard-boiled Calvinism seems to have passed out of sociology altogether but has been retained in the conservative wing of American politics.

Sumner, who had already seen that the use of violence in the abolition of slavery did not solve the race problem, could not accept Marx's idea that the class struggle could be ended by a proletarian revolution. More generally, Sumner did not develop any definite telos for society and history as Marx did. Like Darwin, who felt that evolution followed its own laws, Sumner contended that industry and capitalism would develop according to their own processes. Marx had supposed that modern industrial capitalism would ultimately self-destruct, producing a secular utopia; Sumner subscribed to no such vision. Marx's utopia would be achieved only after the dialectical processes of history had worked themselves out by means of violent forms of political action. Sumner differed from Marx on precisely this point; he found political action neither appropriate nor efficacious for creating a new society. In fact, his vision of the politics of industrial capitalist society was closer to that of Max Weber. Both Sumner and Weber foresaw the tendencies to bureaucratization under systems of modern state capitalism or socialism, but unlike Weber, Sumner did not see the increasing prevalence of bureaucracy as an independent problem.

Writing at a time when the entire federal budget was less than half a billion dollars and 70 percent of the labor force was still agricultural, Sumner at first hoped that the residual values of Puritanism might still be strong enough to define a social character and shape society's institutional structure. If only the best of Puritanism could survive and triumph over its materialist adversaries, American society, by its own inner workings, could provide true justice, social harmony, and public order. But his observations of men and events led him to the view that the Puritans were guided by excessively rigid religious ideologies that ultimately could not overcome the material forces they attempted to resist. Sumner saw only a small chance for a worthy social order to emerge that would be superior to that now developing under crass worldly values. Neither religious revival, industrial progress, nor social reform would be enough to replace the fractured covenant.

NOTES

1. Herbert Spencer is usually credited—and criticized—for formulating just such a theory of social evolution. For a spirited and well-argued corrective see Fletcher, 1971, 316–22.

2. Nowhere is this better expressed than in the biting opening pages of Sumner, 1890, 2–5, in which Andrew Jackson is portrayed as a sinner par excellence whose rise in politics is attributable to pure chance: "Jackson was gay, careless, rollicking, fond of horses, racing, cock-fighting, and mischief. . . . There is no proof that he ever was an ambitious man. . . . It is most probable that he did not get on well with his relatives. . . . A journey which he made to Charleston offers a very possible chance for him to have had his mind opened to plans and ideas."

3. One recent analyst, for example, places Sumner's sociological theory closer to the "social-technological" than to the "critical emancipatory" (Fuhrman, 1980, 44–74).

4. Sumner's position on the race question has usually been misunderstood. For Sumner, relations between Negroes and whites were the litmus test of the mores and folkways. An absence of predictability characterized these relations after 1865, according to him. Unlike Ward, who seemed to countenance the lynching of Negroes in the South as a natural sequel to what he called the "philosophy of rape," Sumner supervised the first dissertation on lynching and saw in those outrages, and even more so in the failure of the government to do anything to halt them, the decline of American civilization. Thus, in the Foreword to Cutler's *Lynch-Law: An Investigation into the History of Lynching in the United States* (1905), he wrote:

> Lynch-law is a very different thing where laws and civil institutions are in full force and activity from what it is where they are wanting. It is not admissible that a self-governing democracy should plead the remissness of its own selected agents as an excuse for mob violence. It is a disgrace to our civilization that men can be put to death by painful methods, which our laws have discarded as never suitable, and without the proofs of guilt which our laws call for in any case whatsoever. It would be a disgrace to us if amongst us men should burn a rattlesnake or mad dog. The badness of the victim is not an element in the case at all. Torture and burning are forbidden, not because the victim is not bad enough, but because we are too good. It is on account of what we owe to ourselves that these methods are shameful to us, if we descend to them. It is evident, however, that public opinion is not educated up to this level.

5. A half-century later Parsons (1951, 189) would reiterate Sumner's findings. Speaking of the effects of certain kinds of primary-group associations of the "universalistic-achievement" pattern of social structure, Parsons described the erosion of friendship among males: "Intrasex friendship as diffuse attachment is much less prominent, probably because it can too readily divert from the achievement complex. Among men it tends rather to be attached as a diffuse 'penumbra' to occupational relationships in the form of an obligation in a mild way to treat one's occupational associate as a friend also. It is thereby spread out, and does not form a focus of major independent structuring."

6. Again, the similarity of Sumner's view of the state to Parsons's is striking, differing only

in the affectively neutral language employed by Parsons (1951, 189) to make the same point: "The state in such a system, it may be remarked, tends to be regarded as any other collectivity, justified only in terms of its service to value goal-achievement. It may very well be, then, that the problem of institutionalizing collective political responsibility is one of the most serious points of strain in such a social system."

7. For a "universalistic-achievement" pattern of social structure, Parsons (1951, 188–89) observed, "Too closely integrated a religious system would be dysfunctional. . . . If the orientation of such a religion were strongly other-worldly it would, like Marxism as a 'religion,' tend to shift the balance over to the universalistic-ascriptive type. . . . The pattern of religious toleration and a diversity of denominations as in the American case seems to be the least disruptive structure."

PART II

From Puritanism to Pragmatism: Sociology at Harvard

CHAPTER 4

Between Puritan and European Thought

After the Civil War, Harvard was the first of the Eastern religious schools to extend and expand its secular and humanistic studies and to open itself to a national constituency of students. Under the presidency of Charles W. Eliot, Harvard became a center of national and international learning, utilizing both American and European social and scientific thought as a basis for its intellectual preeminence. It was during the post–Civil War period that Harvard became a focal point for New England transcendental and pragmatic thought and the then emerging German concept of social science. Having established its prestige as a secular university in the late nineteenth century, Harvard set a framework within which the social sciences would develop in America.

Both European and American social thinkers sought ways to reconstitute the moral unity of Western civilization in the face of ever-increasing materialism and the decay of moral values, and American philosophers hoped to find a secular equivalent to the all-but-shattered Puritan covenant. The European and American social philosophies that developed frequently combined secular aims and theological ideals. For example, Francis Greenwood Peabody (1847–1936), the first professor of social ethics at the Harvard Divinity School, sought to inspire his students with a zeal for reform that derived from the Arminian theology he had learned at the University of Halle. Edward Cummings (1861–1926), a student of Peabody and the first professor to teach sociology courses at Harvard, attempted to synthesize Christian socialism with the social psychology of Gustave Le Bon (1841–1931) and Gabriel Tarde (1843–1904). Other Harvard social thinkers gained their perspectives from such diverse European sources as the Scottish moralists Spencer and Darwin, the English Fabians Beatrice and Sydney Webb, the German historicist Gustave von Schmöller, and economists David Ricardo and Karl Marx. Almost all of the ideas involved in these transatlantic adaptations were redefined to make them relevant to the American condition, and particularly to the fundamental ideas of Puritan theology and their restoration as secular values.

But American Protestantism embodied many separate and conflicting strands, as we have seen. Henry Hughes attempted to apply it to slavery. Lester Ward took it upon himself to supply a substitute for the values of Puritanism in the form of a secular social gospel. William Graham Sumner hoped that the underlying virtues of Puritan character would somehow be strong enough to supply society with its moral fabric. Neo-Comtean movements in sociology such as that at Columbia hoped to create a fully managed secular society based on statistics and mathematical architectonics. Biological reformers hoped to remake the world by transforming the nature of man himself. In economics, especially at Harvard, ideologies of pure market Manchesterian liberalism addressed many of the same problems.

Harvard was a central meeting ground for many of the chief bearers of the Social Gospel. Its scholars included Charles Peirce, Josiah Royce (1855–1916), William James (1848–1910), and George Santayana, who were among the first to make effective contact with European, and especially German, thought. And it was from Harvard that the newest homegrown and imported social and philosophical perspectives were transmitted across American academia.[1]

The extraordinary influence of New England and especially Bostonian culture on the rest of America stemmed from the region's distinctive cultural institutions. The founding in the seventeenth century of the Boston Charity Society, the Boston Historical Society, and Harvard University was a response to both the secular and the theological requirements of Puritanism.[2] Puritan civilization could create a new order of mundane life by means of a covenant with God only by using its own human resources; from the outset it was clear that it could not rely upon England for its supply of religious leaders. Thus, Harvard was conceived as a school of theology in the knowledge that through this institution Puritans could control their own religious and secular destiny. Later, Harvard began to think of itself as a civil as well as a religious institution, whose mission was to supply the nation with leadership in all areas of worldly activity.

The covenanted Puritan community was forced from the beginning to face the problem of social inequality. Earlier and more successful settlers stood above both the Indians and later and less successful migrants, but such differentiation required a justification consistent with the original covenant. Puritan intellectuals built into American culture a moral history and theodicy for all the ethnic, racial, and religious groups that would come to America after them (B. Solomon, 1956). By the act of immigration those groups were held to have rejected their native culture and, willingly or not, to have opened themselves to a revised conception of their past and a new promise of their future. American moral history thus begins with the Puritans, who established their own ideals as the moral basis for a new social order.[3]

The New England Puritan doctrine that found various forms of expression and transvaluation in the words of Harvard's sociologists was derived from that of the English Calvinist William Perkins (Baltzell, 1979, 74–78). Perkins cast his search for a vocational order amid the moral chaos of the sixteenth century into military terms. Order was a duty imposed by God; disorder, anarchy, and social unrest were products of satanic subversion. "God," wrote Perkins, "is the General, appointing to every man his particular calling and as it were his standing: and in that calling he assigns unto him his particular office; in performance whereof he is to live and die." Vocations imposed separate and specific duties, and, because each vocation depended on distinctive talents that were themselves gifts from God, they fostered a theologically justified hierarchical order. Hence, the unequal social arrangements that produced both mundane systems of stratification and worldly forms of authority were just: "God hath appointed, that in every society one person should bee above or under another; not making all equal, as though the bodie shall bee all head and nothing else."[4]

Implicit in Puritan doctrine is the individual's moral responsibility for his own lot in life. The obligation to work in one's calling includes the duty to discover that calling and the discipline to keep at it. The social organization that approved of the moral vocations also recognized men and women who practiced what Perkins called the avocations ("as, for example, such as live by usury, by carding and dicing, by maintaining houses of gaming"), but these were condemned, not to be tolerated within the moral community. "It is a foule disorder in any Commonwealth, that there should be suffered rogues, beggars, vagabonds; for such kinds of persons commonly are of no civil societie or corporation, nor of any particular Church; and are rotten legges, and armes, that droppe from the body." This theology would later supply sociology with its conception of deviance.

Sinners in turn were divided into two categories—those who sought after grace and might be born again deserved charity and compassion, those who were unredeemable were entirely disreputable, unsalvageable human junk deserving of their miserable condition. A duty of the Puritan authority—the magistrate, the minister, the saintly merchant, and, later, the ethically bound social scientist—was to find ways to distinguish between the two classes and to calculate rationally the amount of charity or the degree of punishment due. As Harvard's Puritan sociologists, notably Peabody and Cummings, attempted to graft the new science of society onto the old Calvinist doctrines, they tried to find rational means to effect the heavenly judgment.

The Social Gospel movement was supposed to rationalize through science the hardheaded moral calculus that was required of Calvinist philanthropy. The Harvard Puritans continued to believe in the righteousness of a secular hierarchy through which the virtuous might rise on their road to election. They wished to assuage the suffering of the poor, to find sure ways to distinguish the redeemable from the disreputable and the virtuous from the vicious,[5] to enlist the stewards of wealth in philanthropic Christian endeavor, but they were divided over whether the state was obligated to aid in human redemption or merely to adjudicate among the contending classes. Like Perkins, they believed they lived in a moment of great moral crisis. And just as Perkins had imagined a militaristic God making war on evil, so these first Harvard sociologists sought to recruit an "army" of Christian soldiers who would march into the slums in a "scientific" war on poverty, disease, and general human desolation.

But Puritanism at Harvard had even broader—in fact secular—consequences. Perhaps no one perceived this so well as Hugo Munsterberg, the German experimental psychologist brought to Harvard in 1892, who predicted:

> The intellectual life of the nation which is informed with Puritan and utilitarian impulses, will, . . . after a certain period, advance to a new and national stage of culture; but the highest achievements will be made partly in the service of moral ideals, partly in the service of technical culture. As a result of the first tendency, history, law, literature, philosophy, and religion will come to their flowering; in consequence of the second tendency, science and technique. [1907, 356]

By the turn of the century first New England and then the whole country began to sense that a great crisis had arisen in ideology and theology (McLoughlin, 1978, 141–78). The beginnings of the social and historical sciences in the United States were part of a much larger social process in which men and women sought by various means to gain control over their own destinies in a world where God had become remote and difficult to understand. For social scientists this presented both challenge and responsibility. The challenge was immense and inviting—to remake the world in their own image of God's perfect order. The responsibility was almost too awesome to imagine.

Harvard University was the place where almost all the contradictions of the new social sciences were first revealed and where the philosophical struggles to resolve them were fought. The problems of social and economic stratification, individualism versus collectivism, caste and class, determinism and free will, materialism and idealism, authoritarianism and consensus were projected into the new disciplines of sociology, psychology, philosophy, anthropology, economics, and political science.

The new secular thinkers, compelled to act within the constraints of a this-worldly, secularized Protestantism, brought the values of Puritanism, not Catholicism or Judaism, to their work. It was these values, couched in a new rhetoric of science, that they applied to an emergent world increasingly dominated by growth, prosperity, large-scale organization, and the centralization of institutional life. This juxtaposition of a Puritan world view and a rapidly changing social structure posed two major problems.

First, how could this new society of ex-slaves, immigrants, cities, crime, burgeoning industry, corruption, mass merchandizing, and a national press be reconstituted as a unified community in such manner that its institutions and practices would be consistent with self-discipline, hard work, just rewards, freedom, and equality before the law? This same problem was stated by religious revivalists as: How can a universal—or, at least, an American—Christianity be reestablished in an age of rampant individualism, religious schism, and rising denominationalism?[6] And second, could the sciences, social as well as physical, contribute to the creation of the good, the just, and the perfectible organization of men on earth?

The first is a question for social theory, or ideology, and the second for applied science. Moreover, the second question establishes an "elective affinity" between Protestant-informed thinkers and positivism. In this sense social science can be viewed as originally a Protestant product. If his calling was to be warrantable, the scientist would be expected to make practical social contributions.[7]

NOTES

1. These cross-currents continued well into the twentieth century. Thus Alfred Schutz, upon arriving in the United States, was both surprised and pleased to learn of the close perspectival relationship between his own Husserlian phenomenological sociology and the American pragmatic tradition represented by William James, George Santayana, John Dewey, Charles Horton Cooley, and George Herbert Mead. Schutz also thought that there might be a prospect for intellectual rapprochement between his own outlook and that of Talcott Parsons, but the latter rebuffed him in no uncertain terms. (See Schutz, 1966, 34; Grathoff, 1978, 61–111.)

2. Samuel Eliot Morison (1958, 53) has asserted that the Puritan tradition of East Anglia was the spur to preeminence among the New England settlers and their descendants:

In East Anglia the Puritan movement bit deepest. From East Anglia came the heaviest contingent for the planting of Massachusetts Bay; and Massachusetts as colony and commonwealth, by every known test of eminence, has produced far more distinguished men and women in proportion to her population than any other state of the Union.

3. The only alternative tradition was that of the agrarian cavalier South, delegitimized by the defeat of the Confederacy in 1865. However, this tradition survived in the sociology of the southern emigré to California Joseph Le Conte and among the so-called fugitive poets (see *I'll Take My Stand: The South and the Agrarian Tradition,* by twelve Southerners, 1930; and, in general, Cash, 1941; W. Taylor, 1930). In sociology the tradition finds recognition in Howard W. Odum's development of "regionalism" as a concept for the analysis of customs and institutions (see Jocher et al., 1964). For discussions of this defeated tradition in the sociological literature see Dodd, 1918, 735–46; Bernard, 1937, 1–12.

4. "For example, the life of a king is to spend his life governing his subjects, and that is his calling; and the life of a subject is to live in obedience to the Magistrate. . . . A master of a family is to leade his life in the government of his family and that is his calling." (Quoted in Baltzell, 1979, 75).

5. In the mid-1960s, one sociologist rediscovered the old Puritan distinction and sought to build it into a wholly secular conceptualization of social stratification. See Matza, 1966, 289–302. Richard Cloward and Frances Fox Piven in several books have developed a comprehensive critique undermining the claims of the state welfare sociodicy.

6. In the new scientific terms that would be developed at Harvard, the Massachusetts Institute of Technology, and other places of post-Newtonian physics, the problem could be stated in the way it presented itself to Norbert Wiener, a Harvard Ph.D. at only eighteen years of age (1913) and the founder of cybernetics: "How to reconcile a deterministic world à la Newton with the intrinsically probabilistic universe of Gibbs, the relativistic universe of Einstein and Heisenberg's uncertainty principle" (Rosenblith, [1950] 1967, 274).

7. Cf. the statement by Perkins: "A vocation or calling is a certain kind of life, ordained and imposed on man by God . . . *for the common good:* that is for the benefite and good estate of mankinde. . . . And that common saying, *Every man for himselfe, and God for us all,* is wicked, and is directly against the end of every calling or honeste kind of life" (Baltzell, 1979, 76).

CHAPTER 5

Saving the World: Social Ethics and Applied Psychology

A separate curriculum in sociology as such was not created at Harvard until 1931. In the departments of philosophy and political economy there were powerful intellectual currents concerned with the application of knowledge to the betterment of the world, but conflicts also arose in both departments concerning the moral content of the social sciences. Both departments struggled to find an intellectual foundation for transcending Puritan theology, while retaining the Protestant ethic.

In the philosophy department the study of sociology was associated with the Social Gospel reformism of Francis Greenwood Peabody, the metaphysical foundations for Christian community of Josiah Royce, the philosophical psychology of William James, and the applied experimental and social psychology of Hugo Munsterberg (1863–1916). It was not concerned, as it was in the economics department, with creating "systems" for understanding society and the world. Under Royce's direction philosophy students were encouraged to formulate the grounds for reviving the Christian community that would be consistent with just and harmonious social advance.[1] Peabody's self-chosen mission was to insure that these would be properly instilled into the unlettered, the untutored, and the upcoming generations.

THE URBAN SOCIOLOGIST AS PROTESTANT PROPHET: FRANCIS GREENWOOD PEABODY

Peabody's approach to social ethics (Brackett, 1913, 141; Herbst, 1961; Bernstein, 1963) represented the Unitarian Church's special application of the Social Gospel. It focused on labor, poverty, immigration, and urban problems and employed the inductive case-study approach, but it spoke less to matters of direct legislative improvement than to the positive values of a socially and religiously conscious education and individual moral redemption.[2] Peabody became the first professor of social ethics in the United States when he was appointed to Harvard's Divinity School in 1879, ten years after he graduated. His special brand of sociological Social Gospel found expression in his course "Practical Ethics" (renamed "Ethical Theories and Moral Reform" in 1883 and taught thereafter to both theology and philosophy students) and in his collection of sermons and essays published in 1900 as *Jesus Christ and the Social Question* (Ahlstrom, 1972, 795; Kuklik, 1977, 244–46; Potts, 1965). Courses he established included "Criminology and Penology," "Rural Social Development," "Social Amelioration in Europe," "Moral Responsibilities of the Modern State," and "Selected Topics in Social Ethics" (Potts, 1965). His lectures on "Temperance," "Discipline," and "Charity" along with those on "Labor," "Prison," and "Divorce" (Kuklik, 1977, 245), emphasized the social aspects of prayer (White and Hopkins, 1976, 153).

Peabody praised and promoted cooperatives, proper social planning, the Prussian system of social security, and enlightened philanthropy, and he encouraged the education of Negroes; but all these matters were discussed within the larger context of individual, moral, and social redemption (Ahlstrom, 1972, 795). His academic evangelism stressed individual ethical choice, an Arminian emphasis. A firm believer in translating religious ethics directly into action, he eschewed both structural and historical analyses of current social, economic, and political problems. Social programs were important, perhaps even necessary; but if all individuals would choose the ethical life, social problems would solve themselves and the secular Holy Commonwealth would come into existence.

This attitude represented a distinct schism within the Social Gospel movement, best seen in the opposed views of Washington Gladden and Walter Rauschenbusch (1907). With Rauschenbusch, Peabody stressed man's need to overcome his alienation from God as a prerequisite to establishing the just society; Gladden, pointing to the original kinship of God and man, offered a social theology that "arose out of the pragmatic need to respond to social change in the dawn of a new era" (Knudten, 1968, 225).

It is quite likely that Peabody's work reflected the revivalism that was sweeping the country in the 1880s, a period of intense evangelical fervor. His sociology included a definite constraint on any reform that was not oriented primarily in moral redemption; and moral redemption ultimately depended on individual conversion. His orientation thus was a kind of revivalism in academic garb.[3] But, Peabody wrote in 1886, "The modern minister needs to have been trained in the study of social reform," because the modern world had called the church to an ethical revival that could be realized only through the knowledge and application of the social sciences.

From 1890 to 1918 in Boston, New York, and Chicago, the Social Gospel found one of its most potent forms in the college and university settlement movement. Proponents of this movement emulated the Cambridge and Oxford men who, from their base in London's Toynbee Hall, invaded the slums of Whitechapel and the East End in acts of Christian social endeavor. In the United States the settlement movement was organized around seminaries, the reformist, religious, liberal arts colleges, and a few universities such as Harvard and the University of Chicago. It aimed to put into worldly, ethically motivated practice the biblical injunction "Ye must be born again" (see Peterson, 1964, 177–95); participation in the movement would be an act of conversion and self-renewal as well. By the act of identification with the poor and the destitute—a secular version of the Christian mandate to rediscover one's relationship with Christ—the college student could implement his own conversion, activate his own chance for salvation. The settlement house represented an extension of the Protestant principle of charity (now defined in terms of the relief of social problems), with its attendant claims for prestige through community service.

Harvard had lent early support to the settlement idea. In 1891 Peabody established Prospect Union, a sort of workingman's college combined with a Harvard students' club, run in accordance with redemptionist principles (Mann, 1954, 114). Peabody's conception of the appropriate religion for a college student included "a passion for reality," teaching that was "consistent with truth as discerned elsewhere," and social service, the modern equivalent of divinely inspired "works." He (1901) stated the matter in a manner that clearly indicates the relationship of religion, rationality, and social ethics: "The intellectual issues of the present time are too real to be met by artificiality and too rational to be interpreted by traditionalism. The practical philanthropy of the present time is too absorbing and persuasive to be subordinated or ignored. It is a time for the church to dismiss all affectations and all assumptions of authority, and to give itself to the reality of rational religion and the practical redemption of an unsanctified world." Peabody saw to it that only worthy men like himself were in authority in the Union and that individual salvation took precedence over group advancement. Indiscriminate almsgiving was a sin, and secular socialist persuasions were given short shrift. "I sometimes wonder," he wrote, "why it never occurs to our radicals that a policy of broad patient education—without passionate propaganda—may perhaps be the most revolutionary course that could be pursued" (Potts, 1962, 257).

Peabody's orientation was modified by his student and colleague at

Harvard, Edward Cummings. Cummings criticized some of the grander pretensions of the university and college settlements in England and the United States, observing how naive, sentimental, and patronizing the Oxonian settlement house workers at Toynbee Hall were, despite their admirable motto: "Vain will be higher education, music, art, or even the Gospel, unless they come clothed in the life of brother man." Even these gauche efforts might raise social consciousness and inspire philanthropic effort, but Cummings put his finger on the missing ingredient, essential if a rationalized Christian endeavor in true brotherhood was to succeed: "the lack of system, the great diversity of interests, the absence of thoroughness in the study of problems actually attempted, the unequal and inadequate distribution of men." (Cummings, 1892)

Cummings upheld the old Puritan distinction between the worthy and unworthy poor: "It is . . . by allying himself to the remnants of slum respectability, by bringing strength to indigenous germs of moral excellence, that the settler may hope to multiply his own influence for good." But he urged that the movement turn away from its efforts to achieve individual redemption and concentrate on the slum as a source of otherwise unavailable knowledge and a laboratory for social experiments. The slums could provide a wonderful training ground for "efficient critics and [social] workers. . . . It is difficult to overestimate the value of a brief and comparatively superficial sojourn, which teaches the prospective clergyman or politician or president of associated charity organizations and anti-tenement house leagues how the other half lives,—yes, and smells." Cummings urged his students to go into the slums and ghettos of Boston and New York:

> What is the natural history of your "slum"? It is the natural history of many of the "social questions" and city questions we are so fond of legislating out of existence nowadays—a normal product of inherited weakness and morbid environment. Would you know that life? Then live it—or something approximating it; and in the attempt to do this, the settlement will prove of great value. . . . If our "new ministry to the poor" must call itself a settlement, and a university settlement at that, let it leaven the philanthropy of best living . . . with a scholarly reverence and indefatigable zeal for methods and definite aims. If it shall decide to live in comparative luxury . . . in order to teach the "slums" how their other half lives, let it at least supplement Burne-Jones in the committee room with a colored map from Mr. Charles Booth's new geography of poverty and crime. If it shall meet from time to time for mutual conference and instruction, let the readings from Browning alternate with chapters from *Labour and Life of the People*. (Cummings, 1892)

Cummings hoped to construct the City of God in Boston, but the means for this holy effort were to be scientific and practical. The American settlement movement's leader, Robert Woods (Mann, 1954, 115–23; Peterson, 1964, 177–79), emphasized that at "present, the work must be done by amateurs, for there are no professionals." The information desired could not be obtained by "the mere canvasser or statistician," he declared; the student should proceed something like an anthropologist in a primitive culture area. Moreover, foreshadowing the Peace Corps and Vista volunteers ideology, (Wofford, 1980, 243–316), the college and university settlement movement held that social reform must emerge out of what "the people are accomplishing for themselves both in their individual and home life, and in local organizations for whatever purpose," and affirmed that the "presumption is always against having a Settlement introduce any new institutional scheme" (Woods, 1893, 68, 70). Among the proposals for the hoped-for society-wide social reconstruction were new programs in "healthful recreation,"[4] a slowly and carefully introduced educational plan to establish a workingmen's university, and a "People's Palace" for lectures, concerts, and art exhibits. There would be "experiments in the way of cooperative stores, cooperative industries, building and loan associations, benefit and insurance organizations," all of which would "bring working-men and university-men together, in order that they may learn from each other about social questions" (Woods, 1893, 83–85).

The idea of a university mission to the urban proletariat constituted both a new form and a new agency for missionary activity. It was a clear effort to elevate the lower groups to the moral level of their ethical betters by creating a Protestant brotherhood across sharply drawn class and educational boundaries. As Cummings saw so well, these well-intentioned efforts reflected a sense of guilt derived from superior economic and cultural advantages; but they also revealed a desire to recreate the brotherhood of man in the face of increasing income, class, and ethnic differences.

Moral uplift of the urban proletariat was also a strong theme in the "Third Great Awakening." Dwight Moody, for example, was the first revivalist to systematically work in cities, going to where the sinners lived to convert them (McLoughlin, 1978, 141–45). Other parallels to Prospect Union were the Sunday School movement and the establishment of the YMCA and YWCA.

It was assumed that Harvard's elect, acting as missionaries, could bring the poor and uneducated into the newly defined covenant. These new academic missionaries, however, often sought to inculcate New England culture more than the old-time religious gospel. The older idea of the church's mission gave way to a secularized, this-worldly crusade to promote civic well-being. But, as Harvard's social ethics program illustrates,[5] "civic well-being" was little more than a secular version of the gospel's message regarding ways to achieve moral betterment in the Holy Commonwealth.

The approach embodied in this program lived on long after the social ethics program was dismantled. Its methods became known as field work and participant observation. Anthropological field studies as well as sociological community studies are extensions of this tradition—the work of William Foote Whyte, as reported in *Street Corner Society* (1943), for example, reflects his concern with the moral quality of the lives of Boston's Italian immigrant community. But all religious elements of social uplift, charity, and philanthropy are manifestly eliminated, and the research activity has taken on the quality of objective science and professional work. Peabody could not have accepted such ethical neutrality. He was a missionary committed to the ethical values of Jesus Christ and demanded of himself and his students a dedication to morally charged endeavor— for him, the "calling" would ideally be associated with vows of poverty. For the scientific researchers of the post–Social Gospel era, however, the mere act of "doing science" was sufficient to make the status and class differences between subject and scientist acceptable. They had no qualms about their superior economic and cultural position.

Peabody's sociological theology embraced redemption for both capitalist society and its victims. He was led necessarily to "the application to organization of the personal power inspired by Jesus Christ" (Hopkins, 1940, 210) and to a proposal for an ethical stewardship over wealth. The mere redistribution of wealth would not produce the moral stance required for those summoned to prepare the way for the Kingdom of God. Because "the teaching of Jesus permits in no case the sense of absolute ownership," a man *owes* rather than *owns* his wealth. Jesus "asks the whole of one's gains—and the life which lies behind the gains—for the service of the kingdom" (Hopkins, 1940, 212).

Peabody's homiletic is reminiscent of Henry Hughes's views on slavery: "Property in man is absurd. Men cannot be owned. In warranteeism what is owned is the labor obligation, not the obligee. The obligee is a man." For both Hughes and Peabody there could be no absolute ownership. Thus the slaves owed an obligation to labor and the warrantor (slaveowner) owned only this labor obligation, not the slaves themselves. Moreover, the labor obligation did not redound to the benefit of the slaveowner; he only managed it for the benefit of society as a whole. For both Hughes and Peabody, the beneficiary was the larger community to which all were required to be generous as part of their service to God. Both Hughes and Peabody conceived of philanthropy as a fundamental social institution but also as a source for sociological casuistry: for by Peabody's day the distribution of wealth was so inequitable, and so unrelated to personal achievement, that the original Puritan theology could not justify it in its original terms. The new university-based missionary activity attempted to redefine the mutual obligations of capitalists and workers.

Peabody's orientation was not toward eradicating the structural or institutional foundations of social evil but rather toward chastening man's sinful nature. The danger America faced arose not from the antagonisms between labor and capital but from a "commercialized and materialized civilization, in which the ideals that support Democracy may fail of vitality and strength." Agitation over wages and hours was "the penalty we are paying for not being Christian." Whatever inner-worldly requirements there were for economic, educational, and legislative solutions to the Social Question, essentially it was an "ethical, spiritual, religious [problem], a call to moral redemption, a summons to a better life." (Hopkins, 1940, 246) Peabody incorporated the Spencerian concept of the social organism into his approach, but what he derived from it was a recognition that social problems diffused their negative effects throughout society. Their solution required a reaffirmation of Christian love and the biblical injunction that each person must lose his life in order to gain it. His social outlook culminated in the model of the "moral hero," a person moved to act not by self-interest, prudence, or historical determinism but by "loyalty to an ideal," a loyalty that, Peabody assured his students, would lead to a realistic and rational line of melioristic conduct (Potts, 1962, 121–22).

When Peabody's program was set up as an independent department of social ethics, in 1905, it moved in the direction of ethically grounded but semiprofessionalized social welfare (Kaplan, 1955). Protected with funding from a sympathetic philanthropist, Alfred Tredway White, who donated more than $250,000 to insure continuation of the program and to endow Emerson Hall, the department offered a mélange of social science and problems courses from 1913 to 1920. Under Peabody's successor, ethicist Richard Clarke Cabot, it restored the older moralistic approach (Potts, 1962, 115–23).[6] However, under neither Peabody nor Cabot could the curriculum in social ethics successfully bridge the widening gap between the demands of the secular world and the moral absolutism dictated by its own religious precepts.

After the first World War social ethics became something of an embarrassment to Harvard's ever more professional, secular, and scientific disciplines. Moreover, the religious and reformist élan that had been inspired by the Social Gospel and compelled by the miseries of industrializing America declined all too quickly (Carter, 1971, 31). The Social Gospel seemed out of tune with both the new prosperity and with a hardly realized society-wide democratic pluralism—Catholics, Jews, Asians, East Europeans, and urban blacks did not respond readily to an explicit Protestant sectarian ideology. In terms of both societal utility and university policy, Harvard's manifestly religious social ethicists had outlived their usefulness. The future intellectual development of Harvard was committed to wholly secularized and far more powerfully sublimated expressions of Protestant values.

The secular version of these values was nowhere better stated than in the work of William James in philosophy and Hugo Munsterberg in applied psychology. James, a philosophical social psychologist, hoped to find a pragmatic means to salvation and immortality; Munsterberg, recruited by James to the psychology laboratory, sought to shape or remake all secular institutions by scientific methods. No one has left a deeper mark on the intellectual life of Harvard, and on the disciplines of psychology and sociology, than these two men.

SECULAR PERFECTIBILITY: WILLIAM JAMES

James was a major interpreter of German philosophical and psychological thought to Americans. His interests embraced the range of theories from experimental psychology (Allport, 1966a), which he pioneered at Harvard, to phenomenology, which he came near to adopting as his own outlook (Stern, 1965; Spiegelberg, 1969, 1:66–69). His influence on sociology was transmitted through such thinkers as George Herbert Mead (1863–1931), W. E. B. Du Bois (1868–1963), Robert E. Park (1864–1944), and Horace Kallen (1882–1974), all of whom claimed him as a friend, adviser, and mentor.

Each received something different from James. Mead lived in James's home and tutored his children. Although he took no courses from James and was more directly influenced by Josiah Royce's conception of the absolute self, it appears that James's conception of the "ideal social self"— "a self that is at least worthy of approving recognition by the highest possible judging companion . . . God, the Absolute Mind, the 'Great Companion' " (James, [1890] 1950, 1:315–16)—became in Mead's secular reformulation of James and Royce (Reck, 1964, 371–91) the "generalized other" (see Miller, 1973, 49). Du Bois credited him with curbing his emotions, guiding him to clear thinking, and leading him "out of the sterilities of scholastic philosophy to realist pragmatism" (Du Bois, 1973–78, 2:204; [1940] 1968, 33, 37–39, 259, 296, 322; 1968, 133). Park most admired James's essay "On a Certain Blindness in Human Beings" (James, [1899] 1968, 629–44) because its emphasis on "the blindness with which we all are afflicted in regard to the feelings of creatures and people different from ourselves" provided him with a master clue to the social psychology of racial and interpersonal relations (Park, 1950–1955, 1:vi–vii, 50, 329). Kallen, who studied with Royce, James, and Santayana at Harvard from 1899 to 1903, was James's chosen successor and the scholar entrusted to complete *Some Problems in Philosophy*.

As C. Wright Mills has noted (1964, 215–74), it was the very generality, openness, and breadth of James's idea of pragmatism that made it the philosophical banner of so many otherwise distinct sorts of social scientists. In emphasizing the integrity of every person's experience, it mediated the epistemological demands of "science" and the pieties of "religion," the privileged knowledge of trained observers and the commonsense knowledge of laymen, the rivalry between "rationalism" and "empiricism" (Kallen, 1914, 52–102). James's pragmatism found apertures in closed systems where the "will to believe" helped to liberate the individual from the constraints of generalized objectivity.

James's original role at Harvard was that of an experimental psychologist. Impressed by Wilhelm Wundt's remarkable successes in psychology in Germany,[7] James established an American laboratory to carry out similar and even more advanced experiments. His pragmatic outlook led him to bring Hugo Munsterberg to Harvard as laboratory director, so that he himself could withdraw into philosophizing proper. His linkage of psychology to physiology on the one hand and to sociology on the other provided one more connection between the study of society and the world of natural science. As James Mark Baldwin put it at the Universal Congress of Arts and Science in St. Louis in 1904:

> The position that the private psychic point of view is the only valid one is to grow more and more obsolete, among workers in this field. It will no longer be possible to claim that all truth about mind must be traced in some individual's consciousness, and that the laws of science are to be those of observable psychic continuity alone. Psychic events are intertwined with physical and biological events, and their sequences involve objective as well as subjective terms. The two sciences which will for this reason be brought into vital relation with psychology are physiology and sociology. [Rogers (1906) 1974, 621]

Formerly the soul had been the point of each human's unification, Baldwin explained; now the total being, in its physiological, chemical, psychological, sociological, and social-psychological complexity, could be understood, saved, molded, and brought to full actualization.

Without using the term *sociology*, James and, even more flamboyantly, Munsterberg pointed out the vital relation of sociology to psychology and the promising effects of applying the two sciences to personal and public problems. James apparently felt a moral obligation to be of practical help to all those who needed his assistance, and to supply them with the beliefs and verities they lacked. He had no compunction about entering the world and tending needs. The public platform and the classroom alike offered opportunities to expound his pragmatic philosophy. Man and God were no longer so distinct from each other; man had become God-man with a potential for scientifically guided perfectibility.

> I have found by experience that what my hearers seem least to relish is analytical technicality, and what they care for is concrete practical application. So I have gradually weeded out the former, and left the latter unreduced. . . . In taking my cue from what has seemed to me to be the feeling of the audiences, I believe that I am shaping my books so as to satisfy the more genuine public need.

At times his psychological secularization of the religious brought James close to the mystical. He was receptive to the religious, supernatural, and occult ideas then in popular vogue, lending his scientific name in support of all manner of mind curers, mentalists, and faith healers (Allen, 1967). A believer in spirit mediums, he was the principal scientist active in the foundation of the American Society for Psychical Research. In his Ingersoll Lectures in 1897–98, he seriously entertained a negative answer to the question, "Does this doctrine [that thought is a function of the brain] logically compel us to disbelieve in immortality?" (James, 1899, 10–11). Unwilling to abandon the concept of ever-lasting life, James sought a way to reformulate its promise in scientific terms.

More than any other contemporary American theorist, James believed that psychology, sociology, and philosophy could be applied to the mundane problems of the world, and thus he combined a pragmatic outlook with a desire for secular salvation. At a time when the industrial system had found the means for providing an abundance of the worldly goods he emphasized personal satisfaction and fulfillment. Unwittingly he contributed to the growing culture of consumerism that had begun with what his contemporary, Thorstein Veblen, had recognized as the conspicuous consumption of goods (Veblen [1899] 1973, 60–79).

James and his followers, like no other group of thinkers except, perhaps, the contemporary Neo-Marxists, took God's work out of His hands and put it ever so confidently into their own.

NOTES

1. Royce was more influenced by sociology than has usually been recognized. He completed his undergraduate studies with Joseph LeConte at the University of California. We will present the sources of Royce's thought in chapters 16 and 17.

2. The essence of Peabody's teaching is found in his hyperbolic essay, "The Universities and the Social Conscience" (1908). He writes:

> The most characteristic and significant discovery of the present age is the discovery of the social conscience—the recognition, in a degree unprecedented in history, of social responsibility; the demand, with an unprecedented imperativeness, for social justice; the substitution, on an unprecedented scale, of social morality for the creed of individualism. Never in human history were so many people, rich and poor, learned and ignorant, wise and otherwise, concerning themselves with social amelioration, dedicating themselves to philanthropy, organizing for industrial change, or applying the motives of religion to the problems of modern life. It is the age of the Social Question. A

new phrase, the Social Organism, becomes the description of human society. . . . The social question will not be settled until somehow each life, however helpless or inefficient it may be, finds its appropriate place in the vast organism of social efficiency.

3. It was perhaps because of Peabody's wedding of Unitarianism with Social Gospel that Charles F. Thwing (A. B. Harvard, 1876)—an advocate of a form of Protestant ecumenism in which all the religions of the world were reconceived as variants of or predecessors to Christianity—felt it necessary to defend Harvard against the accusation that it was an irreligious institution. Noting that this charge seemed to originate in those western states that are "filled with Congregational, Presbyterian, Baptist, Methodist, and Episcopal churches," Thwing "acknowledged that many persons identify Unitarianism with irreligion" and that beginning "with the assumption that Harvard is a Unitarian College, they proceed to the conclusion that Harvard is irreligious." But this belief, he replied, along with its corollary that Harvard's "free, hearty, and sympathetic Christian life" is an invitation to immorality, is nothing more than a sectarian prejudice. Thwing predicted that it would disappear as more Harvard men followed him to the West and spread the true word about the university (1893, 200–01). For Thwing's ecumenism and its impact on education in California, see Ferrier, 1937, 367–70.

4. For a critical analysis of the playground movement and the argument that it substituted patterned, rulebound games, a concern for propriety, and respect for private property for the free-forming spontaneous street play of the children of the slums, see Goodman, 1979.

5. For a history of the program written just before it was absorbed into Sorokin's new sociology department, see Ford, 1930.

6. According to Potts, Cabot's approach differed from Peabody's in that Cabot utilized the "moral hero" approach less to instill an ethical idealism than to stimulate students to develop their own personal philosophy of conduct (Potts, 1962, 121–22).

7. James was by no means the only American to be struck by the possibilities experimental psychology held for social reconstruction. Lincoln Steffens (1866–1936) journeyed to Wundt's laboratory in Leipzig in 1890 after being disappointed in what philosophy had to offer in Berlin, Heidelberg, and Munich. Steffens spent a year working in the laboratory and taking lectures "to see if I could find in psychology either a basis for a science of ethics or a trail through psychology to some other science that might lead to a scientific ethic." After a year he left, saying of Wundt: "His logic is untenable, his Ethic commonplace, his system absurd or childish"(Raphelson, 1967).

CHAPTER 6

Puritanism and Economic Theory

POLITICAL ECONOMY, PURITANISM, AND TOTAL SYSTEMS

Sociology was introduced into Harvard's economics department as a "historical" corrective to the static universal models of economic conduct contained in the "classical"—that is, Scottish—school of the eighteenth century and its later interpreters and critics, David Ricardo and John Stuart Mill (Bryson, [1945] 1968). Comte and his American counterparts, Hughes and Ward, treated the science of society as the master social science, interpreting its subdisciplines, history, economics, political science, and social welfare in accordance with its own overarching perspective. The Harvard economists, however, suspicious that sociology—which many of them regarded as confused, value laden, and without a subject matter of its own—sought to appropriate the domain they themselves had already staked out, only grudgingly admitted the new science to their classrooms, and for forty years confined it to the single course first offered by Edward Cummings in 1891.

Harvard's sociology falls into two distinct types and periods. The first, associated from 1891 to 1901 with Edward Cummings and the historical economist William James Ashley, emphasized the application of sociology to socioeconomic problems; the second, associated with the teachings and writings of Thomas Nixon Carver from 1900 to the establishment of the department of sociology in 1931, concentrated on formal, abstract theories and treated social questions in terms of the imperfect state of man and society. In the first case, the redemption of man and society was to be achieved by direct action; in the second it would result from the inexorable evolutionary progress of mankind.

MORAL UPLIFT AND ECONOMIC SALVATION: EDWARD CUMMINGS

Edward Cummings's work reflects the conflict between Manchesterian liberalism and the new spirit of social scientific reform. It also shows his inability to come to terms with social forces that might plunge society into moral decay and economic disintegration, as he sought to combine the ethical values of Puritanism with the economic realities of modern capitalism.

The ravages the new industrialism had made on urban Boston also left their mark on Cummings. The impact of ethnic immigrant cultures had left New England culture on the defensive, and Cummings felt a moral responsibility to uphold its standards. His impulse, as one bound by the duties of the already elect, was to preserve and advance Protestant values against the encroachment of a new materialistic civilization.

For Cummings the key issue was whether human betterment could be brought about by the collective actions of organized groups or through the continued emancipation of the individual (Church, 1965; Brackett, 1913). This same issue had earlier caused a split between the Social Gospelers and Fundamentalists, on the one hand, and the socialist reformers and free-market capitalists on the other. Never an advocate of socialism, deeply influenced by Darwin but unable to accept a purely laissez-faire approach, Cummings sought in vain to harmonize deterministic ideas about impersonal social forces with popular attempts to make society over.

Cummings's version of social evolution begins with the industrial revolution and the gnawing alienation it created between the laborer and the conditions of his work. A new, impersonal relationship rapidly developed between employer and employee, and a distinct and isolated laboring class sprang up with a cooperative united front against capitalists in an attempt to regain control of the conditions of industrial labor. Cummings admired the cooperative spirit expressed in trade unions, and was especially impressed by the studies and methods of Beatrice and Sidney Webb, the British Fabians, and Charles Booth's sociological investigations of London's poor.[1] Nevertheless, he was convinced that a purely collective and deterministic solution to the social question was impossible (Cummings, 1899).

Cummings came to this conclusion partly through the theories of social psychology of Gustave Le Bon and Gabriel Tarde. Le Bon's *Psychology of Peoples*, translated into English in 1896, encouraged Cummings's faith in the ideology of individualism, while Le Bon's seminal analysis of *The Crowd* (1896) discouraged reliance on reason among the agitated masses. Cummings responded to Tarde's theories about the laws of imitation, the preeminence of ideational over materialist forces, and the positive effects of the evolution of popular sovereignty (Tarde, [1899] 1974), finding them complementary to certain principles asserted by William James and Josiah Royce (Cummings, 1890). By 1896–97, Cummings had incorporated Franklin H. Giddings's concept of "consciousness of kind" into his own comprehensive social psychology.

Cummings made careful and comprehensive studies of the effects of labor-arbitration laws, trade-union organization in England and the United States, and cooperative forms of production and commerce in those countries and in France. Arbitration was largely ineffective as a means of resolving strikes and lockouts, Cummings reported: "There have been elaborate laws, and laws that did little more than suggest a special application of generally recognized principles of arbitration; but the former have been charged with 'red tape' and the latter with informality" (1887, 497). Moreover, arbitration, collective bargaining, and other forms of industrial-conflict resolution were guided by neither an enlightened nor an ethical public opinion. The violent outbreaks of labor unrest at Homestead and Chicago revealed a "chaotic condition of public opinion" that required considerable reeducation.

"Unhappily," he went on, "a weak sentimentality sometimes prevails over . . . sober judgment." The belief "that the laborer engaged in a strike has a real grievance is allowed to outweigh the greater grievance which society has against those who . . . resort to war without even [going through] the formality of peaceful overtures." The problem at bottom was ethical and in effect required a science of ethics for the guidance of society.

> If society is to escape the unpleasant dilemma of a prolonged period of industrial warfare or a temporary relapse into the maternal tutelage of stricter regulations, public opinion must concede more duties as well as rights to industrial organizations; it must provide itself with the best means of accurate judgment in blame or praise of contending parties; and it must rouse the public conscience enough to make the praise or blame effective. [Cummings, 1895, 371]

Trade unions and cooperatives were also less-than-effective solutions to the Social Question. Cummings was quite favorably impressed with the development of unionization among the trades and crafts in England. However, in the United States, he believed, "every big strike is certain to be accompanied by hoodlum violence, murder and sedition"; hence, he suggested that "society can better afford to deprive wage-earners of this organized power 'to withdraw temporarily the supply of their labor from the market' than to suffer the graver evils attendant upon its exercise" (Cummings, 1895).[2] Three kinds of cooperative associations had developed side by side the trade unions. Two of these types, workmen's associations and profit-sharing organizations, found their greatest development in France, where Cummings had nothing but praise for them. The third, however, cooperatives devoted to production and distribution, tended to fail, not only because of the "ignorance of the associates, insufficient capital, and lack of confidence in managers" but also because of their managers' refusal to gain the support of labor by sharing profits with them" (Cummings, 1890a). Worst of all, however, was "the persistent failure of the cooperative store." Cummings explained this failure as a product of "premature" development:

> There is scarcely any corporate ill with which it has not been afflicted. It has suffered in the past from entangling alliances with the nebulous program-mers of other movements; from the democratic optimism which believes in the inevitableness of success and the impossibility of attempting too much; from contempt for small savings, contempt for history, and lack of good advice; from instability of population due to immigration from without and migration within; most of all, from instability of leadership, due to the ready outlet for business ability in enterprises where success brings greater rewards, both in money and in social advancement.

Ultimately Cummings was forced to reconsider the effects of the evolu-tionary process on mental and moral development. Cummings believed that the evolutionary process moved unevenly among humans, allowing some to advance while others fell behind. This meant that at any moment the well-endowed and the unfit coexisted in disharmonious and unpro-ductive relationships with one another. Evolution could not be expected to save everyone. Although the long-term trend was away from egoism and toward altruistic feeling, what Cummings called "controlled phi-lanthropy" could be a useful temporary expedient. Ironically, Cum-mings's philanthropic program would aid in the elimination of misfits and deviants, the mental miscreants whose state of mind fosters their own and their neighbor's misery. Cummings's social meliorism found a path toward utopia through elimination of the psychic causes of the Social Question.

His basic desire was to instill into the minds of the masses the social values and mental characteristics essential to mankind's progress. In Cummings, and in the intellectual environment in which he taught, there was a sure sense of class superiority that his son, the poet e. e. cummings, remarked upon more than a half-century later: "In the world of my boyhood . . . before time was space and Oedipus was a complex and re-ligion was the opiate of the people and pigeons had learned to play ping-pong . . . social stratification not merely existed but luxuriated" (e. e. cummings, 1953, 31). But there was also an element of Protestantism's own version of noblesse oblige, moral uplift of the poor; the great un-washed would be helped toward regeneration by those who had already experienced it.[3] Unlike Sumner, who believed that the process of laissez-faire would produce both its own modes of selection and a new set of societal values, Cummings's applied sociology was to be carried out by the state and would create a society in which all would affirm the same values. And the whole would constitute a united commonwealth of virtue.

In such a united commonwealth, moral but not social stratification would be eliminated. Class struggle would be replaced by ethical revolution. For Cummings, Marx's utopia, a classless society of economic equals, would be exchanged for a society in which all could be morally regenerate without being socially or economically equal.[4]

Cummings's sense of noblesse oblige and his ideology of controlled philanthropy led to proposals for harsh treatment for the unregenerate. Addressing a group of Unitarian ministers in 1897, Cummings used the metaphor of a pauper thrown into a tank of water equipped with a pump:

> The tank is a workhouse, run on a reformatory plan, with an indeterminate sentence and every known device for detecting germs of virtue and stimulating its growth—to the end that the prisoner may be reformed and become fit to re-enter society and set free from the bonds of his own vices. The pump is the gospel of work, of opportunity, self-help, and temperance. There are two exits from these tanks. The one is called improvement, and stands forever open. The other is death.

Cummings's metaphor recasts Perkins's Puritan doctrine and recalls Hughes's plantation prison houses—and it also anticipates Skinner's baby box and his image of society.[5] His plan is all-encompassing and describes a benevolent but totalitarian administration with virtual control over the life or death of every designated victim of industrial advance. Those in need of rescue will be scrutinized for physical as well as moral defects, for eugenic engineering was a part of Cummings's hygienic utopia:

> The medical examination is the separation of the weak and incapable, that the utmost may be done for them in hospitals, homes for incurables, asylums, or retreats for feeble-minded. Within the walls of these tanks is no marrying or giving in marriage, or breeding of the unfit. They are the philanthropic monasteries and nunneries of the twentieth century.

Eugenics and hygienics replace God's will; rational natural science becomes the new gatekeeper for admission into the moral commonwealth. In effect, Cummings arrogated the role of gatekeeper to hygienic social scientists like himself; God gave way to the physician as the arbiter of physical, ethical, and moral canons. The medical expert was to pass judgment on the elimination of the unfit, not according to the old-fashioned signs of damnation but rather in accord with the fatefulness of heredity and the rules of rational charity: "Thus shall the hereditary burden of pauperism, disease, and crime grow less, and not greater, from generation to generation. The tramp shall cease to be a burden, the unemployed shall be fewer in the land, and charity shall injure no one whom it tries to help."

Cummings combined the rhetoric of Darwinism with the homilies of religion:

> Thus is . . . the sacrifice of the strong to the weak reconciled with progress, because *intelligent* self-sacrifice of the strong to the weak makes the strong stronger and the weak more strong. To him that hath the capacity to receive shall be given the priceless boon of opportunity, and from him that hath not shall be taken away the power of degrading himself and society. The philanthropy of the future will be wise as the serpent and gentle as the dove.

For Cummings, philanthropy aided by eugenic science was to be the instrument for achieving a virtuous utopia. The role of science was to improve on the selection process of the earlier sectarian community, to weed out more efficiently the unregenerate and the morally unqualified. Thus did Cummings's social science promise to demonstrate its own "warrantability"—a promise echoed in the 1960s with the assurance that social science would end poverty, reconstruct the American city, and provide education for all those possessing the necessary mental qualifications.[6]

BEGINNINGS OF URBAN SOCIOLOGY

Hoping to forge a new social harmony out of new immigrants, slum dwellers, and the redeemable poor, Cummings combined his quest for the moral regeneration of society with a program of social research designed to gather facts about the lives of the new urban masses. The collection and analysis of sound scientific statistics, he believed, could provide knowledge that would guide mankind toward the realization of an ideal society inspired by competitive progress within a framework of social harmony (Church, 1965). In 1893 he praised the annual report of the Connecticut Bureau of Labor as "a valuable contribution to the study of self-help organization and workingmen's insurance" and urged that other states establish similar bureaus so that nationwide statistical collections could be made.

Cummings directed his students to go out into the "sociological arena and laboratory" provided by the slums and immigrant areas of the industrial city. A model for social scientific fact gathering had been provided, he claimed, by Charles Booth's meticulous omnium-gatherum on London's poor, and by the methods of action research employed by the Webbs. Cummings was the first American sociologist to make the link between the methods of urban research being developed in England and the ethnographic study of the urban community. Its first expression was found in W. E. B. Du Bois's *Philadelphia Negro* ([1899] 1967) and its ultimate development in the urban community studies encouraged by Robert E. Park at the University of Chicago. Neither in the *Philadelphia Negro* nor in his essays (1901) did Du Bois acknowledge any influence from Cummings's teachings, even though he had been enrolled in Cummings's "Principles of Sociology: Development of the Modern State and Its Functions" just before the latter published an important article encouraging empirical investigation in the city slums.[7] Similarly, neither Park nor any of his biographers mentions Cummings in describing Park's years in search of a social psychology at Harvard—yet it is difficult to read the writings of Park and his students in urban sociology without being reminded of both the style and the substance of Cummings's observations about the effect on the masses of the modern industrial city:

> The great cities concentrate the great class which are being pushed to the wall. The rate of human wear and tear is dreadful in a great city. The great city draws in the best brains and brawn of the country all about. It is there that the great prizes are won but failure comes there too. Business failure but worse yet the physical failure of bad air, late hours, excitement, bad food, bad amusements, etc. All these tend to destroy mental and moral strength. . . . The cities kill off the masses just as [*sic*] the wars of the middle ages. [Church, 1965, 48]

Cummings failed to find a method for reconstituting the moral community within America's industrial cities. His philanthropic tank remained, at best, a metaphor, containing no leads back into an acceptable social policy. His effort to reconstitute the fractured covenant through employment of Gidding's concept of the "consciousness of kind" was rejected by both Du Bois and the Chicago sociologists in the face of the racial, ethnic, and religious diversity that these authors accepted.

Cummings failed to cement the relationship between English socialism, French social theory, and American redemptionist sociology. He was dismissed from Harvard in 1900, ending the relationship between Harvard's newly developing sociology and both English Fabianism and post-Comtean French social theory. But the salvational ethics so central to his work disappeared from neither sociology nor social praxis, finding their several directions in the eugenics movement, the early urban investigations of Du Bois, and the later sociology of the city at the University of Chicago.

POLITICAL ECONOMY AND TOTAL SYSTEMS

Cummings's departure was a signal for the resumption of abstract theorizing in economics and sociology at Harvard.[8] He was replaced by Thomas Nixon Carver (1865–1961), who for three decades would dominate the sociological scene at Harvard. During this time Harvard's economics department became more closely identified with the aims of business. In 1908 the university established a graduate school of business administration (Faulkner, [1931] 1971, 197), subsequently coordinating courses in that field with those in economics. Courses on such problems as "maximizing profits, double-entry bookkeeping, and industrial organization" (Church, 1965, 85) grew in importance. In the next two decades Hugo Munsterberg supplied the psychological apparatus for Massachusetts's school vocational guidance program. In 1923 banker George F. Baker saluted Harvard's role in professionalizing the administration of business with a gift of $5 million (Faulkner, [1931] 1971, 198). Harvard's economists had entered a joint venture with American business, hoping to supply the vision and leadership that would order society. They turned over virtually the entire range of other social issues to sociology.

Under this division of labor, economics appropriated to itself the fields of economic ideology and economic policy, leaving sociology to seek substitutes for the now inadequate theologies of Puritanism. Carver's sociology—still confined formally to a single course in the economics department—gained a considerable reputation within the university. It set about the task of providing moral underpinnings to economic ideology, which would mean ordering society within the framework of a progressive evolutionary schema and coping with its diversity by supplying rationales for the existence of morally inferior economic actors, races, and ethnic groups. Firmly believing that the destiny of American civilization rested on the superiority of its moral character, Carver set out to rationalize the earlier Puritan conception of the elect (1893; 1894). Included in his theory is the notion that this character had to be protected from morally inferior groups in the society. Carver (1905) built his world view on themes taken from the works of Comte, Spencer, and Adam Smith, together with selected elements of the English perspectives represented by Buckle, Macaulay, Darwin, Pearson, Bagehot, Galton, and Mill. His attitude toward history is clearly indicated by his adoption of Comte's famous "comparative method" as his own:

> To indicate the order of importance of the forms of society which are to be studied by the comparative method, I begin with the chief method, which consists in a comparison of the different coexisting states of human society on the various parts of the earth's surface,—those states being completely independent of each other. By this method the different stages of evolution may all be observed at once. Though the progression is single and uniform in regard to the whole race, some very considerable and very various populations have, from causes which are little understood, attained extremely unequal degrees of developments, so that the former states of the most civilized nations are now to be seen, amidst some partial differences, among contemporary populations inhabiting different parts of the globe. [1905, 56]

It was precisely this approach, transposing contemporary geographically separated peoples and cultures into a temporal series that masquerades as a developmental history, that would inspire the later works of Talcott Parsons and evoke the critical assaults of Frederick J. Teggart (1941, 82–140) and his students, especially Kenneth E. Bock (1948; 1966) and Robert Nisbet (1969, 189–208) of the department of social institutions at the University of California at Berkeley. For Carver, however, this approach permitted a sociology that avoided the onerous task of studying what actually had occurred in the past. Carver compared his own version of sociology to the task undertaken by Darwin, who, he said, "went beyond history and description and became what might be called a dynamical biologist." For the student of social change to become "a dynamical sociologist," he too would not settle for "a description of forms of social organization at different times and places" and would instead learn to "understand the factors and forces which produce social change." Carver concluded about the primacy of studying these factors and forces that transcend history, "that is what it means to be a true social evolutionist" (Carver, [1935] 1974, 11–12).

Talcott Parsons began his *Structure of Social Action* (1937) with Crane Brinton's rhetorical question, "Who now reads Spencer?" Clearly, he and his senior colleague at Harvard did. Moreover, in his final major historical works, Parsons employed the evolutionary approach associated with Spencer together with a very complex and refined variation on Comte's (and Carver's) comparative method. Thus, in a discussion of the transition from "primitive" to "advanced primitive" society, Parsons begins: "Socio-cultural evolution, like organic evolution, has proceeded by differentiation from simple to progressively more complex forms" (1977). For his example of "primitive" society Parsons relied on Durkheim's, Lloyd Warner's, and Levi-Strauss's descriptions of the Australian Murngin—a *contemporary* people; for his "advanced primitive" societies he reviewed the findings of Firth on certain contemporary Polynesian peoples, and those of Nadel, Forde, Fortes, Schapera, Evans-Pritchard, and other anthropologists on several contemporary African tribal forms of social organization. These contemporary peoples, distributed over the earth's surface (and because of the ease of air travel nearly all available to today's observer), were rearranged to form a general *historical sequence* of societal evolution. To his credit, Parsons admits, "I am able to say little about the detailed sequence of events in the course of which primitive societies begin their differentiation into more stratified societies." But it is precisely this "detailed sequence of events" that is required to verify what Parsons—and Carver before him—asserted was "the pressure [on a primitive society] to adapt more successfully to its physical, biological, cultural, social, and psychological environments" (Parsons, 1977, 48)—the pressure to change. The modern usage of the "comparative method" circumvents history altogether, as various identifiable peoples are abstracted into sociological types ("primitive," "advanced primitive," etc.), and the types are then arranged according to an imposed deductive logic as a "history." What actually happened to the Murngin, Polynesians, Bantus, Nuer, and Tallensi is of course known: Their transition to modern life was punctuated by violent and socially disruptive clashes between Western civilization and nativistic resistance. These were disorderly, abrupt, and often destructive processes that were overlooked or glossed over by the evolutionary perspective. Parsons presents an orderly evolutionary scheme that disconnects social processes from the actual history of colonialism, imperialism, and the natives' responses to them. Furthermore, Parsons's theory reclassifies certain contemporary peoples as ancestors of Western civilization.[9]

Parsons's and Carver's theories of civilizational evolution provide a secular account of the Christian march to utopia. At the time of Carver's evolutionary sociology, industrial capitalism threatened to undermine the moral foundations of Western historiography. Concrete histories and theological constructions inevitably come into conflict; abstract evolutionary theories circumvented this conflict by constructing conjectural "histories" consistent with their theological world views. Implicit in Carver's theory, but more visible in Parsons's, is the assumption that America constitutes the highest stage of world evolutionary development—America becomes the City of God, the symbol of perfection and an object for emulation. Moral and economic superiority is identified with the highest stage of evolution. By definition the most advanced industrial society is also the worthiest.

Theories that attempt to achieve closure, however, also have an inherent tendency to seek consistency and comprehensiveness. This thrust to construct a totalistic social theory demands consideration of all issues subsumed under a sociodicy—inequality of occupational rewards, racial discrimination, conflicts between classes, and the problems of suffering and opportunities for salvation. This also requires development of moral and ethical attitudes. Both religious and secular theories presume the existence of a standard for distinguishing between the worthy and the unworthy, between acceptable and unacceptable conduct. Parsons's sociology virtually attempts to duplicate the Puritan index of reputability. The concept of deviance, especially as developed by Parsons's student Robert K. Merton, provides an index and taxonomy of disreputability. A peculiarly American contribution to social theory, the concept of deviance presupposes a national normative consensus, a nationwide covenant of visible saints.

Carver, like Cummings, was concerned with how America might dispose of or absorb its new slum dwellers and recently arrived immigrants.

Or, in theological terms: How can a morally superior society deal with the great mass of unregenerates in its midst? Carver's standard for inclusion or exclusion combined moral virtue with economic productivity, and allowed for the influence of environmental conditions. Referring to slum dwellers, he observed ([1935] 1974, 405) that it is the "height of absurdity . . . when it is argued that an individual who grows up in a slum environment can never have anything but slum incidents in his memory background, and that he is therefore a slum product." Some kinds of slum experience could stimulate "chastity, sobriety, 'generosity, courage, chivalry, and devotion." This carefully circumscribed environmental influence was modified for Carver, as it was for Cummings, by genetic inheritance. Social progress was to be achieved in part by programmatic controls over birth and heredity.

> A community which has more ditch diggers than it can use in combination with its limited supply of competent engineers will always be in a bad way. . . . Any process which would increase the proportion of ditch diggers would have to be called dysgenic. The question becomes, therefore, are we likely to get as large a proportion of competent engineers from the progeny of ditch diggers as from the progeny of engineers? . . . It seems to depend upon the percentages of economic successes among the children of the two classes. This, in turn, seems to depend upon the extent to which the qualities which make the parents high or low producers are transmitted to their children. [431–32]

Unskilled workers of whatever race or ethnic group, immigrant or native, were to be judged on the basis of their productive capacity, inherited and acquired. This was, of course, one more expression of the distinction between the worthy and the unworthy poor, and, like the theological version, it was based on a person's willingness to work and to be productive. In *The Essential Factors of Social Evolution*—written in 1935, twelve years after the Omnibus Immigration Act established quota systems that encouraged immigration from northern and western Europe but virtually cut off admission of migrants from Asia and southern and eastern Europe—Carver reasserted the Puritan means test as a criterion for social acceptance and community respect.

Carver approached the race question solely in eugenic terms, offering almost no possibility for redemption to any of the nonwhite races. "Indiscriminate mixing" of races and nations through intermarriage would be no guarantee of improved American stock, because the immigration process had brought both the best and the worst to the United States: "Immigrants who are driven from their homes because of revolt against an irrational or superstitious religion, because of an intolerable political situation, or because they are persecuted for their righteousness, presumably represent the best of their race. Immigrants who come because they have failed to make a living in their own country, are not likely to be the most capable and resourceful citizens of their home country." Even so, Carver placed his reliance on a biological sociology and its possible applications to population policy. "The eugenic or dysgenic effects of race-mixture are still under investigation," he wrote. "It is not improbable that, in time, it may be found that certain race mixtures produce desirable crosses and others not" (444). However, "the safer policy seems to be to maintain racial purity until we have convincing evidence that race-mixture is desirable." Carver presumed that he had uncovered a scientific basis for rationally determining who would be accepted and who would be excluded from the community of the redeemed.

One additional point worth examining is Carver's special treatment of anti-Semitism. *The Essential Factors of Social Evolution,* published two years after Hitler came to power in Germany and more than a dozen years after the establishment of fascism in Italy,[10] elaborates his opposition to dysgenic amalgamation. In Zionism he saw an ideological basis for establishing permanent territorial separation between Jews and Christians, thereby reducing both intermingling and anti-Semitism. However, apparently ignorant of the Christian roots of anti-Semitism and of the early Church Synod's prohibitions on Christian-Jewish intermarriage (see Isaac, 1964; Parkes, 1969, 57–73; Lyman, 1978, 62) he singled out Jewish endogamy as the principal cause for persecution of the Jews:

> The[ir] persecution is traceable to the determination of the orthodox Jews not to amalgamate with the Gentile population. They realized that nothing could prevent such amalgamation except the studied cultivation of a dislike of non-Jews. . . . The cultivation of a positive dislike was very naturally reciprocated, with the result that, in a country where the Jews were numerous enough to make an impression on the public mind and yet not numerous enough to be strong, they were persecuted and subject to pogroms. ([1935] 1974, 447–48)

In other words, in a remarkable instance of blaming the victim for his condition, Carver holds the Jews responsible for their status in the Christian world because they had originated the dislike for Gentiles and refused to intermarry. He begs the question of genetic election[11] into the new secular covenant and at the same time condemns altogether those who voluntarily opt out of it.

The ultimate objective of Carver's system of selection was to admit into the community only those most likely to contribute to the peace and harmony of its social and economic life. To this end Carver formulated a fourfold table similar to the logico-deductive formulations that would later characterize Parsons's sociology. He used as one of his variables Franklin H. Giddings's concept of consciousness of kind.

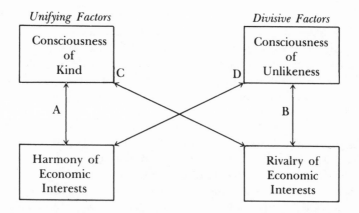

Figure 1. Carver's Graph of Race Relations

Carver hypothesized that a combination of "consciousness of kind" and "harmony of economic interests" produced the "most favorable" chances for "peace and harmony"; a combination of "consciousness of unlikeness" and "rivalry of economic interests" produced the "least favorable" chances; and combinations of "consciousness of kind" and "rivalry of economic interests" or of "harmony of economic interests" and "consciousness of unlikeness" produced situations "somewhere between the two extremes."

At no point did Carver test his propositions over the record of American history, or even the record of race relations in the United States that the graph purportedly sought to depict. Instead, he presented an illustrative instance of each combination, and achieved plausibility by means of supposedly self-evident reason. An abstract logic that produced general principles had triumphed over concrete historical investigations.

Carver identified those unifying and divisive factors related to the realization of the American covenant. His vision of American society was neither pluralistic nor laissez-faire; instead, it foresaw a hierarchy of the biologically elect, each accorded a just rank, place, and station in the new commonwealth.[12]

CARVER, TAUSSIG, PARSONS, MARX

Carver rested his system on the assumption that all social conflict is founded upon economic scarcity of one kind or another, thus laying one more stone for the foundation of an American sociology that has as its goal industrial productivity, elimination of class conflict, and appropriately graded prosperity for all. But productivity could be achieved only by those who by virtue of their genetic inheritance[13] or their voluntary acceptance embraced the Puritan values of hard work, self-control, discipline, and moral purity. Therefore, election into the new covenant would wait on the discoveries of the new scientific sociologists. Biologists and positivists would provide the measures to determine qualifications for inclusion or exclusion—intelligence tests, personnel screening, genetic manipulations.

In the new order projected by Harvard's economists and sociologists the criteria for admission were the motivation to work and the desire to achieve. Frank Taussig (1906, 3), in his search for the psychosocial basis for the "desire for wealth," had determined that this was "not a simple motive, but a very complex one, made up of all sorts of differing passions and interests." Taussig's orientation toward economic motivation was introduced into sociology by Talcott Parsons, who in 1936 praised Taussig's work and four years later incorporated it into his own theory of motivation. In his 1936 essay, Parsons, whose problem was to find a theoretical link between personal motives and institutional patterns, posited "net money advantage" as the critical variable. The individual actor, or even the "social unit" in whose name the individual acted, was measurable by the standard of economic achievement.

> The fact that concretely economic activities take place in a framework of institutional patterns would imply that, typically, such disinterested elements of motivation play a role in the determination of their course. This is not in the least incompatible with the strict requirements of economic theory, for that requires only that, as between certain alternatives, choice will be made in such a way as to maximize net money advantages to the actor, or to the social unit on behalf of which he acts. [Parsons, 1940, 187–203]

By binding Taussig's theory of motivation to his own theory of action, Parsons brought together Carver's Comteanism with a secular restatement of the Protestant ethic. When Parsons attached his theory of the social system to the development of world societies, he enlarged the evolving covenant to incorporate all historical societies and civilizations within a single unified system. Eligibility for admission into that system was established in accordance with Comte's graded hierarchy of civilizational levels. The measure of civilizational admissibility is economic motivation: the need to achieve embraces the moral component that separates the regenerate from the not yet regenerate. Achievement, however, can be activated by the functioning of the system itself, thus guaranteeing the fostering of need-achievement in its social actors and units. Ultimately, all would be admitted into the worldwide covenant when the need to achieve had become a universal motivation.

Parsons claimed that he derived his system from his amalgamation of Weber, Durkheim, Marshall, Pareto, Freud, and other European thinkers, and that his "action theory" represented not only a synthesis but a forward step. His work can be better understood as an extension and elaboration of the work of Carver and Taussig.[14]

In one fundamental respect, he was deeply influenced by Weber's book

The Protestant Ethic and the Spirit of Capitalism (1930), which he had translated while still a young scholar and to which he returned in "The Symbolic Environment of Modern Economics" (1979). In this essay, one of the
last he wrote, Parsons states: "My particular interest is in calling attention
to some of the themes of religious orientation which have figured very
prominently in the history, very particularly, of Western society." He did
far more than call attention to these themes, he took on the Christian
orientation as his own and proclaimed a secular equivalent of the Protestant ethic as the source of both salvation and sociodicy for the modern
world. It was Carver, Taussig, and the American heritage of Protestant
sociology that provided Parsons with this perspective on Weber and
Marx.

Parsons treats both Marxism and Christianity as eschatologies, one
materialist, the other ideal:

> The Marxist scenario portrays modern man . . . as faced with a basically evil
> social order, although, in the background this status as evil is mitigated by the
> fact that it has advanced what Marxian theory calls the "forces of produc-
> tion." There is, however, in spite of this mitigation, a crying need for radical
> change, which may even be likened to "salvation." This change is to be
> brought about by a collective act, that of the new working class created by
> capitalism, the *proletariat.* The act of reorganization or regeneration is thus to
> come about through revolution, the result of which will be to introduce an
> ideal state of affairs, in Marxian theory called the state of *communism.*

Both Marxism and Christianity contain an eschatology of salvation and
damnation:

> In that of Christianity, it is that between the saved and the damned. Those
> anchored in the existing society are, in the nature of the case, not saved, since
> they have either not been exposed to or have not acted upon the mission of
> Christ. In the Marxian case, the analog of heaven is clearly the state of com-
> munism, and only those who have made the transition from the bourgeois or
> capitalistic society to the state of communism by way of socialism can be said,
> in this sense, to be saved.

However, the central weakness of Marxism proceeds from the fact that
it "is confined in substantive references entirely to this world." Christianity, on the other hand, has been able to transcend its specific history
and sublimate its ideals so that its enduring strength derives from the
evolution in which its supramundane concepts "have . . . dropped out
and [been] replaced by concepts derived in particular from economic
theory." It was the Reformation that made this sublimation possible, in
that "it collapsed the duality of previous forms of Christianity as between
the empirical world of this life and the transcendental world." But the
ending of the bifurcation separating this world from the next introduced
a new moral and historical dilemma; namely, "that the question could not

be avoided how far they had in fact succeeded in fulfilling the mission of building the Kingdom of God on Earth." Marxism, from this point of view, becomes a critique of the failure of the Christian promise. Thus, the Protestant position brought the problem of the moral quality of life into this world, whereas Marxism projects the moral regeneration of the world into a utopic future.

For Parsons all this led to a sublimated variant of the worldly rejection of religion. The problem of salvation remains, but it is to be solved by a species of moral rather than political economy, stressing justification through work for capitalists, bourgeoisie, and proletariat. Rejecting Weber's vision of the irreversible disenchantment of the modern world, Parsons offers a secular theodicy of salvation through work and evolution.

NOTES

1. Cummings used as texts in his courses Beatrice and Sidney Webb's *History of Trade Unionism in England* (1894) and *Industrial Democracy* (1898) and was much impressed by the research carried out by Charles Booth in his seventeen-volume *Life and Labour of the People in London* (1889–1902). For a discussion of the relation of these works to the beginnings of sociology in England, see Abrams, 1968. For the history of the Fabians, see MacKenzie and MacKenzie, 1977.

2. After this position had become firmly entrenched among the canons of industrial sociology, it was vigorously criticized as a part of Herbert Blumer's reconceptualization of the nature of labor-management conflicts. See chapter 14 for an analysis of Blumer's approach to industrial relations.

3. The commitment to class and status stratification combined with the obligation to give charity in a rational and calculated way are parts of the subculture of "proper Bostonians" and their Harvard scions. For a discerning portrait of this group see Amory, 1957, 167–86, 291–311.

4. The well-known affinity between Marxist and socially conscious Protestant thinkers is partly explained by the fact that each promises a utopia. Their frequent quarrels and failure to understand each other no doubt stem from the difference between moral and economic utopias and the fact that Protestantism withholds regeneracy from the unworthy poor, whereas under Marxism all can be saved. In Marxist praxis, however, the unregenerate turn out to be the lumpen proletariat.

5. It is worth noting that Bannister (1979, 155, 271) regards Cummings's essay on "Charity and Progress" as an assault on the new alliance of religion and natural selection and as a tongue-in-cheek rejoinder to Benjamin F. Kidd's *Social Evolution*, published in 1894. Church (1965, 44), on the other hand, treats the same essay as "Cummings' resolution of his own dilemma and . . . his answer to the primary question posed by economists across the Western World."

6. When the promises made by the positive social scientists of the 1960s failed to be fulfilled, the sociobiologists, the present-day equivalents of Cummings's eugenic meliorists, took the opportunity thus presented to establish their own claim to regenerate mankind by means of a genetic fix. At present it finds expression in sperm banks for the reproduction of geniuses, proposals for regulated breeding to improve educational achievement, and the continued practice in some states and localities of sterilizing the "unfit." These are instances in which the biological criterion is used to separate the regenerate from the unregenerate. Because genetic engineering takes an unspecified amount of evolutionary time, sociobiolo-

gists are less vulnerable to discreditation than have been the positive social scientists who thought they could produce quick results.

7. Du Bois's dismissal of Giddings's most famous concept—"I could not lull my mind to hypnosis by regarding a phrase like 'consciousness of kind' as a scientific law" (1968, 205)—may have been a slap at Cummings, who employed the concept in his own theory of regeneration.

Cummings taught three courses during his nine years at Harvard. In addition to "Principles" he introduced "The Social and Economic Condition of Workingmen in the United States and Other Countries" (1892–93) and "The Labor Question" (1896–99). (See Church, 1965, 48).

8. Writing about economics at Harvard a quarter of a century later, Karl Worth Bigelow called attention to the "socialist," "realist," and "interventionist" challenges to the classical discipline, but pointed proudly to a healthy "revival of abstraction" that still, however, needed defense; moreover, Bigelow wondered whether "historical," "institutional," and other "realist" schools could find their way out of what he called "Schmoller's confusion: deterministically excusing the economic past as inevitable, while damning the order of the present for not being other than it is, and proposing to mold the order of the future in [a] most undeterminist fashion?" (1925, 394).

9. For a study that takes a historically specific rather than "evolutionary" attitude toward a non-Western society, see Vidich, (1981).

10. Carver's discussion of anti-Semitism can also be seen as a belated response to the scandal that erupted in 1922 when Harvard became the first major university to openly introduce quotas on the number of Jews admitted. Harvard's "Jewish problem" arose from the increasing admission of the offspring of recently arrived Eastern European immigrants, most of them Jewish. For a good discussion of this and later episodes in the context of American racial and ethnic thought see Steinberg, 1981, 222–52.

11. Two years later, the Chicago sociologist Ellsworth Faris would urge Jews to marry Gentiles because "there are excellent eugenic arguments for crossings of this sort, and . . . the gesture and example would count for much" (1937, 352).

12. Today, genetic engineering brings the older eugenic programs of social thinkers such as Cummings and Carver into the forefront of modern secular eschatologies. Genetic engineers and gene splitters hope to refashion and presumably improve the biological and social characteristics of those in the society who remain unregenerate.

13. It is worth noting that Carver's colleague William Z. Ripley had replaced Edward Cummings's brother, John Cummings, at Harvard in 1900 after Cummings had critically assaulted Ripley's "anthroposociology," a species of anatomical radicalism celebrating the relative superiority of dolichocephalic Nordics. John Cummings, a true historical sociologist, refused to accept any biological, physical, or anatomic theories. (See 1900; Ripley, 1900.) Ahistorical biologism has recently resurfaced at Harvard in the works of E. O. Wilson, who analogized his picture of society from the study of ant communities (1980, 1979; Oster and Wilson, 1978). Anthroposociology, or its modern form, sociobiology, has been subjected to a devastating critique by the leading representative of the University of California's Department of Social Institutions (Bock, 1980), where John Cummings would have felt more at home than at Harvard.

14. Parsons, who had begun his career in the department of political economy, became increasingly interested in sociology and in the general system built by Carver. When Parsons joined the Harvard faculty in 1927, Carver, Taussig, Ripley, Edwin F. Gay, and Joseph Schumpeter were among the senior professors who profoundly influenced the early development of his own thought (see 1977a, 23). It would appear that Parsons, in *The Structure of Social Action* ([1937] 1949), substituted Marshall for Carver and Taussig as an exemplar for the concept of economic society and the incentive derived from justification through work.

CHAPTER 7

The "Rational" Management of Society: Hugo Munsterberg

Hugo Munsterberg was the first social scientist at Harvard who sought to merge the Protestant orientation of American philosophy, psychology, and sociology with German positive and experimental science.[1] In doing so, he affirmed an independent social utility for science in a way that emphasizes positivism's essential assumption that social "causes" exist, are discoverable by objective experimentation, and can be rationally utilized to construct a better society. His work complemented Harvard's Protestant conceptions of social science with a technicist, laboratory-oriented science.

Munsterberg believed that a science of society could not develop in the United States until the university system, and especially Harvard, developed a professoriat committed to the values of science. His view heralded a new claim by professional social scientists to societal importance. Through their research they would proclaim a mandate to manage modern society. A practical public philosopher, Munsterberg sought to establish the university's privileged position as the creator of a new sociodicy. Harvard was prepared to send social science missionaries into the world to enter into a cooperative relationship with the new men of power in business, government, education, law, and mass communications.

A major protagonist in the *Methodenstreit* of late nineteenth- and early twentieth-century Germany, Munsterberg argued for a psychophysical parallelism. "Being" (*Sein*) belonged to the realm of science and was governed by laws of cause and effect; "willing" (*Sollen*) belonged to the everyday world and was governed by principles of an illusory teleology. Armed with his scientific knowledge of mind states and their relation to brain states, Munsterberg felt confident about psychologists' ability to apply the methods and findings of experimental psychology to practical problems. Munster-

berg argued against confusing the predictive and controlling powers of a
Naturwissenschaft like psychology or sociology with the willful understanding involved in a *Geisteswissenschaft* such as history or the religiously based
Social Ethics of Francis Greenwood Peabody. When, in 1914, Munsterberg allowed that there might be a *Geisteswissenschaftliche* psychology, he
referred this new psychology to the experts and their collection of the
relevant "psychological facts," admitting that "at present it would be a
vain undertaking to present even in outline the facts of purposive psychology" (1914a, 313).

Munsterberg, who regarded science as on the rise in America and
"psychology [as] the most favoured of all the philosophical disciplines at
the present time" (1907, 437), scoffed at the variety of popular and unscientific proposals for social reform. The Social Question in America, he
pointed out, consisted of debates about the Negro, women's suffrage,
"the half-economic and half-social problem of the extremes between poor
and rich," and the "unspeakable misery in the slums of New York and
Chicago, in which the lowest immigrants from Eastern Europe have
herded themselves together and form a nucleus for all the worst repro-
bates of the country" (158). He observed with disdain that "somewhere
nearer the periphery of public thought there are various . . . social propa-
gandas, as that for the relief of the poor and for improving penal institutions." There was no place for sentimental philanthropy or misguided
compassion in the social sciences, and Munsterberg expressed this opinion in his blunt condemnation of his colleagues in the social ethics department. In 1903 he wrote to Peabody that his "Special Department" of social
ethics was certainly "very pleasant company" but "from the standpoint of
pure philosophy, it lies of course somewhat on the periphery of the field
and . . . we should regret, therefore, if it should give too much the real
stamp to the whole building." The issue was not pure versus applied social
science but rather the cultivation of a dispassionate social science separate
from Christian ethics or any other moral concern. Munsterberg hoped to
eliminate the settlement house as the agency of social reconstruction and
replace it with the laboratory.

The prerequisites for developing a truly applicable social and psychological science already existed in the universities, Munsterberg believed.
Reviewing the status of American science education in 1907, he reported
that "everything necessary to the modern cultivation of historical science
[is] to be found abundantly" (1907, 439). In American philology was to be
found "scientific work of the strictest sort" and "the country looks like a
tremendous experimental laboratory of political economy" (441) while
"in the natural sciences . . . the American by no means favours only practical studies" (442), and "the theory of knowledge, ethics, and above all
psychology, are very prosperous" (437). Munsterberg pointed out that

"the actual achievements [of these sciences in America] are very uneven; . . . in some directions [they are] superior to those of England and France—in a few directions even to those of Germany" (447). He was pleased that in recent years the conditions suitable for the cultivation of science, once so unpromising, "had given way to more favourable factors" (447).

Endowments to the universities had supplied "appliances . . . books, apparatus, laboratories, and collections for those who wish to study, but all that never makes a great scientist. . . . For, after all, science depends *chiefly* on the personal factor; and good men can do everything, even on narrow means" (448). The "personal factor," however, was being aided by two distinctively positive socioeconomic processes.

> The more important factor . . . improves the social status of scientific workers, so that better human material is now attracted to the scientific career. . . . Science has been recognized by the nation; scientific and university life has become rich in significance, the professor is no longer a school-teacher, and the right kind of young scholar is stepping into the arena. [448]

The other factor was a matter of generational development. For Munsterberg, in 1907, the decisive change in the generation of scholars coming of age in his era was the occupational shift "from trade to art and science," and the activation by the new men of science to the New England variant of the Puritan ethic (448). By his time a large part of the inner reorganization of Harvard and other universities had taken place, establishing career lines in both teaching and research. Aspiring and committed scientists could expect to find employment and status within the university and research laboratories of the country and to enjoy close relationships with business and government. Munsterberg was ready to move into the further development and application of his science; for "this social reappraisement of science, and its effect on the quality of men who become productive scholars, are the best indication of the coming greatness of American science" (448).

NEW SOCIODICIES OF SOCIETAL GUIDANCE

Insofar as he tried to develop scientific means for adapting man and industrial society to each other, Munsterberg's work had a significance far beyond its immediate topics. His experiments in the areas of justice, personnel selection, industrial management, and the controlled administration of culture were conducted in the expectation that their results would be applied to societal management. In each area, his science hoped to supply sociodicies of guilt and innocence, redemption and salvation, acceptance or exclusion, self-denial or self-actualization.

THE SCIENTIFIC BASIS FOR FAITH IN JUSTICE

For Munsterberg the new European, especially German, psychology had "made a new discovery. It has found out that men are not alike." Human differences are manifested in memory, and hence in testimony. His class-room experiments showed that suggestibility had to varying degrees influenced his students' abilities to evaluate the intensity of colors, and that the same students who erred in color judgments also had highly selective perceptions of ordinary activities. He concluded that a color test "can pick out for us those minds which are probably unfit to report, whether an action has been performed in their presence or not" (Munsterberg, 1908, 63–64). Eyewitness testimony or oath-bound means of securing reliable statements in a courtroom could no longer be regarded as valid or reliable. In their place Munsterberg offered the techniques developed by the experimental scientist.

America's judicial system had in effect empowered the judge and jury to act in place of the Puritan magistrates, to distinguish the regenerate from the unregenerate, the innocent from the guilty. Munsterberg argued that a jury could not be counted upon to mete out justice. Science would replace the failed theodicy of adjudication with an infallible sociodicy of experimental psychology. That justice could be made certain and not subject to human foibles was within the power of science. He hoped to establish a method capable of determining truth or falsehood, guilt or innocence, without reliance on the imperfect judicial system.

In 1907 *McClure's Magazine* sent Munsterberg to Boise, Idaho, to ascertain the truth in the hotly contested trial of IWW leader William "Big Bill" Haywood and his two colleagues for conspiracy to murder Governor Frank Steunenberg (see Foner, 1965, 40–59; Busch, 1962, 13–43). Utilizing his "chronoscope," Munsterberg administered word-association tests to Frank Orchard, Steunenberg's confessed killer and the state's key witness against Haywood. The Boston *Herald* quoted Munsterberg as stating that his tests had proved "Orchard's confession is every word of it true." Because this remarkable statement was published before the jury had reached its verdict, Munsterberg was censured in some quarters for improper interference in the trial process. In addition, to his chagrin, his scientific technique was challenged by fellow psychologists with respect to both its reliability and its validity. In an unpublished article, he defended his method:

> No witnesses for the prosecution and no outside evidence could have such convincing character as the results of the tests, and no witnesses for the defence and, of course, no opinion of twelve jurymen could have shaken this scientific finding. . . . As far as the objective facts are concerned my few hours of experimenting were more convincing than anything which in all those weeks of the trial became demonstrated. [Hale, 1980, 117]

When the jury found all the defendants innocent, Munsterberg modified his position to assert that his tests showed that Orchard certainly *believed* he had told the truth. His belief in the powers of his "lie detector" were undiminished: "To deny that the experimental psychologist has indeed possibilities of determining the 'truth-telling powers' is just as absurd as to deny that the chemical expert can find out whether there is arsenic in a stomach or whether blood spots are of human or of animal origin" (1908). He insisted that his application of experimental psychology to criminal justice was proper, even humane, because it would eliminate the police tendency to extract confessions by beating and torturing prisoners. Science would serve to humanize the system of criminal justice and induce criminals to testify against themselves. An accused party could not refuse to take the tests: "An innocent man will not object to our proposing a series of one hundred associations to demonstrate his innocence. A guilty man, of course, will not object either, as a declination would indicate a fear of betraying himself; he cannot refuse, and yet affirm his innocence" (1908, 82).

Among some social scientists, today, the desire to place justice in the hands of the expert overrides any faith in a judicial system served by judges, attorneys, witnesses, and juries. As recently as 1974, psychologist Robert Buckhout lamented the failure to adjust jurisprudence to Munsterberg's scientific findings:

> It is discouraging to note that the essential findings on the unreliability of eyewitness testimony were made by Hugo Munsterberg nearly 80 years ago, and yet the practice of basing a case on eyewitness testimony and trying to persuade a jury that such testimony is superior to circumstantial evidence continues to this day.

The continued search for a way of ascertaining guilt or innocence other than by having men and women sit in judgment of their peers reveals the depth of many skeptics' distrust of present juridical practice. Attempts to justify social scientific and technological intervention in the criminal justice system continue to the present day and are exemplified by the recent clandestine "bugging" of juries by one team of sociologists (Strodtbeck, 1962), by the ethnomethodological and sociopsychological simulation of jury procedures in the small groups laboratories of major universities (Garfinkel, 1967, 104–05; Mills, 1967), and by the increasing employment of lie detectors in industrial and commercial personnel-management procedures.[2] For such researchers science promises a foolproof alternative to human judgments. Munsterberg's experiments and applications were prophetic beginnings of what promised to become an administrative science of justice, a science that would exonerate or condemn with as sure an eye as that of God.

FAITH IN APTITUDES, INTELLIGENCE, AND WORK

A central problem for America's emerging industrial order was how to place the right worker in the right job. Like Veblen, who coined the phrase "instinct of workmanship," Munsterberg assumed that all individuals have a propensity for creative expression and an aptitude for work. As a sociodicy this assumption required coming to terms with such issues as inequalities between blue- and white-collar workers, the numbing boredom that accompanies certain jobs, mistakes in career selection, and the anomic loss of identity created by so much of modern work. Munsterberg turned his attention to each of these problems.

The practical problem of how to fit person to job and job to person provided Munsterberg with an opportunity to test his theory of the harmony between mind and setting. In 1907, he was invited by Frank Parsons, founder of the Boston Vocation Bureau (an organization designed to "aid young people in choosing an occupation, preparing themselves for it, finding an opening in it, and building up a career of efficiency and success" [Parsons, 1908]), to formulate mental tests for measuring occupational capacities. He entered into the task with the same zeal he had brought to criminal trials. The mental attitude of Parsons's clients was the key to their aptitude, but it could not be apprehended by self-reports, interviews, or surveillance of their everyday life. "The ordinary individual," Munsterberg pointed out, "knows very little of his own mental functions: on the whole he knows them as little as he knows the muscles which he uses when he talks or walks. . . . [But] half an hour's experimenting in the laboratory may tell us more about a man's attention than half a year's living with him" (1913, 43–45). The tests he designed for the Vocation Bureau were the forerunners of the questionnaires routinely administered today for educational and occupational placement (Mann, 1954, 141–42; Kett, 1977, 239–43).

A major problem after the Civil War was to find a means for bringing new members (youth, immigrants, ex-slaves) into society's existing institutions, and especially for filling jobs and finding the correct career. Instead of measuring the individual's religious qualifications for participation in a community of the elect, new techniques were designed to measure his fitness for specific jobs, giving him a rightful place in the mundane community. The Puritan God's incomprehensible justice and predestined life plans were replaced by the results of aptitude and intelligence tests and by the distribution of ascertainable skills and talents. Under this logic, a man's fate could be both acknowledged and justified as the result of a particular interplay of biological and environmental processes that only the scientist could discover. The occupational structure stratified with respect to both prestige and rewards, lent itself readily to differential distributions of aptitude and intelligence as measured by the industrial psychologist. In terms of the new sociodicy, therefore, each individual could find some solace in his or her particular situation. An inscrutable God had been replaced by a rational, visible, comprehensible, and universal system of placement and reward.[3]

Munsterberg took the same approach to the problems of American business and industry, seeking to apply his nomothetic science to the rational administration of already established work norms and reward values. The Taylor system of time and motion studies had already become a bone of contention in labor–management relations. Munsterberg proposed that his psychotechnics could bypass the conflict by fitting the appropriate mental state to the particular industrial task. He conceived of psychological tests for almost all kinds of workers—for trolley-car drivers, telephone operators, salespeople, advertising executives. Although fellow psychologists were skeptical, major industries and many businesses were impressed, and his tests were much in demand.

Munsterberg was the first to suggest that changes in color scheme and the kinds of sound workers heard could have profound effects on morale and performance. The novel idea of the importance of job satisfaction— even happiness—reconceived the very meaning of work. No longer was it merely a burdensome means to achieve salvation according to God's ordinances. Under Munsterberg's logic, work became a source of self-actualization, and its own reward.

Adapting an idea of the German industrial psychologist Adolf Levenstein,[4] Munsterberg proposed in 1913 that a massive psychological attitude survey be made among some fifteen thousand factory and mill workers. The results, he wrote Harvard's President Lowell, "would form a kind of sociological background for certain investigations on monotony and similar questions which are being examined at present in our psychological laboratory." Although the project was never carried out, certain of its questions foreshadow those of the famous Hawthorne studies, begun at the Western Electric Plant in Chicago in 1927 (Roethlisberger and Dickson, [1939] 1966).

> "Do you think it important for the factory to provide good health conditions, good light, fresh air, cleanliness and attractive grounds, or do you not care for that?"
>
> "Do you feel any pride in or loyalty to the company for which you work, or is it indifferent to you for whom you work?"
>
> "Do you enjoy your work as something which helps the progress of the country, or do you not care for that?"

Work-associated boredom and monotony interested Munsterberg. In *Psychology and Industrial Efficiency* (1913), he asserted: ". . . [E]xperimental psychology offers no more inspiring idea than this adjustment of work and psyche by which mental dissatisfaction in work, mental depression and discouragement, may be replaced in our social community by overflowing joy and perfect inner harmony" (309). However, such an adjustment would require a precise knowledge of the mental skills requisite to each type of job in the factory, business, or office. Munsterberg sought to obtain such knowledge by a survey of a thousand diverse manufacturers.

Munsterberg's approach ran counter to the trend toward standardization. He suggested, for example, that typewriters be chosen according to the mental attributes of their users, as revealed by his tests; but the implied rejection of the notion of interchangeable, immediately replaceable operators won him few friends in business. For Munsterberg, man rather than the machine was the center of the universe. The world of industry could be adapted to individual limits, aptitudes, and ability; he spoke not of behavior modification but rather of the duty of every worker to labor in behalf of building up modern civilization. He believed that workers would become "inspired by the belief in the ideal value of the work as work and as a necessary contribution to the progress of mankind. [Then] the social question will be solved, as all the differences which socialism wants to eliminate . . . [will] appear trivial and insignificant (1914, 108).

Munsterberg envisioned a dutiful body of cooperating workers whose collective efforts would create fulfillment for all within the framework of a unified American culture. The integrity of the worker's mental state, he believed, ought to be of major concern for political leaders, industrial managers, and businessmen.

CULTURAL CONSENSUS AND THE NATIONAL MIND

After the Civil War the challenge of how to assimilate the flood of unacculturated European and Asian immigrants and recently emancipated Negroes preoccupied Social Gospelers, urban missionaries, and sociologists.[5] They turned their attention to the content of immigrant newspapers (Park, 1922), to questions asked and answers given in their editorial columns (e.g., Metzker, 1971), to the street games of immigrant children (Goodman, 1979), and to the newest vehicle of mass entertainment, persuasion, and culture, the movies (Jowett, 1976). For Munsterberg such instruments of culture might provide the clues for forging a unified American society.[6] The media of public opinion, popular entertainment, and mass appeal would, willy-nilly, produce a social, if not a moral, consensus.

In his first years in America, Munsterberg had treated popular culture with disdain. "If the ordinary citizen is prosperous enough to indulge frequently in an evening at the theatre," he observed in 1907, "then, of course, melodrama and farce will become the regular thing, since the common man must always either laugh or cry" (149–50). However, as he immersed himself in the issues and problematics of the American consensus and the science that would reveal the dimensions of its social psychology, the mass media became of increasing interest to Munsterberg and his Harvard laboratory. His 1916 book *The Film: A Psychological Study*, the first full-length study of its kind, provided a trenchant analysis of the social effects of films as well as their psychological potential. In Munsterberg's view, movies not only revealed the basic operations of the mind but also offered America an opportunity to forge a national "soul." He had discovered the potential for a powerful relationship among mind, propaganda, assimilation, and national culture.

"The photoplay," argued Munsterberg, "obeys the laws of mind rather than those of the outer world." The basic process of mind had suddenly been made available through the combination of technological innovation and artistic insight. The silent photoplay forced the viewers to concentrate on the *action* depicted on the screen in order to grasp the *meanings* and *motives* involved, guided to a surer understanding by the filmmaker's techniques. Film, he observed, objectified mental states at the very moment that it made them visible. The process of memory is objectified through the use of the "cut-back," while that of attending is manifested in the use of the "close-up." "In both cases the act which in the ordinary theater would go on in our minds alone is here in the photography projected into the pictures themselves."

Because these movies were silent, Munsterberg believed they had the power to excite unarticulated feelings in the audience in two distinct ways: "On the one side we have those emotions in which the feelings of the persons in the play are transmitted to our own soul. On the other side, we find those feelings with which we respond to the scenes in the play, feelings which may be entirely different, perhaps exactly opposite to those which the figures in the play express."

The "intensity with which the play takes hold of the audience cannot remain without strong social effects," Munsterberg noted. He pointed to the possibility that the "sight of crime and of vice may force itself on the consciousness with disastrous results." However, by the same token, the potential influence of films provided "an incomparable power for the remolding and upbuilding of the national soul." Hence, the "intellectual, the moral, the social, and the esthetic culture of the community may be served." Just as he feared for the use of science unless it was protected and subsidized by a disinterested state apparatus, so Munsterberg saw a danger to culture unless appropriate managers governed the making of popular films. He hoped for the establishment of a "Universal Cultural

Lyceum" that would issue "moving pictures for the education of the youth of the land, picture studies in science, history, religion, literature, geography, biography, art, architecture, social science, economics, and industry."

Munsterberg recognized the enormous propaganda potential in mass culture, and perceived film technology as an important asset for producing and holding together the national soul. He wrote about the core cultural background appropriate to any photoplay: "There must be a moral wholesomeness in the whole setting, a moral atmosphere which is taken as a matter of course like fresh air and sunlight." His definition of this moral atmosphere combined Puritan and German ideas of duty: "an enthusiasm for the noble and uplifting, a belief in duty and discipline of the mind, a faith in ideals and eternal values must permeate the world of the screen." Only when assured that the national covenant was strong should American filmmakers show the seamier and sordid sides of life, but his vision of a deeply embedded culture precluded any need to shun vice, sin, or evil. "There is no crime and no heinous deed which the photoplay may not tell with frankness and sincerity." Once a new national ethics was established, each individual American would be self-steering, and each would voluntarily make a scientifically ordained contribution to the social welfare.

THE MANAGED SOCIETY AND MASS COMMUNICATIONS

Munsterberg's applied experimentalism, emphasizing the functional and static mental traits that fixed every worker in an appropriate task best suited to the individual, did not correspond to that of other American pyschologists of his day. He assumed that the managers of society would accept these mind states as givens, limiting their aspirations for total control. Most notably his experimental psychology was at variance with the approach taken by John B. Watson (1878–1958),[7] whose image of a managed society went even beyond Cummings's societal "tank." Watson emphasized human malleability and the effects that careful scientific conditioning would have on workers' performance:

> Psychology as the behaviourist views it is a purely objective experimental branch of natural science. Its theoretical goal is the prediction and control of behaviour. Introspection forms no essential part of its methods, nor is the scientific value of its data dependent upon the readiness with which they lend themselves to interpretation in terms of consciousness. *The behaviourist, in his efforts to get a unitary scheme of animal response, recognizes no dividing line between man and brute.* The behaviour of man, with all of its refinement and complexity, forms only a part of the behaviourist's total scheme of investigation. [Watson, 1913, 158]

Watson claimed that if behaviorist scientists were given control over the socialization of children and authority to design the entire social environment, they could construct utopia. He rejected altogether Munsterberg's idea of fixed mind states.

> Give me a dozen healthy infants, well-formed, and my own specified world to bring them up in and I'll guarantee to take any one at random and train him to become any kind of specialist I might select—doctor, lawyer, artist, merchant, chief and, yes, even beggar-man and thief, regardless of his talents, penchants, tendencies, abilities, vocations, and race of his ancestors. [(1924) 1970, 104]

Watson's behavioristic psychology was ultimately to find its fullest expression in modern advertising's attempts to manipulate consumption patterns.[8]

The managerial science developed at Harvard combined Watson's and Munsterberg's experimentalism. The application of behavioristic social science to problems of management became most closely identified with Harvard's Business School, where, in 1927, L. J. Henderson (1878–1942) became the first director of the new fatigue laboratory (see Barber, 1970, 5–8). Initially the laboratory focused on worker efficiency and productivity, a concern derived in part from the time and motion studies pioneered by Frederick W. Taylor. But whereas Taylor had assumed that the problem was one of machine efficiency and that the worker could adapt to any machine, Henderson realized that efficient machines could be made inefficient by unhappy workers. The fatigue laboratory did not adopt Munsterberg's perspective that the machine should accommodate the fixed mental state of the worker; nor did it accept Watson's premise that the malleable worker could be trained (conditioned) to any task just as a rat could be trained to run a maze. Rather, Henderson's laboratory sought to discover the optimal interactive relationship between man and machine.

In contrast to Watson and later experimental rat psychologists such as Skinner, who created their own world in their own laboratories, Henderson and his researchers—Elton Mayo, F. J. Roethlisberger, W. J. Dickson, T. N. Whitehead, and George Homans—treated the work site as their laboratory. They attempted to recreate the conditions of the laboratory in the everyday world, studying workers in the factory and in the office, assuring themselves that experimental controls would be operant.

The fatigue laboratory's crucial study was conducted by Roethlisberger and Dickson at the Western Electric Hawthorne Plant in Chicago, beginning in 1927. The company's previous efforts to improve productivity had failed; its officials wished to discover the causes for low productivity. When the Harvard researchers experimented with manipulating various aspects of the physical environment—lighting, ventilation, location of work materials—productivity improved markedly, but inexplicably. Finally the researchers concluded that their very presence, and the attention they addressed to the workers, had improved morale by making the work more meaningful. They had discovered not only the "human" factor in work but also the fact that the norms of conduct in an organizational setting could be defined by the group itself. The Puritan concept of work as a calling for the glory of God had been transvalued into work as a calling for the glory of the work group.[9]

This discovery was extended and elaborated into a general principle of administration used in the management of offices, businesses, bureaucracies, and corporations. It became an article of social scientific faith that employees' motivation could be improved by group psychology, and that the harmonious reciprocality of worker-management relations would contribute to larger common organizational goals. George Homans, author of *The Human Group* (1950), became a champion of this new managerial ideology. His objective was to locate the functions of authority for sustaining the moving equilibrium. The principles of authority and harmony could be extended to the management of society as a whole.

For Homans, managers occupy a special place in organizational administration. He points, for example, to young American engineers, who are frequently insensitive to the human factors in productivity; their purely technical education leaves them deficient in their ability to manage workers. Explicit managerial training is needed to sustain the morale and productivity of the work force, he suggests. The function of the sociologist would be to teach and train these managers: "History is still the school of the statesman, [but] sociology may be the school of the businessman." In a world in which the meaning of work had become fully secularized, managers were God's surrogates. By insuring the moral commitment of the worker to his work, they would assist him in realizing God's intentions.

Harvard's thinkers approached the problem of reconstituting the covenant from two directions. Individual salvation could be achieved by restoring the soul (mind, psyche) of the individual; anyone who accepted society's core values could experience a secular version of rebirth. Societal salvation could be achieved by developing sociopsychological technologies for the administration of industry and business and for spreading and indoctrinating everyone with the values necessary to sustain overall harmony in America. In the spirit of a democratic ethos, all were eligible for participation in the new industrial order of society. Membership in the secular covenant, however, would be based on other measures of saintliness than those required earlier of the pagan seeking entrance to the Christian community. The Christian missionary would grant membership to the pagan who demonstrated a complete conversion; full membership in American society, in the case of immigrants and blacks, turned on proof of assimilation. The industrial worker, the clerk, and the manager could be "saved" by still a different set of proofs: if (1) his aptitudes could be discovered, (2) he was placed in his appropriate role, and (3) he performed according to his superiors' expectations. Only those who successfully achieved each step could expect to become part of the elect; those who failed were held back or demoted or excluded. They remained in the functional equivalents of Cummings's tank—prisons, mental institutions, psychiatric centers, drug rehabilitation programs, hospitals, slums, and ghettos. The specific way in which proofs could be measured became the central problem of societal management. The theologian was replaced by the social theoretician, who undertook to supply society with a moral system against which deviance could be measured.

However, the efforts of Harvard's thinkers to create a fixed moral system succeeded theoretically at the very moment that they failed empirically, thwarted by changes in the society they intended to portray and control. The diversity of values held by various age, sex, racial, ethnic, religious, occupational, professional, and regional groups undermined their claim that the new secular community could share a common set of values.

At the same time the national coordination of mass communications has created an audience united in its consumption of mass culture. The fragmentation of the older covenant may have found a resolution in the forging of a new national viewpoint by propaganda experts, filmmakers, and television producers, the new magistrates of the national soul. The possibility of this occurring, already implicit in Munsterberg's work on film, was not pursued at Harvard; or for that matter in sociology as a whole, except by Herbert Blumer. Instead, motivated by a rigid puritanical Comstockean attitude, film studies have concentrated on whether or not cinematic drama is conducive to immorality (see, e.g., Blumer and Hauser, 1933). Further, the electronic "wiring" of the nation's central banking, credit, and personal-identification systems cuts across all layers of social and economic stratification. The new electronic mass-communications system produces its own covenant.

Except for Munsterberg, Harvard's social theoreticians were loathe to look for core values in something so ephemeral as propaganda or so crass as mass culture. They overlooked the possibility that the unification of American culture might in fact already have occurred.

NOTES

1. Munsterberg, born in the cosmopolitan multiethnic city of Danzig in 1863, became part of the Jewish "enlightenment" of that era but interpreted his new outlook along the lines of German national Kultur, a point of view he carried until his death (Keller, 1979,

71–120), even going so far as to make a vain attempt at preventing America's entrance to World War I (1915).

2. That technological advances in measuring physiological aspects of emotional states have improved the search for a "lie detector" is today a matter for rejoicing among scientists, businessmen, and prosecutors, but worry and dismay among the remnant of Enlightenment thinkers, civil libertarians, and American constitutional scholars and lawyers. (Pear, 1980).

3. The well-known and much debated functional theory of stratification associated with Kingsley Davis and Wilbert Moore is a sophisticated restatement of this secular theodicy, as is Talcott Parsons's analytical theory of stratification.

4. The appropriation of Levenstein's approach to industrial sociology was part of Munsterberg's debate with Max Weber. It began when Weber devoted an important part of his critique of the German economists Wilhelm Roscher and Karl Knies to an assault on Munsterberg's psychological science (1975, 130–51). According to Anthony Oberschall (1965, 99–106, 111–33), Munsterberg had come to appreciate Weber's methods in the latter's factory study undertaken for the Verein für Sozialpolitik in 1907. Weber had given some critical advice to Levenstein, proposing a more systematic analysis of his questionnaire data. Weber's and Levenstein's studies appeared within a few months of each other. (For an English translation of a portion of Weber's study, see Eldridge, 1971, 103–58.) Munsterberg did *not* borrow from Max Weber's survey of German industrial workers in 1908, which in fact proceeded from a point of view quite opposed to his own (see Eldridge, 1971, 103–55).

5. The concept of assimilation appears to have been imported into American sociology via the writings of the Austrian sociologists Ludwig Gumplowicz and Gustav Ratzenhofer and the Russian social thinker Jacques Novicow. Its first thoroughgoing analysis was made by Sarah E. Simons (1901; 1901a; 1901b; 1902), who, in contrast to the later Chicago sociologists, emphasized what was clearly the German attitude about Kultur—"assimilation as a social activity, consciously directed by the state." Simons disdainfully dismissed any "considerations of spontaneous assimilation in groups that have achieved nothing, that have contributed in no way to the world's fund of established knowledge" (1901, 793).

6. Munsterberg's concept of Kultur was that associated with Germany's drive toward nationalism and Prussian hegemony, which had reached its height under Bismarck, with the patriotic histories of Treitschke and Ranke, and with the development of sociology in Germany. As early as the late eighteenth century, German intellectuals had supposed that the assimilation of the Jews, the one people who seemed to bar the way to a German victory in the Kulturkampf, might be accomplished by distinguishing the "enlightened" from the ordinary members of that group and inducting them into German Kultur via the salons. (See Arendt, 1958, 56–68; 1974). American sociologists—such as W. E. B. Du Bois, Robert E. Park, and Albion W. Small—were impressed with the Kultur concept and sought to adapt it to the American situation, expecting the absorption of an American Kultur to uplift the masses. However, the more pervasive if subtle adaptation of the German Kultur concept occurred when it was transvalued, democratized, and converted into the formal American sociological term—and process of—*assimilation.*

7. Watson was born in Greenville, South Carolina. The son of a prosperous farmer, he received an M.A. from Furman (Baptist) College in Greenville in 1900 and entered the University of Chicago, then also a Baptist college, from which he received his degree in 1903. He appears not to have been influenced by European thinkers. Watson's brief academic career at Johns Hopkins ended when he became an advertising executive, first with the J. Water Thompson Company and later the William Esty Company.

8. Another expression of Munsterberg's applied psychology, one that went beyond his original utopic statement, is found in the work of Robert Yerkes. Yerkes, who was Munsterberg's student, assistant, and colleague, chaired the newly formed National Research Coun-

cil's Committee for Psychology and was a principal scientist in the construction of the Alpha and Beta tests, used by the US Army in examining recruits during World War I. These tests purported to be able to classify inductees according to innate intelligence and were used to decide on inclusion and exclusion in the armed services as well as for the assignment of specific duties. In effect they enunciated the doctrine that only those who were among the biologically elect could participate in the project to make the world safe for democracy. The surrogates for God's missionaries had now become selection officers for the national crusade. (Chorover, 1980, 58–75.)

9. For a discussion of the broader implications of this discovery for the meaning of work in American society, see Vidich, 1982a.

PART III

**The Administrative State and
Social Science at Columbia:
The Frightful Symmetry of Statistics**

CHAPTER 8

Positivism and the Perfectibility of the World: Franklin H. Giddings

At Columbia University sociology began as a graduate study in the faculty of political science. Its later development as a discipline in its own right was largely due to the writings and teachings of Franklin Henry Giddings (1855–1931).

Giddings's background was that of old Anglo-American Congregationalist New England (Odum, 1951, 86–94; Fuhrman, 1980, 100–83); his father, the Reverend Edward Jonathan Giddings (1832–94), was a strict evangelical Puritan, who had entitled one of his studies *America's Christian Rulers*. Introduced in high school to the work of Spencer, Huxley, and Darwin, Franklin Giddings adapted his father's world view to their scientism. He received an A.B. in engineering at Union College in Schenectady, New York and for eight years thereafter wrote for various Massachusetts newspapers, especially the *Springfield Republican*. In 1885, he began writing articles for the official publication of the Massachusetts Bureau of Labor Statistics and for such academic journals as the *Political Science Quarterly*. These articles led to his appointment in 1888 as Woodrow Wilson's professorial successor at Bryn Mawr, where for six years he taught courses in political institutions, political economy, and methods and principles of charities, corrections, and administration. After 1890, he also conducted a graduate seminar on modern theories of sociology. In 1894 Giddings joined Columbia's political science department and for the next thirty-four years dominated Columbia's sociology program, becoming Carpentier professor of sociology and the history of civilization in 1906.

Giddings's theory of the developing social order was challenged by his recognition of the growth in diversity and complexity of American society. He used three key terms to address the rational ordering of both the national and world society and their respective moral and ethical foundations: *consciousness of kind, voluntary association,* and *social personality.* His idea of the consciousness of kind recognized the individual's inclination to seek out his own kind and to form voluntary associations on the basis of mutual likenesses. At one level this meant accepting the permanence of the ethnic, racial, religious, and class differences brought about by immigration and industrialization; at another it meant forging a unified social order (or, in theological terms, a covenant) for this diverse world. Paralleling his stress on mutuality of interest as a basis for group formation, Giddings saw society as evolving toward greater individualism and free choice of association. The ultimate outcome of this evolution would be a social personality having the capacity to be responsive to others. Before this social personality could emerge, a number of what Giddings called "public utilities" would have to be realized, including the reconciliation of clashing interests among individuals, classes, and races. A eugenics program would have to be established to insure the biological prerequisites for a good society; its social prerequisite would be proper socialization within a "pure and sane family life, which disciplines the welcome and untrained child in the robust virtue of self-control, and in an unswerving allegiance to duty" (Giddings, 1896, 352).

Fundamentally Giddings was concerned with the secular management of morals and ethics. Such management was possible through a secular variant of the Puritan covenant, according to which "the effectual call of each elect saint of God would always come as an individuated personal encounter with God's promises" (Ahlstrom, 1972, 131). Each true Puritan, at God's initiative, enters into a voluntary covenant with God, involving an "inward, overt, and obedient preparation, appropriation, dedication, gratitude—and a commitment to walk in God's way according to his law." The individual "hath liberty only to do that which God lists"; in other words, he agrees to live according to the sect's—or the association's—ethical and moral standards. Thus, individualism is firmly located within the collective context, whether this be the religious sect, the voluntary association, the business organization, or the public bureaucracy. This balance of individual freedom and obligation to the collectivity, central to the whole concept of civic morals in America, has frequently been misunderstood by radical libertarians who have assumed that American liberty and freedom are unqualified.

The Puritan concept of the invisible saint posed the practical problem of how a congregation could decide who should be elected to membership in its ranks. This problem was solved by inventing the category of the visible saint. The Church, as ideally conceived by the Puritans, was a "congregation of 'visible saints' who had covenanted with God and with one another." True saints would be known to others by "infallible signs";

the identification of these signs, a central feature of New England theology, was the subject of endless sermons.[1] Those who were already members of the congregation could pass judgment on the acceptability of applicants for membership, selecting new members according to the principle of like-mindedness.

Giddings transvalued these Protestant "ways of seeing" into his secular concepts of voluntary association and consciousness of kind; the image of the sect becomes the model for all of social organization.

The sect characteristics of voluntary commitment and acceptance of the terms of participation are, of course, central features of secular voluntary associations. The idea of acting according to one's conscience was the basis for the creation in the nineteenth century of hundreds of voluntary associations such as the Elks, the Moose, the Odd Fellows, Voluntary Fire Fighting associations, burial societies, mutual aid societies, and, in the economic sphere, the business corporation. Giddings's theory hoped to embrace secular sectlike associations within a sociological version of the Puritan framework of authority (Giddings, [1900] 1972, 23).

> Only through the rationalistic habit of mind can men come to understand how important it is, on the one hand, to assert the rightful supremacy of moral authority, and, on the other hand, to deny the rightfulness of any external authority other than a common or social consciousness of the reality and rightfulness of the moral authority in each individual. . . . [It is of] supreme importance to continue without quarter to fight that obscurantism which is still endeavouring to keep the control of thought and conduct within the hands of those who assume to rule the spiritual domain by right of divine anointment.

This is Giddings's attack on Roman Catholicism and papal authority and his affirmation of the Protestant idea that moral authority resides in the individual rather than in the Pope. This statement is also Giddings's way of saying that the fear of Catholic contamination of the covenant is not restricted to American Know-Nothings. Expressed in positive terms, it implied praise for the Protestant virtues of autonomy, responsibility, and voluntarism.

Ethical motives could be strengthened "by teaching and by activity." One way in which these ethical motives might be made more firm reflects the late-nineteenth-century American Protestant emphasis on strength and health:

> The ethical motive . . . springs from physiological conditions; and as power, it is derived from vitality. To neglect bodily development, therefore, is not merely to do wrong in a sense which all intelligent persons now recognize, by impairing the health that is in itself a good, but in the much deeper sense of impairing the very springs of moral conduct. [24]

The secular expression of this principle is found in the contention that competitive sports and wholesome recreation foster good moral character.

Giddings goes on to decry the categorical Puritan strictures against pleasure, affirming the value of some of its forms: "Morality without pleasure of some kind . . . is unthinkable. . . . We must frankly admit the essential goodness of pleasure, and deny that asceticism is in any sense ethical." Asceticism for Giddings implies an antisocial and individualistic attitude. Asceticism ran counter to the high value that he placed on voluntary associations, which by their very nature deemphasize independent individuality, isolation, or withdrawal. Being a "joiner" in Giddings's world is the antithesis of the cloistered individual who rejects the world, or of an independent individual who zealously engages it: "the overzealous Puritan, the moral or religious fanatic, the uncompromising political radical, when they refuse to recognize any interest in life other than the ones to which they are devoted, are . . . as immoral as the drunkard or the libertine" (25). Unwillingness to compromise is to Giddings a form of immorality common to all fanatics and principled ideologues who threaten the moral fabric of the group and of society.

Finally, Giddings affirms the Christian duty of every man to have faith in a finer future, to cultivate learning, and to actively support the advancement of his fellows.

> He should care about the well-being of other classes than the one to which he belongs. He should be interested in the progressive civilization of other nations than his own. Above all, he should be interested in the history and development of thought, in the broadening of the mental horizon of the races, and in the expression of its struggles and aspirations in the enduring forms of literature and art. [25–26]

This homiletic calling on man "to form and cherish ideals" is a central part of a faith in a perfectible world: "We must believe that many things can be made better than they are at present, and that life in many ways can be made more desirable" (26).

Progress and perfection are to be attained by rational, systematic—indeed, it appears, mathematical—effort: "But these ideals . . . must be brought into harmony, order, and measure. In fine, the ethical motive must be both strengthened and directed by reaffirming the Platonic doctrine of correlation, subordination, and proportion in all that we think and in all that we do."

In conceding the ethical desirability of pleasure Giddings recognizes the values of consumption. More important, while he retains the Puritan God's qualities of "harmony, order and measure," he emphasizes that God's intentions are discoverable. The Puritan God was inscrutable, his intentions forever hidden; Giddings's God yields his secrets if one asks the right questions. Mathematical equations and entities provide the appropriate means of discovering the Light, a way of changing the world for the better, a kind of functional equivalent of prayer. Giddings replaced theodicy with the sociodicy of mathematics, opening a way to perfect the social order. The intellectual foundations for this order would rest on the mathematical conceptions of correlation, subordination, and proportion.

Since ultimate values are no longer legitimated by theological authority and mathematics cannot even ordain them, Giddings was forced to find a secular grounding for ethical and moral values within the structure of society itself. He did so by linking ethics and morals to voluntary associations and to consciousness of kind: society was at its apex when a reflective, rational, and selective consciousness of kind formed the basis of voluntary association.

God's effectual call was replaced by sympathy, instinct, and thought:

> The substance of society at first is sympathy and instinct mainly. At its best estate, society may rise to a level where thought has for the moment completely subordinated feeling. But usually, and throughout the greater part of its career, society is sympathy and instinct more or less organized, more or less directed, more or less controlled by thought. [39]

At the lower end of the evolutionary spectrum—among the primitive communities of the nonwhite races,[2] for instance—brute sympathy was the basis of social relationships. Ethics and morals are associated with those societies in which there is a recognition of the rational organization of consciousness of kind. This is an evolutionary reformulation of the idea of a covenanted association of visible saints, whose members were expected to extend sympathy, recognition, response, and (as Max Weber observed in his description of the Protestant sects in America [1946]) credit to one another and to be far less trusting of that vast otherhood beyond their company of believers.

Giddings's evolutionism, which begins with brute, sympathetic, involuntary association and ends with rational, voluntary coming together, is a substitute for the means by which a religious communion is formed. This complex secular transvaluation includes three separate but interrelated arguments. First, *society* is the ultimate outcome of the evolution of psychic phenomena and finds its perfected form in the pluralistic association of individuals in families, friendship groups, religious associations, labor relationships, and, embracing all these, the state. Second, the volitional and rational exercise of consciousness of kind, which can appear only in the final stage of social evolution, opens up the possibility for multiplicities of associations, including those dedicated to one or several social or economic purposes. Third, the degree to which any individual is attached to one or another of the several associations to which he belongs is problematical. Indeed, this is the basic topic for psychical sociology. Whereas the Puritan magistrates required a demonstration of each puta- tive church member's degree of saintliness, Giddings would replace their judgments with standardized measures that would directly evaluate the inward states themselves. Thus, the degree of "regeneration" of each "socius" could be known by application of the statistical method; and the responsibility for evaluation and selection would be transferred to a new group, the sociologists.

The ethical and moral values of a given person were expected to be congruent with those of the group(s) to which he or she belonged. Gid- dings and his followers at Columbia did not postulate, as did George Herbert Mead, a conception of a "generalized other" which represented "societal" values as expressed through the multiplicity of groups experi- enced by each individual. Mead's generalized other allowed for the pos- sibility that the individual might develop a unified self—his or her own distillation of societal ethics and values. The theory of reference groups, on the other hand, implies a multiplicity of norms and values that do not necessarily combine to form a unified self. Reference-group theory as- signs the responsibility for selection of ethical norms to the individual who chooses to become part of the group and thereby adopts its perspective. According to this conception choice is conditioned by peer-group pres- sure and status aspirations, and conformity to group values is brought about by rewards and punishments: status conferral or denial, admission or expulsion. The social bond of this kind of "covenanted" community is sustained in accordance with instrumental values. Voluntary associations and reference groups are the denominations and sects of secular society. Setting out to find a way of governing such a pluralistic entity, the Colum- bia sociologists first devised methods of attitude and opinion measure- ment to discover the degree to which individuals are attached and com- mitted to their reference groups. Using the knowledge so gained to index the consciousness of kind, they could then chart the degree of consensus in society and advise policy makers on the potential consequences of any proposed reform programs. By combining the statistical study of consen- sus with predictions about the effects of public policies, the Columbia sociologists laid their claim to participate in the management of a rational social order.

STATISTICS AND CERTAINTY: THEODICY AND PRAYER

Like Comte, Giddings held that "empirical generalizations in sociology may be made by two methods, namely, the comparative and the histor- ical," and regarded each as a form of the logical "method of concomitant variations." Thus, the "comparative and the historical methods may become precise when they can become statistical ([1896] 1970, 64). Again like Comte, he distinguished between the abstract and concrete sciences, placing sociology among the latter. As a concrete science, sociology "must usually begin its investigations with observation and must conclude them with deductive confirmation and interpretation" (51). Although "empirical generalizations . . . even when made according to the most cautious statistical methods, and from abundant statistical data, are only probabilities," these probabilities are superior in their truth value to "the haphazard observation of the blunderer." Thus Giddings claimed a privileged position for the statistical sociologist.

Though Giddings did not employ statistical procedures very often in his own work, he set the terms under which statistics became the hallmark of scientific sociology in America. It is not well known to sociologists today, even to those who followed Giddings into a mathematicized social science, that the original introduction of mathematical language into science had religious foundations. In the sixteenth and seventeenth centuries mathematics was recognized as the divine language in which the Book of Nature is written. Hence, science could proceed in its discovery of God's truths only by recognizing the limitations of ordinary speech and undertaking the mastery and application of mathematics. As Galileo (1564–1642) put it: "The book [of nature] is written in the mathematical language, and the symbols are triangles, circles and other geometrical figures, without whose help it is impossible to comprehend a single word of it; without which one wanders in vain through a dark labyrinth."

Scientists like Galileo were certain of two things: first, not every person could master the language of divine nature, and hence truth could be known only by a few; second, as Morris Kline (1980, 46) puts it, "Of course, the divine intellect knows and conceives an infinitely greater number of mathematical truths than man does, but with regard to objective certainty the few verities known by the human mind are known as perfectly by man as by God." Prior to the Reformation, mathematics was a priestly function. After the Reformation the ability and responsibility to know God were transferred to the individual. Under these terms the secular scientist adopts the Catholic priest's role as God's interpreter. Humanity continues to wander in the dark labyrinth of inner-worldly ignorance, while the few scientists illuminate a small portion of God's knowledge.

When Calvin's conception of life and afterlife revealed a mysterious omniscient God who oversees a world whose meaning is known only to Himself, the Puritans responded by undertaking risky ventures the outcomes of which would signal their posthumous election or damnation (see Scott and Lyman, 1970, 129–31). Much like Weber's Puritans, science, including the mathematically oriented social sciences, set out on a risky journey that would enable it to execute God's intentions.

Social science in nineteenth-century America was sufficiently secularized to pay less attention to what seventeenth-century Puritan scientists had insisted on as a first priority—engaging in scientific endeavor for the glory of God. Nevertheless, nineteenth- and early twentieth-century social scientists insisted, with rare exception, on the second principal tenet of the Puritan ethos: working for social welfare in a warrantable calling and serving the good of society as a basic scientific goal (Merton, 1936). This tenet was, of course, reinforced by the impetus of the Social Gospel and constitutes the secular extension of the Puritan desire to build a Holy Commonwealth. There still remained, however, the problem of general and perhaps irremediable human ignorance.

Giddings's approach to human ignorance was not different from that of Francis Bacon (1561–1626), although less systematic. Bacon, seeking a "great instauration" (i.e., a fundamental reconceptualization of the nature, classification, and methods of science), had warned of the poor quality of all forms of information improperly conceived and collected,[3] and of the imperfections of the human understanding occasioned by the "idols of the mind."[4] Giddings, concerned to establish the truths of sociology on a sound scientific basis, also conceived of an instauration of the social sciences and warned against either acceptance of a Jamesian phenomenological chaos[5] or premature scientific maturity.[6] Like the elitist scientists who followed in the train of Bacon's apprehensions, Giddings put his faith in a "relatively few minds [who] have enough curiosity and doggedness to make the effort painstakingly" (1924, 2). However, he located an inner-worldly limitation on the findings of science:

> The scientific tradition is the sum of our actual knowledge of the world and of man, as distinguished from our conjectures about them. It is the sifted record of observations, experiments, and classifications. Making no attempt to penetrate the final mystery of existence, it explains the constitution of the world only to the extent of showing how one thing is related to other things, in sequence and in coexistence. [(1896) 1970, 145]

Sociology thus becomes the penultimate science; ultimate knowledge is left to God, ultimate outcomes to evolution.

Giddings left the general emancipation of human reason to the processes of evolution. For him the social mind, dedicated to the balanced encouragement of equality and liberty, emerges as the final outcome of the evolution of consciousness. This evolution required sociological endeavor not unlike that of Christian missionaries; its "modes . . . are missionary effort, philanthropy, and education . . . [and] are an expression of the passion of the highest social types to extend themselves among the lower races, and among the poor, the unfortunate, and the ignorant" (149). In effect social science would replace missionary endeavor with scientifically grounded programs of social engineering.

To develop a truly scientific sociology without statistics was impossible. Indeed, it was statistics that had already proved the truth of social telesis: "The study of societal phenomena by statistical methods has now, for those who understand them, terminated controversy over this hoary question of societal self-determination by demonstrating that the societal process is telic as well as fortuitously and physically evolutionistic" ([1924] 1974, 142). But the application of these statistics to social engineering was possible now because the evolution of the social mind at last permits deliberation, and deliberation, in turn, recognizes the rule of reason (i.e., science) over passion (1896, 150–52). The ideas of the social engineer should take precedence in planning for social change.

> Engineering of any description, civil or military, mechanical, chemical, or electrical, ecological or societal, is an acceptance of scientific principles as the basis of practice, and a following of technical methods of applying them. It is hard and expensive work. Imagination has a place in it, but wishful thinking has not. [(1924) 1974, 165]

Giddings hints that the social scientist should form a power base in order to compete with and eventually overwhelm the power bases of other societal groups (155–56). "In every sovereign state there are would-be states," (155) including priesthoods, armies, landed aristocracies, trading and manufacturing classes, peasantries, and proletariats. To such power-hungry entities Giddings credits every form of political machination. Each type "initiates and foments class struggle. It experiments with insurrection and rebellion. When opportunity offers it goes on to revolution. At other times it falls back upon conspiracy, plotting, agitation, and the tamer political methods" (155). Moreover, each of these entities aims at nothing less than "a dictatorship, whether this ugly word is frankly used or religiously tabooed. . . . The aim is to organize the state, to institute, define and administer government, to shape policies" (156). Thus, it "is the would-be state which unceasingly does things *to* the sovereign state. . . . Thus far in history a succession of would-be states has done but little *for* the sovereign state" (156). The sociologist-cum-social-engineer alone possesses a consciousness of kind whose professional aims include a perspective on the totality of society.[7] There is here a sotto voce call for the secular successors to America's "Christian Rulers," who rule on the basis of reason and science, rather than the power-grabbing proclivities of other elites.

SECULAR SAINTS OF SCIENCE: COST-BENEFIT ANALYSIS

A comprehensive sociology that was both theoretical and applicable to social amelioration, Giddings believed, would have to subsume ethics under its all-embracing scientific curriculum. Ethics, he insisted, was related to integrity, not to utility; and integrity in turn was inextricably realized in the wholeness of the properly developed personality: "The integrity, the unity, the internal harmony of the consciousness is therefore the first necessity" (1893, 21). But, although "utility must for the moment give way" when it comes into conflict with integrity, "there can be no enduring integrity without development, no permanent conservation without progress" (212). Ethics, therefore, must enter positively into the contradictory dialectics of integrity and utility. It could do so through the medium of a scientific sociology that works "out the laws of that cumulative happiness which is the reward and the confirmation of well-doing" (212). Such laws might be discovered once we abjure the idea that "life is . . . the whirl of a constant number of jugglers' plates, balanced on the sword-points of the players" and accept in its place the thesis of stability in the midst of change. "New plates and new motions appear at every instant, compelling ever most delicate readjustments throughout the entire system, and yet without once disturbing seriously the approximately perfect balance of the whole" (210). This dynamic equilibrium provides the basis for a scientific practice of social ethics. "The large and difficult conception, then, to which we must attain, is that of a world in which there can be no true ethical phenomena except through a process, at once progressive and orderly, of mutual modifications and adaptations of man and society by each other; in which each acquires, stage by stage, a more delicate complexity of organization" (210).

Giddings plunged into the social problems of his day, finding in each an application for a cautious scientific approach to social reform. He insisted, however, that certain conceptual difficulties took priority over policy. Progress, he asserted, was a common faith, and although "science must rectify it at a thousand points . . . such faith *in se* is the beginning of righteousness" (215). A righteous sociology founded on a secular faith might, then, be scientific and practical, melioristic and efficient. "The first law of life is the law of motion" (215), but that motion "must be developmental; mere change is not evolution but confusion; and the nature and limitations of an evolutionary process, imperfectly recognized as yet in ethical discussions, are practically unknown to popular thought" (215). The sociological approach to the Social Question must begin with a clarification of the distinctions among such conceptually confused terms as "change," "development," "evolution," and "progress." So, "it is here, then, that the rectifying work of social science must begin."

Giddings's contribution to the rectification was a general procedure of social cost-benefit analysis for measuring the price of progress in the past, present, and future. He applied this procedure to such issues as wage labor as a form of slavery; the race question; the immigration question; the woman question; suicide, crime, and delinquency. He proposed certain general policies that might be implemented to encourage social development and inhibit the worst features of social decay and moral deviation.

Giddings's social-bookkeeping approach begins with the observation that "all progress . . . is conditioned by cost, and if the law of conservation holds good in these matters, as we have assumed that it must, the cost will increase with the progress; not however, necessarily in the same ratio as the gain, since riper knowledge should enable us to get more from physical nature with a given expenditure of human effort" (217).

Progress entailed both an economic and an ethical problem, and it was to the latter that Giddings directed his antiutopian scientific meliorism. The price of progress was that someone or some group had to suffer:

> There can be no social gain that does not entail somewhere, on the whole community or on a class, the breakup of long established relations, interests, and occupations, and the necessity of a more or less difficult readjustment . . . ; there can be no social progress, and therefore no evolution of ethical personality, except at the price of an absolute, but not necessarily a relative, increase of suffering. [217, 218]

Moreover, the absolute character of the pain or injury was distributed in such a manner that "the classes who are displaced, whose interests and occupations are broken up by the relentless course of change, are not the ones who secure the joys of richer and ampler life. That which enormously benefits mankind is too often the irretrievable ruin of the few" (218–19). This law of the social cost of progress warned against unthinking speedups in evolution: "[I]f the increase of social activity, which is one phase of progress, becomes disproportionate to the constructive reorganization of social relationships, which is the complementary phase, the increase of suffering will become degeneration and moral evil" (234). Assisting progress and resisting evil required scientific and policy skills of the highest order.

Giddings's sociology supplied both a remedy to and a sociodicy for the specifics of the Social Question. Capitalism, urbanization, the depopulation of the countryside, and the creation of wage labor were all evidences of progress. And the price was paid by those least able to bear it—the lazy, improvident, unintelligent, nonadaptive sectors of the population. "And so, while this comparative freedom of enterprise stimulated activity in a hundred ways, . . . it destroyed the old economic footing of the less com-

petent members of society, and left them to struggle on, thenceforth, as a
wage-earning class" (220). Giddings's theory of the progress of civilization
celebrated individualism, locating both grace and its absence in the distribution of character traits. As great changes in social organization upset
the older order, individuals who possess initiative, daring, and adapt-
ability will succeed economically and gain in social status and political
power; those who are weak, fearful, and maladaptive will lose. There is no
way to prevent this cycle of civilizational advance and its concomitant
redistribution of social misery.

The productive methods of advancing industrial capitalism and the
socioeconomic condition of the workers had diminished the extent but
not the fact of human misery. "So enormous has been the net gain from
improved methods of production that the consequences of displacement
[of the worker by the machine] are immeasurably less serious than they
were a century ago. The chances of finding re-employment quickly are,
for competent men, far greater than they were in any former time, and
the period of search is made endurable by accumulated savings and varied forms of aid." Hence, "industrial history discloses a progressive diminution of the proportion of inevitable suffering mixed with the gains of
progress" (223). However, the condition of misery would never be totally
eliminated. "The personnel of the displaced class changes more rapidly
than in earlier times, but the class, as a class, is endlessly renewed. . . . It
can never disappear as long as progress continues" (223).

What was to be done with and for the impoverished, the unemployed,
the immigrant? A proper sociological understanding of civilization and
progress refuted the popular view of the miserable poor as *oppressed;*
rather, they constitute a surplus population. "These people continue to
exist after the kinds of work that they know how to perform have ceased
to be of any considerable value to society" (226–27). The "drudgery of the
needle-women or the crushing toil of men in a score of life-destroying
occupations" (226) are not needed in modern industrial societies. Such
people are able to earn any kind of living solely because "society continues
to employ them for a remuneration not exceeding the cost of getting the
work done in some other and perhaps better way" (227). Giddings's society, kinder than the forces of nature postulated in the Social Darwinists'
vision of inexorable struggle, left room only for scientifically managed
social welfare policies.

Giddings proposed restrictions on immigration and legislative control
over "those industries in which free competition displaces the better man
by the inferior" (246). He abhorred

> those political policies that so often force vast hordes of destitute people into
> migrations that have no definite destination, as in the case of the Russian
> Jews, [whose settlements abroad result in] a cruel and ruinous substitution of

the lower for the higher grade of workmen. . . . [It] would not be unfortunate that the Irishmen . . . displace the native American, . . . the French Canadian . . . the Irishman, and that finally the Hungarian or the Pole . . . the French Canadian, if the men of the higher standard of life could immediately step into industries of a higher grade. [237]

Without restrictive immigration and the selective regulation of employment, the higher elements "can live only by sinking to the level of their more brutal competitors" (237).

Giddings's argument against economic mongrelization parallels those regarding biological mixtures of "lower-immigrants" and superior Anglo-Saxons. The "superior" group, made somewhat defensive by immigrant encroachments, feared the diminution of its own privileges and esteem. The myth of Anglo superiority constitutes one reaction to immigrant claims for membership in the covenant, and supplies an ideological justification for maintaining a restricted covenant.

Inequalities among men, said Giddings, sprang from basic human inequality and necessary competition.[8] For the Puritans and their religious descendants, to explain how apparently righteous men could be unequally rewarded was always a problem. Casuistries to account for such inequities included either the devaluation of material reward—"you don't need money when you have Jesus"—or references to the unfathomable nature of God's will. In Giddings's sociodicy, inequities were accounted for by inherent inferiority, evolution, and the price paid for progress.

Those who made proposals for the abolition of poverty, misery, and want were naively "philoneistic" (247)—that is, devoted unreflectively to the course of progress. Society, on the other hand, "is on the whole misoneistic; therefore we can mend its ways but slowly" (247). The pace of social amelioration must be governed by the physico-mathematical law: "With a given amount of energy you can go in an hour or a day a given distance. Prolong the time and you can increase the distance" (232). Applying this theorem to the Social Question in much the same way that Taylor later applied it to time and motion studies, Giddings stated: [S]ince the conservation of energy is a fact of social . . . phenomena, the essential nature of progress . . . is a conversion of lower, . . . more simple, imperfectly organized modes of energy into higher." (213) Hence, if a policy was meritocratic it would most probably require that "society in its corporate capacity . . . assume the responsibility of finding new work" for the technologically displaced workers; it would continue to reward labor "according to performance only" (230). In these respects Giddings's thinking parallels that of Sumner when he speaks of the struggle for survival. Unlike Sumner, however, Giddings did not abandon the "unfit" to the wisdom of fate but held society responsible for finding them work or otherwise sustaining them, thus managing to retain the notion of Protes-

tant charity within the framework of nineteenth-century Social Darwinism and setting the stage for the welfare state in which work could be
replaced with a right to assistance.

Intense competition—the very engine of capitalism—was another
cause of the displacement of the "inferior" by the "superior" man in
industry and, by extension, of the "frightful wreckage of physical and
moral degeneration" that piles up in every progressive community. Employing statistical analysis, Giddings sought to prove that the "seemingly
anomalous" social fact which struck every sociologist—"that suicide, insanity, crime, vagabondage, increase with wealth, education, and refinement"—occurred only "when the rate of social activity exceeds the rate of
constructive reorganization" (238). The remedy, then, must be contained
in the scientific regulation of the pace and ratio of social activity in relation
to the introduction of innovations in social reorganization (a phenomenon that Giddings's student William Ogburn later named "cultural
lag"). Giddings here managed to find a middle ground between Sumner
and Marx. He contradicted Sumner's insistence on individual self-reliance by arguing for social intervention and opposed Marx's "to each
according to his needs" by arguing that resources should be distributed
according to utility.[9]

"The practical solution of the problem depended on a difficult combination of two very difficult things. . . . to convince one set of people that
society ought to assume the cost of its programs . . . and . . . another
set . . . that at all times a portion of mankind must be relatively useless to
the community, and, for that reason, relatively poor" (242–43). The condition of the ever-re-created useless portion of the population could be
ameliorated only if it were "held for the while in practical subjection to
other individuals or to the commonwealth" (243). Such a progressive
form of subjection was an institutionalization of the "most important
single doctrine that Christianity had to contribute to social science"—the
doctrine of stewardship, which recognized "the distinction between those
who are free from the law and those who are under bondage to the law"
(244) and provided the "key to the solution of the social problem." The
population segment above the law embraced "the progressive resourceful, creative [and those] capable of self-mastery and self-direction" (244),
while those consigned to temporary but possibly long-term servitude included the poor, the technologically displaced, the inferior races, and the
degenerate. In effect Giddings's version of stewardship was a variation of
Hughes's system of warranteeism. In both the issue is the relationship
between the *regenerate* and *unregenerate,* and the social control of the latter.

In the Puritan theocracy, church membership conferred the rights and
privileges of citizenship, and unregenerate nonmembers had virtually no
political voice. Moreover, the Puritan divines thought it their God-given

responsibility to rule over the unregenerates and to prevent their sinful-
ness from encroaching on the community. The distinction between those
belonging to the covenant and those not is one of long standing. In
Giddings's argument, however, the elites above the law are the social
engineers who replace the older magistrates.

THE NEW MAGISTRATES IN THE IMPERIAL STATE

Under the guidance of the new social-engineer magistrates a measured
sociological telesis would unfold, effected by the virtuous actions of a
rational, voluntaristic citizenry. Giddings believed the national state to be
the inevitable, as well as the appropriate, outcome of historical movement. And the highest form of the national state, he argued, was the
democratic empire ([1900] 1972, 1–12). Unlike Hobson and Lenin, who
regarded imperialism as a social process related to capitalism and treated
the colonial scramble of the late nineteenth century as the beginning of its
downfall, and more like Bismarck, Giddings argued that the rise of the
democratic empire heralded a moral millenium:

> Only when the democratic empire has compassed the uttermost parts of the
> world will there be that perfect understanding among men which is necessary
> for the growth of moral kinship. Only in the spiritual brotherhood of that
> secular republic, created by blood and iron not less than by thought and love,
> will the kingdom of heaven be established on earth. [357]

In 1900, buoyed by the outcome of the Spanish-American War, Giddings developed a theory of the origins and development of the democratic state and its attendant empire (3–12). Like most developmental
theories since Comte's, Giddings's formulation included an ethnogenic
history that unfolded in three stages that could also stand as a national
ideology.

The first period saw the invention of "a legal fiction, whereby all who
lived within the territorial boundaries occupied by a localized tribe became nominally—for political, military, and fiscal purposes—members of
a purely nominal tribe, irrespective of their blood relationship." This
consciousness of kind emphasized "mental and moral qualities" rather
than blood or race. However, the men of power in these regimes sought to
perfect and enforce the recently emerged like-mindedness through a
policy of religious unification in which the "medley of ancient faiths was
blended in a national, organic religion, which by its sanctions was made to
uphold the authority of the central power." Religious unification was at
length followed by an enforced conformity in which "manners and
customs, forms of dress and ceremonial, even amusements, were in like
manner subjected to a minute regulation, all in the interests of that per-

fect homogeneity of mental and moral type which now was believed to be the requisite basis of a true and strong national unity."

The second stage emerged out of an antithesis with the first: "Men became critical: They began to demand release from formal bonds which were no longer necessary to their well-being." By becoming more sophisticated, they weakened the moral unity of the state. This weakness facilitated barbarian invasions. The state disintegrated. But "chaos and anarchy slowly gave way to the formation of a new order of personal liberty, freedom of contract, and constitutional law." However, the homogenizing principle of consciousness of kind found new expression in the "conviction that liberty and social cohesion could coexist only in states of relatively small dimension, with well-defined boundaries, and peopled by men of substantially one blood and type of mind."

In the third and present epoch, "men were stimulated to put forth their energies to the utmost. . . . Investigation, discovery, and exploration revealed possibilities of material well-being of which the race had never dreamed . . . [and soon] the new enterprise and the growing population began to threaten to overflow the relatively narrow bonds that had been set by the political philosophy of liberalism to the republican state."

The free society has the mission of bringing its moral structure to other countries. In England and the United States, which Giddings insisted were the freest societies, liberty led to a fundamental reorganization. For England the result was imperial expansion over so much of the world that "the homogeneous population of English blood was becoming the most heterogeneous admixture of nationalities of every speech and faith and political tradition to be found on the face of the earth." For America, almost "before the most far-seeing of men realized what was happening, the compact little nation of the thirteen original states had become a continental domain." The consciousness of kind associated with this new democratic empire was based on pluralism of manners and faiths combined with a unity of ethics. "No suggestion was made that, throughout this vast domain, men should be compelled to confess the same faith, to worship in the same way, to dress in prescribed costumes, or to amuse themselves according to forms prescribed by state authority." The ethical like-mindedness that bound together the subject-citizens of the new democratic empires consisted "in a common loyalty to the common judgment and will, in a common willingness to share a common destiny, and in a common conviction of the priceless value of individual, religious, and local liberty." Having established its own internal unity, the United States was prepared to carry its message to the rest of the world.

Democratic empire, Giddings believed, could extend rather than restrict the liberties and opportunities of the peoples brought under its sway. "Given mental and moral agreement . . . a nation of any territorial extent, of any admixture of blood, of interests, of religions, can wax strong generation by generation, while yet becoming more free and more diversified in its social organization" (10–11). However, the preservation of democracy within an empire hinged entirely "on the one inviolable condition that, *as it lengthens the reach of government, it must curtail the functions of government.*" The imperial government must leave such tasks as protecting life and property, building roads and bridges, operating street railways, waterworks and lighting, and maintaining schools and libraries to the local authorities who, "homogeneous in nearly every respect—in blood, in traditions, in beliefs, in interests, may successfully conduct a local or municipal government of highly diversified functions."[10]

In Giddings's image, American imperialism would be the agency for creating a world Christian brotherhood; the ultimate "consciousness of kind" would be nothing less than a global acceptance of the Puritan covenant or its secular surrogate, the American system. If such acceptance was not forthcoming, Giddings was prepared, like Cromwell and Cotton Mather, to achieve "perfect understanding" by the imposition of a brotherhood. In suggesting that America should export its social system by national missionary activity, Giddings reveals his Puritan ancestry. Ethnocentrism of this type could come only from an unexamined identification with the dominant group of American society and its ideals—the covenanted community of white Anglo-Saxon Protestants.

The mature democracy that was fitted for empire—that is, sufficiently perfected in its social organization so that class, racial, and ethnic conflicts had given way to a socially purposeful harmony—had also to be prepared to act jointly in defense of that harmony. Giddings observed in "superior types of society . . . a high degree of individual mobility combined with a marvelous power to mobilize enormous numbers of individuals, in moments of emergency, upon any work needing to be done" ([1906] 1974, 797). Empire and the capacity to make war effectively depended on a sufficient amount of compromise among the diverse interests within a pluralistic society—among the policies of unification, liberty, and equality—to make social mobilization and patriotic endeavor possible.

The boldness and high purpose of his imperial project led Giddings to think of himself as a radical, but not a revolutionary. He regarded his social engineering as more progressive and—more important—more effective than either the amateurishness of the philanthropic do-gooder or the destructive irrationalism of the incendiary:

The feasibility of the projects of amelioration receives little enough consideration from untrained and unchastened uplifters, and none whatever from our phosphorescent ignorati of revolt and revolutionism. The engineer knows that feasibility is limited and is grimly conditioned by human constitutions, nerves, and energies, and by the costs which must be met out of finite incomes. [(1924) 1974, 166–67]

Avoiding the extremes of right and left would insure an equilibrium that was at once moral, social, historical, and progressive. These were the greatest virtues.[11] The achievement of a societal middle way[12] would involve an evolution toward mixed or emergent socioeconomic systems, combining the egalitarian and welfare institutions of state socialism with the preservation of individual liberty under democratic capitalism.

> If social evolution is to continue, and the ethical life of man is to become larger and richer with increasing happiness, social organization in the future will be not simpler than it is now, but immeasurably more complex. In its larger being individualism, socialism, and communism will not be the mutually exclusive things that they now seem to be. There will be not a narrower but a wider field for individual effort, not less but more personal liberty. At the same time, more enterprises will be brought under public control, and more of the good things of life will be distributed, like the sunshine and the air, in free and equal proportions. The displaced men and women will be more quickly reestablished than now, their services will be made of greater value, and society will assume a larger portion of the burden of their misfortune. [1893, 233]

MAGISTRATES OF THE NEW SOCIOLOGY

For Giddings, social science had two interrelated roles to play in the development of the democratic and imperial state. The first was to chart the evolution of that type of society in an historical and comparative measurement of statistically exact concomitant variations: "Following the historical method, we search for a given social fact at each stage in the historical evolution of a given society, and thereby determine what social phenomena are continuous . . . [and] we systematically search for a corresponding fact or correlation in all contemporaneous societies, animal and human, ethnic and civil." These procedures will lead to the discovery of "those resemblances and differences in social phenomena that are the bases of scientific classification." This classification will set the terms for the establishment of a "complete scientific theory of natural causation." Such a theory, however, will have to wait until "our knowledge becomes quantitatively precise," because all too often "the law that we seek to formulate eludes us until the correlations of phenomena have been determined with mathematical exactness." The moment of that quantitative millenium will soon be at hand, Giddings believed, because it "is to the scientific students of sociology that the world owes the discovery and development of an inestimably valuable form of the comparative and historical methods, namely, the statistical method." The immense and far-reaching possibilities of statistics "were first demonstrated in the epoch-making social studies of Jacques Quetelet" and had been employed by Danish, German, English, French, and American social scientists. Statistics had become and "will continue to be, the chiefly important method of sociology; and assuredly, in the course of time, it will bring our knowledge of society up to the standards of thoroughness and precision comparable to the results attained by any natural science" ([1906] 1974, 798–99).

The second task was social engineering, in which the sociologist was to be an enlightened magistrate, utilizing statistics as his basic tool. It was essential for Giddings that social engineers take Protestant values as their guide in effecting social change. "Spasmodic attack upon prevailing conditions, evil and reprobated, has recurred throughout recorded history. Systematic and organized effort to abate them is a characteristic of modern times" ([1924] 1974, 156). Writing in 1924, he called attention to the great advances already made in improving health and lowering death rates, preventing industrial accidents, reducing illiteracy, treating insanity, and alleviating the miseries of the poor. The maintenance of this civilization was to be achieved by the joint "energies and the financial resources of all the agents and agencies of amelioration: individual, social, societal, and governmental" (156). Giddings singled out charitable organizations and, even more significant, labor organizations and taxpayers as bearing "the burden of big effort and expense" (158). Social engineering was to be a collaborative effort between public and private institutions.

Several unresolved social problems remained, each requiring social scientific study and deliberate action as a remedy. Among these were delinquency, vice, and crime, ever threatening to the moral community. Still another problem, "the possible degeneration of an entire population," had received some "sober attention" in the new laws ending unrestricted immigration to the United States and outlawing miscegenation; nevertheless, "notwithstanding fifty years of public and private effort to ameliorate them, the relations of white and coloured races in the United States have never been more perplexing than they are now" (159). Moreover, the perfected harmony of diverse interests had not yet been completed:

> The desirability and the possibility of assimilation (always to be distinguished from amalgamation) of the native and foreign born elements of our population came sharply to attention with our participation in the European war. There has been legislation against the teaching of foreign languages in the schools and against a foreign language press, but some of it has been repealed. Religious prejudice, which has a way of flaring up and dying down, has of late been unfortunately strong. [159]

Social engineering was required to solve these social, racial and religious problems and to move the evolving secular society of scientifically guided saints forward to its inevitable posture of guided, rational, beneficent, and conflict-free democracy. Filled with the optimism of the great potential inherent in linking positivism and perfectibility, Giddings still saw the Holy Commonwealth as a possibility.

NOTES

1. The idea of "infallible signs" is a latent element in the theories of assimilation, accommodation, and acculturation that sociologists and anthropologists would later develop to measure a given group's degree of Americanization.

2. "From the standpoint of the observer of animal and primitive human societies, it is difficult, if not impossible, to establish a line of demarcation between the more highly organized bands of animals, like troops of monkeys, or herds of elephants, or bands of wild horses, and the simplest hordes of human beings, like Bushmen or Australian Blackfellows" (Giddings, [1900] 1972, 38). These "animal and primitive human communities in general are reflective societies. The reflective stage corresponds to the appearance of the perception of kind and to reflective sympathy" (29).

3. "The information of the sense itself, sometimes failing, sometimes false; observation, careless, irregular, and led by chance; tradition, vain and fed on rumor; practice, slavishly bent on its work; experiment, blind, stupid, vague, and prematurely broken off; lastly, natural history trivial and poor:—all of these have contributed to supply the understanding with very bad materials for philosophy and the sciences" (Bacon, 1939, 19).

4. "The . . . false notions which are now in possession of the human understanding, and have taken deep root therein, not only so beset men's minds that truth can hardly find entrance, but even after entrance obtained, they will again in the very instauration of the sciences meet and trouble us, unless men being forewarned of the danger fortify themselves as far as may be against their assaults" (Giddings, [1896] 1970, 68–69).

5. I.e., "the world upon which a baby looks forth as a big and buzzing confusion" (Giddings [1924] 1974, 1).

6. "Then there are minds that almost grow up. . . . One part of the world in particular they find so comprehensible that they want to take it to pieces and put it together again, with improvements" (Giddings [1924] 1974, 1–2).

7. At this point Giddings's conception of the sociologist parallels that of Karl Mannheim's unattached intellectual (1953, 137–39) whose lack of commitment enables him to see the higher social good. But where Mannheim tried to define a free-floating intellectual, Giddings attached his social engineer to the values of Christianity. Giddings wrote from the perspective of a member of the American covenant who accepted its fundamental tenets; he was very much attached and expected his engineers to be no different.

8. Giddings suggested that women's elimination from the labor force might be a boon to social order because female crime, according to statistics he adduced, showed an increase directly proportional to the expansion of job opportunities for them (1893, 241).

9. When, under the influence of Ogburn, the New Deal later attempted to effectuate this proposition, Sumnerian businessmen objected because the immoral poor were being pampered, and the Marxist left objected because New Deal policies saved capitalism by dampening the revolutionary ardor of the poor and destitute by supplying them with welfare.

10. When he wrote *The Scientific Study of Human Society*, ([1924] 1974), Giddings was no longer so sanguine about democratic empires. By that time World War I had dashed many

hopes for the spread of American democracy by means of imperialism. Giddings's model of imperial democracy reflects the manifest destiny of the Spanish-American War and is a foreshadowing of American foreign policy after World War II, when the message of democracy in opposition to communism was carried over the globe and when the United States sought to uplift the rest of the world through foreign aid in the pattern of Puritan philanthropy pursued on an international scale. It was in this sense that Giddings had hoped to internationalize the covenanted community.

11. In recent sociology this same idea reappears as inherent in the American social system in Columbia-educated Seymour Martin Lipset's "stability in the midst of change" and in Talcott Parsons's concept of "dynamic equilibrium."

12. Giddings located the path to social amelioration in Aristotle's ethical imperative, "the middle way." As Giddings put it, "The middle way, which Aristotle described as the only true road of virtue, is indeed such; and no one can wander from it to the right hand any more than to the left, without falling into wrong" ([1900] 1972, 25). For Giddings, as Charles H. Page (1969, 174) has observed, the "middle way" combined an "emphasis upon evolutionary gradualism, the contempt for socialism, the belief in individualistic liberalism and progressivism, [and] the desire for an ethical consciousness directed toward social ends."

CHAPTER 9

Rationalizing Christian Endeavor: The Social Survey

At Columbia society was to be saved by the rational and scientific efforts of an elite of Gospel-inspired men. Whatever else the words "rational" and "scientific" might mean, they in fact came to be equated with numerical measures, statistical surveys, and the ever-expanding use of quantitative methods. However, with its ever-more-costly demands for large-scale surveys, comprehensive analyses of enormous quantities of facts, and mechanized techniques for collecting, assorting, and interpreting data, the new salvational social science would require its own financial saviors. Led by Columbia-educated sociologists, it found its first patron in the Russell Sage Foundation and, soon after, in the Rockefeller family. Committed to stewardship over his wealth, John D. Rockefeller entered into a variety of corporate philanthropic relationships with the incipient social sciences, the most significant of which was the Social Science Research Council. The rationalizing of Rockefeller's charity in turn facilitated the rationalizing of sociology, giving even greater impetus to statistical orientations and reinforcing its image as statistical technique. By the time private philanthropy in the social sciences gave way to public subsidy, the quantitative approach had become nearly coextensive with the discipline of sociology. The rationalizing of the means, moreover, ultimately led to a deemphasis, if not abandonment, of sociology's ends.

We can trace the process that slowly turned sociology away from direct Christian endeavor and toward massive, statistical social-policy research by analyzing the tendencies in the college settlement movement and observing the rise and legitimation of the social survey at Columbia. The rationalizing of social research and its linkage to social policy in America was carried forward by a small, sectlike group of Columbia-trained sociologists who came to be known as the "Giddings Men."

FROM THE SETTLEMENT MOVEMENT TO THE SOCIAL LABORATORY

Although the college and university settlement movement had been inspired by a renewed zeal for religious charity and Christian compassion, it soon adopted the outlook of the professionalizing social sciences. Harvard's Peabody (1908, 18) saw the change as part of a necessary cycle of development: "The administration of charity . . . has passed beyond its sentimental period, and in the complex life of our great cities the call for sympathy is succeeded by the call for expert knowledge." Robert A. Woods, a foremost leader of the movement, urged that "science and sympathy must unite if we are to have any living knowledge of the poor," but when statistical methods emerged as the simulacrum of scientific sociology, compassion would have to give way: "The close scientific study of the social conditions in the neighborhood about a settlement is indispensable to its success" (Woods, 1893, 68–69). As early as 1892 (272) Edward Cummings had supposed that the "painstaking study, assistance, and criticism" offered by the settlement house workers would serve primarily as a social scientific resource for "the great network of organizations and agencies already developed." Peabody's, Woods's, and Cummings's acceptance of the shift toward quantification of charities and rationalization of philanthropy was consistent with the Protestant Church's use of social surveys to achieve reform and uplift.[1]

The college and university settlements followed in the wake of social science developments and sometimes pushed ahead of them, converting their urban missions into social laboratories. In 1889, there appeared the socioreligious census of Hartford's immigrant poor; in 1895, the standard-setting *Hull House Maps and Papers;* in 1897, the survey of the Fifteenth Assembly District of Manhattan, sponsored by the Federation of Churches and Christian Workers of New York City. Both the Church and the sociologists began to sense the need to centralize, subdivide, and bureaucratize their efforts at reform, rehabilitation, and uplift. This trend found representative expression in W. E. B. Du Bois's *Philadelphia Negro* ([1899]1967), the first American urban community study.[2] The plight of Philadelphia's black population had aroused the sympathy of Susan P. Wharton, a leader of the University of Pennsylvania's college settlement. She requested "the cooperation of the University in a plan for the better understanding of the colored people, especially of their position in this city." Pennsylvania's provost Charles Curtis Harrison agreed, and Samuel McCune Lindsay—later professor of social legislation at Columbia and a leader in expanding sociological research into regional, national, and colonial policies—became the overall supervisor of the project. Du Bois, who had taken his first course in sociology under Edward Cummings at Harvard, was research director. To Du Bois, as to the university professors and settlement-house workers, the collection and analysis of social facts were as much a religious as a scientific activity offered as a form of prayer for the redemption of dark-skinned people.

Graham Taylor was singularly responsible for changing what had begun as sympathetic and sentimental programs of uplift among the immigrant and laboring classes into socially efficient experiments. As early as 1889 Taylor had directed the Connecticut Bible Society's socioreligious survey that counted not only Hartford's families, boarders, and domestics according to nationality and religious denomination but also the "destructive forces"—saloons, prostitution, criminals—in its immigrant neighborhoods and slums. He summed up the relationship between Social Gospel and social science:

> This is an age when the study of social science is in inception. It should be the science of Christian society. Its field is the world, including all classes and conditions of men for all nationalities. Its work is to investigate the conditions of social and personal life, discover the causes of suffering and the sources of inharmonious relations. When Christian sociology has done all this, it will be more possible to adjust differences, and harmonize the varying elements by applying the principles of Christianity.

When Taylor left Hartford to become the first professor of Christian sociology at Chicago Theological Seminary, he brought his ideas of sociology as an instrument of missionary activity to that school and to the University of Chicago. He also opened Chicago Commons (White and Hopkins, 1976, 139), a settlement house that he sometimes spoke of as a "social laboratory," organized

> to discover, demonstrate and interpret needs; to initiate, try out, test and approve efforts and agencies to meet these needs; to ascertain the facts and causes of deterioration and supply the conditions or apply the forces which will prevent or remedy it; to promote the ideals of progress and help correlate all the personal and public resources available for their realization. [Quoted in McClymer, 1980, 20]

The new settlement-house social laboratories, together with the urban and socioreligious surveys, became the first major extra-university loci for the merger of two strands of fin-de-siècle sociology—Social Gospel theology and rational, planned, scientifically grounded municipal action. "Rational," "scientific" societal reconstruction soon emerged as the order of the day among Progressive reformers, socially conscious, religiously inspired sociologists, and urban community builders. This approach stood against both the sentimental, softheaded attitude attributed to naive but well-meaning charitable organizations and individuals and the radical and revolutionary solutions espoused by such groups as the Socialist Labor Party, the Socialist Party of America, the Industrial Workers of the World (Kraditor, 1981) and crimino-labor sects like the Molly Maguires (Broehl, 1968; Foner, 1980, 150–200).

MORAL REFORM THROUGH SOCIAL POLICY

Under the intellectual leadership of Giddings and Samuel McCune Lindsay, sociology at Columbia embarked on a project to disseminate the technique of the social survey and to establish linkages to government and business. The social survey soon displaced the older philanthropic means of Christian endeavor.

At the time the social survey was invented, the United States was undergoing a vast transformation in its urban and industrial life; yet it was still a politically decentralized society. Great fortunes were being accumulated by a new generation of business entrepreneurs who, in contrast to the corporate managers of today, lived in the cities where their businesses were located: Philadelphia, New York, Pittsburgh, Cleveland, Chicago. Hence, the businessmen had an interest in the quality of life among the urban masses and in the social problems that plagued their own communities. In the expanding urban world in which they did business, the settlement house and its localized, direct methods of social reform were inadequate, a handicraft approach to machine-age problems. The social survey, on the other hand, employing a mass-production method, paralleled the mass-production processes in industry.

The first major sociological survey was conducted by Paul U. Kellogg (1879–1958), a student of Giddings who also pioneered the development of welfare journalism.[3] His Pittsburgh Survey, conducted from 1907 through 1909, marshaled the interviewing, statistical, and analytic tools of the new science of sociology for professional public service. And it did more; it was the first experiment in social *engineering* in the strict sense of that term.[4] It proceeded on the assumption that industrial society was itself a great mechanism and that melioristic sociologists could apply the laws of social physics and social mechanics to its adjustment. The laws themselves were deducible from the statistical facts collected. Kellogg's Pittsburgh Survey sought to do for the United States what Charles Booth's study of London had done for England: place charity and reform on a sound, scientific basis.

Pittsburgh was chosen because it seemed to be both microcosm and portent of the future of industrial America (Kellogg, 1908, 1668–69). Statistical methods were employed because, as Kellogg put it, they would "clamp our facts in so that they cannot be shaken off and so that they will have national interest and, within the limits *we consciously set for them,* scientific values." Further, Kellogg supposed that a statistical rendering of the social facts would "make the town real—to itself," avoid both "goody-goody preachment of what it ought to be" and "sensational discoloration," and—strangely, in light of the actual multivolume compendium finally produced—eschew "a formidable array of rigid facts." Reflecting the Social Gospelers' belief in obtaining *useful* facts on the one hand, and Giddings's as well as his own suspicion of yellow journalism on the other, Kellogg urged his survey staff to regard "the standard ahead of us" as "piled-up actuality." Ultimately the findings would be used to establish "relations," to "project" the survey's work "into the future," and to suggest practical solutions to particular problems. These solutions, in turn, would be carried forth by "local initiative . . . to shoulder the responsibilities which the facts show to be obvious." The facts were to speak for themselves to the makers of social policy.

The Pittsburgh Survey was financed primarily by the newly founded Russell Sage Foundation. Ultimately that foundation provided $47,000—only a small part of which was recovered from the sale of the six compendious volumes that reported the survey's findings—to subsidize research and publication (Chambers, 1971, 34). It was an auspicious beginning for both social science and for its new patron, which subsequently financed further surveys in Scranton, Atlanta, Topeka, Ithaca, St. Paul, and Springfield, Illinois. Not only did this provide the kind of continuity in social research that experimental sociologists favored, but also it helped to cement the relationship between the discipline and the foundation. Moreover, the Russell Sage subsidies had spin-offs of positive advantage for both sociology and social reform. Other cities, including Cleveland and Rochester, were surveyed by local or outside groups, and as urban historian Blake McKelvey (1963, 260) has observed, "These surveys . . . culminated in elaborate exhibits that performed an educational function and stimulated improvements in public health, welfare and the schools." Concrete problems of uplift and social improvement were believed to be resolvable by the new method.

The Pittsburgh Survey epitomized the new statistical scientism that had replaced the early and short-lived enthusiasm for local Christian endeavor in the settlement houses. As the Protestant denominations began to concern themselves with such national social issues as labor's right to organize; sickness, accident, and old-age insurance; workmen's compensation; child labor; the eight-hour day and the six-day work week; the calculation of the living wage; and the precise measure of the poverty line, they hired specialists in collecting and interpreting social and economic facts to head their various agencies and to staff their Gospel-inspired social studies. Through the survey, American sociology set its feet firmly on the ground of statistical study and started on a road toward "practical" social reform. At the time, this meant an alliance with the Progressive movement and a cooperative attitude toward those entrepreneurs and captains of industry who sought to soften the prevailing "tooth and claw" version of Social Darwinism with their own Protestant-inspired steward-ship.

The Pittsburgh Survey provided the first major opportunity to develop and experiment with the organizational techniques appropriate to large-scale social research. Kellogg, for example, provided a model for later directors of sociological urban and community surveys:

> He had to coordinate the work of literally hundreds of persons, not only his chief staff aids who wrote the several volumes, but all those statisticians, social workers, engineers, lawyers, physicians, economists, labor investigators, and city planners who made significant contributions at every point of the Survey. He had to keep his lines open to community leaders, for without their support the work could not continue. He had to keep community agencies, businesses, churches, civic leaders informed of his work at every phase and stage. He had, of course, to manage the budget. He had, finally, to edit thousands of pages of studies and reports, for the results of the investigations found publication in a number of . . . periodicals. [Chambers, 1971, 37][5]

Management and coordination of research became professional so-ciological skills in their own right, on a par with if not superior to the use of pure reason to solve scientific problems. The recruitment and supervi-sion of staff and line personnel, the designing of questionnaires that would be administered by apprentice and journeymen field-workers, the attention to budgetary matters, and the editing and rewriting of one's subordinates' works would become mainstays of the survey sociologist's practice.

But statistical sociology also claimed a role in the formation of social policy, and again it was the sociologists at Columbia who provided the rhetoric and technology that supported this claim, a secular derivative of the Puritan legitimation of a this-worldly magistracy. These social scien-tists hoped by means of their knowledge and technology to perform acts of social-minded stewardship addressed to the new urban, industrial, and welfare problems of the society. Their efforts were aided by the other Christian stewards, the great American philanthropic families who re-garded their wealth as held in trusteeship for God. It was the meeting of these social engineers and the possessors of the new industrial wealth that shaped the character not only of sociology but of the social sciences in the United States. Their interconnections determined the intellectual and technical directions that would be taken by the new secular theodicies.

EXCURSUS: BUREAUCRATIZATION OF CHRISTIAN STEWARDSHIP

The idea animating stewardship was that wealth is ordained by God for human welfare. As Joseph Cummings, president of Wesleyan University, put it in 1886, "The great remedy for social wrongs will be found in the Christian use of money." The consecration of capital to God required the capitalist to regard his talent to obtain and increase capital also as a calling to use it for the benefit of the community. As an alternative to socialist and other collectivist proposals stewardship was a central principle advocated by the Social Gospel movement—and by such captains of industry as Andrew Carnegie and John D. Rockefeller. "God gave me my money," Rockefeller once proclaimed, and it would have to be looked after with that in mind.

John D. Rockefeller's religiously grounded sense of civic responsibility has had a deep and lasting impact on American society. His version of stewardship moved according to the principles of horizontal monopoly; it extended over a variety of institutions affecting foreign missions, medical education, Negro advancement, and, most important for the present study, the statistical approach in sociology (Collier and Horowitz, 1976; Hawke, 1980; Brown, 1979). Whereas both Christian Socialists and secular radicals emphasized the *redistribution* of wealth, Rockefeller, Carnegie, and other industrial giants, guided by the plutocratic version of the Social Gospel, considered its *rational management* to be appropriate expression of their special calling to holy stewardship. "The problem of our age," wrote Carnegie, "is the proper administration of wealth, so that the ties of brotherhood may still bind together with the sick and poor in harmonious relationship." Rockefeller used this theme to reorganize his own philanthropy to meet the new standards of "scientific giving." In 1891, he hired the Reverend Frederick T. Gates as his chief almoner. Gates conceived of wealth in terms of corporate structures—bureaucratized charities that would rationalize philanthropy in the same manner that his employer had rationalized the extraction, production, and sale of oil. "I saw no other course," he later recalled, "but for Mr. Rockefeller and his son to form a series of great corporate philanthropies for forwarding civilization in all its elements in this land and in all lands; philanthropies, if possible, limitless in time and amount, broad in scope, and self-perpetuating" (Collier and Horowitz, 1976, 60).

The rationalization of philanthropy was to follow the same path as that taken by capitalist institutions in Max Weber's well-known analysis (1930). Ultimately, a number of "immortal" (Lyman, 1979, 243–45) foundations, boards, institutes, and universities would superintend the scientific administration of major aspects of education, health, human welfare, and social uplift in America. Even while it was to be centralized and bureaucratized, the plutocratic pattern of giving was to retain the Protestant desire to uplift unregenerate souls and encourage their committed participation in and for the benefit of society.

The age of corporate philanthropy would attempt to retain the essential character of the original Calvinist conception of charity. For the earlier, small-scale steward—the successful businessman and the professional of Main Street America—the important element of charity was social control. Recipients were expected both to be grateful (loyal to the "booster" values of the town) and to conform to the small-town standards of decency. The same expectations were built into large-scale philanthropy. In effect, the values of Calvinism were built into a nationally organized philanthropic industry for the production and distribution of small-town Protestant values.[6]

GIDDINGS AND HIS MISSIONARIES

Rockefeller's corporate stewardship eventually turned its attention to social science, and particularly sociology. Giddings's statistical sociology had by then begun to reach out for control over basic research and influence on public policy. The interests of the Rockefellers and the "Giddings men" coincided, and over the years they collaborated in a project to insure the triumph of statistical social science.

Giddings's commitment to the mission of American sociology, linked to the world-wide expansion of America's democratic and Christian empire, was both challenged and reinforced by World War I. During the war he became increasingly patriotic, xenophobic, anti-intellectual, and distrustful of non-Christian and immigrant groups (see Gossett, 1963, 312–13). His idea of the consciousness of kind was being put to the test by international wartime alliances that divided the allegiances of Americans, and his response was to redouble his efforts to define the secular mission of the social sciences.

To this end, early in the war he sent a memo to Columbia University president Nicholas Murray Butler, calling for a reorganization of the tasks of the faculty of political science. He proposed that each discipline be reconstituted for patriotic service (Summerscales, 1970, 64):

Department	Purpose
History	How to Make the World Safe for Democracy
Sociology	How to Make Democracy Safe for the World[7]
Public Law	How to Establish and Safeguard Peace
Economics	How to Pay the Bill

In Giddings's conception the social sciences would become an instrument for national security as well as national policy. His powerful and single-minded sense of mission led him to categorize his colleagues as either believers or apostates, patriots or traitors. Consciousness of kind became a yardstick for the measurement of morality and patriotism.

Giddings applied the same yardstick to his relationships with colleagues and students. He expected his students to adopt his ideas and remain loyal to them during the rest of their careers, in return for which he furthered their careers within the profession. In the thirty-four years during which he dominated Columbia's department, Giddings created a group of dedicated and committed disciples[8] eager to spread his message throughout the universities and colleges of the United States and the world.[9]

Among the most important "Giddings men," were William Fielding Ogburn (1886–1959), Howard W. Odum (1884–1954), and F. Stuart Chapin (1888–1974). Each served as president of the American Sociological Society (1929, 1930, and 1935, respectively), as did three others—James P. Lichtenberger in 1922, John L. Gillin in 1926, and Frank H. Hankins in 1938. Giddings himself served two terms (1910, 1911). He placed his students in the major social science centers in the country: Lichtenberger at Pennsylvania, Hankins at Clark and then at Smith, Chapin at Minnesota, Gillin at Wisconsin, Odum at North Carolina, Ogburn at Chicago. These centers, plus Columbia, produced the next several generations of sociologists who occupied positions in new and expanding departments of sociology around the country. In the old mode of missionary endeavor, the Giddings men operated like a sect throughout the East and Midwest.[10] Their message was that statistical sociology, when linked to the social survey, would supervene all other approaches, and would help solve local, state, and national problems.

Cultural Lag: Ogburn's Monodimensional Gospel

William Fielding Ogburn followed up leads in Giddings's original sociology to develop his own hypothesis of "cultural lag." He also worked to rationalize sociology through universalizing the statistical method, to give sociology a corporate organization through the Social Science Research Council, and to make it an arm of national policy through his directorship of President Hoover's Research Committee on Social Trends. His sociological outlook made possible the shift from the old Social Gospel to the new statistical positivism. From his time onward, the language of Christian endeavor was expunged from sociology, but its spirit remained part of the science's catechism.

Ogburn's basic approach to a statistical sociology and its application were established in his doctoral dissertation *Progress and Uniformity in Child-Labor Legislation* ([1912] 1968), conceived as a pioneering effort in both techniques of measurement and legislative applications. Ogburn "hoped that this subject will be of practical value, especially to legislators, who, it is believed, can better frame their laws on child labor after a thorough knowledge of the status of child labor laws of the various states." However, he insisted, his "investigation is not a study to determine causes, but it is hoped that it may be used as a basis for a study of causes." Before causes could be ascertained, accurate description and careful measurement were essential: "No science has progressed far without basing its conclusions on measurements." Moreover, the "science of measurement becomes more difficult, the more complex the nature of the measurement. Child labor laws were particularly complicated and difficult to measure, and Ogburn knew of no previous attempt to measure them quantitatively.

The hypothesis of "cultural lag" was taken from Giddings's observation about "the seemingly anomalous fact that suicide, insanity, crime, vagabondage, increased with wealth, education and refinement" and that this increase occurred "when the rate of social activity exceeds the rate of constructive reorganization" (1893, 237–38). "Constructive reorganization" suggested that the deviancies occasioned by these inverse rate changes in different spheres of the social order might be reduced or prevented altogether by scientific intervention in the social process. Ogburn's restatement of this idea was an argument in behalf of bringing the nonmaterial elements of culture into a constructive relationship with the more rapidly changing material ones.

Ogburn presented quantitative evidence that the increase in industrial accidents varied with the growth of major industries in the United States, but that appropriate compensation practices lagged far behind. "It is therefore quite clear that between the time when the number of industrial accidents became significantly large due to the growth of machine industry and the time of the adoption of workingmen's compensation, there was a very unsatisfactory adjustment to the accident situation" ([1922] 1966, 235–36).

Prior to Ogburn, melioristic sociologists had spoken of the general tendencies of whole societies to change and had proposed (or opposed) particular policies designed to hasten (or to slow down) the movement. Much of the earlier sociology approached amelioration indirectly, preaching and practicing an unbounded faith in progressively educating the next generation toward a rational and scientific approach to producing positive social change (e.g., Ellwood, 1910, 371–87). Ogburn, in contrast, provided an outlook compatible with the brooding disappointment with human rationality that had arisen among social thinkers after World War I. His statement was a rejection of the optimistic and global evolution of enlightened reason associated with the neo-Comtean sociology of Lester F. Ward (see Hinkle and Hinkle, 1954, 21–22). Central to his outlook was a belief in the inherent social, cultural, and moral propriety of the American system of government and economy, coupled with an assurance that the human problems of an industrial civilization could be solved by piecemeal applications of government-sponsored social science.

As Ogburn defined them, social problems arose because of a maladjustment between human nature and culture. "Human nature is really a factor in all social problems, in the sense that if our human nature were different the social problems would either not exist or else would be different, because all social phenomena involve the two factors, human nature and culture" ([1922] 1966, 325). Ogburn's science postulated a nonrational element at the base of this troublesome human nature and selected "selfishness" as the fundamental element of human nature and the basic source for societal difficulties. If "we were less selfish or more considerate, in some effective social manner, of the interests of others, many of our present-day social problems would be minor ones" (334–35). How to adjust human selfishness effectively became the hallmark of Ogburn's early proposals in applied sociology. Replacing the sin of greed with the secular term "selfishness," Ogburn launched twentieth-century positivistic sociology into the practical activity of making a world safe from sin.

Holding that social problems manifesting themselves in individual acts of deviance arose out of the rapid advances of industrialization, Ogburn suggested mass psychotherapeutic modifications that might rechannel overstimulated emotions away from their more or less uncontrollable urges. He stressed the utility of recreation:

> In certain types of recreation, there is a satisfactory stimulation of the feelings but apparently very little provision for any motor expression; at least, the drive does not work out through much bodily activity. Where an individual participates in a boxing match or a football game or in various athletic contests, such is not the case, for there is abundant provision for motor outlet. This does not appear on the surface to be so true of a recreation such as attending the theatre, except as there is expression in tears, laughter, or applause. The theatre is a wonderful invention for arousing the emotions. . . . We do not know very much about the motor outlet in connection with many of these emotions; it is conceivable that there may be outlets or expression with little bodily activity. . . . We are not, however, in a position to speak positively concerning the recreations involving little movement. . . . Some types of recreation, such as, for instance, those that appeal to the sex instinct, apparently arouse the instinct but do not provide for the completion of the act. . . . An inventory of the recreations further reveals many such as dancing, card-playing, gambling and talking, concerning which it is not very clear what happens psychologically when one takes part in them. [359–60]

In his attitude toward "passive" recreation (i.e., theatre, sex, card playing, dancing, talking, gambling), Ogburn restated in scientific terms the language of Main Street Protestantism, with its later nineteenth-century emphasis on sports and other forms of "muscular Christianity" (see Kett, 1977, 130, 189–90, 243). But here, too, his concern was less with religious moralizing than with its secular counterpart: curbing the disruptive effects of "vices." Sin and vice became issues that might be resolved by means of properly guided recreation.[11]

For all his secular hardheadedness, Ogburn was a true believer in the redemptive qualities of quantitative methods. His concern for the propriety of measurement over theory led him to champion the quantitative study of social trends. "Science grows by accumulation," he pointed out, and there "is some doubt as to how much social theories help in the . . . process." He was certain that "statisticians are engaged in adding exact knowledge to the existing stock, and thus solidly helping its [i.e., sociological science's] growth." In a 1929 book on recent social changes in the United States, Ogburn recognized that "these are certainly years of great and rapid change" and that the "social sciences ought to render aid in these times of change and uncertainty." However, he pointed out these "sciences . . . are young [and] their achievements in the exact measurement of the relationships of social phenomena are meager, too much so for much reliable prediction" (Duncan, 1964, 100–01). He looked forward optimistically to the day when, with "more complete statistics and with better measurements, we shall attain fuller knowledge of what is happening to us and where we are going." Optimistic about the prospects for a statistically oriented social science and the social controls that might be adduced from it, Ogburn also was sure that intervention in the social process would require much more detailed and precise research.

Ogburn launched into the practical world of planning, organizing, and directing national efforts to rationalize social research. As a founder of the Social Science Research Council and director of the President's Research Committee on Social Trends, he embarked on a project to coordinate the scientific efforts of two of the most powerful stewards of society's wealth, the Rockefeller Foundation and the federal government.

THE STATISTICAL SYNTHESIS OF THE SOCIAL SCIENCES

The Rockefellers had for many years applied their convictions about Christian stewardship to the rational administration of the emerging social sciences. At first, they worked through the economics department at Harvard. In 1914 Edwin F. Gay and F. W. Taussig served on Harvard's committee to explore the feasibility of establishing an interdisciplinary research group under the sponsorship of the Rockefeller Foundation (Church, 1965, 80). The committee's efforts appear to have been unsuccessful. It was not until 1923 that Rockefeller's stewardship over social science was firmly implanted. In that year Beardsley Ruml, who directed the Laura Spelman Rockefeller Memorial Fund, put money "behind the efforts of Charles E. Merriam, head of the Political Science Department at Chicago . . . [and thereby] helped underwrite the conquest of the academic world by Merriam and his 'behaviorist' school" (Collier and Horowitz, 1976, 143). This group founded the Social Science Research Council (SSRC).

Ruml's aim was to use the fund "to make a concentrated effort to reform the social sciences and make them more applicable to the problems of social management and control as encountered by the expanding government and corporate bureaucracies." Merriam, together with Wesley C. Mitchell and Shelby M. Harrison, served on the Council's policy-making administrative board.

Ogburn, who served on the Council from 1924 to 1941, used his position to turn the methodological stance of Columbia's sociology into the single most significant criterion for judging social research and for unifying the social sciences. Under his and Merriam's guidance, the SSRC sought to achieve unification of the social sciences by means of quantification. Merriam, following in the wake of Giddings's earlier methodological preachments, championed the use of statistics in all social sciences (Merriam, 1925, 184–219). Ogburn preached the gospel of statistical redemption not only from the pulpit of the SSRC but from the rostrums provided by his presidencies of the American Sociological Society and the American Statistical Association. In 1929 the SSRC established a subcommittee on mathematics as part of its Committee on Social and Economic Research in Agriculture. The subcommittee "construed its mandate broadly and published recommendations . . . concerning the courses in mathematics that prospective social scientists in general ought to study" (Sibley, 1974, 2–3). Through its Committee on Scientific Method in the Social Sciences, established in 1923, the SSRC commenced a rather one-sided discussion of what constituted truly scientific research, and sponsored publication of a compendium of statistical procedures by Stuart A. Rice.[12] In 1949, in an attempt to reinforce its commitment to statistics, the SSRC established a Committee on Mathematical Training of Social Scientists. From 1952 until 1958 the committee's chairman was William G. Madow, a statistician from the University of Illinois, who dreamed of "a community of social scientists whose mathematical strength was equal to its mathematical problems" (Sibley, 1974, 21). That dream, according to SSRC historian Elbridge Sibley, "epitomizes the Council's aim."[13]

Rockefeller, Ogburn, and the other zealots of statistical social science shared a naive optimism about the scientific solution of social problems and the malleability of human societies. They supposed that moral and political issues might be transposed into technical, quantifiable problems with equally technical and calculable solutions.

Following the missionary style of Ogburn, the SSRC established an important beachhead for spreading the word at the University of Chicago. Immediately upon arriving in 1927 Ogburn began to undermine the ethnographic, qualitative, case-study, and sociopsychological approaches that had given sociology at Chicago its special imprint. Not only his student Samuel Stouffer but Stuart A. Rice as well relegated the case-study method to a prestatistical phase of investigation, useful only for defining a social entity, in preparation for exploration by statistical methods (see Wirth [1940] 1974, 165). In December 1929, a "Social Science Research Building" financed by the SSRC was opened on the university campus at 1126 East Fifty-ninth Street; "1126" soon became a shorthand reference for SSRC-sponsored research at Chicago. Carved on the bay of the building was the quotation from Lord Kelvin: "If you cannot measure, your knowledge is meager and unsatisfactory."[14]

Conversion of the entire discipline to the statistical gospel never succeeded; some "pagans" held out against its promise of scientific salvation and refused recruitment into the army of quantitative Christian manqué soldiers who sought to march sociology ever onward and upward. When in 1939 a seminar called "Quantification: The Quest for Precision" was held at "1126" as part of its decennial celebration, not all the participants would accept the terms of reference limiting the discussion. Talcott Parsons inquired of the chairman whether what he preferred to call "non-numerical quantification, where one can only make judgments of a 'more-and-less' type," might not be more significant than the precise methods of quantification under discussion. Frank H. Knight, translator of Weber's *General Economic History,* proposed that speculation might be of equal or even greater importance to social science than quantitative precision. "In most problems and in all human problems, to a very large degree, the formulation proceeds along with the solution," he declared, and "if the interest is in the realization of ends or the achievement of purposes to a maximum degree, we have both quantitative and nonquantitative problems. . . . It is doubtful if it ever makes sense to talk about an objective or empirical measurement of any subjective attitude." He concluded that his own discipline, economics—certainly in the SSRC's eyes a safer convert to statistical sectarianism than sociology—could "only within fairly narrow limits . . . be a positive science . . . [because] fundamentally we are not dealing with empirical data."

However, such skeptical voices did not deter the quantifiers from their mission. The SSRC continued its struggle to save social science from subjectivity and sentiment, employing organizational strategies more often than intellectual debate.

Designed, like a holding company, to coordinate the work of lower-level specialists and experts who no longer had a comprehensive view of society, the SSRC hoped to bring the technical expertise of academic researchers into the service of national public-policy administration. At the university level—including Harvard, Columbia, Yale, and Chicago—it sponsored local chapters of the national organization and encouraged the establishment of interdisciplinary research institutes. Where Giddings men had already established independent research institutes—the outstanding one was Odum's Institute for Research in Social Science at the University of North Carolina at Chapel Hill, opened in 1924 (See Johnson and Johnson, 1980)—the SSRC cooperated, providing funds for joint ventures in social research. In the words of Rockefeller's aide, Raymond Fosdick, the SSRC became "the most important instrumentality in America for furthering intercommunication between students of social problems and sponsoring cooperative research among the several disciplines" (Collier and Horowitz, 1976, 142–3). To further coordinate the social sciences, it recruited its members from the national professional social science associations, including the American Economic Association, the American Sociological Society, and the American Statistical Association, and extended its offer of services to anthropology, psychology, and history. However, the first opportunity to engraft its comprehensive quantitative perspective on national public policy arose when President Herbert Hoover established his Research Committee on Social Trends.

SECTARIAN STATISTICIANS IN PUBLIC ADMINISTRATION

Work on the thirty separate studies sponsored by the President's Research Committee was dominated by Giddings men.[15] From its inception the committee became virtually a branch of the SSRC, with Merriam, Mitchell, and Harrison serving as its chairman, vice-chairman, and secretary-treasurer respectively, and with Ogburn as director of research and Odum as assistant director. The fact that policy-related research was being subsidized by the government of the United States suggested that Ward's dream of a technocratic sociocracy might be about to come true. More immediately, the federally sponsored research provided job opportunities for sociologists just as the Great Depression set in, suggesting that social science might relieve its own unemployment problems at the same time that it delivered the nation from poverty and joblessness. Moreover, the new positivist orientation might be employed to reconstruct a society almost shattered by economic collapse and threatened by radical revolution. A technological revival of the Protestant ethic might serve as a prop against alien and revolutionary ideologies.

Hints about a new American covenant, rooted in a scientifically managed democratic commonwealth, are contained in Merriam's contribution to the committee, a study of "Government and Society." Pointing to "the feasible forms both of social control and of emancipation through education, preventive medicine, mental hygiene, medical treatment, social work, guidance of leisure time, eugenics, [and] semi-custodial care, that are far reaching in their implications for the social and political order," Merriam, while voicing some inconclusive concerns for individual liberties and human rights, urged that a "modern government must be prepared to deal intelligently and judiciously with these new controls and releases as they are perfected, and understand how to utilize them for the enrichment of the lives of its citizens in the commonwealth to come" (*Recent Social Trends*, 1933, 1540).

How a modern government might deal with these new social, psychological and medical technologies was suggested in Ogburn's "Review of Findings," which introduced the committee's final report. The kind of social science encouraged by the SSRC, he proposed, might be nationalized through the constitution of a National Advisory Council,

> including scientific, educational, governmental, economic (industrial, agricultural and labor) points of contact, or other appropriate elements able to contribute to the consideration of the basic problems of the nation. Such an agency might consider some fundamental questions of the social order, economic, governmental, educational, technical, cultural, always in their interrelation, and in the light of the trends and possibilities of modern science. [*Recent Social Trends*, 1933, lxxiii]

Ogburn, the SSRC, and their fellow missionaries of positivist advance hoped to insure the existence of a rational public administration and an equally rational, unified, and statisticalized science of society from which its policy advisers would be drawn.

> The Social Science Research Council, representative of seven scientific societies, and devoted to the consideration of research in the social field, may prove an instrumentality of great value in the broader view of the complex social problems, in the integration of social knowledge, in the initiative toward social planning on a high level. . . . It is within the bounds of possibility that this Council might care to take the initiative in setting up other machinery for the consideration of *ad hoc* problems, and for more and continuous generalized consideration of broader aspects of social integration and planning. It would further be possible for this Council to organize sponsoring groups in which there might be brought together the technical fact finding, the interpretation of data in a broader sense, and the practical judgment of those holding the reins of authority in government, industry and society. [lxxiii]

Social science and society would be administered by a giant holding company, legitimated by popular adherence to the new religion of technoscientific progress, funded by a joint venture of private philanthropy and public subsidy, powered by federal authority, and supervised by a watchful but benevolent neo-Comtean elite. Much of the older dreams of nine-teenth-century sociology is contained in this proposal. Hughes's division of labor under warranteeism is given unacknowledged recognition in the placing of the "mentalist" elite at the administrative apex of the social order, while the new technologies of social control envisioned in so many of the committee's reports would undoubtedly bring about the appropri-ate compliance of whatever groups would make up modern America's "warrantees." Ward's sociocracy is also represented, but in Ogburn's vi-sion the technoscientific administrators are working hand in hand with businessmen, religious leaders, and politicians to bring about a guided and scientifically graduated movement toward the democratic cosmopoli-tan commonwealth. Albion Small's vision (presented in chapter 12) of a born-again capitalism, given a Christian soul to ameliorate the faults so clearly delineated by Marx, is transvalued: For Christian conversion, read scientific management; for social and economic amelioration, read tech-nical readjustment and application of the techniques of social and psychic control; for the investiture of soulfulness, read administration by right-eous but efficiency-oriented scientists. The Giddings men had found the group that their mentor's father had longed to search out: They them-selves were to be America's Christian rulers.

Like biblical prophecies, Ogburn's proposals were couched in dire terms. Although the committee did not "wish to assume an attitude of alarmist irresponsibility," it did sound a doleful tocsin. Unless a "new synthesis" emerged in which the agricultural, industrial, scientific, and governmental "factors" were coordinated, American society faced either stagnation or dictatorship. A continuation of the current policy of "drift" would fail to excite the "constructive social initiative" needed to apply "conscious intelligence" to "social action"; it would not only risk social and cultural decline but also encourage the forces favoring "dictatorial sys-tems in which the factors of force and violence . . . loom large (lxxiv).

The "Review of Findings" prophesied sociocultural destruction:

> Unless there can be a more impressive integration of social skills and fusing of social purposes than is revealed by recent trends, there can be no assurance that these alternatives with their accompaniments of violent revolution, dark periods of serious repression of libertarian and democratic forms, the pro-scription and loss of many useful elements in the present productive system, can be averted. [*Recent Social Trends*, 1933, lxxiv]

Despite such dire warnings, Ogburn and his committee failed to con-vince Roosevelt's new administration of the need to fuse social science with public policy. Although he employed the talents of a great many social scientists in formulating and administering his "New Deal" for America, Roosevelt never established the kind of national advisory coun-cil envisioned in the committee's report.

The rationalization of sociology, begun as an act of bureaucratic stewardship, reached its apex in the President's Research Committee on Social Trends. Thereafter for fifty years, a sociology "establishment" existed under the aegis of the SSRC and the informal groupings of second-, third-, and fourth-generation Giddings sectarians that clustered around it. This "establishment" reinforced statistical sociology and sought to absorb other paradigms—Parsonian structural-functionalism, for instance—within the quantitative realm.[16] Also, it reopened and continued its search for foundational support and federal patronage. Sociology's rationalization took on a purpose similar to that which Rockefeller's General Education Board had set for medicine: To coordinate and integrate the different elements of the system so that it performs its designated functions. In medicine, the main obstacle to that complete coordination and integration was the private physician (Brown, 1979, 194–95); in sociology, it was the independent thinker—the scholar who carries out research in accordance with an autonomous interest that comes from a self-activated sociological imagination. However, the idea that sociology might be a free and independent discipline, inherently unorthodox and nondoctrinaire, had been virtually overwhelmed by the secular orthodoxy of Giddings's sectarian social engineers.[17]

NOTES

1. One Episcopalian clergyman, James O. S. Huntington (1893, 135) of Maryland's Order of the Holy Cross, objecting to scientific almsgiving as a menace to true philanthropy, invoked a popular ditty:

Organized Charity scrimped and iced
In the name of a cautious, statistical Christ.

2. Du Bois's was not the first ethnographic study of an urban ethnic group in Philadelphia, however. Ethnological studies at the University of Pennsylvania had been pioneered by Daniel Garrison Brinton. Brinton's colleague R. Stewart Culin had done a careful participant-observation study of Philadelphia's Chinatown during the 1880s (1903, 493–500). Culin's work, however, was animated not by Christian endeavor but rather by his remarkable quest for the origins of civilization. Ultimately, on the basis of his own studies of Chinatown and Frank Hamilton Cushing's studies of the Zuni of the Southwest, Culin would put forth the hypothesis that Asiatic civilization had derived from that of the ancient Amerindians. For the implications of this work for sociology see Lyman, 1979, 91–115.

3. Welfare journalism attempted to use sociological data gathering to bring to the public's attention the need to reform the sordid life conditions of the urban poor, destitute, and evil—in a word, the unregenerate. Welfare journalism is a direct ancestor of modern investigative journalism that attempts to expose, among other things, the corruption of "unregenerate" bureaucrats caught in the malfeasance of office. The moral dimensions of nineteenth- as well as twentieth-century American journalism have their sources in the moral norms of the early settlement house, urban surveys, and ethical foundations of the covenanted community. (See Chambers, 1971.)

4. The immediate practical results of the Pittsburgh Survey have been described by Ernest S. Griffith (1974, 122):

One of the earliest tangible results of the Survey was the popular vote (1909) for a bond issue of $6,775,000 for a new tuberculosis hospital, playgrounds, an additional filtration plant, garbage incinerators, new sewers, a new boulevard, and a new street widening. There was a great awakening of the civic conscience. By 1910 the majority of the [city] council were indicted for bribery, together with a number of the bribing bankers, middlemen, and jury-fixers. By 1911 the city had a new and model charter, in the campaign for which the Voters' Civic League played a major role. The Survey continued its leavening effect for many years thereafter.

5. It is illuminating to contrast the methods used by Du Bois as research director of the study of Philadelphia's Seventh Ward with those used by Kellogg in his foundation-subsidized Pittsburgh Survey. As Du Bois (1968, 198) recalled many years later:

I started with no "research methods" and I asked little advice as to procedure. The problem lay before me. Study it. I studied it personally and not by proxy. I sent out no canvassers. I went myself. Personally I visited and talked with 5,000 persons. What I could, I set down in orderly sequence on schedules which I made out and submitted to the University for criticism. Other information I stored in my memory or wrote out as memoranda. I went through the Philadelphia libraries for data, gained access in many instances to private libraries of colored folk and got individual information. I mapped the district, classifying it by conditions; I compiled two centuries of the history of the Negro in Philadelphia and in the Seventh Ward.

6. As philanthropy took on rational and bureaucratic forms it also became a mechanism for socializing the new wealth acquired by America's later immigrants. Social and civic acceptance into a community could be measured by a willingness to "give" to the arts, education, medicine, and even to the poor, who were embraced by the United Way. Protestant and Judaic philosophies of charity especially could meet on these terms, since both religions are characterized by this-worldly orientations. Insofar as status competition could be measured by the absolute amounts given, givers and receivers could be measured across religious and ethnic lines by assessing philanthropic contributions. Philanthropy thus became a basis for status claims and for inclusion in a new kind of covenanted community. Giving became a secular equivalent of showing proof of visible saintliness.

7. The anti-German feeling that swept over America after the sinking of the *Lusitania* overwhelmed much of Columbia's faculty. Giddings became a foremost patriot, sacrificing the scientific content of his lectures to propagandistic service in behalf of the war effort. On May 7, 1916, he addressed a public meeting in Carnegie Hall, sponsored by the American Rights Committee, denouncing Woodrow Wilson's policy of neutrality. On February 6, 1917, speaking before what the *Columbia Spectator* called "the largest and most impressive gathering in the recent annals of the University," he asserted that there could be only "one strongest nation" in the world, and that nation had to take the responsibility to "enforce the peace." By April of that year Giddings, who was professor of the history of civilization as well as of sociology, was warning that the West faced the greatest threat to its survival since the invasion of Attila the Hun. He wondered aloud whether "the sons of the patriots have grown soft" and asked whether recent immigrants had come to the United States "for conscience or liberty, or for income only." In October, he attacked German Kultur and claimed that his sociological investigations had discovered its "fundamental misfortune in the exaggerated self-importance which is a notorious trait of all primitive and isolated peoples."

8. Of special historical importance is the fact that a Giddings man, Howard Brown Woolston, dominated the sociology curriculum at the City College of New York, a school that attracted numerous Jewish students in the 1920s and 1930s. (Gorelick, 1981, 146–59). The City College of New York proved to be most important for Jews in the 1930s because of its centrality for hotly contesting factions of Trotskyists, Stalinists, and other splinters of the

socialist tradition in America. The most important of the radical Jewish sociologists went on to Columbia, where Robert S. Lynd and Robert K. Merton took them in hand and guided them toward creating a synthesis of Marxist and functionalist perspectives (Page, 1982, 13–103).

The roles of Lynd and Merton in acculturating the sons of Jewish immigrants to sociology cannot be underestimated. Lynd, a Protestant ministerial student who had been deeply influenced by Dewey and Veblen, had clashed with Ogburn over the latter's insistence that sociology should become a science for its own sake; Lynd insisted that social scientific knowledge had to serve a social purpose (see Smith, 1979–80; Lynd, [1939] 1964). His socially meliorative and critical outlook resonated with the outlook of Jewish radicals who sought a science that could be used for social reconstruction (see, e.g., Lipset, 1969). And they could identify with Merton's ironic style of sociological writing. The ironic is a semiotic of the less powerful, who, though unable to overturn the system that oppresses them, nevertheless only appear to accept their situation while knowingly revealing that they are not taken in by its pretensions. In Merton's work this appears formally as the study of "latent functions" and "unintended consequences," an approach that suggests that the sociologist, at any rate, is the person in on the secret (see Schneider, 1975).

9. One effect of the war crisis at Columbia was the founding of a separate private, independent institution of higher learning that was intended to be free from administrative control over its professoriat. The New School for Social Research, established in New York City in 1919, grew out of both the academic disaffections at Columbia and certain discussions among the editors of the *New Republic*—notably Alvin Johnson and Herbert Croly—about the need to establish in America an institution similar to the London School of Economics (see Johnson [1952]1960, 272–88). Founded with the aid of philanthropy but no permanent endowment, "The New School" attracted in its first decade a number of distinguished if dissident historians, philosophers, and social scientists, including James Harvey Robinson, Charles Beard, John Dewey, W. I. Thomas, W. E. B. Du Bois, Harry Elmer Barnes, Thorstein Veblen, Alexander Goldenweiser, Sandor Ferenczi, and Wesley Clair Mitchell. Robinson, who had resigned from Columbia, explained the educational philosophy of The New School as one that confines

> our studies to mankind and his present predicaments—to public affairs and human organizations;—all, of course, in the light of man's history and nature as now understood. History, anthropology, psychology, biology, economics, sociology, public law and the rest of the disciplines which have man, his nature and social organization for their theme are not set off in departments but are concentrated into a common effort to state and explain so far as may be human conduct, aspirations and organizations. [Barnes, 1927, 324]

That academic freedom was to be a central concern of The New School for Social Research was indicated in Robinson's justification of its faculty's refusal to confine critical analysis to the policies and conditions of historical societies—a clear slap at Butler's policies of 1917–18:

> We in The New School can venture to be shamelessly interested in current conditions just because we can treat them without reservations imposed by the educational *mores*. We can think as freely as we are capable of thinking just because we are not afraid that too much thinking is likely to be done either by ourselves or by our students.

Moreover, Robinson insisted on a skeptical orientation toward received truths, manners, and morals. The "policy of the Hanseatic League can be treated with a freedom impossible in the case of the United States Steel Corporation," he noted, and a professor "may venture to say all he knows of such long-dead pacifists and radical reformers as Pierre Dubois and

Marsiglio of Padua"; but in the climate of unprotected opinion that prevailed at the time "an equally fair statement of the contentions of Lenin or Victor Berger would obviously be offensive and tend to create intellectual 'unrest'." At The New School, Robinson asserted, freedom of scientific opinion would take precedence not only over ideologies, manners, and morals but also over social reconstruction itself:

> Our object is not to allay doubts and rationalize what exists, but frankly to stimulate questioning and investigation among the men and women that come to us. Our only fear is that the questioning and investigation will not be thoroughgoing enough, not that it will be dangerously free. The New School is no guardian of the morals of the young; it does not function *in loco parentis*, or even *in loco almae matris*. Its instructors are scientifically interested in the subjects they deal with; they all believe that fundamental social readjustments are inevitable, but they are pledged to no program of social reform, old or new; they are simply looking for light, and encouraging others to do so. Facts are not classified in their minds as sacred or dangerous; radical or conservative; suitable for the young or adapted only for the old and settled.

Columbia's President Butler, according to Alvin Johnson ([1952]1960, 167), savaged the social science curriculum at The New School for Social Research as the product of "a little bunch of disgruntled liberals, setting up a tiny fly-by-night radical counterfeit of education." After Johnson had founded the University in Exile (1933)—later the Graduate Faculty of Political and Social Science of The New School for Social Research—President Butler commissioned Frederick Keppel, then of the Carnegie Corporation, to persuade Johnson to allow Columbia to take over The New School. The University in Exile was composed entirely of refugee scholars—many of them Jews—whom Johnson and his colleagues had rescued from the Nazi regime. Keppel explained to Johnson how Butler had decided to take control over but keep separate the traditions of European and American scholarship:

> You know, Alvin, Nicholas Murray Butler is great on consolidations. If he had been in business he would have consolidated all the corporations in America. He proposes to take the New School under the wing of Columbia. . . . He sees a fruitful combination between your University in Exile and the Columbia faculty, your faculty to take care of the European point of view, ours to take care of the American (Johnson [1952]1960, 167–68).

Johnson refused Butler's offer—even though the graduate faculty was then, as frequently, in dire financial straits—because Keppel had warned him that the Columbia trustees would not tolerate two graduate faculties and would soon absorb a few of the Exile faculty and then let The New School perish.

10. Among the strategies employed by Giddings and "Giddings men" was encouraging their students to debunk rival schools of thought. Thus, Giddings assigned his new graduate student, Howard Odum—who had matriculated at Clark College under Giddings's disciple Frank Hankins—to criticize Ward's *Psychic Factors of Civilization* (Odum, [1951]1969, 187). Years later, Ogburn supervised Samuel Stouffer's dissertation at the University of Chicago, which purported to show that case studies, the staple of Chicago's sociology program, were "a prescientific heuristic, rather than a source of valid knowledge in their own right" (Wiley, 1979, 60; see Stouffer, 1980).

11. Ogburn's discussion of selfishness ([1922]1966) suggests that it combines envy, pride, and even lust as well as greed. For a discussion of the sins and their relation to sociology and the other social sciences see Lyman, 1978.

12. Perhaps the most famous publication of the SSRC was Herbert Blumer's appraisal of W. I. Thomas's and Florian Znaniecki's *Polish Peasant in Europe and America* ([1918–20]1958), in which Blumer concluded that the authors' generalizations could not be derived

from or proved by their data and that they had arrived at them through deep knowledge of and close association with Polish peasants and emigrés (see Blumer, [1939] 1979, esp. 50–53). The council seems to have taken this conclusion as further support for its advocacy of even more quantitative efforts, though clearly that was not Blumer's meaning or intention (79, 114–15, 168–71, 184–86, 187–91, 196–202; Sibley, 1974, 19–21).

13. The council also commissioned mathematically oriented works in historical scholarship that "had wide circulation and have doubtless given considerable impetus to the efforts of . . . historians to apply more rigorous and scientifically valid methods in interpreting the past" (Sibley, 1974, 27).

14. We have reprinted the quotation as stated by Frank H. Knight in his sharp disagreement with its implications in the roundtable discussion, held on December 1, 1939, at Building 1126 ([1940]1974, 169). According to Norbert Wiley (1979, 60), Kelvin's original statement read: "When you cannot measure . . . , your knowledge is . . . meagre . . . and . . . unsatisfactory" and had been intended to be restricted to the physical sciences. Ogburn, Wiley contends, had not seen the original and was unaware that he had taken it out of context and omitted ellipses.

15. "Ogburn," recalled Odum ([1951]1969, 148), "not only was mainly responsible for the outlines and arrangements for this study but the appropriation of more than a half million dollars for the study by the Rockefeller Foundation was facilitated by Ogburn's directing the study." The networks linking Giddings's and Ogburn's sociology to institutions of research, universities in the East, South, and Midwest, private philanthropy, and public policy are well illustrated in Ogburn's choice of authors for the special studies that formed the bulk of the committee's final report. "Giddings men," SSRC leaders, and representatives of Rockefeller-funded foundations dominate the report and give it its peculiar messianic-scientific tone. Ogburn himself elaborated his hypothesis of cultural lag in two reports, "The Influence of Invention and Discovery" and "The Family and Its Functions"; Odum provided a study of public welfare activities that concluded with a call for "social planning which will bring to bear the fullest utilization of social science and social research and their application through social work and public administration" (*Recent Social Trends*, 1933, 1271). Three other students of Giddings contributed their specialized talents to the committee's final report: Warren S. Thompson coauthored "The Population of the Nation"; T. J. Woofter, Jr., a colleague of Odum at North Carolina, wrote "The Status of Racial and Ethnic Groups"; and C. E. Gehlke, a member of the original F.H.G. Club, composed of Giddings devotees, joined Edwin H. Sutherland in an analysis called "Crime and Punishment." The older connection of the Rockefeller foundations to Harvard's economics department was reaffirmed in Ogburn's selection of Edwin F. Gay to be senior author of the committee's report "Trends in Economic Organization." The Rockefeller-funded Institute of Social and Religious Research was represented in three studies: "Changes in Religious Organization," by C. Luther Fry with the assistance of Mary Frost Jessup; "The People as Consumers" by former ISRR member Robert S. Lynd; and "Rural Life," coauthored by Edmund de S. Brunner. Rockefeller's General Education Board was permitted to voice its opinions in Lawrence K. Frank's "Youth and Childhood." The Rockefeller Foundation employed a Columbia Ph.D., Sydnor H. Walker (whose dissertation had been published by the press of Odum's University of North Carolina), to present the committee's report, "Privately Supported Social Work." The Chicago tradition that had developed under Park, Burgess, and Mead was hardly represented: Stuart A. Rice, a Chicago Ph.D. who had become an SSRC statistical stalwart, coauthored "The Agencies of Communication" with a fellow SSRC man, Minnesota's Malcolm M. Willey. Of the original Chicago School sociologists, R. D. McKenzie, who had migrated to Michigan and was a rather hard-nosed representative of the human-ecology school, wrote the committee's report "The Rise of Metropolitan Communities," while former Chicagoan Jesse Steiner's "Recreation and Leisure Time Activities" was, at

Ogburn's insistence, overseen by University of North Carolina's statistical sociologist, Clarence Heer. Chicago's Leonard White, a sometime student of Park, contributed "Public Administration" to the committee's final report, but he already leaned in the direction of Merriam and the SSRC. Underscoring most vividly the Columbia/foundation network that dominated the committee, perhaps, is "The Arts in Social Life," by Frederick P. Keppel, who had left Morningside Heights for the Carnegie Corporation.

16. In the late 1940s Samuel Stouffer was appointed to Harvard University, where he joined Frederick Moesteller, a pure mathematician, in the department only recently created by Talcott Parsons, who had displaced Pitirim Sorokin as chairman of the sociology department and disbanded it to create the social relations department. Sorokin, who had originally been brought to Harvard in 1931 for the purpose of introducing quantitative sociology, had chosen not to give the department a statistical and mathematical orientation, which Stouffer and Moesteller now brought to it. In 1950–51, Paul Lazarsfeld was a visiting professor in the same department, and he brought with him his graduate assistant from Columbia, Peter Rossi. In 1970, several years before Parsons's retirement, the Social Relations Department disintegrated into a Sociology Department chaired by George C. Homans, a Social Psychology program that rejoined the old Psychology Department, and a Social Anthropology program reintegrated into the Department of Anthropology.

17. The half-century of positivist sway was evaluated in 1982 by Francis X. Sutton, deputy vice-president of the Ford Foundation, when speaking before the SSRC's Area Assembly held in 1983 at Airlie House, Airlie, Virginia:

Positivism . . . was a set of doctrines relegated, with its errors exposed, to the history of philosophy and social thought. . . . Having lived through an era that reeked of positivism—in its faith in planned and controllable development—I wondered how I and so many other expensively educated people could have been so inattentive to what we were supposed to know. . . . By now, the bright optimism that colored the decades after World War II has faded. . . . Confidence that the affairs of nations can be controlled and steered briskly toward better futures has been badly shaken. The positivistic faith that human troubles and imperfections are mere "problems" that have solutions based on scientific inquiry and rational action has receded, and we now—in doubt and disquiet—ponder what we can and cannot do. (1982)

PART IV

Christianity, Social Conscience, and Sociology in the Midwest

CHAPTER 10

Secular Evangelism at the University of Wisconsin

The secular ideologies and programs that had begun to develop in the East—philosophical pragmatism, theories of social and moral uplift, and social programs for the socialization of newer immigrant and older racial groups—were refracted in the work of sociologists in the Midwest. Midwestern sociologists addressed themselves to the region's ethnic, racial, and religious groups and to its problems—crime, delinquency, prostitution, and other vices. Cities were being built even as they were being studied, enabling the universities to play a central role in shaping the political and social culture. In contrast to eastern schools, where students were exhorted to be reborn through encounters with the urban masses, at the University of Chicago the urban masses were brought into the university as students and awarded higher degrees.

The state universities embarked on a program for the democratization of culture, the Americanization of immigrant urban populations, and the moral, economic, and spiritual elevation of rural life. They regarded the farm family, the small businessman, the merchant, the rural minister, the local official, and the small-town newspaper editor as the beneficiaries of their educational mission. The activist and reformist elements in this-worldly Protestantism based their mission on the belief that the university was God's instrument for making a better world. The ideology, institutions, and peoples of the region placed their special stamp on the new discipline of sociology, ensuring its attentiveness to the society then developing on the former frontier.

The eastern version of the Social Gospel melded with midwestern populism; an egalitarian but xenophobic communitarian ideal replaced the elitism of New England salvational ethics. In the Midwest, proposed solutions to the Social Question took

151

new directions and evoked further contradictions. Theorists and activists were divided over encouraging the growth of industrial democracy or preaching individual redemption; extending civil and social rights to Negroes, Asians, Jews, and new arrivals from southern and eastern Europe or urging selective emancipation, rapid assimilation, and restrictions on immigration; opposing the liberation of women or urging new conceptions of work, marriage, and the family. Ultimately, the Midwest selectively absorbed the modified versions of both the Harvard and the Columbia styles of sociology, the latter most prominently at the large state universities such as Wisconsin, the former at the privately sponsored University of Chicago.

A period of new agricultural and industrial development began in the Midwest after the Civil War. Steeped in abolitionist pride and encouraged by its agricultural strength and northern European traditions of yeomanry, the boosters of the Midwest thought of themselves as both the successors of and the superiors to eastern paternalism and plutocracy (May, 1959, 91–106). Their democratic egalitarianism rested on a base of small farms and rural communities of Norwegian, Swedish, and German immigrants who had moved beyond the Alleghenies and into the Ohio and Mississippi valleys. The city of Chicago had become a new point of confluence between East and West, trading the grain and livestock produced on the extended frontier for the ideas and culture of Boston and New York. Chicago was not merely a point of transit, however, but a self-proclaimed center of culture in its own right, a city that represented and hoped to lead a new America forward to democratic secular salvation (H. Duncan, 1964).

One year after the founding of the university, Chicago—which until that time had been known more for its stockyards, its fire in 1871, the great strike of 1877, and the Haymarket bombing of 1886 (see P. Foner, 1977, 139–56; 1969)—hosted the World's Columbian Exposition. Its exhibits, architecture, displays, and shows were designed to proclaim the city's global cultural status. Precisely because the city's commercial and industrial elites lacked social and intellectual sophistication, the University of Chicago could fill the void with its civic-minded professoriat. Its faculty played a civic role similar to that of an eastern city's upper class, staffing or advising its artistic, literary, scientific, and philanthropic institutions, serving on the boards of its museums, helping form its welfare and penal systems, and acting as consultants to urban political and community leaders (see H. Duncan, 1964; May, 1959, 101–06). Professors delivered public speeches, sermons, and homiletics and later, after the advent of radio, broadcast lectures and discussions. Professors in sociology and the other social sciences and the humanities joined with the rising midwestern Realist school of literature, the new urban architects, the

Social Gospel preachers, and the leaders of settlement houses to create an urban center of culture and social reconstruction in Chicago.

By asserting its claim to being a metropolis and the Midwest's cultural center, Chicago challenged the small-town ethos that prevailed in the hinterlands and that energized the state universities. Traditionally suspicious of eastern business, banks, and culture, rural Midwesterners were also apprehensive about a metropolitan business and cultural center in their own midst. Eastern influences were strong in Chicago. Many of its civic and intellectual leaders were born and educated in the East, including all of the first professoriat at the University of Chicago. From the beginning, then, there was in the Midwest a contrast in outlook between urban and country life that found expression not only in the different self-conceptions of the University of Chicago and the state universities but also in the way in which they represented the social gospel in sociology.

Sociology and the Social Gospel made their appearance in the Midwest in 1892 with the appointments of Charles Horton Cooley (1864–1929) to the University of Michigan, Albion W. Small (1854–1926) to the University of Chicago, and Richard Theodore Ely (1854–1943) to the University of Wisconsin. Each was an apostle of the Social Gospel, but in each that movement took its own special form.

For Cooley, the societal covenant was virtually restricted to the family and the "primary group"—a term he coined (see Clow, 1919)—and to the intimate settings in which the individual might hope to acquire a wholesome self and self-image.[1] For Small, the new gospel required nothing less than a Christianization of capital, a moral crusade against Marxism, and the incorporation of all immigrants and racial and religious minorities into a revitalized Protestant America. For Ely, Christianity provided all that was required for the solution of the Social Question: The latter part of the commandment to "Love the Lord thy God with all thy heart and thy neighbor as thyself," he wrote, is "in its elaboration, social science or sociology" (quoted in Everett, 1946, 81). Small's sociology aimed at a new covenant of Christian capitalism; Ely's at a populist version of Christian socialism. Their differences in attitude toward the Social Gospel pointed sociology at the University of Chicago and at the University of Wisconsin in different directions.

RICHARD T. ELY'S CHRISTIAN POLITICAL ECONOMY

Ely had been brought to Wisconsin to build a program in economics, history, and political science that eventually embraced anthropology, sociology, and social work as well (Curti and Carstensen, 1949, 1:502; 2:342–44). "The Christian religion is assigned an important work in this

field," he wrote, "and political economy becomes a Christian science. . . .
Professorial socialism must become Christian socialism" (quoted in Everett, 1946, 92). As John R. Everett has pointed out, "Ely's whole assumption involves the conception of a brotherhood of free men following Christ." Hence, a logical as well as a sociological prerequisite to the new covenant was conversion of those who had not yet accepted Jesus as their saviour. As a professor of political economy, Ely was hardly in a position to conduct a mass evangelization. But he could and did influence the religious character of the professional associations with which he was associated. The American Economic Association, which he founded, was established virtually as a Protestant and ministerial organization: its original membership included twenty-three ministers, and its credo stated, "We hold that the conflict of labor and capital has brought to the front a vast number of social problems whose solution is impossible without the united efforts of church, state and science." Later, Ely, Ulysses G. Weatherly, and John R. Commons formed an American Institute of Christian Sociology (Odum, 1951, 59, 126). Christian social science became the first step toward forging a Christian society. The early economists and sociologists at the University of Wisconsin were committed to a Christianization of the social sciences as part of a larger effort that would make professional social scientists responsible for creating a new social covenant.

The purpose of the new covenant would be to cement Christian brotherhood in the new industrial society. Ely's commitment to a national and ultimately universal Christian brotherhood—representative, he insisted, not only of the highest state of social but also of the appropriate stage of ethical evolution—was sometimes overlooked by those who were outraged by his sympathy for workingmen's associations, his friendly advice to strikers, and his encouragement of state intervention in the economy. Wavering between the social agitation of the domestic and foreign-born radicals and the Christian socialism advocated by the left wing of the Protestant reform movement, Ely's brand of the Social Gospel aroused the suspicion of entrenched business interests and the apprehension of university boards of trustees. However, Ely was a meliorist, not a socialist, in his attitude toward social reform, and a gradualist, not an agitator, in his approach to social action. His approach was less that of a politician with a program than that of a missionary with a message: "I felt I had a mission that I must fulfill," he recalled in his autobiography. "In the words of St. Paul . . . 'Woe is me if I preach not this gospel'" (Everett, 1946). He admonished businessmen to replace the profit motive with altruism and laborers to seek Christ in their hearts before they took clubs in their hands. He prophesied that the Kingdom of God would find expression in a benevolent state society:

Looking forward into the future we may contemplate a society with real, not merely nominal, freedom, to pursue the best, a society in which men shall work together for common purposes, . . . and in which this wholesome cooperation shall take place largely through government, but through a government which has become less repressive and has developed its positive side.

Ely's conception of the state as an instrument for achieving a Christian brotherhood based on altruism and cooperation endowed government itself with a spiritual quality. In so doing it reconceptualized civil authority as "a delegated responsibility from the Almighty" and looked forward to the day "when men come to look upon their duty to the State as something as holy [as] their duty to the church," regarding the State as one of God's chief agencies for good. Then, Ely prophesied, "it will be easy for government to perform all its functions." In his catechism the state was to be granted an element of divinity. Thus, Ely's actual teachings were not to radicalize sociology, as his critics charged (Curti and Carstenson, 1949, 1:508–27; Hofstadter and Metzger, 1955, 426–27)—but to invest it with a self-righteous, populist, and evangelical mission: to fulfill the promise of the Christian Kingdom on earth.

Opposing the First Amendment, Ely modified the Constitution itself: "The state has divine rights conferred upon it just as much as the church." A religiously inspired public policy would ensure the fulfillment of the Gospel promise, because "states do not accomplish all we want, and no scheme of [political] socialism meets our needs. Religion is needed for enlightenment and for strength, and without the aid of religion there is little hope for social progress." As Everett (1946, 97) points out, Ely "never seems to raise questions regarding the validity of the Christian revelation in Christ or the accepted Christian ethical precepts." Nor did he show any regard for the peoples and creeds in America that were outside his version of Social Gospel: "Yes, we are speaking about religious reform, and all reform *must* become religious reform." Thus Ely's Christianization program for America came into conflict with the constitutional requirement for a separation between church and state and with the social fact that many Americans were not willing candidates for conversion—Jews, Catholics, and Asians, for example, who were fast becoming the basic labor force in American factories, mines, and farms. The First Amendment forced some Protestant thinkers to transform the faith into a secular "civil religion." Protestant social science, constitutionally prevented from forging an ecclesiastical state, could only go in the direction of a sublimated secularization with the state as its central focus.

Ely's high-minded conception of a religious state based on an ideology of Christian altruism contained an incipient rejection of those who would not change their religion and could not change their racial background. For Ely the task was to "Protestantize" the state, not to absorb the diverse groups in American society. His sociology reinforced rural midwestern provincialism and xenophobia. This aspect of his work became a central focus of attention for his disciples at the University of Wisconsin, for whom the labor question was indissolubly linked to race and religion.

John R. Commons, Selig Perlman, and Edward Alsworth Ross each addressed the labor problem, and each made judgments about who was to be admitted to the new social covenant, a joint venture of church and state. Commons (1862–1945) insisted that a Nordic Protestant America had a basis in the first formation of the society: "It is the distinctive fact regarding colonial migration that it was Teutonic in blood and Protestant in religion" (1920, 27). Other followers of Ely wished to extend the covenant to embrace Jews. Perlman (1888–1959), who had fled the pogroms of Russia to come to America in 1908, had sympathy for his fellow Jewish immigrants and admired Samuel Gompers, the immigrant Jewish labor leader who had organized the trades where eastern European Jews were employed but who excluded Asiatics and, later, Negroes from the ranks of the American Federation of Labor (see Seligman, 1962, 241–43). For Gompers, membership in organized labor turned on the question of assimilability. The Chinese and Japanese were "unassimilable," hence proscribed; the eastern European Jews were able to be Americanized, and thus were welcomed into the unions (Gompers, 1925, 1:216–17, 278–79; 2:151–73; see also H. Hill, 1967, 265–402; 1973; and Lyman, 1977, 30, 46, 253–54). Perlman extolled organized labor's role in the anti-Chinese movement and Gompers's policies on the Chinese question as central to the substitution of class for race in American labor relations:

> The political issue after 1877 was racial, not financial, and the weapon was not merely the ballot, but also "direct action"—violence. The anti-Chinese agitation in California, culminating as it did in the Exclusion Law passed by Congress in 1882, was doubtless the most important single factor in the history of American labor, for without it the entire country might have been overrun by Mongolian labor and the labor movement might have become a conflict of races instead of one of classes. [Perlman, 1922, 62]

Ross, himself a product of the Midwest, became sociology's most demagogic champion of a Teutonic America, vigorously opposing Chinese and Japanese immigration (Ross, 1911, 47–48; 1927, 285–355) and derogating eastern European Jews[2] and Latin and Catholic immigrants from southern Europe (Ross, 1914, 95–194). His new Protestant covenant would admit to membership only Nordics and native-born Americans (Ross, 1901, 438–42), who alone possessed the right physical appearances, adhered to the right kind of religion, and would be hardworking and public-spirited. Ross's idea of the covenant was Calvinist in its orientation. For the Calvinists, grace—and therefore admission to the covenant—was the gift of an inscrutable God who had predestined the fate of all souls. Race and ethnicity for Ross were a social marker of predestination, the unchanging sign of one's state of social grace. The old Calvinist virtues, especially that of hard work, remained as proof of acceptability, but only if they were linked to an acceptable ancestry.

E. A. ROSS'S POPULISM AND NATIVISM

Sociology proper began at the University of Wisconsin in 1906 with the appointment of Edward Alsworth Ross (1866–1951), an ardent champion of midwestern Progressivism, populism, and nativism (see Weinberg, 1972). Born in Illinois and reared in Kansas and Iowa, Ross grew up in a strict Presbyterian atmosphere, against which he revolted when he came across Darwinism and other rationalistic perspectives in Berlin in 1888–89 (Ross, 1936, 1–10, 115–19). But unlike Lester F. Ward, his uncle by marriage, Ross did not make atheism a cornerstone of his sociology. Instead, he hoped to build a Christian society, using sociology as a major resource. Ross's conceptions of Protestantism and its missionary endeavor[3] were a corollary of his understanding of Social Darwinism:

> Will the *social idea* ever again be so beautifully set forth as it is in the Gospels? . . . A people may be rescued from a low or debased religion by teaching them a higher religion. A Chinese Taoist who turns Christian is at once released from a host of needless fears, his eyes become brighter and a new light shines in his face. Observe that what is nowadays sent out is *the highest form Christianity has ever assumed.* Even the Apostles were puzzled over what position to take concerning weather, crops, blights, sickness, witchcraft, demon possession and the like—matters which the contemporary missionary leaves to science. *Now for the first time the Christianity carried to the "heathen" may be as spiritual as is the Sermon on the Mount.* [1936, 117–18]

In Ross's evolutionary scheme of things, Christianity was the highest stage of religion in a civilization that had reached the highest stage of development. Science working together with religion fostered a new division of salvational labor. Religion was relieved of its worldly burdens while science assumed the responsibility for material uplift. Ross defined the role of a scientist as one in service to the *social idea* found in the Gospels. When he applied this conception of the Gospel to the moral improvement of midwestern society, he declared his mission to be nothing less than a new secular salvation.

A leader of the movement to eliminate what he regarded as the modern version of "sin in society" by breaking up trusts and introducing state regulation in business (Ross, 1907), Ross also gave sociological legitimacy to the populist Progressive ideology of the Midwest: opposition to eastern plutocracy and the big city; support for the local church, the family farm, and the small town; prohibition of the manufacture and sale of alcoholic beverages; restriction or exclusion of "unassimilable" peoples—Asiatics,[4] eastern European Jews, Slavs, Italians, Greeks, and others. Ross's anti-Semitism is evident in virtually all of his writings, including his general text on the *Principles of Sociology* (1920).[5] His attitudes toward foreigners, business, cities, and cosmopolitanism echoed a ubiquitous theme of mid-western populism—what Arnold Rose (1948) would later characterize as a form of city hatred. Sociology at Wisconsin became a discipline in service to Ross's vision of an America remade and covenanted in the image of rural and small-town Wisconsin celebrating the ethos of farm and village Protestantism that R. Richard Wohl has called the "country boy" myth (1969, 77–158). Associated with this covenant would be a new and more democratic religion, "obliged to become simple and graspable." The cler-gyman, "expected to give his people solace, counsel, and instruction," became in effect priest, public teacher, personal counselor, and social worker (Ross, 1940, 181).

The public university was to play a central role in upholding and ex-tending the virtues of this scientifically perfected society. It would not undermine religion; democratic Christianity thrived in universities like Wisconsin: "Student and faculty denominations build their hostels and maintain their student pastors, religious leaders with a message are brought in, and no one fears lest . . . the things of the spirit are falling into neglect and decay" (Ross, 1912, 198). Thus the secular gospel could up-hold the virtues of rural life, support the use of science to enhance the lives of rural folk, and promote democratic values—but only for those admitted to the covenant. Americans of Anglo-Saxon descent, making common cause with immigrant German and Scandinavian farmers, would exclude Orientals, Jews, and Catholics but support popular de-mocracy, equality, social justice, prohibition,[6] and scientific progress.

Ross regarded his Christianized populism as a replacement for New England's Puritan democracy and an exemplar for the whole nation. While the once-proud bastion of Puritanism was deteriorating in culture, social organization, and vitality, the Midwest was not merely growing but becoming superior to the old America. The progress and democracy of the Middle West, as he saw it, were attributable to recent Nordic immigra-tion, which provided the region with an ablebodied yeomanry and a powerful tradition of self-assertion. He contrasted these "Germans, Scan-dinavians, Mennonites, Poles, Bohemians, and even Icelanders, [who] landing at Castle Garden, journeyed straight through . . . and . . . settled on government land" with the Jews, Italians, Hungarians, and Armenians who were "marshaled in gangs of miners, shovelers, or concrete-mixers, or lodged in certain pockets—a Ghetto, a Little Italy, or Little Hungary or

Little Armenia—the later aliens form[ing] as it were, insoluble clots."[7] These "clots" menaced the progressive democratic society emerging in Wisconsin, Ohio, Iowa, and the Dakotas.

Ross's exclusion of certain minorities from the populist covenant carried over to his sociology of women and the family. He encouraged the practice of birth control among the unregenerate lower classes and the unworthy foreigners; he favored "more progeny left by the gifted, and fewer by the dull; less prudence in the good homes, and less recklessness in the hovels and tenements" (1922, 33). Ross's interest in birth control was related to his concern for the emancipation of women:

> Cave, hut, hovel, and shack do not fit into the modern scene; nor do their large broods of neglected, infected, ill-nourished, half-clad, unschooled children fit into the modern democratic community; no more do illiterate, ignorant, overburdened wives, without a gala dress, who never go anywhere or hear anything, whose only recreation is gossip with other women at the village well or while driving up the goats! [1927, 252]

The right kind of propagators were to be found in only two collectivities: native-born white Americans and Nordic immigrants. Jews, Italians, southeastern Europeans, and Asiatics would have to be disregarded as marriage partners by the favored Anglo-Saxons (see Ross, 1914; 1927), and their fecundity reduced substantially. Contrasting their large families with the smaller ones of American Midwesterners, Ross observed that "among the native-born the worn-out mother of a dozen children is almost unknown." He assured Americans that "with parents of the right kind and with enough children of the right age accessible in the neighborhood nursery, kindergarten, or playgarden, the three-child family may socialize its members quite as thoroughly as the family with a dozen." The reconstituted democratic family of the Americanized Nordic Midwest would lend support to the developing democracy: "Provided it pulsates to humanitarian ideas, it ought to prove a school of social service" (1920, 587, 588–89). Democratic values were to be propagated within the family, with the midwestern family set out as a model for the nation.

The superiority of the midwestern family was also demonstrated in Ross's discussion of divorce. Equality for women, for Ross, was a necessary condition of populist democracy. This position required him to defend divorce and uphold a new form of democratic morality. His argument supporting the legitimacy of divorce rested on the expectation that a stronger family would emerge if equality between the marriage partners prevailed. Ross thought of the family as a working unit, in the image of the yeoman farm family, upholding the hallowed values of rural democratic America. The pair should merge their individuality into the family unit, forming a covenant between husband and wife the strength of which would reside in the exclusion of all others from their world. Imbalance in the sex ratio had beneficial consequences: "Any shortage of women that makes the men eager suitors alters the terms of the marriage partnership to the advantage of the wife and betters the lot of the married man. Accordingly, the codes of the Western States treat the wife with more liberality than did the codes of the older States, the fairness to women seems to be a Western practice that spreads East" (1912, 161).

Ross's views were not shared by other sociologists in the East or the Midwest.[8] The single most important figure propounding the idea of the family as a "sacred" unit of secular society was Charles F. Thwing, a Harvard graduate, Congregational minister, and ultimately president of Western Reserve University. Thwing provided as thoroughgoing an argument against divorce as might ever be produced; with the publication of Charles and Carrie Thwing's *The Family* in 1886, "Never again would it be necessary to explore at such tiresome length why orthodox Christianity was fully justified in condemning divorce." (O'Neill, 1966) Ross's argument ran counter to the Thwings' influential study. He followed the line developed by James P. Lichtenberger, who in 1909 had argued that high divorce rates were but one temporary index of the twin forces of rapid industrialization and female emancipation. Once the transition to a fully developed industrial democracy had been completed, the family would become stable again, based on a far greater degree of freedom and equality.

Ross saw divorce as necessary at this stage of development of the American moral community, but did not argue with the Thwings' belief that divorce threatened civilization with a dangerous amount of individualism and selfishness, the two fundamental evils in the eyes of orthodox believers. He assumed that declines in divorce would occur if only the *right kind* of people were entering the country and marrying one another. In line with his activist and interventionist attitudes toward social reform, he further believed that the high divorce rates would diminish as institutional reforms—especially the suppression of plutocracy, immigration restrictions, temperance laws, the establishment of domestic-arts instruction and marriage-ethics courses in public schools, and enforcement of a waiting period between the declaration of intent to marry and the granting of a marriage license—reduced excessive egoism and avarice.[9]

The issue of divorce and the family was only a small part of Ross's larger theme of the social idea as set forth in the Gospels. For him higher education and the university as a whole were to be committed to social service. As the family was an institution in the service of raising children, the university was an institution in the service of all spheres of life. Its function was to promote the this-worldly, scientific gospel and to work hand in hand with the clergymen, whose function was spiritual guidance. This division of labor between university and ministry aided the state government in achieving a coordinated approach to the problems of the state. Ross envisioned a democratic, consensual society that would be total in its approach to those economic and populist reforms that were consistent with the ideals contained in the Protestant social idea. The university could appropriate to itself the responsibility for bringing the good life to the inhabitants of the state; that was its mission, and the professors were to be its missionaries.

THE PROTESTANT ETHIC IN THE TOTAL STATE

In 1913, the *World's Work* wrote admiringly of "A University That Runs a State." Professors at Wisconsin had served on a variety of commissions, prepared regulatory legislation, enhanced the efforts of the Legislative Reference Service (May, 1959, 100), and, with the expansion of its extension service, the university announced its willingness to teach virtually anything to anyone in the state.[10] Especially significant was its mission to rescue the farm family from the physical and cultural hardships of rural life. John Commons defended the university against charges that its emphasis on agricultural education and practical idealism had abrogated the age-old obligation of higher education to teach the classics and educate the elite: "Of course a cow is just a cow, and can never become a Winged Victory, but within her limits she is capable of approaching an ideal. And, more than that, she is an ideal that every farmer and farmer's boy—the [modern equivalents of the] despised slaves and helots of Greece—can aspire to" (quoted in May, 1959, 101).

While Social Gospel movements in the eastern schools sought to uplift the new urban immigrants, Christian-inspired reform in the Midwest sought to ameliorate conditions in the Protestant community as a whole. The scope of this program, to attempt to transform the Social Gospel into a statewide system for the rational ministrations of ethics, culture, socialization, life-styles, technology, and labor, vastly expanded the role of the university in the state. Family, school, farm, factory, judicial system, economy, all were seen as areas that could be brought into the orbit of university-proposed social policy and public administration. The university's task was that of research and development and the training of future experts in politics, administration, the professions, the arts, and culture. This represented the organizational rationalization of the Social Gospel in a bureaucratic state administration. At bottom, the *social idea* contained the germ of a totally rationalized social order that the Progressive sociologists thought might first be achieved in Wisconsin.

While Ross's sociology and the Wisconsin idea were both rooted in midwestern populism, progressivism, and Protestantism, the Wisconsin covenant was open to a wider membership than Ross would have liked. Its secularized this-worldly Protestantism contained a strong sense of missionary endeavor that allowed for the possibility that anyone might enter the Kingdom of God on earth and might ultimately be admitted into the new statewide covenant. The price of admission was simple: a willingness to work, a positive attitude toward social betterment, and pride in the accomplishments of the state. Excluded or subjugated were those who flouted the dominant ideology by being lazy, unclean, impractical, critically opposed to the ordered rational life of decent people—or, as in the stereotype of Asians and Jews, too interested in hard work and their own group and family life to be worthy and selfless contributors to the covenant.

The state's objective, utilizing the university as its brain center, was a benevolently administered society in which everyone shared the fruits of the collective effort. Only differences in education justified social differentiation, legitimating the professoriat as an appropriate managerial elite. The university, and ultimately the state, repositories of the social wisdom, were to use this wisdom solely for social betterment and the enhancement of society and its institutions. Society was to be a kind of brotherly bureaucracy of the like-minded.

As Wisconsin became more urban and industrial, such social problems as crime, delinquency, prostitution, truancy, illiteracy, strikes, racial upheaval, corruption, and political alienation became major concerns for the state university's sociologists. The xenophobic and pastoral themes in the older populism became less salient, even if they did not entirely fade away. Technical specialists began to replace social philosophers.

The new concerns of Wisconsin's sociology brought it closer to the statistical emphasis and social outlook that had developed at Columbia under Giddings, even though Ross, like Ward and Small, had considerable misgivings about Giddings's sociology (Stern, 1932, 1933, 1935b, 1936, 1937, 1938, 1946, 1947, 1948, 1949). In 1912 Ross invited a former high school pupil, ex-Congregational minister and Columbia Ph.D. (1906) John Lewis Gillin (1871–1958), to join him in the sociology program. Gillin took over the chairmanship of sociology after Ross retired and remained active at Wisconsin as an emeritus professor even after his own retirement in 1943 (see Odum, 1951, 135–41). He carried Giddings's message that sociology had begun as social philosophy but matured into a statistical science (Gillin, 1931). However, for Gillin, who had been trained in statistics and surveys when they were being introduced, even Giddings had been too influenced by philosophy and logic. He denied a role for social philosophy, maintaining that methods alone were all that were necessary to guide sociology in the task of social reform. Statistics, he felt, was the basic scientific tool uniting the social sciences. "Modern sociology gives meaning to the raw material provided by the statistical treatment of data in the field of social pathology," Gillin wrote in 1931. These words, totally lacking the passion and prejudice that characterized the work of Ross and Giddings, reflect the emotionally flat rationality of the technician for whom there was no longer an issue about the goals of society but only a question of the means. As the Great Depression set in and problems of race, class, and political conflict loomed large in the United States, Gillin urged sociology's "recognition as a science which has a contribution to make to the understanding and solution of present-day problems." The separation of sociology from social work and social reform was coming to an end, he asserted. When he stated that "the world certainly needs what sociology can give," he spoke in behalf of a secular technoscientific salvation that was far removed from the original spirit of the Social Gospel.[11] Ross also was influenced by the new direction sociology took during the years of the Depression. He abandoned his strident populism and made a leap into scientism and expertism. Henceforth sociology at the University of Wisconsin would focus on applied practical research.

When the Social Gospel, which had already been rationalized into a comprehensive state administration full of benevolence and good intentions, was transformed into positivist science, social theory lost its connections to theology and philosophy and attached itself to a statistical technoscience. The next step was to rationalize methods for identifying social needs and for distributing social benefits. The Wisconsin idea found a national formulation in the aims of the New Deal and post–World War II Keynesianism.[12] The latter aimed to secure the secular salvation of the United States and the non-Communist world. The University of Wisconsin had become a national resource in a project to reconstitute a much larger covenant than one confined to a single state.

Wisconsin and other universities placed themselves in service to the national and international crusade to defeat fascism, contain communism,[13] and develop the Third World. State universities enlarged their range of services, extended them throughout the world, and committed themselves to an ideology of international societal management and world policy formulation. In so doing, they extended intellectual resources to their outer limits, but failed to replenish their intellectual capital.

The Wisconsin experiment, applying the new scientific gospel in behalf of the extended social idea, had given sociology an opportunity to be used. Only later did it become apparent that while being used, positivist sociology had used itself up, lost understanding of its intellectual roots, and surrendered its independence to the makers of public policy.

NOTES

1. Cooley was always painfully shy, contemplative, and withdrawn. He made use of these apparent drawbacks in his sociology, choosing to study his own children in order to work out the theory of socialization within the primary group. He refused Giddings's offer of a professorship at Columbia and remained in Ann Arbor, his birthplace, for virtually all of his professional life. In one sense his Social Gospel was more Catholic than Protestant: he favored an ascetic life, admired Thomas á Kempis (about whom he wrote an early essay), and eschewed city life in favor of the small university town. His social psychology in effect compressed the covenant into a cloister and found its secular expression inside the individual mind, within the confines of the family, or in the intimacy of a small group. (See, in this regard, Jandy, 1942, esp. 9–80). Cooley's nephew, Robert Cooley Angell, continued his search for a moral community in a self-enclosed local institution, the University of Michigan. Cooley supervised Angell's dissertation, on *The Campus: A Study of Contemporary Undergraduate Life in the American University* (1928).

The major works by Cooley are *Social Organization and Human Nature and the Social Order* (1956); *Social Process* (1918), and *Sociological Theory and Social Research: Selected Papers*, ed. by Robert Cooley Angell (1930). See also Reiss (1968).

Cooley's sociology would have little effect until it branched out in the direction of Meadian social psychology (Mead, 1930) or was incorporated into F. Stuart Chapin's graphic and statistical measurements of the social psychology of social institutions (see Chapin, 1928; 1935; 1935a; 1950, 263–67). It is doubtful that Cooley would have approved of Chapin's usage of his concepts and theories. Cooley was suspicious of the false scientism contained in the statistical fetish. He once wrote: "Use diagrams, by all means, use classifications, use maps, curves, statistics—and forget them! . . . Nothing is more illuminating or more fallacious than statistics. If the underlying material is trustworthy they may reveal its meaning; but numerical exactitude is often the only thing scientific about them" (1927, 156).

2. A typical example: "Confined behind the walls of Jewry, forbidden to own an estate or practice a profession or intermarry with Christians, they [Jews] kept alive a jealous, exclusive, tribal spirit, foreign altogether to the demotic character of modern society. As if Canon Law and Civil Law had not done enough, the Jews maintained between themselves and the Christians a hedge of their own, viz., their religious and ceremonial observances. The practice of their rites obliged them to live in closest contact with one another and to shun the uncircumcised. They might not eat the same food as the Christians, or food prepared in the same way. Regulated in the minutest details of life by the six hundred and thirteen commandments binding on an orthodox Jew, they were obliged to keep aloof from the Gentiles, with the result that they became in the last degree clannish and conservative" (Ross, 1912, 228).

3. Ross wrote to Ward on July 20, 1912, that while the Catholic missionaries in China "craved power," the Protestant missionaries "were trying to build up the Chinese converts to the point of running their own affairs as a separate congregation. There would be no exploitation, financial or political. Their work therefore amounted to a man with a high and broad *Weltanschauung* trying to bring to his view people with a low, narrow and dismal *Weltanschauung*. In such cases, where there is no question of self interest, I am for the bigger *Weltanschauung* every time—although neither may be scientific and true to reality" (Stern, 1938–49, 14:117).

4. Ross's exhortations against Asiatics threatened international relations. On May 7, 1900, at a mass meeting in San Francisco sponsored by the American Federation of Labor, he was reported by a local newspaper to have said that "should the worst come to the worst, it would be better for us if we were to turn our guns upon every vessel bringing Japanese to our shore rather than permit them to land" (quoted in ten Broek, Barnhart, Matson, 1954, 35).

Ross later recanted his belief in the inherent inferiority of Asiatics. *"Difference of race* means far less to me now than once it did," he confessed in 1936 (1936, 276). This shift had been brought about by a religious experience: "One Sunday in a tiny mission chapel on the Coast of Fokien I noticed a young Chinese with the face of St. John. Our eyes never met, but I felt he and I might be comrades for life" (276). The covenant could now be extended across racial lines because Ross had always "seen blue eyes that glowed with a Divine Light" but now, at last, he could "say the same for brown eyes and black eyes" (276–77). However, even this new covenant had its limits for Ross: "So far I have met with no such mute appeal in the eyes of a red man or a black man," but here Ross attributed his failure to have yet discovered Negro or Indian comrades to the fact that "their faces are a script I have not yet learned to read" (276).

5. Ross's hostility toward Jews was part of his larger rural midwestern thesis, emphasizing that the Jews were a subject people, incapable of agriculture, immoral, clannish, plutocratic, cosmopolitan but not public-spirited, capable of Orientalization but not Americanization: "The Jew's distaste for farming is seen to be a traditional attitude caused by confinement in the Ghetto for several centuries and debarment from owning farm land. . . . The East-European Hebrews also show much moral deformity from subjection to the will of aliens. . . . It is noteworthy that through the Middle Ages the rich Jews, being obliged to keep their wealth in *unseen* mobile form—money, jewels, etc.—never got from it the considerations which land ownership conferred. . . . Among the Jews the publicans [i.e., tax collectors] could not enter a court of law to give testimony, nor fill offices of judicature, nor engage in public prayers. No money was to be changed at their treasury, their contributions to charity were not accepted, and they were ranked with thieves and murderers. . . . The Jews of Kaifeng-fu lost their language and their religion and became Chinese in all but physiognomy" (Ross, 1920, 59, 113, 349, 469, 558).

6. A lifelong temperance advocate, Ross was outraged by the repeal of the Eighteenth Amendment: "The current outcry against what is stigmatized as 'sumptuary legislation' is out-and-out dishonest. The pretense that the endeavor to curb the liquor trade by law has anything in common with the seventeenth-century attempt of the nobility to dictate what the lower social grades might indulge in is a hollow fraud. Not class jealousy is behind the anti-alcohol drive but the realization of the harm intoxicating, habit-forming beverages do to the higher life of man. The failure of the Eighteenth Amendment in the United States was the triumph of 'moderate' drinkers, plus the organized liquor interests, over a social idea" (Ross, 1937, 461–62).

7. The contrast between sociology at the University of Wisconsin and at the University of Chicago is no better illustrated than in Ross's designation of non-Nordic immigrants as "insoluble clots." For Robert E. Park these "insoluble clots" were the raw human materials for his race-relations cycle, which promised their ultimate absorption within urban civilization.

8. One generation earlier, Stephen Pearl Andrews, who together with Henry Hughes and George Fitzhugh had been one of the major antebellum sociologists, became a champion of abolitionism, anarchism, universalism, international language, and, most notoriously, free love (Andrews, 1975, 1–55). With Victoria Woodhull—whom he supported for president of the United States in 1872—he organized a free-love, feminist, and spiritualist chapter of the International Workingmen's Association that was expelled from the International by order of Karl Marx. Marx railed against the fact that "the social conditions of the United States, though in many other respects most favorable to the success of the working-class movement, peculiarly facilitate the intrusion into the International of bogus reformers, middle class quacks, and trading politicians" (Padover, 1973, 225). In notes he made on the matter, Marx referred to Andrews, Woodhull, and their supporters as "middle-class humbugs and worn out Yankee swindlers in the reform business" (231). In fact, the "woman

question" had reopened the debate over priorities within the socialist movement in America, pitting the German and Irish followers of Friedrich Adolph Sorge, who advocated a strict working-class alliance, against the American- and English-born followers of Andrews and Woodhull, who favored a covenant uniting workers with Negroes, spiritualists, feminists, and free-love "pantarchists." Marx favored the German faction and led the fight in the International against those who gave "precedence to the women's question over the question of labor" and advocated "the women's franchise, and . . . all sorts of nonsense" (Gerth, 1958, 177–78, 194–95, 248, 264–67). The Andrews faction was expelled by a vote of 49–0–9, despite the fact that it had published the first English translation of the *Communist Manifesto* to appear in America (1871) and that Andrews's and Woodhull's campaign for the American presidency in 1872 had sought to reconstitute the Negro-abolitionist-suffragette alliance behind the Equal Rights Party ticket of Woodhull and Frederick Douglass. Douglass, however, supported Grant in the campaign (see P. Foner, 1955, 79–86).

The incident is significant for the development of sociology in the United States, for it provides one more illustration of how, in their advocacy of either sacred or secular covenants, American sociologists have ever been divided over the priorities and place of women, racial and ethnic minorities, and socioeconomic classes. For a view sympathetic to the class priority see Herreshoff, 1967, 79–105; for one sympathetic to women, see Shively, 1975, 1–13. For documentation on how the Woodhull faction affected the attitudes of other feminist leaders, see E. Du Bois, 1981, 101–09, 152–65. For a sociological analysis of this incident emphasizing the differences in outlooks that separated the European generations that had grown up in the 1840s from the American generation that had matured just prior to or during the Civil War, see Gerth, 1962.

9. This idea was to find its way into state university departments of rural sociology, home economics, and child development and family relationships. It ultimately was enshrined in textbooks on marriage and the family. Extension and home-demonstration agents carried this image to small towns and rural areas, where it reinforced the already existent belief in the superiority of the rural farm family to that of the urban, ethnic, and foreign way of life. The marriage and family curriculum in state universities and sectarian colleges became the official bearer of this image of the family and transmitted it to generation after generation of pink-cheeked youth attending the nation's institutions of higher learning.

10. The University of Wisconsin's focus on social service and its interest in populist, democratic, economic reforms were consistent with the Progressive politics of Robert La Follette during the early part of the century. When La Follette was governor (1902–08) there was a particularly close relationship between the university and the Progressive's state political machine.

11. In the post–World War II period this technoscience was sustained by the appointment of William Sewell to the chairmanship of the department. Sewell had been a student of Giddings's student F. Stuart Chapin at the University of Minnesota and later, with Paul Lazarsfeld and Harold Wilensky, edited *The Uses of Sociology* (1967).

12. The economists of Wisconsin had developed a program for the state that anticipated both the theory and the policies of the New Deal. Its Keynes-like economic thought was utilized in the formulation of Wisconsin's policies on unemployment insurance, industrial safety, workingmen's compensation, taxation, transportation, rural welfare, and much of the program that would later be regarded as basic to the welfare state.

13. Communists were excluded from membership in the covenant. When the social idea was extended from the state to the nation and finally to the world at large, they were to play the role of the unregenerate, which had previously been assigned to Jews, Asians, foreigners, and Catholics, groups that by this time had been made part of the larger crusade. It was not an accident that the attack on American communists at the beginning of the Cold War was carried out by Wisconsin's Senator Joseph McCarthy. As a Catholic, he himself had

only recently been admitted to the status of regenerate and was eager to display his credentials to his new reference group. However, as a latter-day midwestern populist in the tradition of E. A. Ross, McCarthy had also adopted the antieastern, antiplutocracy elements of Wisconsin's progressive populism and therefore included in his attacks not only un-American communists but also such eastern institutions as Harvard University and such havens for the sons of the plutocracy as the State Department. These attacks could still find a positive resonance among his constituents.

CHAPTER 11

Lutheranism as Positivist Evangelism: Luther Lee Bernard and George A. Lundberg

The positivism at Wisconsin, linked first to the reform of the state and then to the New Deal, stands in sharp contrast to the strict evangelical brand of Comteanism developed by Luther Lee Bernard (1881–1951) and strongly identified with George A. Lundberg (1895–1966). The central feature of Bernard's and Lundberg's positivism is its projection out from its regional sources in rural Lutheranism onto a national and international stage. Such elements of rural populism as opposition to eastern monopolies, centralized government, and global interventionism became the leitmotiv of their sociology. Their orientation stressed democracy, strict codes of public morality, and an obligation to be ethical in scientific endeavor. Never detached from its religious or regional foundations, their positivism foundered upon the uncompromising quality of its ethical standards. Its moral spirit was lost to sociology even as the substance of its techniques became the new sociological faith.

Luther Lee Bernard's work was based on his postulation of a distinction between the theological and the religious. In 1922 he announced:

> It is asserted both by friends and opponents ... that the Christian Church of today is moving in the direction of becoming a great social service and instructional agency, abandoning for the most part its theological and metaphysical predilections, or at least relegating them to the category of the aesthetic and ritualistic. Certainly, through its embodiment of the principles of the social and other sciences, the church is coming under the domination of the scientific method and content. ... The principles of sociology, psychology, economics and political science come to be embodied in the fabric of Christianity as it changes its character. [Bernard, 1922, 86]

Bernard believed that modern Christianity had become an important force for social progress because it had rejected superstition and dogma and replaced them with science. He proposed that sociology reject not religion, but magic, metaphysics, theology, and utopian idealism. He clarified his position while discussing what he regarded as an opposed sociological perspective, that of the Scottish Moralists, which he claimed had been integrated "into Christian ethics, Christian sociology, social ethics, social work, and journalistic reform." However, this rival perspective did not ignore social facts. "It simply did not develop its technique of discovering and generalizing data *pari passu* with its interest in the content and technique of reform." The Scottish moral philosophy would have to give way in the face of the "methodology the schools of Le Play and Quetelet accomplished, the one by the use of a survey technique and the other by means of statistical generalization" (1931, 204). In Bernard's positivism there was less a worldly rejection of religion than a scientific sublimation of Christian ethics.

Bernard's statistical positivism was quite similar to that of Giddings and Ogburn. However a midwestern stamp differentiated it from its eastern counterpart, most notably in Bernard's attitudes toward the role of the church in rural society, the functions and responsibilities of national leadership, and the attainment of world peace. Whereas the eastern positivists considered their orientation compatible with worldly urban secularism, Bernard's reflected the rural and regional mentality of midwestern Lutheranism. The problems of the rural sector of American society, he noted, differed from those of the city. For him, the rural ministry had a special role to play in social reconstruction. In 1917 he observed that the Protestant adoption of the scientific outlook had not yet penetrated rural areas of the United States, where what he called rural attitudes still prevailed. Bernard concluded that the rural ministry required further education so that it could maintain itself as part of the leadership stratum in agricultural communities.

If rural society was to be redeemed, the minister would have to be the agent of redemption. However, before he could take up this calling he would have to be educated in science as well as religion.

Because the social and economic problems of the country are different from those of the city . . . the rural minister must be trained in the college of agriculture. . . . He must have his background of rural science . . . but to this he must add a superstructure which will fit him for the special work he is to do. . . . For him the courses on the rural church, the rural school, farm accounting, marketing and cooperation, community organization, rural health and sanitation, and the like will be of the greatest interest. Without these he will not be adequately equipped for rural leadership. . . . The spiritual leader should also be the community leader. [1920, 72–73]

Bernard's attitudes toward rural society and its moral and social uplift were closer to those of Ross than to the eastern version of the Gospel as it had been transmitted to the Midwest by his own mentor at the University of Chicago, Albion W. Small. However, Bernard accepted Small's vision of a national and international social order, superimposing his own populist orientation on it. He championed the interests of "the little man" throughout the world, and he opposed those leaders who did not respect the wisdom of the common people.

Bernard linked his faith in the common man to grass-roots democracy and to his distrust of militarists, big business, and centralized government. He rejected Spencer's evolutionary thesis that as society changed from a military to an industrial form, it became more peace loving (Bernard, 1916). Contrary to Spencer's line of reasoning, Bernard doubted whether modern industrial states that claimed to be democratic actually were so. One year before Woodrow Wilson led America into the war raging in Europe, Bernard observed that "if the United States were a truly democratic state it is scarcely conceivable that it would be involved in war or would need to make very active preparations for war. . . . We may therefore safely conclude that if the United States engages in a foreign war it is not likely to be in one democratically initiated." Bernard's commitment to democracy led him to adopt an isolationist attitude toward America's involvement in the international struggle for world markets, imperialist forays into Latin America, and involvement in global conflicts. He attributed war making to the competition among the economic elites of industrial states to control world markets. In 1928 Bernard, who included Latin America in his area of expertise (see Bernard, 1927a; Bernard and Bernard, 1928), severely criticized U.S. military and economic imperialism in Latin America and complained about America's tactless, unsympathetic, and heavy-handed diplomacy in that region (Bernard, 1928a).[1] In 1933, he and his wife, Jessie Bernard, suggested that "perhaps a growing number of sociologists are becoming convinced that war is an inherent element in our highly competitive capitalistic system, and that the only way to abolish war is to abolish or transform the system (Bernard and Bernard, 1933, 33). A careful reader of Marx, Bernard expressed doubt as to whether capitalism, with its inherent tendency to imperialism, was compatible with democracy and peace.[2]

Nowhere was Bernard's political philosophy better illustrated than in his sociology of war. Opposing the government's co-optation of sociology in World War II, his own international conception favored a sociology that would be used to achieve world peace. As war clouds darkened the

sky in Europe and Asia, Bernard spoke out against American involvement. The failure to abolish war, he wrote in 1936, was clearly attributable
to the fact "that we have not been able sufficiently to socialize and to
control the formation of the attitudes and ideals in the larger industrial,
cultural, and political groups that now dominate modern society." Social-
control devices had not been sufficiently advanced to redirect either bell-
icose attitudes or belligerent conduct. As early as 1931 Bernard had asserted that "in the United States at the present time there is more opportunity for free thinking religiously than politically. . . . This condition . . .
result[s] from . . . the fact that the avenues of political propaganda or
conditioning are relatively much more controlled through economic
means than is the case with religion." Political and economic elites, he
noted in his comprehensive critical analysis of the justifications for war,
now possessed the means to gain popular support for any war.

"The *salvaging of democracy,* to which is closely allied the purported
desire to protect the fighting peoples against slavery and in the enjoyment
of liberty," provided a convenient and effective rationale to mobilize
public opinion in support of America's entrance into the Second World
War, Bernard pointed out. America's proclaimed war aims were as suspect as those of the Axis powers: "No one has asserted more unctuously
and persistently than President F. D. Roosevelt that the United States
participated in the Second World War in defense of democracy and freedom." Moreover, "Vice-President Wallace declared in an address in Chicago, September, 1943, that 'we must fight not merely to make the world
safe for democracy but to give democracy first place in the world' "—yet,
as an editorial in the *Nation* had commented: "We see no sign as yet that
the President and his advisers on foreign policy are determined to give
democracy 'first place' in the world, much less attack the basic economic
evils which Wallace boldly enumerated as the enemies of democracy"
(Bernard, 1944, 254–55). In Bernard's view, Wallace, himself a midwestern populist, had forsaken his legacy by making the goals of democracy secondary to war and domination. The government's policy of linking democracy to war violated the spirit of populist democracy and
vitiated the Christian dictum of peace on earth, good will toward men.

Bernard explored various proposals put forward to insure world peace
after the war had ended. He was not optimistic about the efficacy of any of
them except for a United States of Europe that would include Russia,
Scandinavia, England, Greece, France, Germany, Italy, and Spain, and
the establishment of a truly international mechanism to spread Roosevelt's "Four Freedoms" throughout the world. Convinced that science
could be an instrument for achieving peace, Bernard asked whether
"human intelligence, aided by the social and political sciences and the
social technologies, has . . . reached such a degree of development that

we can consciously replace the method of force—i.e., consolidation by conquest—with peaceful social planning." He believed it could. But he conceded that it was not likely that benign social engineering would take over where coercive aggression had proved so effective. In fact, he foresaw that the United States would "take over the responsibility for world peace and enforce it." To carry out such a program, Bernard warned, "would mean transforming ourselves into a world empire and the policing of this world empire, not for several years, but until we fell crushed by its weight as did the Romans by their empire." And "our task would be never-ending, for in the very nature of the thing we could not turn loose our responsibility once we have taken it on."

Bernard went on to rehearse a parade of horribles that would occur if the United States assumed the role of world policeman:

> Not only would it transform us into a world imperialistic power, but it would make us imperial-minded and destroy our democratic institutions, social as well as political. It would make of us just such a people as those we have set out to eliminate. . . . Our liberties would disappear. Militarism would replace democracy. We should have to load ourselves with unbearable taxes or take them out of our conquered wards, thus goading them anew to rebellion. We should acquire a superior feeling about ourselves which would render us as intolerable to the rest of the world as the German "Aryans" now are to us. We should quickly consume our vast natural resources, upon which our great prosperity has been based. . . . We should be compelled to subordinate our higher cultural interests . . . to the mere material requirements of existence. [1944, 153–54]

Bernard believed that an internationally oriented positivist science could save the world. The positivism he advanced differed in one major respect from that advanced by the Columbia school and the members of the Social Science Research Council. The SSRC believed in harnessing sociological science to the national state in order to achieve rational controls over amelioration, reform, and progress, and had delegated to political leaders the responsibility and the right to define the state's role in international relations. Bernard, however, sought a role for sociology in international affairs as a science that could provide techniques for global social control and the prevention of wars; he did not join in active support of the subordination of sociology to the interests of American foreign policy in the 1930s and 1940s. In 1939, Bernard quoted approvingly from the Belgian sociologist Paul Otlet's proposal for an international sociology—"a general science of international relations, which ascertains, plans, and synthesizes from the special social sciences, social hygiene, economics, law, history, those universal conditions essential to the development of civilization and culture." This international sociology would in turn administer a "universal plan capable of coordinating the . . . objectives of survival, peace, and progress" in accordance with a "world constitution so constructed and proclaimed as to give to the international community such juridical norms as are provided constitutionally for every rational community" (Otlet, 1932). Bernard placed his proposed new science above governments; in effect he borrowed from Comte a secular means for social reconstruction and global order.

As a scientist, Bernard felt it would be possible to organize and manage the world to achieve the goals he considered desirable. But he regarded politicians as not yet sufficiently socialized to recognize the necessity for the reorganization "of society and the manipulation of the formative institutions in such a way as to habituate people to the performance of the functions which will make for social progress" (Bernard, 1922a). To assure progress politicians were to share the labor of societal management with scientists. He believed that the "twentieth century is developing the technique of the environmentally based social psychology and social sciences and will add these to the agents serving mankind intelligently, for it will be the function of the one to create an effectively planned psychosocial environment and of the others to administer it" (Bernard, 1927). A statistical and laboratory social science (1919), that emphasized a search for valid and effective methods of collective mind control (1923a; 1924; 1926; 1927; 1929; 1931; 1940) would legitimate the authority of scientists.

Bernard's conviction that a social scientific contribution to social progress was possible (see Bernard, 1922; 1923; 1925; 1926a) led him "to reassert the [sociologists'] intellectual right to generalize and the[ir] moral right to offer guidance to the members of society" (1932). However, he worried about the residues of metaphysics, utopianism, and idealism still to be found in sociological pronouncements and had grave misgivings that the discipline would become "chained to the Scylla of business and the Charybdis of professional politics." In reference to the eastern sociological establishment, he had expressed as early as 1932 his concerns about self-serving sectarian interests within the profession. "There is perhaps some danger among us," he noted in his presidential address to the American Sociological Society in that year, "that only the 'orthodox,' that only those who have been blest with the laying on of the hands of a foundation and have been admitted to membership in some Royal Order of Knights and Ladies of Research, or at least who have been invited to membership on national research committees, will be regarded as true researchers by their more fortunate, or, perhaps, more politically adept, brethren of the cloth." Bernard was not confident that he could trust those sociologists whose faiths were based on other convictions. Eastern, southern, and midwestern Protestant theologies each had a different vision of the positivist utopia. Unable to accommodate the elitism contained in the eastern and southern perspectives with his own international populism, he was caught in the dilemma of disapproving of the ethics of the eastern positivists whose statistical sociology he admired.

Bernard regarded the Easterner's claim to the possession of an orthodoxy as suspect because its market orientation violated his conception of a sociology that would be both ethical and intellectual. By linking themselves to big government and big money, the eastern positivists had surrendered their right to define the mission of sociology. He worried that, controlled by bureaucratic administrators and foundation-supported technocrats, the discipline of sociology would be populated by "statisticians, questionnaire makers and mongers, and machine operators instead of . . . rich and penetrating personalities" (1932). He feared that "the man . . . best able to secure an appointment to a position of administrative power . . . [would be] least able to administer his charge to social advantage" and that the appointments would be made by those "not . . . able to grasp the possibilities of the most brilliant research plans" (1932). He sympathized with the kind of qualitative social psychology advocated by Herbert Blumer: "Blumer has more faith in the ability of a 'rich personality' to interpret and estimate so complex and subtle a thing as personality than all the quantitative mechanical devices that can be brought to bear in testing and measuring it. With this I agree in general. I should rather trust the genius of a Cooley or a Vincent to detect motives, attitudes, and behavior than nine-tenths of the laboratory equipment" (1932). However, Bernard doubted that the discipline would attract exceptional scholars: "There are so few Cooleys and Vincents and so many little men who measure . . . and are compelled to use machines and mathematical formulas." (1932)

Trapped in a dilemma of his own making—commitment to both the charisma of interpretive creativity and the bureaucratic mentality of statisticians—Bernard reluctantly placed his faith in the development of a quantitative social science. His ambivalence was expressed on one occasion when he chastised Ogburn for expressing doubts about the uses of statistics for sociological research (see Ogburn, 1934; Bernard and Bernard [1943] 1965, 677–80). He finally placed his faith in statistics, becoming the acknowledged leader of the coup that in 1935 replaced the University of Chicago's *American Journal of Sociology* with a new journal, the *American Sociological Review*, dominated by quantitative positivists (see J. Bernard, 1973; Kuklick, 1973).

No twentieth-century figure deserves more credit for the revival and legitimation of a statistical version of Comtean positivism. Because he would not compromise his intellectual, political, and populist ethics, Bernard was never able to secure a permanent position at a single university and became a veritable circuit rider throughout the South and Midwest, firing up the spirit of his version of the Comtean science at such universities as Western Reserve, Florida, Missouri, Minnesota, Cornell, Tulane, North Carolina, and Washington (St. Louis), and eventually Pennsylvania State College (see Barnes, 1968). His essays, books, and reviews hammered home the importance of objectivity, experimental methods, and properly gathered statistics, and the necessity for scientifically guided social control (see Bernard, 1928; 1942).

Because he was so peripatetic he never gathered a body of loyal followers. His one disciple, George A. Lundberg, would continue the struggle to emancipate social science from metaphysics and its idols. But although Lundberg succeeded Bernard as America's leading apostle of positivism and statistical sociology, insisting that only his own brand of science could save America and indeed the world, he compromised Bernard's ethical humanism. Lundberg (1947a, 5) wrote that "Science is not a substitute for ideals. . . . It is the most effective instrument for their attainment." For Lundberg ideals were not to be set by sociologists but by politicians and policy makers. However, the exception to his belief in the separation of ideals from sociology was his refusal to cooperate with America's participation in World War II.

During the war Lundberg continued to speak out in behalf of positivist social sciences, but in answer to the question "What should scientists do in wartime?" he replied, "In general, and as far as possible, they should go about their business as scientists" (Lundberg, 1944). Though he believed that the social sciences ought to be placed in the service of any government for any purpose, he drew the line at accepting the justifications for supporting what he regarded as Roosevelt's war. A subscriber to Harry Elmer Barnes's and Charles Beard's thesis that "Roosevelt lied us into war" (see Lundberg, 1953), he discounted as so much obfuscating propaganda the ethical purposes that officially justified America's all-out assault on Nazi and Japanese aggression. As late as 1944 he doubted whether the "testimony of displaced politicians, refugee scholars, and others who have suffered personal misfortune and injustice at the hands of the regimes in question" could be trusted. He dismissed Roosevelt's "romantic talk about freedom from want and fear," holding that "it should be recognized that such 'freedom' is only partially attainable and that it is always a relative matter." The president's "Four Freedoms" were beyond attainment. Proclamation of America's social ideals, in Lundberg's perspective, amounted to "unbridled social idealism, . . . unbalanced by scientific criteria as to possibilities and cost, . . . and in effect [was] a kind of fraud on the body politic." Science, he concluded, "has the decency to stipulate also the degree of probability of their attainment in given circumstances and periods of time." Wartime propaganda violated his vision of positivistic idealism.

Lundberg's opposition to the war brought him into conflict with sociologists who accepted America's war aims and were eager to put their science in service to them (see Lundberg, 1968). In 1943 his presidential address to the American Sociological Society—a polemic that denounced "organized and articulate Jews . . . [for] devoting themselves to legalistic and moralistic conjurings . . . about inalienable rights," ridiculed the National Catholic Council's "Catholic Statement on Peace Essentials," dismissed public concerns over "justice, authority, and freedom" as so much verbiage deriving from "primitive theology," criticized sociologists who confused "their own cultural preferences for democracy" with sound "scientific conclusions" on the subject, and opposed the "legalistic and moralistic viewpoint anchored in theology . . . [that] operates in our international relations"—aroused a clamor of opposition. The eastern cosmopolitan urban positivists saw no contradiction in putting their sociology in service to the war effort and thus linked their brand of science to America's emergence as a world leader. Lundberg's gospel of midwestern populist positivism, originally derived from his membership in the Farmer-Labor Alliance of North Dakota, reflected the isolationism and xenophobia of that region's agricultural mentality. Chained to the ethics of populist American Lutheranism, he became an anachronism in postwar American sociology.

As his outspoken statements continued to find their way into professional and popular journals, Lundberg's fellow-positivists began to criticize him. Ogburn pointedly suggested that Lundberg write under an assumed name when he wanted to have fun (see Larsen, 1968). Jessie Bernard (1949) suggested that he had threatened the integrity of the discipline by his zeal in selling its products. Harry Alpert (Larsen, 1968) exclaimed, "Good grief, George! Aren't you saying that democracy is incompatible with the requirements of technologically advanced society?" Although Lundberg would continue his jeremiads against sociology's failure to reject legalistic, moralistic, magical, superstitious, and idealistic orientations and demand that the discipline accept science as a religion (see Lundberg, 1948; 1950), his populist Lutheranism was rejected even as his positivism was celebrated by those Calvinist sociologists who saw in it an opportunity to penetrate the corridors of power.

NOTES

1. Bernard's criticism of American policy in Latin America also reflected his opposition to the ideas of George Frederick Holmes, the antebellum Comtean sociologist. In 1856 Holmes had written, "If the United States should, in the course of time, absorb Mexico, annex Cuba, spread over Nicaragua and the rest of Central America, and overflow the wide llanos and pampas of South America, they will only repeat on a grander scale the same series of phenomena which has been exhibited in the past by every nation and every race which has

been signally instrumental in furthering the progress of humanity. Conquest, extension, appropriation, assimilation, and even the extermination of inferior races has been and must be the course pursued in the development of civilization. Woe may be unto those by whom the offence comes, when there is a real offence—but such is unquestionably the plan prescribed for the progressive amelioration of the world" (Holmes, 1856, 529).

2. Bernard wrote his critique of Marxism in the same period that his mentors, Charles Ellwood and Albion W. Small, also published critiques of the European doctrine that seemed to challenge almost all American sociological formulations. (Bernard, 1913; Ellwood, 1911. On Small, see chap. 12 below.)

Bernard's Lutheran-based revolutionary inclinations were compatible with and sympathetic to those of Marx, but his attitude had its origins in religion, while Marx's were located in an eschatological vision of history. Latter-day midwestern radical sociologists who attack the entire system of corporate capitalism and the welfare state and who see the warfare state as a major obstacle to peace are more likely to be the moral descendants of Bernard than of Marx. The Marxism of contemporary midwestern sociologists has separated itself from Bernard even while being truer to his evangelical radicalism than to Marx's radical revolutionism. Midwestern Lutheranism in its sublimated forms can accommodate utopian Marxism, complex mathematical and statistical methodologies, the peace movement, industrial democracy, and hatred of Eastern banking and political plutocrats. Positivistic opponents of the military industrial complex have forgotten their earlier mentor, Bernard, and adopted the currently more fashionable Marx.

CHAPTER 12

Small's Transvaluation of Marxism into Christian Sociology: Civil Religion and Societal Consensus

Sociology at the University of Chicago began with the invitation of Albion Woodbury Small (1854–1926) to found and chair the first department of sociology in the world, in 1892. Small, the son of a Baptist minister, was graduated from Colby University in 1876 and matriculated at Newton Theological Seminary in 1879. He then studied at the universities of Berlin (1879–80) and Leipzig (1880) and in the British Museum (1880–81), taught history and political economy at Colby (1881–89), and obtained a Ph.D. under Richard T. Ely at Johns Hopkins (1888–89). Small served as president of Colby, from 1889 to 1892, when the University of Chicago's president, William Rainey Harper, called him to join the nine college presidents who would initiate Chicago's first professoriat.

Sociology, as Small conceived of it, would address the burning question of the day with both a Christian homiletic and a reformist zeal. Somehow Small hoped to infuse Progressive reconstruction with pious reverence. His goal for sociology was to supply a secular theodicy for industrial capitalism, just as Henry Hughes earlier had provided one for slavocratic agrarian feudalism. Small shared with Hughes the vision of an impending crisis threatening America. However, the debate over slavery and the labor question inspired in Hughes a vision of totalitarian utopia, while for Small, the threat of a world-wide Bolshevik revolution required a new crusade that, by combining a Marxian economic ethic with a Christian social ethic, would lead to the salvation of modern industrial capitalism.

Small sought to distinguish Chicago's sociology from that being developed by Sumner, Ward, and Giddings. Constructing the discipline as an expression of enlightened Protestantism, Small wanted its pure form to answer the question, "What is worth doing?" and its application to show "how

... the thing worth doing [might] be done" (Small, 1905, 663). He rejected the pessimistic sociology of Sumner altogether; a social scientist who could not envision the practical remaking of the world was by Small's definition no sociologist at all.[1] Ward's sociocratic meliorism did attract Small's interest and admiration, but its vast system of psychic, evolutionary, and neo-Darwinian apparatus and, more disturbing, its author's unabashed atheism made it unacceptable.[2] He considered invalid Giddings's claim to have developed a scientific sociology based upon the concept "consciousness of kind."[3] Small's sociology required both Christian ethics and rigorous empiricism. At Chicago he hoped to build a department that would employ social science for the purpose of making America a unified community, a covenant in which common values would be shared by all.

During his first two decades Small tried to make the department a center for disseminating his sociological outlook, including provision for the social uplift and cultural needs of the city of Chicago, its region, and the nation as a whole. His goal was the cultural homogenization of America's ethnic groups, the humanizing of business and industrial corporations, the Christianizing of capitalism—and spreading the message of America world-wide. But because the university had been founded originally as a Baptist institution and in accordance with the principles of stewardship that guided its founder-benefactor, John D. Rockefeller, Small's freedom to make the faculty appointments he desired was severely constrained. Only those who could pass muster with Rockefeller's surrogate, President Harper, were hired. Nevertheless, Small was able to give his program a distinct moral and social character. Moreover, he and his colleagues and students could draw on the intellectual resources of other departments: theology, where Shailer Matthews (1863–1941) built a program in liberal-minded religious studies; economics, where for its first thirteen years Thorstein Veblen (1857–1929) taught while editing the *Journal of Political Economy;* and philosophy, whose lecturers included George Herbert Mead (1863–1931) and, for a decade beginning in 1894, John Dewey (1859–1962).

The Christian spirit of uplift seemed to be the principal prerequisite for appointment to Chicago's sociology department, just as it had inspired the appointments of Edward Cummings and Francis Greenwood Peabody at Harvard. Every member of Small's faculty during its first fifteen years—until Harper's death—was associated with ministerial work, settlement houses, Chautauqua, and Social Gospel. Perhaps the two most significant appointments were those of Charles Richmond Henderson (1848–1915) and George Edward Vincent (1864–1941). Henderson, whose courses at Chicago have recently been compared more than favorably to those of Cummings at Harvard (Shils, 1980, 220), left his Detroit pastorate to become associate professor of sociology and, in 1894, university chaplain. He had a powerful influence on graduate students and on Marion Talbot, the department's first instructor in "sanitary science" (Wright 1980, 110, 121–22, 150, 161). In keeping with Small's inclinations and his own principles, Henderson became chairman of Chicago's short-lived program in "ecclesiastical sociology." Assenting to President Harper's recommendation that Henderson be appointed to the sociology faculty to introduce "charities" into the curriculum, Small asserted that the "whole subject of the sociological facts and possibilities of organized Christianity should be treated by a man of broad intellectual outlook and practical pastoral experience" (quoted in Diner, 1975, 520).

Harper's admiration of Chautauqua and its contribution to a public-spirited but religiously correct liberal arts education was satisfied when George E. Vincent, son of the Methodist Episcopal bishop who had founded Chautauqua, became first a graduate student and then a member of the sociology faculty. Even before he obtained his Ph.D. in 1896, Vincent had been associated with Small in teaching sociology and writing a major college textbook in that subject (1894). The interconnections between sociology, Christian uplift, Chautauqua, the Rockefeller stewardship, and the spread of the new gospel to the Midwest are amply illustrated in Vincent's teaching and administrative career. After teaching sociology for two decades at Chicago, he accepted an appointment as president of the University of Minnesota, where he served for six years (1911–17), playing a major role in establishing that institution's sociology department (Martindale, 1976, 20–25) and becoming the sixth president of the American Sociological Society in 1916. From 1914 to 1929, Vincent occupied a seat on Rockefeller's General Education Board, and, upon leaving his post at Minnesota, became president of the Rockefeller Foundation (1917–29). Chautauqua always remained as important to him as it had been to his father and Harper; from 1907 to 1915 Vincent presided over that educational association, and he continued as its honorary president from 1915 to 1937.

Small and Vincent (1894, 365) had established the credo of the new sociology that they were developing at Chicago in 1894: "In the apparent conflict between self-interest and the collective welfare, the religious motive exerts a most powerful influence in securing social or altruistic conduct." The faculty—with the exception of the agnostic W. I. Thomas—shared this point of view. Graham Taylor (1851–1938), the founder of Chicago Theological Seminary's Department of Christian Sociology in 1892, influenced the development of Small's department in its early years (G. P. Taylor, 1930, 385–406; Wade, 1964, 78–82, 99–100, 166–67). Ellsworth Faris (1874–1953), who had been a missionary in the Belgian Congo before he took his Ph.D. in philosophy and psychology in 1914, joined the sociology faculty the following year. After teaching at the State University of Iowa for three years (1916–19), Faris returned replacing Thomas, who had been forced to resign. Harper's superintendency over Small's appointments led to the appointment of Frederick Starr as the department's first anthropologist (Diner, 1975). Starr had been curator of the American Museum of Natural History and a former teacher at Chautauqua. Anthropology remained a part of the sociology curriculum until 1929, when it withdrew to form its own department. Charles Zeublin (1866–1924), an erstwhile divinity student under Harper at Yale, was appointed as a sociologist. Zeublin had studied Old Testament theology at Leipzig before coming to Chicago to found the Northwestern University settlement house. He became a spokesman on housing, city planning, and labor matters and taught from 1894 to 1907 in Small's department. Although Zeublin's liberal-minded politics displeased Harper's successor, Henry Pratt Judson, and ultimately led to his resignation from the faculty and withdrawal from the discipline, his concentrated search for the ethical solution to urban problems helped establish Chicago sociology's later emphasis on the city. To Small, who had promised his readers in the *American Journal of Sociology's* first issue that he would be respectful of Christianity but suspicious of "Christian sociologists," civic reformers who applied Christian precepts were the right sort for the faculty.

Even after Harper's death, when Small was able to assume greater control over teaching appointments in sociology, the faculty continued to represent the spirit of activated Social Gospel and a public-spirited civic ideology. During the decade after 1906, most of the men whom Harper had appointed either departed or died: Graham Taylor and Charles Zeublin left the department in 1908; Jerome Hall in 1909; Ira Howerth (Ph.D., 1893) in 1911, the same year that George Vincent left to become president of the University of Minnesota. Charles Henderson died in 1915. Small's subsequent appointments, though given to men further removed from religious life than those of the first two decades, reflected the transvalued version of Protestant uplift that had found expression in Chicago's civic improvement ideology and the transition to secular professional education in sociology.

THE SACRALIZATION OF MARX

"It would seem to be axiomatic," Small observed in 1914, "that in the degree in which partnership of other men besides the proprietor is necessary to make a type of capital possible and efficient, corresponding partnership of those other men in control of that capital is indicated" (1914, 752). More than any other American sociologist, Small epitomized the ethos of American Christian socialism, in both its ethical criticism of capitalism and its unwillingness to become politically revolutionary. Small's "socialism" combined a Protestant moral attitude with a program for converting private business into a public trust.

Small's sociology was guided by a lifelong dialogue with Marx.[4] Indeed, his responses to Marx's challenge to both social science and civil society constitute virtually the only explicit debate by an American sociologist on the subject. Although convinced that Marx was wrong in socioeconomic theory, ethical outlook, and proposed revolutionary practice, Small (1912) nevertheless was sure that the author of *Das Kapital* belonged with Galileo in the pantheon of "the world's great discoverers" (1912, 810). As early as 1895, inaugurating what he called "the era of sociology" with the first issue of the *American Journal of Sociology,* he wrote: "Within the last thirty years a theory of social development founded on an economic conception [has been] put forward by a worker quite outside the ranks of the official exponents of this science." This theory—"Marx's view of modern society, and the theory of surplus value on which it is based"—had already earned its discoverer a place "alongside . . . Darwin in influencing the thought of the nineteenth century." Yet, Small asserted, Marx's perspective "is a view so utterly out of proportion, so evidently only partially true, and so clearly demonstrative at every point of the author's ignorance of the method of action in human society, of existing evolutionary forces larger than any he has taken account of, that it can hardly have any prominent place reserved to it in a future science of society." The appeal of Marx's theory, Small was sure, lay in the fact that in the present state of knowledge there had been absolutely no science of society to which the world could look for help and guidance in the problems with which it is "struggling in a kind of agony that gives a note to the entire literature of our period" (1895, 11–12). Small was more impressed with Marx's implicit secular theology than with his social science, but he thought that neither would be sufficient to resolve the Social Question.

Both Marxism and religion had failed, Small contended: neither had put forward a coherent theory or a coordinated program of action. Each had splintered into opposed sects and sectarian denominations. Protestantism alone was so divided into "infinitesimal gradations of religious theory—from the one extreme of belief virtually identical with that of the Pope . . . to another extreme which eliminates nearly everything that the Pope would call Christian or even religious" that it could offer no unified creed. Similarly, "both friends and enemies of socialism are laboring under a delusion when they imagine that socialism is a perfectly definite thing." Socialism consisted of the disparate thoughts and varied practices of widely scattered groups of people. "The socialism professed by other groups of people, at the same time and in other places, may be different in kinds and degrees, ranging from trivial points of order to irreconcilable differences of principle." Small declared that "nobody since Martin

Luther has done as much as Karl Marx to make the conventional-minded fear that our theories of life may need a thorough overhauling" (1912, 805, 811). What was needed now was that overhaul.

Small credited Marx with contributing five particulars to the reconstruction of social theory: he "alleged that *the world must set itself right about the economic interpretation of history*"; he "called attention to *class conflict, as a* primary factor in human history, and he tried to rouse the classes that have no resource but their labor to open their eyes to their own interests in the situation, to become 'class conscious,' and to pursue their own interests as intelligently and as completely as other classes pursue theirs; he "put a new emphasis on the rudimentary economic fact of *surplus value*"; he assumed "that *the laboring class and the capitalistic class may be sharply distinguished and precisely divided*"; and he offered as "the keel of his proposed ship of state . . . [the] *socialization of capital* (1912, 811–16). Small regarded these five points as of the utmost importance but at the same time hopelessly and irretrievably one-sided. He particularly criticized Marx and other socialists on the issue of the sociology of profits (1925). "[If] pushed to its logical limits, the Marxian conception of profits would even make it necessary for us to regard every penny which each laborer receives for his work in excess of the amount necessary to support himself and his family in accordance with their attained standard of living as parasitism and piracy." Such logical absurdities suggested to Small that "the Marxian theory furnishes no means of discriminating between those types of profit which might more reasonably be classed as wages and those types which are piratical" (1925, 440–41). Small pointed out the contradictions in Marx's theory of relative surplus value by showing that part of the worker's wage also could be part of that surplus value.

To Small it was German social theory, so often mistakenly equated with socialism, that started with the correct ethical assumption, "that men are more important than capital, and that all political and legal and economic practices must be held accountable to that principle" (1912, 818). American sociologists, however, had not yet grasped this principle. "It is a symptom of social punk-mindedness," Small remarked acidly, "that all our best equipped thinkers are not as seriously intent as the socialists are upon the unresolved problems of society." But, he complained, the socialists approach these problems with "more zeal than discretion" (1912, 819). A revival of the original social scientific mission, rededicated to what Small in 1897 had called "this rudimentary idea of the paramount dignity of persons, regardless of their social state" (1897, 349), was required.

Although Small pioneered the introduction to America of Gustav Ratzenhofer's (1842–1904) interest-conflict theory (see Small, 1905), he firmly believed that the perpetuation of competing and contradictory interests could produce only temporary compromises or, worse, the temporary hegemony of one constellation of interests over another. Such solutions to social conflicts could never promise any permanent social good. What was needed was a basic moral vitalization, fueled by Christian values. A sociology that was at the same time an ethical science could provide the moral calculus necessary for attaining the socially good. Armed with his vision of social unity and moral reform, Small proposed a new "Great Awakening." The world could be saved from unregenerate capitalism and unethical communism by a Christian victory in the war over the faith and minds of men.

The Protestant churches of America required rededication to their missionary crusade. Writing an open letter to the Laymen's Committee on Interchurch Survey in 1919 Small spelled out the terrible dangers of the new Bolshevism, now making its appearance in Russia, and the need for Christian action lest it spread to America. Because the Russian Revolution would challenge the credibility of both capitalism and democracy, he feared a revolt of the masses. "The moment that the ideas which . . . previously held society together lose that controlling power," he warned, "competing ideas take possession of the unsettled minds, and these ideas do not stop with correcting the errors of the old ones. They not only drive out the oldest ideas, and newer ones which may be better, but they do not stop there. Before equilibrium is restored the ideas in circulation and control may have flown to the opposite extreme of futility and perhaps fatality" (1919, 494). Events and portents of Russia provided Small with an awesome example:

> The same inverted progress from worse to worst is now visible in Russia, where the Bolshevik Communist Party, as Lenine [sic] now calls it, proposes to redeem Russia and the rest of the world by the 'dictatorship of the pro-letariat.' This means the suppression by violence of everyone who resists the exclusive rule of those who work with their hands. It means a regime in which . . . no one shall have more property or income than the average work-man has. It means a regime in which no one shall have any more influence upon any business, whether economic or political, than the average workman has. It means a regime in which . . . anyone who has less has license to take, if he can, from him who has more, and not merely to get all the enjoyment there is in goods thus acquired, but to pronounce a benediction upon himself as a servant of righteousness besides. [Small, 1919, 494]

Small urged the church to recognize, however painful it might be, "that *capital, as it is legally established in modern industrial countries, is bound to answer to the charge of having acquired legal rights which Public policy cannot permanently concede*" (1919, 495). Small had already concluded that this aspect of the critique of capitalism was correct, but he proposed a new basis for governmental policy—that private business be required to act as a utility (1895a) and that corporations carrying on business of a "semi-public" character be placed under some type of public, collective, or democratic control (1895b).

The problem facing the church was even greater than that challenging the legitimacy of capitalism: "*A church which has no positive attitude, no definite policy toward the group of problems thus indicated, can scarcely hope to impress men whose lives pivot upon these problems as dealing with anything very close to reality*" (1919, 496). In effect, Small believed that Protestant doctrine suffered from a failure to make its beliefs and perspectives relevant to the great social issues of the day. The class struggle had reached world-wide proportions, and challenged the Christian with an "irrepressible conflict" certain to erupt.

The true Christian must face this challenge armed with the "clue which Jesus offered to the divine scheme of things . . . not a belief, not a creed, but a moral attitude, or, as the good old pious phrase had it, a spiritual frame." This spiritual frame amounted to following Jesus' basic teaching as paraphrased by Small: "Thus and thus must we be *in our hearts;* so and so must we be disposed toward one another and toward God; after this manner must we bear our part in life, or else we are counting against realization of the divine scheme of things" (1920, 678).

For Small the moral order turned on the issue of property ownership and property rights and duties. "The property system of every civilized country, our own for example, may be described as a fabric of devices to serve everybody's need of protection against the selfishness of everybody else" (1920, 693). However, what had gone wrong in America was the reversal of authority permitted by the introduction of unbridled *corporate* property.

> In one aspect a corporation is a deathless superpersonal selfishness vested by the state with superpersonal powers. This monster is commissioned by the state to exercise its superpersonal powers within the society of plain persons. Thus we have unconsciously converted our property system from a protection of similar natural persons against one another, into a licensing system of supernatural persons. . . . The invention is not, and cannot come to, good, unless the society of plain persons can either endow corporations with souls, with souls' liabilities, or create and operate in its own interest an adequate superpersonal control of the superpersonal enginery of corporations. [1920, 693]

Small would have America retain the corporation as an economic form, but he proposed that it be put to work in the service of God. The soulless corporation was to be imbued with a soul of its own.

To accomplish this objective, he proposed a "new crusade" that would "accept the mandate to carry Christianity, with all it may involve, into settlement of those issues of economic righteousness which stand between our generation and the Kingdom of God" (1920, 694). By Christianizing all of the members of the corporate world there would be ushered in that world which "Jesus tried to convince [the people of] his time" to establish. "The only way out of this mess must be acceptance of the world as the domain of a beneficent Father, and adoption of the belief that the only economy which can fit this world permanently is the economy of brotherly love" (1920, 683). Small's crusade would eliminate the Marxist necessity for revolution; it would also achieve the Christian aim of world brotherhood. It was the duty of the true believer to reach out to America's corporate rulers and inspire a Christian soul within them.

Small wished to infuse capitalists with the same spirit of sectarian Puritanism that Max Weber had observed in America in 1904; but, he believed that the current crisis required an end to sectarianism. The old sects and creeds had lost their inspirational force by competing with each other; he scoffed at those "both inside and outside the church [who] can see no Christianity at all except in social settlements, or Red Cross drives, or purifying municipal politics or 'abolishing the capitalist state'" (1920, 680).

Revived, the old Protestant ethic would infuse the now fallen capitalist spirit with a new morality, helping it to stand against the rising tide of Bolshevism. The new mission of Protestantism was to combat communism.

> The irrefutable bad of the Russian revolution, the central reason why every just man who is also clear headed hates it, is that essentially it is *no revolution at all*. It is simply a transfer of that old guilty *dominance* of the Czar to the even more guilty hands of Lenin. . . . The tragedy of Russia was and is the absence of a middle class able and willing to create a real revolution by abolishing all dictatorship and introducing a regime of justice to all interests. [1920, 692]

America *does* have a middle class, and hence it need not experience the violent pseudorevolution that had wracked Russia. "Middle class Americans today are rapidly reaching the conclusion that the typical good man for our time is contrasted with the bad man of our era by his will to do his part toward finding out what this property wrong is and how it may be righted" (1920, 691). But for this good middle class to triumph over its adversary, Christianity must volunteer its forces for an all-out spiritual struggle. "Christianity cannot be a neutral. Christianity cannot be a noncombatant. In spite of itself, whether it will or no, Christianity must give aid and comfort to one or the other of the belligerents" (1920, 692).

Small's Christian crusade was a call for militant collective action in behalf of the Protestant idea of individualism. It required the lay Christian as an individual to pledge full-fledged support to the cause: "If the Christian laymen of America should in effect take the position that economic justice is no pressing business of organized Christians, that attitude would amount to another betrayal of our Lord with a kiss" (1920, 691). Each Christian must search his or her soul for the answer to "the central human question, and probably for generations to come . . . *What is right, and how may we realize the right in economic relations?*" (1920, 686). Newly reborn Christians would give the correct answer not merely in words, but, far more significantly, in works. "Then it is the business of these Christians . . . to find their vocations and to live their Christian spirit into the vocations until, as the New Testament phrase has it, they 'leaven the whole lump' (1920, 685).

Calling for a second Protestant Reformation to do for the twentieth century what the original had done for the sixteenth, Small hoped that the new solidarity he envisioned among American Christians would spread to salvage the entire world. "Ever since Christendom ceased to be one, the dream of reunion has had a place among Christian impulses" (1920, 685). The united Protestant actions during the war had fostered a spirit of ecumenism and also introduced new organizational practices, resulting in "more business-like budgets for the several denominational groups than the Congress of the United States has ever been able to adopt for the operations of our government for a single year" (1920, 689). As Small perceived it, "American Christians have unwittingly acquired a mental and moral unity which is equipment for still more tremendous responsibility, and it is assurance of an output of personality, touched by the spirit of Christ, more lavish and more precious than the dedications of money" (1920, 689). However, Small was not loath to call for new money for the church, and for even better organization for making even more money.

"The church is bound to be a failure unless it is first and foremost not a master but a spiritual incubator. Its main business is to bring to life a Christian in every man and woman" (1920, 685). The task of reaching souls had been made easier by the fact that "the mechanism for exchange and aggregation and direction of Christian impulse is far more sensitive, far more penetrating, far more pervasive, far more comprehensive, than it has ever been before" (1920, 688). Recent vast improvements in mass communications meant that "up to the twentieth century no Roman pontiff . . . commanded means of instant and circumstantial intercourse with the churches of Europe equal to those today at the service of every intelligent Christian in the United States about every part of the world" (1920, 688). Commercial organizations for the gathering and distribution of news now made it possible that "if an Anglican bishop in Africa or a Baptist missionary in Asia says or does something out of the ordinary today, it will be talked about tomorrow at ten million breakfast tables all over the world, and the day following it may divide a church council or a national denominational convention" (1920, 688). A new Christian ecumenism was now realizable, Small believed, aided by means of mass communication and catalyzed by means of modern organization.

Small's commitment to restoring the Christian consciousness of kind within the framework of industrial civilization was unflagging. Both he and Giddings thought that they could achieve an American covenant and an American world mission with the aid of philanthropy, the one through individual tithes, the other through corporate subsidies and foundations; for each, money would be the vehicle taking modern man and industrial society down the road to salvation. Giddings thought to reach his objectives through America's industrial might and military power, Small through reaching the souls of humankind.

CIVIL RELIGION AND SOCIETAL CONSENSUS

The obverse side of Small's Christian concern with economic equality was his preoccupation with community and consensus, a theme that has appeared and reappeared in American sociology in conceptions of the covenanted community and the Holy Commonwealth. Small framed this dimension of his sociology around the concepts of civic community and national consensus. In his day, these issues were exacerbated by the ethnic, racial, and religious diversity of the country. As clouds of war appeared over Europe in 1914 and threatened to engulf America, Small grew concerned over the nature and fabric of Americanism, the bonds of nationality, the degree of national preparedness, and the structural prerequisites of democracy. In a series of essays published between 1915 and 1919 he pointed to themes that would preoccupy the sociologists at Chicago for many years.

In August of 1914, as editor of the *American Journal of Sociology*, Small conducted a survey of 250 American men and women representative of "the widest range of vocations . . . from officers of local labor organizations to Justices of the federal Supreme Court . . . [to] leaders of thought in all the large religious bodies, in . . . learned professions, in manufacture, engineering, banking, trade, transportation, journalism, philanthropy, criminology, and the most prominent reform movements" on the question, "What is Americanism?" (1915, 433–86). To his chagrin, forty-four of the 250 surveyed plus an additional ten labor leaders, part of a supplemental survey, responded (Small, 1915 and 1915a). Even more disappointing, Small could discern no core American values in the responses:

> Very few Americans furnish credible evidence of sharing very largely in the knowledge, belief, and purposes of all Americans. . . . There are no Americans in whose minds the abundance of American thinking is so organized that their combination of American judgments is recognized by the rest of their

fellows as standard Americanism. . . . Except in certain vague superficialities, American minds are anchorages for a heterogeneity of ideas. American life is correspondingly uncorrelated. [1915, 483]

Small's response was to call for a resurgence of nationalism. "It is conceivable that the time may come when all nations may have melted into a world-citizenry. Meanwhile, it is certain that nationality . . . must be one of the tools with which humanity must work out its larger salvation" (1915, 484). The larger problem of world unity as a brotherhood of man must await America's resolution of its internal problems, Small seemed to suggest; but, contrary to Giddings's promotion of a plan for American empire resting on a confederation of consciousness of kind, he addressed his attention to the problem of securing national unity.

Small spoke from the perspective of an American assimilationist: "The nation consists of people of a State developed into a linguistic and cultural unity." Moreover, the nation so defined was a cultural and moral imperative: "So long as the nation and the State are coextensive, the national and the civic interest are also one. . . . [The] more highly the national interest is developed, the more will the tribal or racial interest merge itself into the national interest" (Small, 1905, 255–56). However, this vision of a national, secular, covenanted community of common interest was threatened in the United States by the desire of some immigrants to preserve their original language and culture and by the absence of a national culture that could surmount ethnic and racial diversity.

Small's preoccupation with assimilation had been stimulated by Ratzenhofer's prediction that competitive racial and ethnic interests could not be made to disappear by America's industrializing and democratic processes. Small attempted to adapt Ratzenhofer's theory of society as a cockpit of competing interests to the United States, but he believed so strongly in the solidarity principle implicit in the *Kultur* concept that he could not accept Ratzenhofer's thesis of American exceptionalism. The *Kultur* concept, supported by such Prussian chauvinists as Treitschke, Ranke, and Droysen, framed Germany's drive for nationalism under Bismarck. The problem that faced eighteenth- and nineteenth-century Germany was how it might incorporate its many indigenous nationalities—and whether it should integrate its Jews—under the banner of *Kultur*. The prenationalist German Enlightenment (*Aufklarung*) had responded to the issue in an elitist fashion: it would admit the "enlightened" Jew into its salons if he proved himself worthy, as an exception to his own people's alleged characteristics or as a paragon of selected virtues,[5] but it would not permit him to amalgamate. The German assimilationist approach would have to be democratized for the American situation, Small and other American sociologists came to believe, its elitist *Kultur* traded for mass culture. Yet for an American "core" culture to triumph, the values of Puritanism also would have to be democratized and diffused. Calvinism would have to become Americanism, the Protestant ethic the spirit of capitalism.

Small treated America as if it were a democratic Bismarckian society in the making. Therefore his adaptation of Ratzenhofer's theories did not go so far as to compare the United States to the Austrian sociologist's homeland—a multinational empire whose unity rested uneasily on the limited capacities of a traditional monarch. The possibility that the disintegrating Austro-Hungarian Empire might be a closer counterpart of America than Germany was lost on Albion Small. Ratzenhofer had predicted that once the struggle for existence in America became intense, ethnic divisiveness would reassert itself as a powerful force for intergroup conflict.[6] Small and almost all American sociologists insisted that America would not disintegrate, its people would be assimilated.

Newcomers to America had an obligation to Americanize themselves, Small asserted, and "immigrants of all nationalities who propose to cast in their lot with Americans . . . should as soon as possible become assimilated with the whole of the population." Small was adamant on this point: "Anything that tends to keep them a group by themselves is unfortunate both for themselves and their children" (Dibble, 1975, 248, n.2). Small asked how and of what cultural materials the bonds of nationality could be constructed. American institutions appeared too weak to provide the supports for what he called a new social ethic. The family had lost its capacity to inculcate values and insure ethical permanence from generation to generation. Religion had become so overlaid with doctrinal disputes, schisms, and separate churches, denominations, and sects that its fundamental truths could not penetrate the consciousness of individuals and organizations. A newly formulated ideal of national consciousness was required (1919a, 259).

The Germans of the *Aufklarung* had set a standard of intellectual attainment and demanded that all true Germans reach or surpass it. Though revolted by this elitism, Small opposed intermarriage (see Dibble, 1975, 247–48). He put forth a theory of assimilation that would produce consensus around a secular ethic but would not include sexual intercourse between persons of different nationality or race. Small called his theory of assimilation "race solidarity," but made it clear that this did not necessarily include interracial or interethnic unions (1915, 643).

In effect, Small's "purely secular ethic" was to be the basis for a new American civil religion. "By a *purely secular ethic*," Small wrote in 1919, "I mean a concept of *ends* which are within the range of the visible career of men, and which are the most convincing correlation of the lesser and the larger purposes that are found to have a place in human life" (1919, 295–96). In the face of an alleged society-wide moral chaos and divisiveness, Small sought to implant a secular, ecumenical,[7] yet essentially Protestant ethic as the stem:

My own Pillar of Fire and Pillar of Cloud, in this wandering toward the Kingdom, is a vision of *the American Religion*. . . . The Jew, the Catholic, and the Protestant might graft this religion each on the trunk of his peculiar faith, and each might contribute to his rendering of religion all the spiritual force there is in his distinctive beliefs. The documents of this religion are every scripture, canonical or uncanonical, in which a seeker after God or an avoider of God has set down an authentic truth encountered in the experience of either. Its ceremonial is not a single prescribed ritual. It is every outward form of worship by means of which anyone feels himself brought nearer to God and to his fellow-men. Its polity is the concerted purpose of every American, from Eastport to San Diego, to join in a perpetual league for finding out the quality and program of life which gives sincerest heed to the spiritual possibilities in every one of us. Its work is dedication to an ideal of life in which each shall give his best to all others, and receive his best from all the others in promoting a method of life in which our dealings with one another, from the most trivial individual act to the most momentous public policy, shall do all that is possible toward realizing the most and the highest of which each and all of us are capable. Its last appraisable outcome will be the utmost refining of our spirits for everything which may hereafter answer to our most aspiring thought of "the inheritance of saints in light." I do not know of anything short of *The American Religion* which can be more than a settlement of preliminaries to the genuinizing of our lives. [1915, 682–83]

Small's basis for the new national consensus, a modern secular but covenanted community, required the conversion of America's materialistic individualism into altruistic ethical teamwork:

As a sociological proposition, the initial problem of American civilization is how to fill all sorts and conditions of men with this knowledge of the ethical medium in which all relatively advanced progress lives, moves, and has its being. It is the problem of getting every range of life, from the humblest home and the commonest employment, to the largest economic, governmental, scientific, and religious operation, moving in response to this radical ethical impulse, the obligation to make one's self all that one can be made as a factor in the functioning of the whole. [1919a, 273]

In this vision of society, the highest form of altruism was the subordination of self to society, "the obligation to make one's self and all that one can be made as a factor in the functioning of the whole." The similarity to George Herbert Mead's ideas about the relationship between mind, self and society is clear. Mead's ideas are a social psychological restatement of this same idea of the integration of the individual into the covenant, in which the generalized other becomes the moral arbiter for the self. Small's new American religion would not only replace the sectarian schisms of Protestantism but also embrace the new immigrant groups in Chicago and, ultimately, in the nation.

Yet Small, like others before and after him, was aware that the situation of blacks in America constituted a special problem. The inequality of races seemed to make such collective spiritual effort extremely difficult if not altogether impossible. Indeed, Small made this point embarrassingly clear in his analysis of the differential distribution of America's "social resources." He felt that the character traits of self-mastery, self-direction, and self-realization were the most esteemed of the nation's resources. The strength of the nation rested upon having an abundance of these resources. However, "the total of our social resources . . . would be relatively small if our population were made up . . . chiefly of individuals of the type of the plantation negro. The total would be relatively large if our population were chiefly of the type of the early New Englander, or of 'the southern gentleman of the old school' "[8] (1915, 634). Unfortunately, the plantation Negro now loomed large in American society, Small implied, while the influence of the early New Englanders and southern cavaliers had diminished.

Yet Small was not wholly pessimistic about blacks. Their situation only *appeared* to prove that emancipation had been a mistake: "Perhaps this condition sums up now as worse than it was under slavery. Perhaps, however, as a result of the alleged actual regress concealed under the formal progress alleged in the deceptive terms 'emancipation' and 'enfranchisement,' [the Negro] may presently reach a consummation of self-mastering and self-direction and self-realization" (1919a, 264). The Negro too could be admitted into the community, Small affirmed, but the terms of admission would recognize that the deficiencies of his character could be obviated by following the precepts of a socially conscious ethic.

However, the new ethic required revising some of the maxims of the Puritan ethos: "We are becoming conscious of the task of converting the ideal 'Every man the architect of his own fortune' into that of 'every man in his place in building the city efficient and the city beautiful.' We are facing the problem of convincing ourselves that 'God helps those that help themselves' much less than he helps those who most systematically help one another" (1915, 637). The Negro would have his place, particularly in the city beautiful—the hallmark of later sociology at the University of Chicago—not as a victim of the cruel system of laissez-faire—'God helps those who help themselves'—but rather within a community where whites and blacks helped each other. Small was convinced that a common coordination of feelings, sentiments, and opinions was a sine qua non for survival. He did not believe that equality for all members of society could be achieved, but that the life chances for all groups could be improved. Strength lay in national solidarity. Unassimilated minority races would not survive: "Races which are found today within the confines of civilized States, and which can neither consolidate themselves into nations nor become integral parts of nations, must inevitably disappear. Such, for instance, are the Gypsies in Europe, and the North American Indians" (1905, 257).

Small's basic idea was to instill in the individual the sense of character that would integrate self with society. Character and social structure were to be unified and a sense of civic and national unity achieved. The vital question for American society was "whether we can achieve a controlling sense of responsibility of the individual to the whole; whether we can develop a type of citizenship which feels bound to share the common burdens, or whether we must grow apart and disintegrate, because the different groups of us have no care beyond the particular interests of each" (1917, 151).

If social scientific knowledge—as opposed to religious doctrines, political ideologies, sentiments, prejudices, or ignorance—was to become the basic tool for social reconstruction, social scientists would search "not for one element of good, nor for the solution of the problem of life for a single class, but for means by which the conditions of life for all classes may be improved" (Small and Vincent [1894] 1971, 78). Small believed that class and race problems were subject to the same kind of solution: namely, a change in the hearts and minds of men.

NOTES

1. "To this day," Small wrote in 1916,

I have not succeeded in thoroughly revising the opinion I formed of Professor Sumner while reading his *Social Classes* shortly after it appeared in 1883. It came to me consequently as a surprise and a shock that he was thought of as second president of the American Sociological Society. At that time (1907) he was not within my field of vision as even nominally a sociologist. I had forgotten that he had by implication referred to himself as a sociologist in the book which still seems to me a moving picture of what a sociologist should not be. [1916, 732–33n]

2. Small (1916) criticized Ward for the limitations imposed on his social science by his career in paleontological botany, for his Comteanism, and for his evolutionist psychology, which, Small said, "has never been accepted in detail by sociologists who were scrupulous about their psychology." As early as September 18, 1890—two years before he went to Chicago—Small admonished Ward for expressing his "opinion so freely upon religious subjects" and urged him to cease his acerbic assaults on religion so that Christian sociologists "would have . . . no occasion for suspicion of your methods." Ward replied that he "did not write for the feeble-minded." (Stern, 1933–37, 1933, 165.)

3. In his letters to Ward, Small never lost an opportunity to criticize Giddings, to applaud Ward's criticisms of the Columbia sociologist, and to "wonder more and more as I think over Giddings that a man can have been within a call of positive science . . . & appreciate so little of its spirit & method" (Stern, 1933–37, 1935).

4. Two of Small's students provided additional critiques of Marx and Marxism at this time. See Ellwood, 1911; L. L. Bernard, 1913.

5. Gotthold Lessing set a tone for this new ethics of tolerance that would later find resonance in American practice. In his play *Die Juden* he offered as hero a cultural stranger who performs remarkably selfless and courageous deeds and saves a Christian baron and his daughter from more than one dire calamity. When offered the hand in marriage of the lovely lady he has rescued, the stranger admits his Jewishness as both a stigma and a ground for nobly refusing. (See Gay, 1970, 100–01.)

6. According to Ratzenhofer:

> The time will come when the population will have become dense. The struggle for existence will have to be more carefully planned. Then the people of America will be forced to stop and reflect. There will be need of attaching themselves to the several political groups into which their individual interests naturally divide them, in order to gain the reinforcement of the group interest for each one's individual interest. When that situation comes about, the memory of racial extraction may at last be reawakened. The different languages may become the rallying centers for the different interests. Thereupon for the first time will America confront decisively the problem of its national unity [quoted in Small, 1905, 256].

Small rejected this element of Ratzenhofer's argument, despite the fact that he had generally subscribed to the Austrian's central idea about group and creedal interests. [Salomon, 1934] For Small's admitted reliance on Ratzenhofer, see Small, 1916.

7. "It is altogether thinkable that Manu, and Buddha, and Moses, and Isaiah, and Jesus may each have made, in some more or less important particulars, unsurpassed and even unsurpassable contributions to permanent and universal world-consciousness. . . . It is probable that when the barbarian superimpositions upon insights of Jesus have been cleared away, the actual content of Jesus' consciousness which will be recovered will hold a key position in the final world-consciousness" (Small, 1915).

8. To the best of our knowledge this is the first statement by a major sociologist that the North and South had reconciled the differences that led to the Civil War at the expense of the Negro. Henry Hughes's totally institutionalized utopia could accommodate the Negro in a manner that northern Protestant sociology could not.

CHAPTER 13

Toward Moral Brotherhood: Robert E. Park and the Chicago School

Robert Ezra Park, William Isaac Thomas (1863–1947), and George Herbert Mead separated themselves from the explicit Christian gospel that had guided the work of Albion Small. While there were significant differences among them in emphasis, starting assumptions, and direction, they shared a common concern for the problems of individual morality and the brotherhood of humankind within the framework of an emergent urban and industrial civilization. Park saw the city and civilization as a great crucible in which all the races of mankind would ultimately become brothers. Mead attempted to locate the mind and the self in the social process and believed that both morality and conscience are conditioned by interaction with the values of American civilization. Thomas attempted to locate the fulfillment of the human personality in human wishes and needs that transcended specific civilizations and cultures. Their intellectual responses were informed and otherwise affected by conceptions and understandings that with varying degrees of sublimation, transvaluation, and secularization, were derived from the Protestant heritage.[1]

THE PROTEST AGAINST PROTESTANTISM

Robert E. Park was part of a generation of American thinkers who attempted to transcend some of the basic values of their own civilization. He stated his earliest dreams for intellectual and personal liberation as a quest: "I made up my mind to go in for experience for its own sake, to gather into my soul, as Faust somewhere says, 'all the joys and sorrows of the world'" (Baker, 1973). In his desire to experience life in all its vitality, Park was similar to other cultural rebels of his generation who wished to shed the constraints and pieties of small-town American Protestant culture and morality.

That generation turned for moral support to such writers as Freud, William James, Nietzsche, Shaw, Ibsen, Dostoevsky, and Bergson. They sought an intellectual-political stance that would permit them to criticize capitalism and experiment with self-actualization and liberation from social constraints.[2] Park was determined to see and report life; to discover and interpret "the long-term trends which recorded what is actually going on rather than what, on the surface of things, merely seems to be going on" (Park, 1950, iv). Unlike his predecessors in Chicago's department of sociology, he did not think of himself as a missionary of moral uplift.

Park's experiences as a journalist and crusader for the causes of the American and the African black led to his disenchantment with piety and his disillusion with reform. He thought the world was in a period of general institutional crisis and believed he foresaw the consequences for civilization that would arise from war, the garrison state, bureaucracy, imperialism, and the world-wide upheaval of peoples and races. In spite of these dramatic developments, Park could prophesy an ultimate world brotherhood: "I became convinced . . . that I was observing the historical process by which civilization, not merely here, but elsewhere, has evolved, drawing into the circle of its influence an ever-widening circle of races and peoples" (vii). Where Small had thought in terms of a world that could be Christianized within the framework of a Social Gospel, Park believed that the social process itself would resolve problems of racial conflict, social inequality, urban disorganization, and ethnic integration. In place of the Social Gospel, with its overtones of charity and noblesse oblige, Park substituted the workings of a dynamic and inexorable civilizing force.

While at the University of Chicago, along with many of his colleagues, Park committed himself to both the understanding and the re-creation of the city of Chicago. Chicago provided him an opportunity to construct a mundane version of the Heavenly City on the shores of Lake Michigan. Park's secularization of the idea of the Heavenly City occurred in the same period in which William F. Ogburn and his colleagues were beginning their own transvaluation of Christian rhetorics. The differences in perspective between Ogburn and Park represented two of the directions Protestant thought could take. It is perhaps ironic that it was at Chicago rather than Columbia that transvaluations of the Social Gospel should have found their most cosmopolitan and worldly expression. In part, this was true because Park's outlook on the world had been more deeply influenced than Giddings's by European thinkers.[3]

Park's earlier education with Dewey at Michigan and with James and Munsterberg at Harvard oriented his studies toward such specifically American concerns as race, the community, and the city, while his Euro-

pean education gave him a philosophical and historical outlook on international and global problems. The city of Chicago, the American South,
and the Pacific Coast became the strategic sites for researching integrative
processes occurring throughout the world; he made America his laboratory for elaborating his vision of the larger world. The xenophobic varieties of the Gospel, as they had appeared in the works of Giddings, Ross,
Carver, and Lundberg, were absent in his work. For Park the Gospel
message had been transfigured—mundane social processes would produce a world brotherhood.

Park's studies of the bureaucratization of the Prussian military forces,
of the racial and financial atrocities by King Leopold as businessman-king
of the Belgian Congo, and of the Protestant-based assistance to "good
Negroes" in the South, where northern charity hoped to create "a city of
racial peace," revealed new directions being taken by a more deeply secularized Christianity. Modernization, Park felt, had almost irredeemably
compromised Christian ideals and civilization, sunk them in violence and
murder. His concern for racial emancipation had been aroused by the
blood that had been spilled in the Congo and Booker T. Washington's
struggles to avoid bloodshed in the American South. Brought together in
his various studies are the implicit themes that underlie all of his later
work: the crisis of political and moral legitimacy in modern nation states,
the rise of nationalistic, business-oriented imperialism and the responses
it provoked, and the painful interacial accommodations in urban and
colonial settings.

Park rejected the attitude of Protestant moral self-righteousness that he
had first experienced in the small towns of the Midwest. That self-righteousness was in part a defensive reaction to the breakdown in the Protestant mores and folkways that had occurred since the Civil War. Park, who
recognized this theme in Sumner's works, made the absence of deep
cultural roots in the United States a fundamental part of his perspective
for understanding the emerging institutions of urban industrial society.
To take one example, in his doctoral dissertation he characterized the
conditions and consequences of modern crowd manifestations in terms
strikingly similar to those Sumner employed in *Folkways:*

The crowd . . . seldom arises where there is social stability and where customs
have deep roots. In contrast, where social bonds are removed and old institutions weakened, great crowd movements develop more easily and forcefully.
From a sociological standpoint, this explains, at least in part, the significance
of the strike . . . whose first goal is to draw the public's attention to a condition
considered unjust and unbearable by the workers. It is an appeal to the
judgment of the whole because no existing court has jurisdiction. This means
of appealing to the public results in the interruption of normal activity for

large numbers of people. Thus it provides the conditions for a crowd movement and eventually for a popular riot. [Park, 1905, 376–95]

In contrast to European thinkers, who treated the labor movement as
part of class conflicts or a product of socialism, Park considered the conduct of dissatisfied crowds of workers as an aspect of the problem of the
public interest. Like Cummings, he stressed Le Bon's fears about the
crowd. He claimed to see the crowd process manifested in the strike, but
more important, he thought that the strike, labor's major weapon against
employers, reflected a fundamental moral and social instability. Europeans saw in the labor movement a socialist brotherhood of workers; Park
saw the breakdown of the societal brotherhood of man. The residual
moral system of Puritanism that Sumner hoped might provide a basis for
consensual values in the new industrial civilization could not embrace the
world Park had witnessed.

THE WARFARE STATE AND IMPERIALISM

In his dissertation, completed in 1903, Park remarked, "War, a crude
form of social competition, has as its goal . . . the drive for domination
that causes a nation to test its power in war against other nations" (Park,
1972, 53). His neglected study three years earlier of the German army—
"the most perfect military organization in the world"—is an analysis not
only of the bureaucratization of the Prussian armed forces but of the
moral redefinition of the aims of the German nation as a whole. In it he
shows how Germany had modernized its goal of domination by means of
a thoroughly organized and bureaucratized division of military labor,
including the creation of a military intelligentsia—the general staff.[4] He
quotes chief-of-staff General Moltke's claim that the national spirit could
be embodied in war: "In [war] the most noble virtues of men find their
expression—courage as well as abnegation, fidelity to duty, and even love
and self sacrifice. The soldier offers his life" (Park, 1900). War as the
highest purpose of the nation requires the state to embody the national
spirit. In turn, the state becomes "an individual . . . [with] a destiny which
its actual existence serves to realize" (1972, 70–71). Self-sacrifice for the
preservation of the state becomes the ultimate duty of every citizen and an
expression of the noblest human virtue, the secular equivalent of
salvation.

As a personification of an individual, the German state had asked itself:
"What is necessary in order that the state, in the emergencies that arise,
may defend itself with all the force and all the resources it possesses?" The
answer, given in the plan put forth by generals Schornhorst, Hardenberg,
and Stein after 1806, and carried to perfection by Moltke after 1858, was a
wholesale reorganization of the society such that every individual would

share in the sacrifices required for national preservation. This reorganization entailed democratizing the military services and a rational reordering of education, science, production, and basic human discipline. Democratization took the form of universal military training and conscription—the creation of the citizen soldier, the disestablishment of the officer corps as an exclusive monopoly of the nobility, and the declaration, "instead, that not prestige, but education and natural talent should fix the rank and determine advancement in the army," thus allowing "the position of highest command [to be] open equally to the son of the *bauer* and the son of the prince." Rational reordering took the form of the division of the army into regular forces, the reserves, the *Landwehr* (militia), and, most significantly, the *Landsturm*, the ultimate national reserve of all persons from 17 to 50 capable of bearing arms—in short, the conversion of the German people into a nation in arms; and the promotion of its chief of staff to the position of "Commander-in-Chief in time of war," subject only to the authority of the king and the strategic intelligence provided by the German general staff. This reorganization made possible the establishment of a meritocratic garrison state led by a bureaucratic militaristic intelligentsia. The militaristic ordering of society democratized the distribution of sacrifice and eliminated feudal inequalities (Park, 1900, 376–95). Every German in effect became a member of a new national church. The religious ethics that had helped to transform feudalism into capitalism were now themselves transformed into a civil religion, with generals as its ministers.

Park detailed the effects that this new state organization would have on German education, on the military bureaucracy and its leadership, and on criteria for the allocation of prestige. The opening of the officer corps to educated and talented men regardless of background or birth required the opening of new military schools in which such knowledge could be acquired, strategic and tactical talents demonstrated, and official certification of one's ability obtained. Restratifying military rewards was accompanied by the specification of duties for each rank and by special training for them. Meritocracy in the military led to a new kind of army in which achievement was the sole basis for promotion: "Henceforth, position and rank were to be left to the decision of a merciless and impartial competition that spared no man" (1900). The democratized military had in effect become a calling. Recognition of diligence in that calling substituted the judgment of military superiors for God's.

The ultimate consequence of the military reorganization of German society, Park perceived, was the creation of a garrison state[5] prepared to wage all-out war on civilian populations as well as enemy forces. Park laid bare the organizational principles and conditions that would usher in the century of total war (see Aron, 1955). He located the new conception of war enunciated by Moltke in a speech to the Reichstag:

In a war begun, the greatest benefit is to end it quickly. To that end, it should be established that all means without exception are good, no matter how odious. I do not agree with the declaration made at St. Petersburg, that the weakening of the enemy's forces constitutes the only proper method of warfare. No; we should direct our attack against all the means and resources that the enemy possesses—against his finances, his railways, his food supply, even his prestige.

The idea of total war was based not only on what Park called the "ancient Teutonic faith in the trial by battle" but also and even more significantly on a transfiguration of religion: "War [according to Moltke] is an institution of God, a principle of order in the world." In Moltke's eschatological vision the force of God achieved its aims through the force of arms (1900). War, directed by the rational intelligence of man, would accomplish God's ordering of His Kingdom on earth.

The new military intelligentsia embodied in the general staff, Park observed, differentiated sharply between the mental work of military planners and the physical efforts of the combat soldier. It was in the arena of command that the outcome of war would be determined. Moltke, the bureaucratic genius of the general staff, believed that "the next war will be a war in which strategy and command will play a leading part. . . . Our strength will be in the command, in the directive—in a word, in the general staff." The new German army was a giant organism with a centralized brain located in Berlin and its limbs strategically quartered throughout the state. Moltke had converted God into the Supreme Commander with the general staff as his ministry.

Park's essay addressed some of the most profound problems affecting the application of Christian morality to modern society. In German society the Christian ideal of the brotherhood of man had been subordinated to the national ideal of the otherhood of the enemy. The expedience of war gives rise to moral expedience, and an independent Christian morality had been eliminated as a factor in international affairs.

Park extended his interpretation to the moral problems attendant upon the introduction of capitalism and imperialism into the non-Western world in turning his attention to the Congo Free State. As recording secretary for the Congo Reform Association, he examined the personal administration of King Leopold II of Belgium in the Congolese colony in Africa (see Raushenbush, 1979, 36–42). A peculiar synthesis of traditional authority and capitalist enterprise accounted for the special immorality of King Leopold's administration of the Congo. "A new figure looms large in the horizon of Europe! A figure strange, fantastic, and ominous—the king who is capitalist, *le roi d'affaires;* the man who unites in himself the political and social prestige of a reigning monarch with the vast material power of a multi-millionaire" (1906, 624). Emphasizing the special power that flowed from combining absolute authority with unlimited finances, Park contrasted Leopold with John D. Rockefeller. If Rockefeller had somehow become permanent president of the United States, if he had used his office to increase his wealth, if he had wrested personal control of America's colonies—Puerto Rico, the Philippines, Santo Domingo—from the administrative bureaucracy that ordinarily governed them, if he had converted the colonized peoples into something between tenants and serfs—then and only then would he have achieved the position and exercised the power already in the hands of Leopold II, who in the "thrifty little country of Belgium . . . is king, business manager, and general superintendent" (1906, 624). Leopold II became "a royal Captain of Industry" as part of a shrewd resolution of the problem presented to him in 1865 when he became the constitutionally limited monarch of "a little kingdom, made up of heterogeneous elements, Catholic and Protestant, Germanic and Gallic, patched together and presented to his father by the Powers in 1830" (1906, 632). Belgian imperialism could be exercised without any moral or ethical constraints.

Leopold exploited the Congo not for personal benefit, Park saw, but as an act of dedicated stewardship for kingdom and God. King Leopold II was a virtual Puritan who arose at 5:00 A.M. each day, worked diligently on state papers and international finance, punctuated his labors with brisk walks, ate plainly and lightly, drank only pure water or warm tea, and conducted all matters by the clock. Neither his work space nor his private rooms were opulent. "The chamber in which he passed the night shows none of the refinements of an effeminate luxury. The furniture is simple and not for show. The bed is that of a soldier rather than that of a king and a millionaire." And, Park concluded, "the whole atmosphere . . . reflecting, as it does, the dominant note in the king's character, is quite middle class" (1906, 625). Park had linked entrepreneurial Protestant asceticism and middle-class propriety to capitalist imperialism.

How was it possible for a nation that called itself civilized to condone the atrocities committed in the service of Leopold's capitalist imperialism, Park asked? Despite the world-wide publicity campaign, designed to arouse the conscience of humanity (1906a, 763–72), staged by Park (1906a) and other members of the Congo Reform Association (see Louis and Stengers, 1968, 158–70; Inglis, 1973, 19–106), the moral-minded Belgian middle classes did not condemn the king's excesses. Park explained this apathy in light of the peculiar character of capitalism and the public attitude toward its bureaucratic entrepreneurs. "Leopold says that the results [of colonizing the Congo] are civilization. The missionaries say they are Hell. *But everybody admits they are profitable*" (1906, 632). Leopold, he pointed out, was more of a general manager than a king. "The fact of the matter is that it is easier to sit tight and not murmur under a General Manager than it is under a king or any other form of government. . . . We ask only one thing of a General Manager—dividends. The crucial question is: 'Has he the goods?'" (633). The managerial ethic of the modern corporation or the corporate capitalist kingdom separates the manager from responsibility for his deeds. The profitability of the imperial enterprise could be admired by all who were its beneficiaries, and took precedence over its immorality.

Another moral compromise derived from the competition between Protestant and Catholic missionaries. Park's zeal for reform abated when he realized that the jurisdictional struggle for the souls of the Congolese natives meant more to the members of the Congo Reform Association than the reforms themselves. This discovery did much to reinforce his distrust of Protestant social reformers. Connecting imperialism, the missionaries, and the middle classes, he pointed to the relation between religion and the interests it might serve on the international stage. He evaluated missionary endeavor by its objective consequences rather than by the intentions its practitioners voiced.

In his analysis of the relationship of modern capitalism to imperialism and racism Park had formulated a thesis of the interlock between business, the media, managerial bureaucrats, and religion. He placed little hope in the social reform that this constellation of elements might produce, but he did not abandon his own effort to find a moral solution to the problems of modern civilization. In a world rent by war, imperialism, racial conflict, and national divisions, Park put his faith in "foreign missions and . . . other cultural agencies in this field . . . [whose function] is to bring those people who are already in physical contact with one another into . . . more intimate personal and cultural association—not, to be sure, of a single sect, but at any rate of a single world religion" (Park, 1924, vi). Religion ultimately could provide a moral foundation for a world brotherhood of humankind.

A MORAL FOUNDATION FOR RACE RELATIONS

Park's analysis of the total state and capitalist imperialism made him critical of most of civilization's central institutions and historical tendencies. When linked to capitalism the social ethic of Protestantism had resulted in racial barbarism, technocratic managerialism, and the centralized bureaucratic state. But despite his pessimistic view of the world, Park believed that the immorality of modern civilization could be overcome. He hoped that inexorable social processes would transcend the moral compromises into which the Gospel ethic had been pushed by its own secularization. Park rooted his solution in democratic and equalitarian sentiments of the local community, in a cultural ideology that romanticized the common man who lived on the land, and in the inevitable intermixing of races and cultures.

Park believed that character, culture, and civilization were rooted in the interaction of soil and people. As early as his Congo investigations (1905) he noted; "The race issue in its most concrete form, that is, in the case where you have not merely the race, but its appropriate environment, the soil on which it lives, . . . [is] an element in the problem." This naturalistic orientation, with its focus on indigenous areas of settlement, found its way into Park's sociology of the Negro community in the South and of immigrant communities in the city.[6]

"In the great cities and outside," Park stated in a Founder's Day address at Tuskegee Institute in 1942, the United States "is made up of little racial and cultural units, existing in, but not wholly incorporated into, a life of the total community"[7] (Matthews, 1973, 62). These islands of ethnic and racial solidarity, living together symbiotically—a condition Park later dubbed "accommodation"—survived through intercommunity cooperation and the formation of a subsociety of their own.[8] It was this brotherhood of locals that was the starting point for constructing a moral world, and, Park believed, interactions within and between them should not be forced by external agents. Those who interfered in their affairs disrupted the natural social processes. Just as the missionaries, meddling in Africa in the name of uplift, contributed to the moral subversion of the very peoples they sought to save,[9] so white philanthropists and educated black leaders (Park had W. E. B. Du Bois and Monroe Trotter in mind), seeking to liberate rural southern blacks, succeeded only in patronizing and overwhelming them. "One thing that reconciles the leaders to segregation and keeps the Negro leaders adapted to segregation is that in every movement in which they represent whites, they are controlled by whites" (quoted in Hill, 1953). Each community must generate its own leadership from within: Negro leaders obtained much greater prominence when they were able to represent and control their own people. Park therefore opposed all those processes of colonial administration, absentee leadership, and outside penetration of a community that might interfere with its indigenous moral development. Racial and ethnic conflict could be resolved and civil order achieved if each community reached a condition of mutual cooperation among its own members and made its accommodation with the outside world.

Park developed and documented this hypothesis in two studies in which he sought to locate the social values that would produce institutional arrangements of racial accommodation: one in 1905 of the separate black community of Columbia Heights in Winston Salem, North Carolina; and the other, three years later, of Tuskegee Institute's mission station to rural black families (Park, 1905, 1908). In these communities Park discovered the effectiveness of the values of self-sufficiency, hard work, and inner-worldly asceticism, for economic development, community improvement, and interracial peace.

Columbia Heights, founded in Salem in 1752, was "an old Moravian settlement, . . . one of those many communities that the missionary enterprise of Count Zinzindorf and his followers have scattered over the earth, in which thrift and industry have united with pure religion to give the world a true example of the 'Simple Life'" (1905, 898). Established to "carry Christianity to the Indians and negroes," the Moravian church community took the black children into its Sunday school, and, though as adults these men and women entered other Protestant denominations, "this kindly people . . . [was] well-disposed to efforts of the colored people to better their condition" (1905, 898). As missionaries, the Moravians believed in the superiority of their Protestant values and expected others to adopt them. Park admired the fact that the Negroes in Columbia Heights had internalized these values. Columbia Heights was a city of racial peace that revealed the triumph of religious creed over racial division.

Blacks in Alabama, on the other hand, were the despised element in a racial caste system. "To say that the Negro is not assimilated means no more than to say that he is still regarded as in some sense a stranger, a representative of an alien race" (Park, 1930, 2:282). No missionaries were available to aid in the regeneration of the Negroes in Alabama. Booker T. Washington had enunciated an alternative method for black redemption in his famous "Atlanta Compromise" speech in 1895. It proposed a two-step approach to black liberation, placing acquisition of an economic foundation ahead of achieving political rights and accepting social segregation as the price of interracial peace. It approved a separate black community at the same moment that it looked forward to biracial participation in the industrial and other economic sectors (Washington, 1903, 5–6). Washington laid out a practical program for southern blacks based on thrift, agriculture, mechanical arts, small business, and the ethics appropriate to them, and founded a university at Tuskegee dedicated to Negro uplift through the inculcation of these values. Tuskegee, Park understood, was the secular counterpart of "that most modern expression of the missionary spirit, the University Settlement," attempting to combine moral uplift with economic advance. Hard work, frugality, personal hygiene, and individual initiative constituted a moral kit of credentials by which blacks could "prove" their right to be part of a secular covenant rooted in Protestant virtues.

Tuskegee in effect provided new forms for the more benevolent aspects of the despotic ethical program that had been advanced by Henry Hughes, combined with the docile, hardworking stance associated with Edward Cummings's ideology of the tank. Tuskegee's program adapted the racial folkways of the postbellum South to the technicways of the northern Social Gospel. Washington did not entertain grandiose utopic

visions but rather located Negro redemption in everyday economic activities, which were to be the starting point for a practical politics aimed at
securing equal rights.

THE DIALECTICS OF RACE AND CLASS

Park's sociology of races, classes, and the city was part of his larger idea of
a dialectic between civilization and culture.[10] Urban processes would
erode traditional rural, ethnic, and folk cultures, but would not eliminate
them. Culture for Park always referred to local, ethnic, religious, or sub-
national ways of thinking and acting.[11] The rationalization of thought,
the division of labor, and an impersonal money economy in the metropolis led to ever-increasing individuation (see Park, 1950, 15–23).

The form of any temporarily fixed social order could be interrupted
and broken down by migration, urbanization, and commerce. Park's Congo studies and his analyses of Negro life in the American South illustrated
the dilemmas and contradictions of such cultural and societal collisions.
The city was seen as a congeries of "natural areas," places where local
cultures, ethnic communities, and racial solidarity might flourish for a
time, but eventually would succumb to the inexorable force of civilizational processes (Park, 1919).

The dialectic of civilization and culture added a new voice, a special
nuance, in each epoch.[12] In the present era, as Park saw it, the civilizational struggle to realize its form against the resistances of local, ethnic,
and class cultures would resolve one aspect of the Social Question: race
and labor. Marx's class struggle became part of the general civilizational
dialectic of social forms, of which the race struggle was an equally significant component. Park's race relations cycle and Burgess's hypothesis of
the concentric zonal growth of the city provided in their separate and
intersecting dynamics a slow, patterned sequence of the general historical
cycle (see Park, Burgess, and McKenzie, 1925; Burgess, 1926). The race
relations cycle—contacts, competition, accommodation, and eventual assimilation—was continuous, until a single race would emerge.[13] When
race relations became a feature of city life, it perforce became intertwined
with the processes of concentric urban expansion and social mobility. As
different races and ethnic groups "invaded" a newly opened neighborhood, they succeeded another racial or ethnic group that had moved out
of the area and up the social ladder. Such urban population movements
had an order that could be perceived in the long view as the working out
of the civilizational process in which ultimately all groups would move out
and upward, until all had achieved full incorporation within an international covenant.

Park's dialectic of civilization and culture addressed itself to the Social

Question in universal terms: classes could not develop until all the "diverse and distant peoples of the earth [were brought] together within the limits of a common culture and a common social order." Unlike Marx's theory, which postulated a proletarian world revolution that would eliminate classes, Park's required prior elimination of the struggles between racial and ethnic groups:

> The same forces which brought about the diversity of races will inevitably bring about, in the long run, a diversity in the peoples in the modern world corresponding to that which we have seen in the old. It is likely, however, that these diversities will be based in the future less on inheritance and race and rather more on culture and occupation. That means that race conflicts in the modern world, which is already or presently will be a single great society, will be more and more in the future confused with, and eventually superseded by, the conflicts of classes. [Park, 1939, 41]

Park's conception of secular historical processes is consistent with Christianity's moral, humanitarian, and brotherly ethic. The community becomes a natural moral region in which a limited brotherhood thrives in the midst of industrial, bureaucratic, urban society. Originally limited to kinship, ethnic, and racial communities, this brotherhood will spread to embrace all races and peoples in a single civilizational covenant. However, the elimination of racial barriers would reveal another barrier standing in the way of true brotherhood: the class struggle. Park's dialectic of history ends rather than begins with class conflict.

NOTES

1. W. I. Thomas, despite his subsequent renown, played a marginal role in Chicago's sociology department before being fired in 1918. In our discussion of Chicago sociologists we use Park as a crucial case to exemplify the development of that school's orientation and later history. We have elected to treat the work of Mead in the context of our discussion of the sociology of Herbert Blumer (chapter 14).

2. Daniel Aaron's description of the revolt against Puritanism by Max Eastman, Floyd Dell, and John Reed, in his book *Writers on the Left* (1977, 8–9), is also applicable to Park:

> By Puritanism, they meant "repression," "bigotry," "prudishness," "Comstockery," attitudes which they attributed to dry and arid New England, and they detected its confining influence in politics, economics, religion, education and art. . . . The Young Intellectuals felt no pity toward these [Puritan] formulators of the American mold and even less for the genteel men of letters, with their White Protestant, Anglo-Saxon, "schoolmarm" culture who applied their absolute moral values as rigorously to poetry as they did to politics. In contrast the young intellectuals intended to be "freely experimental, skeptical of inherited values, ready to examine old dogmas, and to submit afresh its sanctions to the text of experience. . . . This was the program of a generation trained in the pragmatism of William James with its sympathetic receptivity to emotion and innovation, and in the instrumentalism of John Dewey, which provided a basis for "social and intellectual reconstruction."

3. Park completed his doctoral studies in Germany in 1903. There his work was influenced by Georg Simmel ("it was from Simmel that I finally gained a fundamental point of view for the study of the newspaper and society. . . . With the exception of Simmel's lectures I never had any systematic instruction in sociology"); Windelband ("he described philosophy as a 'science of sciences', fundamentally a science of method based on a history of systematic thought. There is, in my opinion, no other way of getting an adequate conception of scientific method"); the economist Knapp ("his lectures on the development of agriculture and particularly his accounts of the German peasant and the German peasant community . . . had given [me] the best possible introduction to an understanding of the plantation Negro"); the geographer Hettner ("who . . . led me to the conclusion that every student of sociology should have to know geography, human geography particularly, for after all, culture is finally a geographical phenomenon"); and by his reading of Hugo Munsterberg, whom he had met and admired at Harvard ("the approach presented in this study ['Masse und Publikum,' Park's doctoral dissertation] is that of Wilhelm Windelband and Hugo Munsterberg").

4. This point would later be noted by Thorstein Veblen, who saw that the general staff had combined the methods of modern social organization with the aims and atavisms of a feudal dynastic state (Veblen, 1917).

5. Park did not use the term *garrison state*. We have adapted it from Harold Lasswell, "The Garrison State" (1968).

6. This attempt to ground the moral order in nature was to lead Park's students to carry out a number of sociological studies of urban ecology. Currently, ecological studies have been revived in both sociology and anthropology, but the new ecologists seem to have forgotten the original connection of ecological studies to the moral foundations of social order.

7. Park's idea of the "little racial and cultural unit" was developed by Robert Redfield, his student and son-in-law, in a series of books culminating in *The Little Community* (1960). Redfield's works have been conventionally classified as anthropology. Anthropologists have not ordinarily recognized that his theoretical perspective on communities and cities derives from this sociological tradition.

8. It was precisely these elements of intracommunity cooperation that inspired W. I. Thomas to team up with the Polish sociologist Florian Znaniecki to explore the community institutions of Polonia, the Polish community in Chicago. (Thomas and Znaniecki, [1918–1920], 1958).

9. Park was to discover that his work for the Congo Reform Association was not unconnected to the situation of blacks in the United States. The Congo question had become embroiled in the debates over the treatment of American blacks after Emancipation. "One American gentleman," reported E. D. Morel, founder and historian of the Congo Reform Association, "sent me an elaborate scheme whereby the United States Government was 'to become interested in the purchase and real freedom of the Congo State and dump its negro population into the Congo Basin'" (Louis and Stengers, 1968, 98).

10. For an early statement combining his civilizational thesis with Washington's toiler ethic, see the article Park wrote but published under Booker T. Washington's name, "Inferior and Superior Races" (1915).

11. Park attributed a nostalgia for folk culture to the popular mind; the tendencies and effects of civilization, on the one hand, were given the force of an historical law. This duality is illustrated in his remark about the fate of San Francisco's Chinatowners. At once inhabitants of an island of exotic culture afloat in the sea of urban civilization and a "nuisance [because] of their tong wars" and other racial eccentricities, "[t]he Chinese population," he wrote in 1926, "is slowly declining in the United States, but San Francisco, at any rate, will miss its Chinese quarter when it goes." (Park, 1926, 196)

12. One of the troubles of contemporary sociology arose when Park's students took his formal sociology too literally and, worse, misread or neglected altogether the dialectic between sociology and society that adumbrated all of his work. All too often they concentrated their efforts on natural history, and when actual happenings showed it to be conjectural— i.e., nondescriptive and unpredictive—they introduced *ad hoc* variables to explain the discrepancies.

13. E. Franklin Frazier, Park's student and disciple, eventually perceived the methodological limitations of his mentor's commitment to an unfalsifiable hypothesis (see Frazier, 1961; see also Lyman, 1972, 55–67).

CHAPTER 14

A Secularization of the Sociological Perspective: Herbert Blumer

Herbert Blumer broke away from religiously derived concepts. Infused with an antipositivist and antibehaviorist stamp (see Blumer, 1940; 1954a), his work stresses the interaction between character and social structure. Social relationships have two intersecting histories: the decisive events that shape and reshape the world in which they are embedded and the elements of the past that actors bring with them to define their own situation.[1] Within this framework Blumer focused on all of the major substantive problems in American society that had been of concern to American sociology since its inception, including those of race, industrialization, mass communications, social interaction, the constitution of the self, ethics and morals, and the problems of macrosocial order.[2]

RACE RELATIONS IN THE UNCOVENANTED COMMUNITY

Blumer transformed Park's theory by separating race relations from a formal linear sequence and from any "historical necessity":

> Any theory of race relations which seeks to gain scholarly creditability must obviously be able to cover and explain the significant happenings . . . in the empirical world of race relations. This means that the theory must be able to identify races and the relations between races; it must be able to handle . . . the diversity of relations existing between races; it must be able to explain the variations and shifts that occur over time between any two racial groups; and it must be able to analyze the interplay of . . . racial factors and other factors in actual ongoing group life. [Blumer and Duster, 1980, 221]

While in his other works Blumer uses such terms as *contacts, competition, accommodation,* and *assimilation,* he treats these not as an irrevocable pattern of development but rather as forms that might temporarily be constituted in various places and different times. "We should clearly understand that . . . the body of race relations is [not] uniform or constant" (Blumer, 1965). Nor can race relations be reduced to the psychology of racial prejudice or the fixity of individual attitudes in any human population. "Attitudes enter into behaviour," he conceded (1958), "but [they] do not account for the behaviour." The "explanation of race relations," he asserted (1955), "must be sought in social conditions and historical experience."

Disappointed by the failure of the assimilative process to have absorbed most of America's minorities and by the apparent insolubility of the "Negro question," sociologists tended to view the issue as a social psychological problem, narrowing it to the study of attitudes held by members of one race toward another.[3] Although the attitudinal survey as a one-sided orientation toward the subjective aspect of human relations had been given impetus in sociology by W. I. Thomas's 1904 distinction between the individual's attitude and the "objective" value[4]—an approach Blumer criticized in his doctoral dissertation in 1928—it became the predominant approach in race relations during the 1930s and 1940s (see e.g., Simpson and Yinger, 1959). Combining Freudian concepts with questionnaire surveillance and clinical interviews, the psychological approach to race prejudice reached its apex in 1950 with the publication of a mammoth research report, *The Authoritarian Personality*, by a member of the Frankfurt School, T. W. Adorno, and his colleagues. Blumer (1939) had opposed such unilateral approaches but did not prevail over the chorus of enthusiasts who thought they might save the soul of the nation by salvaging the psyches of its most virulent and pathological racists. Ironically, once it was disclosed that almost everyone was prejudiced—as Gordon Allport (1966) discovered—the solution of the race problem appeared beyond human possibility unless the entire nation received therapy.

Blumer also opposed the position of the functionalists, who supposed that the problems of race relations would be resolved by the inexorable operation of a social system imbued with its own integrative tendencies, predicating their position on the inevitable coming of an inner-worldly interracial covenant.[5] In Blumer's view, racism was neither a product of an evil individual nature nor the symptom of a sinful world. It would be overcome neither by a sacred millennium nor by the working out of a secular eschatology.

The hierarchical order within which racial relations proceed might come into existence through conquest of one land by the people of another, the dominating group establishing an economic, political, and cultural order that legitimates the relative position and status of the peoples involved (e.g., Anglo-Saxons and American Indians); by the importation of one or more peoples into an already established order of life in which the rights, privileges, and prestige of new arrivals are legally restricted (e.g., blacks, Asians, and southern and eastern Europeans); by the voluntary or involuntary migration of one or more people to an inhabited area in which they must compete with the older established groups for various valued resources (e.g., slaves, exiles, or refugees). In effect, racial relations in the United States arose from all of these modes—the conquest of the Indians, the forced importation of Africans, the solicitation of the labor of Europeans, Asians, and Latinos, and the admission of exiles and refugees.[6] Once the relations between such groups had been established by a political process of discussion, decision making, and dissemination of public opinion, the dominant racial group must also find a way to maintain its position against counterclaims (1958). Hence, the phenomenon of prejudice in race relations, seen as the struggle for position of groups in relation to each other, "has a history, and the history is collective."[7] Attempts to understand race prejudice as an incident in a natural history of preordained human relations or "in the arena of individual feeling and of individual experience" were "clearly misdirected" (Masuoka and Valien, 1961, 227). Race relations were a part of a social organization based on hierarchy and racial group position. The particular relations among races that prevailed at any one time were not irrevocably fixed. Race prejudice was a matter of history and politics, not individual attitudes, psychological predispositions, or predetermined systemic processes.

Blumer offered a new theory of race relations to replace both the nonempirical and the psychologically reductionist orientations he had criticized. Race relations, he argued, are first and foremost a process in which peoples are categorized as belonging to racial groups, and that identification is, in turn, given decisive weight in policies, programs, customs, and attitudes. Status, rights, and life chances are affected by such racial classifications. This classifying process is carried out in the public arena by spokesmen for prevailing interests. The process of establishing and maintaining a racial order is not a once-and-for-all affair but rather ongoing, modified by events and the shifting grounds of interests. Typically, the hierarchical character of race relations fixes for a time one or more dominant groups over one or more subordinate ones. Subordinated groups are caught in either the push toward moving up and into the dominant group or the pull to remain out of and independent from the group of self-proclaimed superiors. The dominant group is caught between maintaining its exclusionary tendency or originating a gate-opening policy that, by carefully monitoring the conditions of entry, justifies the original ideology of the hierarchy while at the same time helping to dissolve its barriers. Blumer's theory is a secular statement, and description of the practices that prevail when the idea of a covenanted Holy Commonwealth is transformed into an ideology of national community that still retains criteria for admission and exclusion.

Blumer (1965a) asserted that the sense of group position could be understood in terms of the "color line," a term first employed by Ray Stannard Baker (1908), which "comes into play when members of the two races meet each other not on an individual basis but as representatives of their respective groups." It "is a collective definition of social position and not a mere expression of individual feelings and beliefs"; it "is not appropriately represented by a single, sharply drawn line but appears rather as a series of ramparts, like the 'Maginot Line,' extending from outer breastworks to inner bastions." The lines were maintained by the entire structure of caste etiquette, residential segregation, social definitions of good and bad "niggers," and ultimately by the use of force and terror—arbitrary justice and the lynch mob.

Since the end of World War II, Blumer (1956) pointed out, the South had been increasingly incorporated into the social, economic, and political life of the nation. One result of this loss of regional and sociocultural isolation was pressure on those echelons of the color line that were in the public arena. "The acquisition of civil rights by Negroes in the South will thus have two stages . . . first being brought abreast of the general level of enjoyment of such rights as exists elsewhere in the nation, and then sharing in the further struggle to extend those rights that is occurring on a national basis" (1965, 329). Race relations in the South were thus governed by the breakdown in regionalism in the United States and by the compromises that dominant groups in the South were forced to make in order to share in the expansion of the national economy.

However, expanding civil rights did not in and of itself dissolve the color line, though "Whites are generally disposed . . . to view the matter in this way." In fact another "band" of the color line "consists of the barriers confronting the Negro in his efforts to improve his economic lot," and the "future of the color line in this intermediate band remains a highly problematic matter" (329–35). Granting civil rights might breech one rampart of the color line without necessarily affecting the economic relations between the races.

There remained what Blumer called "the inner citadel of the color line," the "intimate and private circles, represented by social sets, cliques, private clubs, friendship sets, family circles, courtship, and marriage." Although equalization in political and economic status, should it occur, might be expected to soften the resistance to interracial intimacy, this area lay outside society's formal controls. "Even in a situation of equal social status the Negro group would accommodate to exclusion as a separate racial group—as, indeed, Jews have done in large measure" (335–36). A separate racial identity might be maintained even in a democratic society. Blumer's "inner citadel" preserves a group freedom and a right to collective idiosyncracy.

The repudiation of assimilation as the *final solution* to the race question and the rejection of the race relations cycle as the *natural history* of that question mark the ultimate secular break with sociology's transvalued religious utopias. Blumer's rejection of eschatology and its secular surrogates—Park's utopian assimilation, Parsons's promissory "inclusion" thesis, Adorno's tentative hopes for a society cleansed of prejudice—forced sociology to look at the past and present as the products of human beings acting without divine plan or guidance.[8]

RACE AND INDUSTRIALIZATION

Blumer's open-ended orientation toward race relations also includes a critique of conventional views about the impact on them of industrialization. His analysis takes a relative view of the rationalization process characteristic of industrialization and indicates its differential effects on race relations in various industrializing national and colonial settings. Blumer addressed his criticism to the materialist utopian view, still prevalent in sociological theory, that holds that industrialization will bring down any social order not based on values of universality and achievement.

For Parsons, occupational roles in an industrial society would be rewarded almost proportionally to their functional importance to the system, and race would therefore not figure significantly in the calculation of rewards. For Marx, the class formation superseded and absorbed the problems arising from racial relations, and therefore race members come to identify themselves primarily in terms of their class position. In these theories race, in the long run, "vanishes as a factor which structures social relations. Workers will compete with one another on the basis of industrial aptitude and not on the basis of racial makeup" (Blumer, 1965). Parsons and Marx believed that they had found a sociodicy that would replace theodicies of racial inequality. Blumer rejected both their positions.

Blumer did not accept the idea of an even, progressive evolution. He offered a skeptical view of the rationalizing effects characteristic of industrialization. He pointed out that none of the alleged consequences of industrialization on race relations were proved, and that quite different and varied outcomes could be shown to be just as likely. Industrialization by no means inevitably undermined the traditional or established racial order. "In early industrialisation," he pointed out, "the rational or secular perspective, which industrialism admittedly fosters and stresses, may compel an adherence to the racial system rather than a departure from it. . . . [The] *rational* operation of industrial enterprises which are introduced into a racially ordered society may call for a deferential respect for the canons and sensitivities of that racial order." And, he insisted, "This observation is not a mere *a priori* speculation. It is supported by countless instances of such decisions in the case of industrial enterprises in the Southern region of the United States, in South Africa and in certain colonial areas." Indeed "the rational imperative in industrial operations may function to maintain and reinforce the established racial order" (1956a).

Blumer went on to argue that "the intrinsic structural requirements of industrialism need not, contrary to much *a priori* theorizing, force a rearrangement of the relations set by the racial system" (1960). By the same token, the introduction of rational industrial techniques did not necessarily provoke racial tension. Instead, the "empirical evidence pertaining to this matter presents a very varied picture." The assumption so widespread in industrialization theories—and, incidentally, in Marxist theories about the effects of capitalism on the formation of social classes, of which Blumer's argument is an implicit critique—that rationalization of production and geographic mobility will "open access in such a society to one another's occupations, lines of industrial endeavour, areas of entrepreneural opportunities, and residential areas is not true." If industrialization occurs together with new racial contacts in which relationships are at first vague and undefined, "they come to be defined quickly—defined under the overbridging sway of traditional views of the appropriate position of the races." Racial friction in strongly organized, racially structured industrial societies is more likely to occur, Blumer argued, "at the points of contact between different subordinate racial groups," because in "the reshuffling which industrialization induces, such subordinate groups may be brought into competition at scattered points in the industrial structure with resulting strain and discord." Pointing to such outbreaks of friction as those between Negroes and Mexicans in the United States and between Africans, Colored, and Indians in South Africa, and to the varied modes of accommodation that arise between industrial elites and the peoples brought in to work for them, Blumer concluded that "members of the dominant and subordinate racial groups are not thrown into the competitive relationship that is presupposed by *a priori* theorising." (Blumer, 1965, 235–36)

Finally, Blumer attacked the thesis that industrialization would obliterate the significance of race in modern societies. This claim has in one form or another been one of the most powerful domain assumptions in sociological theory, finding various expressions in the works of Marx (see McLellan, 1972, 178–83), Simmel (1900; 1978, 131–203, 343–51, 419–28), J. S. Mill (see Fletcher, 1971, 215–96) and, more recently, William J. Wilson in America (Wilson, 1978) and Annie Phizacklea and Robert Miles (1980) in Britain. "The view that industrialisation moves ahead naturally to dissolve the racial factor is not borne out by the facts," Blumer wrote; "certainly not in the case of [such] racially ordered societies . . . [as the]

Southern United States, South Africa, and some of the colonial areas."
The facts of history showed that "the hiring and assignment of industrial
workers from subordinate racial groups did not follow the postulates of
industrialism; members of such groups have not found entrance into
managerial ranks; and entrepreneurs from such groups were confronted
by high walls barring them from exploiting opportunities lying in the
province of the dominant group." To those who claimed that the "transfer of the lines of racial patterning to the industrial enterprise" was
"merely a temporary stage in which the forces of industrialisation have
not had opportunity to come to natural expression" and that "with time,
or in the long run, the industrial imperatives would gain ascendency
stripping the racial factor of any importance," Blumer replied: "We do
not know how much time is needed to constitute the 'long-run'; certainly
half a century of industrial experience in both South Africa and the South
in the United States brought no appreciable change in the position of the
races in the industrial structure." On this point Blumer concluded that
the "picture presented by industrialisation in a racially ordered society is
that industrial imperatives accommodate themselves to the racial mold
and continue to operate effectively within it." If there were a set of factors
that would necessarily disintegrate the racial order, it would have to be
found outside of industrial imperatives. (1965)

It would be hard to overstate the implications for social theory of
Blumer's analysis of both race and the relationship between race and
industrialization. Unlike evolutionary thinkers, Blumer freed himself
from the prevailing myths of nineteenth-century progressive, religious,
and romantic ideologies. The idea that industrialism would resolve the
problems of race was merely another secular eschatology.

Like Weber, Blumer, saw that values could be both autonomous and
organized within specific spheres of life. Moreover, he made this discovery within the context of one of the deepest problems in American society—industrialization and race relations. Almost all other thinkers, with
the possible exception of William Graham Sumner, assumed that, given
time, the race question would be resolved within the context of an emerging industrial order, whose integrative processes would also reconstitute
the moral covenant. Blumer, by fundamentally severing the problems of
industrialization and race relations from the several sociodicies to which
they had been attached, placed these problems in a strictly secular sociological framework that offered no hope for ultimate salvation.

INDUSTRIALIZATION AND MODERNIZATION

In the mid-1950s Blumer journeyed to Brazil, where he studied the industrialization process at first hand. The result of these studies was a
series of essays formulating a critique of conventional functionalist and

Marxist thought on the subject. Blumer's position was that it is a fallacy to suppose that industrialization must in the nature of the case have certain definite effects.

Blumer's research on the effects of industrialization is an application of his earlier methodological critique (1956a, 683–90) of the role of the "variable" in sociology: the "idea that in . . . areas of group life the independent variable automatically exercises its influence on the dependent variable is . . . a basic fallacy." What intervenes and is decisive for the actual outcome in concrete instances, is the interpretive process, the forging of a definition of the situation and the organization of attitudes and actions with respect to that definition. Industrialization is a case in point. The dominant sociological theory about industrialization tends to treat it as an independent variable, automatically exercising a specific influence on the dependent variable, social organization. Such procedures are not only methodologically misdirected, Blumer sought to demonstrate, but empirically false.

That "industrialization, by its very make-up, can have no definite social effect" (Blumer, 1960) is the second element of Blumer's critique. Contrary to the conventional theories that have been handed down since Marx, Blumer contended that the belief that "industrialization undermines the traditional order . . . [by] displacing existing occupations, shifting production from the home and the village, producing migration and urbanization, fostering social mobility, introducing monetary and contractual arrangements, arousing new wishes and expectations, and promoting secular and rational perspectives," and the correlative allegation that the consequences of these changes "break down the existing family system, disrupt the prevailing class structure, disintegrate status and role arrangements, undermine paternalistic relations, weaken the established system of authority, transform traditional tastes, and erode established values" are, singly and taken together, "markedly inaccurate" (Blumer, 1964, 129). By announcing his skepticism about the whole of this received wisdom, Blumer virtually invited his colleagues in sociology to abandon the fundamental base from which nearly all their work proceeded and to begin anew—in effect, to reinvent sociology, but this time in accordance with concepts and methods that would be faithful to the nature and character of its subject matter (see Blumer, 1969).

The proposition that the traditional order would disintegrate in the face of industrialization, Blumer argues, took into account neither the diverse empirical realities that lie behind that conceptually vague term *traditional* nor the variety of ordered and organized responses that an industrializing people might make. Although traditional societies vary enormously in the character of the tradition to which they are attached, even more important, they also vary in the degree of their attachment to traditional forms, "great in some parts, moderate in others, and negligible in still other parts" (1964, 131). And the parts of such a society interpenetrate one another in different ways and degrees (Vidich, 1981). The changes introduced by industrialization must be perceived in terms of their interplay with the several parts of society and how workers meet new situations. There are alternative possibilities of great significance for each of the changes introduced:

> Thus the shift in productive functions from the home to the factory may strengthen the family by placing it in a better economic position and permitting parents to devote more attention to the welfare of their children. The migration of people from villages and farms may relieve pressure and distress in such areas. Migrants and their families may find urban conditions of residence to be an improvement over previous conditions of residence, with better opportunities for a less arduous life, for the education of children, and for an elevation of status. Detachment from the extended family may result in a strengthening of the nuclear family, just because it is thrown on its own resources. Adjustments to mobility of employment may be taken in stride as thousands of cases of worker families show. Detachment from paternalistic, feudal, or tribal systems may be a relief from distasteful restraints and an opportunity to forge one's own pursuit of a better life. Participation in a fuller system of contractual and monetary relations may be a means of organizing careers on a more hopeful and solid basis. [Blumer, 1969–70, 57]

Hence, Blumer concluded, it is necessary to recognize "that both the industrializing process and the traditional order are heterogeneous. . . . It is a grievous mistake to presume uniform happenings when industrialization enters a traditional society" (1964, 132). The consequences of industrial penetration into traditional areas cannot be determined in advance.

As Blumer saw it, conventional studies of the effects of industrialization proceeded from a composite, systematic, but a priori perspective, which he outlined as follows:

> There are three fundamental ways in which industrialization brings about a condition of social disorganization: (1) by introducing a strange and discordant framework to which people have to adjust; (2) by disintegrating the traditional order; (3) by releasing sets of new forces which are disruptive. The condition of social disorganization is manifested in (a) a variety of disturbed feelings or psychological disorders, (b) a disruption of groups and institutions, and (c) a variety of more or less violent expressions of protest. [1969–70, 47–48]

Blumer's argument is that this unidirectional analysis assigning weights to specific variables is not faithful to the facts. What happens with the introduction of industrial techniques is quite varied. The newly created labor force, for example, is by no means everywhere made up of rural

agriculturalists living in a custombound society that lacks internal contradiction and is fixed in outlook and habitat. "The recruits . . . may be
tribesmen, dispossessed land owners, members of a rural proletariat,
villagers, city dwellers, or imported aliens" (1960, 10). The situation into
which they enter as industrial workers is by no means uniformly bizarre
and irrevocably disruptive. Members of "the traditional society meet the
situations introduced by industrialization in terms of the advantages and
disadvantages which the situations offer." Making selective usage of the
situation, instead of merely succumbing to or revolting against the al-
legedly alien forces of extramural industrialization, workers "may seize
and exploit the opportunities which the situations offer for the pursuit of
their own interests." In general they "weave divergent patterns of activity
around the industrializing process and bring it inside of the context of
their collective life." It is a "largely mythical notion that industrialization
intrudes as a unitary structural force which pushes aside and displaces the
traditional order" and "false to view industrialization and the traditional
order as naturally standing and moving in opposition to each other." The
contacts of industrialization with different kinds of traditional orders
ought to be perceived as "occasions for diversified accommodations or
diversified modifications for both of them" (1964, 132).

During the late 1950s and the 1960s, as the Cold War accelerated and
peaked, American sociologists were conducting studies of developing
nations throughout the world, and in 1966 Blumer extended his critique
to embrace the "widespread burgeoning of sociological interest in the
topic of social development" (1966a, 3). As in his earlier criticisms of
sociological theory in general and industrialization in particular, he noted
the absence of generic concepts, and reminded his colleagues that, contrary to the rhetoric of positivists about the cumulative character of science and about its autonomy, the new interest in "social development" is
nothing but "a case of sharing in a growing outside concern with the
contemporary position of so-called 'under-developed' peoples." The political scientists had recently become concerned with "political development" and the economists with "economic development," and the sociologists emulated these disciplines by discovering an interest in "social
development."[9] There had been "no break-through in sociological theory, no resetting of research problems because of accumulated findings,
and no other kind of indigenous development to account for this new
interest" (1966a, 3). There had been a growing amount of government
agency-generated research, Blumer would point out a year later, and the
discipline responded to whatever subject area the funding would support—including "Project Camelot" (1967, 153–76), the Department of
Defense-sponsored counterrevolutionary research program that had enlisted hundreds of social scientists and when exposed scandalized the
profession.

"In order to build up generalized propositions centering around the ideas of social development as a process of modernization," sociologists would have to provide "an identification of the characteristic makeup of modern life, and . . . of the mechanisms that bring group life into conformity with this makeup" (1966a, 8). Blumer rejected the stock of sociological concepts associated with the organic analogy, evolutionary theories of change, and the functionalist perspective on society. "No one of the abstract conceptions of society currently accepted by sociologists seems to provide any ground for forming a generic conception of social development. . . . Notions like 'social unity,' 'consensus,' 'social integration,' 'social function,' 'equilibrium of a social system,' 'social control,' or 'social order' are rather hopeless as providing either a goal or a measure of social development" (1966, 6). In addition he charged his colleagues with "neither identifying the goals of social development nor studying the means of their achievement" (1966, 9). Studies of social development were based on the unexamined assumption that the changes being studied moved in a predetermined direction.

Blumer pointed to an even larger theoretical error—the unacknowledged ethnocentrism built into theoretical schemes that held that "the historic experience of Western society in moving into a modern status during the eighteenth and nineteenth centuries . . . is [the model for] . . . the process of modernization among contemporary 'underdeveloped' peoples" (1966a, 9). This issue is not merely normative, nor can it be resolved by recognizing the arrogance of claiming Occidental leadership in modernization: it is conceptual. "The more thoughtful scholars are coming to recognize the importance of the difference in the historical setting in which . . . [modernization] is taking place" (1966a, 10). It is a mistake to assume that the underdeveloped world's ontogeny is a recapitulation of an Occidental phylogeny. Yet, as Blumer pointed out, many sociologists, "are following this line of attack, using such matters as industrialization, urbanization, the formation of political institutions and the shaping of social structures in Western civilization of a century or two ago as the prototypes of social formation among contemporary underdeveloped peoples." But the "modern world which confronts underdeveloped peoples today is very different from the emerging modern world of two centuries ago in Western civilization. Modernization is less a reproduction of the past experiences of other groups and more a preparation for one's own emerging future" (1966a, 10). In effect, Blumer here reminded his colleagues that their modern reintroduction of the discredited Comtean "comparative method" was as misleading in the study of social development as it had been for the history of civilization.

Blumer argued that social effects and consequences are contingent in relation to the particular social milieux in which they occur. For example, industrial technique might be integrated into traditional authority relations, as in Japan, or preexisting despotic bureaucracies might be imposed on industrial organization, as in Russia. No formula existed by which "theory" in itself could predict how a traditional order would receive industrialization, and any general theory of industrialization that purported to supply a priori categories of analysis would foreclose the recognition of data relevant to an understanding of the specific case. Blumer understood this and accepted its consequences. Any sociology freed from a priori reasoning and sacred vocabularies would have to accept an uncertain, unpredictable, and multivalued world. In this perspective, the metaphor of a unified commonwealth (holy, national, or international) and the promise of a secular utopia are abandoned.

THE MORAL FOUNDATIONS OF SOCIAL ORDER

In a world of autonomous and frequently competing values, by what standards could the actions of men be given moral and ethical guidance? In his essays "Science as a Vocation" and "Politics as a Vocation" (Gerth and Mills, 1946, 78–158) Weber attempted to work out the ethical implications of the modern world's moral relativity. Blumer arrived at his formulation of the same problem by an entirely different route—whereas Weber's starting point had been the study of religion and an examination of religious rejections of the world and their directions, Blumer focused on industrialization, work, and character structure in a world in which men already found themselves committed to almost wholly secular values. Like Weber, he located ethics and morality in modern society in social interaction. Blumer saw the quintessential expression of this problem in labor-management relations; he asked, What ethical and moral standards would guide the struggles between competing interest groups?

The relationship between entrepreneurial functions, capital investment, work, and salvation had been central themes in Weber's 1904 work, *The Protestant Ethic and the Spirit of Capitalism*. These themes entered the field of industrial sociology as orientations toward the problems of worker motivation, management–worker relations, the rights of workers, and the relations between workers and other groups in society. At Harvard these issues in industrial sociology had been addressed in Munsterberg's work on vocational tests and industrial morale, which drew in part on Weber's own studies. They were given additional impetus in the famous Hawthorne studies, which had discovered that worker motivation arose less from Protestant ethics than from the social relations that prevailed at the work site. Work was related to social recognition and economic rewards. In secular terms, striving for grace through work had given way to searching for social, psychic, and economic security.

The obverse side of the problem of worker motivation is that of worker dissatisfaction—that is, what conditions might lead the worker to cease his efforts. The strike became a central focus of attention for industrial sociology because it revealed a breakdown in the covenant between workers and employers. From the point of view of the larger commonwealth, the strike seemed to threaten the moral foundation of society; the social compact could not be sustained under conditions of conflict between employers and employees. For this reason industrial sociology focused much of its attention on improving "human relations" in the factory. Since the beginnings of industrialization, the factory had become the site at which men's moral and ethical relationships with each other and with God were put to the test.

Blumer came to his studies of industrial relations from his experience as an arbitrator on major industrial disputes, including that between the United States Steel Company subsidiaries and the CIO's United Steel Workers in 1945.[10] His studies of entrepreneurial organizations, labor–management struggles, the function and control of strikes, and the societal implications of industrial conflict break out of the framework of academic industrial sociology, whose practitioners he regarded as "dreadfully naive with reference to the nature of industrial relations" and who employed "the stock of conventional ideas and modes of research ... [that] are essentially hackneyed, unrealistic and uninspiring" (Blumer, 1947). Industrial relations proceeded according to an inner logic that could not be fathomed by ideological directives, utopian hopes, cultural analyses, the status-conflict outlook, the study of long-term trends, the "human relations" approach associated with the Harvard researchers, or the quantitative studies of attitudes and the construction of sociograms.

"The most noteworthy feature of the relations between workers and management in American industry is that they are dynamic, uncrystallized and changing" (1947, 272). Moreover, these relations are not interpersonal but collective, carried out through representative organizations of workers and managers. Industrial relations, hence, could no longer be analyzed according to the "simple contract between a worker selling his labor and an employer purchasing that labor. . . . That bare fundamental relation has been elaborated in our society into an extensive, diversified, complex and indirect network, of relations in which the individual worker becomes an insignificant and inconspicuous figure. . . . Relations between workers and management become primarily a matter of relations between organized groups" (1947, 272).

Industrial relations could be understood only as relations between organized sectors of society. But precisely because they were "mobile, indirect and [of a] large dimensional character," Blumer likened them to "a vast, confused game evolving without the benefit of fixed rules and frequently without the benefit of any rules." Even their setting was unstable, "shifting and presenting itself in new forms" and putting "strains on the pattern of [the] game." The moves in the game are but "accommodative adjustments largely between organized parties." But "the participants are far from satisfying their respective wishes and objectives in the temporal accommodations which they make to each other" and consequently put "constant pressure on their relations and [look with] an opportunistic readiness to change them." Hence, Blumer concluded, "we deceive ourselves and perhaps engage in wishful thinking when we regard this shifting flow of relations in industry as temporary and transitory, to be followed by a shaking down of relationships into a permanent orderly system." So long as America remained a "dynamic, democratic, competitive society," the "mobile character of . . . [industrial] relations," together with their "degree of tension, . . . rapidity of accommodations, and . . . shifts," would persist (1947, 277). Like race relations, industrial relations promised no harmonious millennium or ultimate resolution.

Blumer made no assumption of a unity of purpose between capital and labor. He did not assume the likelihood of a covenant in which capital and labor would join together in a common endeavor to build the good society. The human relations approach to industrial psychology at least implicitly accepts the covenanted brotherhood; its efforts are directed at restoring or at least preventing the further fracture of that brotherhood. For Blumer no industrial brotherhood could exist; industrial relations are adversarial, and necessarily so, because the two parties have opposed interests.[11] Blumer perceived labor and management as competing organized power groups jockeying for position without fixed rules.

Framing his analysis in terms of the concepts of political sociology, Blumer (1954) distinguished among "codified," "sympathetic," and "power" relationships. The first are governed by "rules, understandings, and expectations which are shared and followed by the parties to the relationship"; the second "are marked by the presence of, and guidance by, personal sentiments and understanding" and may "be found particularly in friendly or intimate relations" but also "between detached, remote, and even alien groups and individuals." Power relations "are set and guided by respective positions of effective strength, . . . marked by an opposition of interests, intentions, and goals, . . . [and characterized by] scheming, maneuvering, the devising of strategy and tactics, and the marshaling and manipulation of resources." Labor–management relations are power relations because they occur within an arena in which "people in pursuit of goals are thrown into opposition to one another, with sanctioned or allowable leeway in the forging of actions to achieve success in the face of such opposition, and where the pursuit is not made subservient to considerations of each other's welfare" (1954, 234–35).

Blumer (1958a) attempted to delineate the pattern of power relations that prevail in the labor–management sector, but his analysis also contained the elements necessary for understanding a society in which almost all groups have come to bargain and negotiate for what they regard as their fair share of social rewards and social participation. Blumer did not assume the existence of either a set of core social values or the need for a social compact among the organized sectors of society.

"Power action" is less conspicuous on the local level, "particularly when local unions enjoy a high degree of autonomy," but it "comes to be pronounced . . . in . . . large international unions which have to function *as single entities* vis-à-vis large corporations, trade associations, and employer organizations." The "power psychology" prevalent here includes "a lively scrutiny of the operating situation to ascertain what threats it holds, what obstacles it sets, what advantages it contains, and what exploitable facilities it yields." With such a psychology in operation among both labor unions and management organizations

> a conspicuous fluidity is introduced into their relations, . . . policies . . . become increasingly subject to compromise, tempering, and redirection under the impact of the passing array of newly developing situations, . . . the relations between tbe parties become tenuous, shifting, and tentative as each views the other and awaits developing action on the part of the other . . . [and, finally] there is an increasing tendency for the power struggle to move over into the political arena. [1954, 238–39]

Each party attempts to exploit the political arena to gain its own ends: through legislation, executive decisions, administrative actions, and the mobilization of public opinion. Other groups in society are then vulnerable to the pressures and manipulations of the vested interests.

The transfer of this power relation to the political arena implied the existence of a referee or a higher judge with the capacity to resolve the conflict. Blumer also saw that "this transferring of the power struggle between organized labor and management from the industrial arena to the political arena marks a major transformation in their relations, with consequences which, while only dimly foreseen, will be momentous" (1954). Here referring to the Taft-Hartley Law, he observed that compulsory arbitration and mediation did not eliminate the industrial problem but only transferred the power struggle to another level. Such political mechanisms could not prevent the strike or insure a resolution of the basic conflict between management and labor. Blumer contended that "the labor strike is indispensable for proper and effective labor–management relations" (1958, 23). Collective bargaining, he insisted, was meaningless and useless unless the union had legitimate recourse to strike when its demands were refused by management. Indeed, "the resort to the strike is . . . natural in arising from a genuine opposition of interest . . . [and] healthy in . . . establishing a workable relation between the parties on an issue on which they are otherwise hopelessly at odds" (1958, 33). By rejecting the idea that the strike was an act of social immorality or a breach of ethical conduct, Blumer introduced an alternative ethical and moral code into industrial sociology. However, he also confronted the problem of supplying an alternative ideological basis for public ethics and morality in societies characterized by large-scale organized groups.

The starting point for Blumer's public ethics was his concern for the public interest—an interest that stands above that of the several vested interests of organized groups that make up the political structure of the society.[12] Park had wrestled all his life with the nature and character of the public interest, exploring its Enlightenment-endowed advantages together with its vulnerability to irrational assaults and emotional distortions by the mass, the crowd, the mob, and the media as these were envisioned by Le Bon and Trotter (see Park, 1904; Le Bon, 1896; 1913; 1924; Trotter, 1916). Blumer also explored its dimensions, distinguishing the public interest from both the private concerns of business, labor, religion, and racial groups and the mass phenomena of fads, fashion, and media. In industrial relations, Blumer located the public interest in the action taken by liberal democratic governments to referee the contests between labor and management, but he understood that the existence of a referee did not solve the problem of ethics unless both parties accepted the rules of play. In the process of exploring this dimension of the public interest, he formulated a further distinction—between the legitimate labor strike carried out for purposes consistent with the employees' inherent interests in job situations, and the unwarranted withdrawal of labor's services for some ulterior purpose. Blumer's theory requires the presence of an authority who can distinguish between legitimate and ulterior interests in behalf of the public good. He recognized, however, that the "line beyond which the public interest is seriously endangered is a matter of judgment and cannot be drawn precisely." Given his image of society as a congeries of competing interests, he could not find an institutional arrangement whereby both the public welfare and the rights of all parties to the competition could be regulated in the public interest.

Nevertheless, there remained the law and the possibility of moving labor–management relations closer to codified procedures. Blumer was not overly sanguine about this matter. Each party to an industrial dispute had not only to satisfy its legitimate needs but also to respond to the pull of ancillary interests that would arise as side products of organization and expansion. The introduction of law into industrial relations was not likely to eliminate the resort to power practices. In the case of management, paternalism might be initiated as a deliberate policy to forestall union organization or mitigate the adversarial situation inherent in employee–employer relations (1951). Labor might utilize the strike "to satisfy extraneous interests," including personal tribute, political advantage, the advancement of political or ideological doctrines, or advantage in business competition. An employer who had rejected or failed to implement a policy of paternalism might exploit the strike to create divisions within a union, to harm a competitor, or to injure a rival union. Recourse to codified law transferred the struggle between labor and management to the courts, where each party would seek to define the law in its own interest.

Every effort to define the concept of public interest pointed to another set of special interests that claimed to represent it. The idea that the central government might play a detached role in representing the public interest was linked with Keynesian doctrine, which assigned to government the role of referee between labor and business (Bensman and Vidich, 1971; Bensman and Vidich, 1976; Vidich, 1980, 1982). In that period, when business had been weakened by the Depression and when labor was organized with the support of the Roosevelt administration, it appeared that the government did indeed represent the interest of society as a whole. In retrospect, however, the compromise between labor and business that was represented by America's version of Keynesian social and economic policy could succeed only so long as both parties would accept the government as a referee. The existence of a public interest presumes a national consensus that overrides group interests. In America such a national consensus has been achieved only in times of extreme national crisis.

Blumer's sociology of power, conflict, negotiations, and bargaining did not look forward to a millennium in which a covenant of cooperating believers would have overcome worldly struggles. His image of society is reminiscent of the relationship of the ancient Hebrews to Yahweh. Bound by the covenant with Abraham to see to the public interest and general welfare of his contractees, Yahweh might be expected to interfere in the name of justice at the appropriate moment, but he could also be called to account for any lapses (see Weber, 1952, 118–24). Unlike the believer in the inscrutable Protestant God, the believer in Yahweh could argue with his God concerning ethics and their violation. Blumer shifted the image of social relations. In effect, in his perspective, they would be governed by the state standing in for Yahweh rather than God. Thus Blumer posed the problem of the locus of morality in the modern state, but he could find no way to insure that the state would in fact administer justice. The state was a creature of interests and had no overarching morality of its own. This was the point at which Weber had left the same problem in his essay

"Politics as a Vocation" (Gerth and Mills, 1946). Blumer recognized and grappled with this problem in his studies of mass behavior and the shifting locus of morality in public opinion.

SOCIAL ORDER AND MASS PHENOMENA

"In folk communities where the forms and scope of life are ordered, mass behavior scarcely occurs, and when it does occur it represents an excursion from the days of such folk life," Blumer wrote in 1935. "The form of mass behavior, as we are acquainted with it historically, is to be found in complex, heterogeneous societies, or in folk societies in a state of disruption" (116). Mass behavior is the central feature of modern society.

Blumer attributed both destructive and constructive consequences to mass behavior. "Things that catch the attention of the mass represent invasions as well as innovations, experiences which do not arise in the texture of local group life and which are not prescribed by local conventions." The interruptions in everyday life created by mass phenomena like "the operation of mass influences can be thought of . . . as tending to disaffect dispositions which are [otherwise] accommodated inside of local culture." But mass behavior has a constructive side as well. It "represents the beginning of efforts to introduce some sort of organization into the area of life touched by mass behavior." Here Blumer pointed to the possibilities of new social moralities: "The very fact that the individual's attention is directed away from local group life means that orientation is being made to the larger world, to a wider scope of existence, and, in a measure, to a new order. . . . Mass behavior seems to represent preparatory attempts, however crude they may be, at the formation of a new order of living."[13] It was in mass phenomena that Blumer saw the problematics of public ethics and social order.

"The mass" is not a definite stratum of society. As Blumer defined it (1935), it is "a population aggregate which cuts across the lines of class, vocational position, and cultural attainment" (114). The arena of mass behavior is outside of local culture; the mass is "a homogeneous aggregate of individuals . . . [who have] no traditions, no established rules or forms of conduct, no body of etiquette adjusting the relations of individuals, and no system of expectations or demands" (118–19). Mass behavior, usually inarticulate and based on vague, confused, and unchanneled ideas, "is frequently capricious and foolish, . . . [sometimes] irrational, disorderly and perhaps vicious, . . . [but at other times] unassembled, quiet, deliberate, selective, brooding, and living in imagination." Mass behavior was always capable of producing new social forms and new codes of conduct.

Mass phenomena included a variety of things and activities. Among these was fashion, a subject to which Blumer devoted considerable attention (see Blumer, 1968; 1969). Fashion was a mass phenomenon—not, as Simmel had supposed, the innovation-emulation-innovation cycle carried on as a status competition between elite and subjacent classes in modern societies—because it partook of the "chief way in which the mass behaves . . . by making choices, selections and adoptions" (Blumer, 1935, 121). Hence, even the prestige of the elite class "does not assure that anything it introduces will become the fashion; instead, its introductions must coincide with the direction of what is acceptable" (Blumer, 1968, 344). In Blumer's conception, fashion represents the radical democratization of society.

Fashion requires both innovation and acceptance. It has something of the character of new regimes that might come into existence by conquest, force of arms, revolution, election, or inheritance but must also be accepted—become legitimate, as the political sociologists say—in order to persevere. However, while regimes may be reactionary, conservative, or traditional "Fashion is always modern; it seeks to keep abreast of the times" (343). "Its origin, formation, and career of collective taste constitute a huge problematic area . . . [for] study" (344). It is a peculiar feature of modern societies, where, "conspicuous in the area of dress, [it also] operates in a wide assortment of fields. Among them are painting, music, drama, architecture, household decoration, entertainment, literature, medical practice, business management, political doctrines, philosophy, psychology and social science, and even such redoubtable areas as the physical sciences and mathematics"[14] (342). Fashion rejects traditional codes of conduct and specifically requires the absence of ideological conviction; it requires, in short, an opportunistic population that does not wish to be left behind. Insofar as modernity lacks any specific content, it is always in the process of being defined in a continuously flowing present. Modern society is placed in the situation of permanent moral ambiguity because morality itself is subject to the dictates of fashion. Consistent standards of morality cannot be maintained, Blumer seemed to say, because modern society is made up of detached and anonymous individuals possessing no culture to evaluate conduct and establish an ethical consensus. Moral standards are shaped by mass media that break down local cultures and introduce fashionable codes of conduct.

It was with this perspective that Blumer approached his study of the relationship between conduct and motion pictures. His film studies grew out of an immediate problem disturbing the relations of the film industry with its clientele, but they also picked up leads and observations from earlier mass media studies by Park and Munsterberg. Commenting on the film's role in breaking down traditional and ethnic solidarities and helping in the inevitable march toward assimilation, Park observed: "The cinema may be regarded as the symbol of a new dimension of our international and racial relations which is neither economic nor political, but cultural" (Park, 1926, 195). In this observation Park followed Munsterberg. Films, as Munsterberg had made clear (1916), objectified the processes of mind, making them available for inspection and evaluation by the masses. Park went even further: since "culture is merely the objective and collective aspect of the inner and personal life of individuals and peoples, and it is in men's minds and in their intimate personal experiences that the most profound and significant changes in the world are taking place today," the cinema might bring "all the peoples of the earth measurably within the limits of a common culture and a common historical life" (Park, 1926, 195–6). The function of the cinema, Park concluded, is symbolic, and, as a symbolic form of communication, cinema "profoundly influences sentiment and attitudes even when it does not make any real contribution to knowledge" (1938). Park saw the purely cultural and ideational potential of the mass media, thus signaling the onset of the modern age of public relations, public opinion, impression management, and propaganda.

Blumer's research on American movies counterposed the mass values of what Park called civilization against the local mores and folkways said to be part of the consciousness of the moviegoer. Carried out in the early 1930s, Blumer's two studies (Blumer, 1933; Blumer and Hauser, 1933) reflected the Chicago school's interest in the interplay between immigrant folk culture and America's mass society. In answer to the basic question, "What is the general influence of motion pictures?" he replied: *"It is a reaffirmation of basic human values but an undermining of the mores. . . .* Motion pictures operate like all agencies of mass communication to turn the attention of individuals outward from their areas of locally defined life." The films affirm such basic human values, or sentiments, as "bravery, loyalty, love, affection, frankness, personal justness, cleverness, heroism and friendship," but they depict these in "social patterns or schemes of conduct . . . [that] are likely to be somewhat new, strange, and unfamiliar." And, Blumer insisted, that is why the films are "an attack upon the local culture." For it is precisely these new forms of life—"colored, so to speak, by the basic human qualities which are placed in them and operate through them"—that "become attractive and understandable, and develop a claim on one's allegiance" (1935, 124).[15] Not only could the media present values as if they were autonomous but they could do so over against the values of the local cultures in which their audiences lived. The media could present a world of competing cultural values and could undermine existing values even where these values were rooted in material or ideal interests.

Blumer pointed out some new social problems that arose because movies had become a basic part of modern culture. The concept of *reverie* was one of them. "The motion picture experience is, itself, a form of reverie—in turn it is a great stimulus and feeder to further reverie." Reverie is the special character taken by the release from everyday reality that is brought about by the intrusive effect of the movie. The consequences of such a release are unpredictable. However, that it had the potential for world building was clear:

> There is an intimate relation between reverie, awakened disposition, and basic taste. The play of reverie, whether ordered as in the motion picture or free as in individual day dreaming, awakens various impulses, furnishes objects upon which they may fasten, sketches schemes of possible conduct, and launches the individual upon vicarious journeying in new social worlds. That this rich play of inner experience has important effects on dispositions and tastes is seemingly true even though the nature of these effects is obscure. [1935, 126]

Blumer's conception of the unpredictable outcomes of reverie suggest that in modern society there is no ethical and moral core to which the individual can turn for guidance. The philosophical pragmatists had always been interested in the moral groundings of society, especially after the processes of secularization had dissipated the religious authority of Puritanism. John Dewey and George Herbert Mead had sought to ground a general morality in education and childhood socialization, but they were unable to locate a code of ethics in anything other than the development of the self. Blumer placed his stress on the problematics of the self that the world of mass communications had opened up. The self, no longer rooted in a faith or guided by a set of fixed moral convictions, was vulnerable to the moral worlds presented by the media. The mass media would become a new agency of public instruction and ethical socialization.

Without core values or any grounds for social consensus, there is no basis for a public morality superior to those of the values guided by self- and group interests. The alternative is a moral consensus based on public opinion. But public opinion is itself plural, reflecting the expression of competing values and interests. The mass media contain the promise of breaking through the several public opinions and forging a mass consensus. However, the morality produced by mass consensus, transient and ephemeral, provides no steady, unambiguous standard for individual conduct. Situating morality in the midst of the stream of action, where presumably it is guided by situational ethics, Blumer took the last step in separating sociology from the rhetoric of its original religious foundations. Having rejected any religious underpinnings for sociology, he investigated historical and existential experience in its own terms. His orientation was thoroughly secular, rejecting the idea that theoretical assumptions can substitute for or function like divine revelation. In his work Blumer not only grounded sociology in a secular perspective; he also challenged the "religious" lines of reasoning of his colleagues, whom he seemed to regard as a sociological clergy.

NOTES

1. Our own position on this matter is fundamentally different from that recently presented by Lewis and Smith (1980, esp. 120–258). Lewis and Smith hold that the principal influence on Blumer was his undergraduate instructor at the University of Missouri, Charles Ellwood; that Blumer's symbolic interaction is a variant of subjective nominalism in contrast to Mead's social realism; and that Blumer is intellectually closer to Thomas and Cooley than to Mead and Peirce. It is worth noting that Blumer (1977) has denied the influence of Ellwood and repudiated the interpretation of Lewis and Smith.

2. One of Blumer's students who followed in this direction is Tamotsu Shibutani, who taught at Berkeley after serving as a participant observer in Dorothy Swaine Thomas's Japanese-American Evacuation and Resettlement Project, carried the symbolic interactionist perspective to the University of California at Santa Barbara, and applied his efforts to general issues in social psychology and race relations and to the residues of the wartime treatment of Japanese-Americans. (See 1966; 1980).

3. Exceptions to this are the disciples of the Park-Thomas approach to the study of race relations, including Doyle (1937); Johnson (1943); Frazier (1957; 1957a); and Hughes and Hughes (1952).

4. Thomas had developed one significant aspect of this point in distinguishing between race prejudice, an attitude, and caste feeling, a product of racial competition (see his "The Psychology of Race Prejudice" [1904], a paper that should be read in conjunction with his "The Significance of the Orient for the Occident" [1907], 111–37. See also Thomas and Znaniecki [1918–20]1958, 2:1831–63).

5. It was this dimension of systems theory and functionalism that made these approaches acceptable to Marxist sociologists, who could construe the brotherhood of races as the prerequisite or the consequence of the brotherhood of the proletariat. By accepting neither psychological nor functionalist theories, Blumer found himself in the same intellectual position that John Cummings had faced when he had to contend with a biological theory of race relations and social development. Just as Blumer argued against the thesis that there was a "normal" state of tolerance, so Cummings disparaged the claim that anatomical features—head size, eye size, skin color—had need of reform in order to resolve the racial question. In his one significant essay on the subject, Cummings (1900) devoted himself to the critical task of clearing the intellectual decks of the claim that some irreducibly obdurate factors—in Cummings's case, the cephalic index—determined to their detriment the nature and quality of social relations among races.

6. For an analysis of America's racial relations that is not inconsistent with Blumer's and that proceeds from the point of view of a comparison of the positional situations of Europeans, Africans, Indians, and Asians, see Lyman, 1977.

7. As a "sense of group position," race prejudice emerges as a form of social hierarchization embracing "four basic types of feeling: (1) a feeling of superiority, (2) a feeling that the subordinate race is intrinsically different and alien, (3) a feeling of proprietary claim to certain areas of privilege and advantage, and (4) a fear and suspicion that the subordinate race harbors designs on the prerogatives of the dominant race" (Blumer, 1958).

8. To do this completely sociology would have to accept the existence and plurality of forms of evil as permanent features of worldly life. For an analysis of this point, see Lyman, 1978, 269–76.

9. Blumer's critique of his colleagues was even harsher than our text suggests. He bluntly stated, for example, "It is clear, that in embracing the notion of social development, contemporary sociologists have fallen under the lure of a term." Social development was merely the current idea that had cachet attached to it. "Lacking markedly any clear idea of what it means [the sociologists] use it as a prestigeful rubric to cover an array of unrelated studies and to conceal a state of obscure thought. They seemed to wish to share in the luster that the term conveys in its current fashionable use" (Blumer, 1966a). Blumer also suggested that they engaged in such studies simply because research funds could be obtained if one used the appropriate terminology in research proposals.

10. "Herbert Blumer" reported *Business Week* in its July 21, 1945, issue, "associate professor of sociology at the University of Chicago, is the impartial member of a new three-man arbitration board for settling disputes. . . . With Blumer, ex-linesman of the Chicago Cardinals [pro-football team], will sit Walter J. Kelly of Tennessee Coal and Iron, representing the corporation, and Eugene Maurice, the union. In the eight years U.S. Steel had had a contract with C.I.O., no permanent board was set up for lack of issues to keep it busy. Its creation now suggests that U.S. Steel and the union intend to make increasing use of the contract's arbitration provisions."

11. In the case of management two interests predominate: directing the work force, and operating the enterprise in a profitable manner. Blumer pointed out that, in contrast to the position taken by Marxists, these managerial interests are by no means confined to capitalistic enterprises or bourgeois societies. In "contemporary worker-states, like that of Soviet Russia, the management of industrial enterprises is juxtaposed to the workers in the enterprises." There, too, "working rules must be established, hours fixed, work quotas set, wages established, assignments given, and work supervised." "These," he went on, "provide abundant sources of dissatisfaction and grievances among employees." Moreover, whatever ideological rhetoric might be used to cover up the fact, "all of these phases of operation are covered by a need to have the industry operate profitably, i.e., yield returns equivalent to or in excess of costs." Such a "financial and accounting requirement removes, further, the possibility of the management of Soviet industrial enterprises acting primarily in behalf of the interests of workers."

Even in worker-owned businesses, such as the Cast Iron Pipe Company of Birmingham, Alabama, management and workers have separate interests. Blumer pointedly quoted a worker-owner from that plant who was busy organizing a labor union: "Sure, this is my plant, but somebody has to protect my rights as a down-trodden working stiff against my privileges as a bloated capitalist stockholder." (Quoted in Blumer, 1958a, 3, 9–11.) Blumer's prescient observations about industrial relations, bureaucracy, and authority in socialist societies anticipates by quite a few years the belated recognition of bureaucratic elements in communist societies by Marxist scholars (e.g., Hodges, 1981).

12. It is possible that Blumer's concern for the public interest is a transvalued version of Jewish ethical concerns as they have been expressed in sociology. (Cf. in this regard Selznick, 1957; Lipset, 1960.) The age-old Jewish concern with law, contracts, bargaining in good faith, and written agreements—originating in the Yahwist orientation to God—also found expression in Philip Selznick's attempts to produce a sociology of responsive law (Selznick, 1959; Nonet and Selznick, 1978). Blumer's interest in codified relations and in bringing the illegal and unwarranted elements of industrial relations under the jurisdiction of a civic, impartial referee—a secular, law-abiding equivalent of Yahweh—is another expression of the tradition.

13. In 1935, Blumer had told the American Sociological Society that mass behavior "can be thought of as constituting the earliest portion of the cycle of activity involved in the transition from settled folk life to a new social order." Thirty-five years later he applied certain aspects of this thesis about mass effects to his critique of theories of industrialization, especially the supposition that industrialization invariably introduced social disorganization

into folk, local, or traditional societies. Blumer noted that at its onset industrialization is often accompanied or followed by the release of new social forces and new demands on life, "such as the wish by women for emancipation, the desire of youth for greater freedom, a general desire for superior living comforts, a search for higher social status, and an elevation of ambition and aspiration." But he attributed the rise of these new demands "more to a complex of social and ideological changes than to the industrializing process" alone. Among the other elements making up the complex are mass phenomena—"modernizing influences such as communication, travel, education, the spread of democratic ideas, and the development of a variety of social movements" (1969–70, 58).

14. The inclusion of social science among the arenas of fashion suggests to us that the very methods and procedures, theories and domain assumptions through which sociology makes its claim to be a recognized and subsidized science may well be subject to fashion and, hence, not to the independent requirements of science. It seems to us that Blumer has, perhaps unwittingly, hit upon the paradox that adumbrates his half-century of criticism of the social sciences: The demand that sociology emancipate itself from the fashionable though egregiously erroneous positions it has taken with respect to science and society is doomed so long as sociology remains an uncritical part of the mass society it seeks to study.

15. Blumer's complex understanding of films was misunderstood by Hollywood and misrepresented to the public. His studies were part of a larger project financed by the Payne Fund and carried out under the auspices of the Motion Picture Research Council, an organization whose executive director was a pious opponent of popular films, Rev. William H. Short (Jowett, 1976, 231, n.48). The research was undertaken to determine "the degree of influence and effect of films upon children and adolescents" (220). The publications appeared in 1933, when the Hays Office, Hollywood's board of self-censorship, was under fire for failing to monitor the moral quality of movies to the satisfaction of several different pressure groups. Blumer's qualified statement about the role of the movies as an intrusive factor on local cultures and on the mores was lost in the clamor for greater censorship. Blumer was mindful of the predominant business mentality that prevailed in Hollywood. Indeed, he took it into account as part of his analysis: "[M]otion pictures, I think, can be said to have no culture. They are the product of secular business groups with commercial interests. The motion picture industry has no cultural aim, no cultural policies, no cultural program" (Blumer, 1935).

PART V
The Fragmented Covenant in California

CHAPTER 15

The Gospel Mission to the Pacific

RELIGION AND RACE

When, in 1951, Herbert Blumer accepted an appointment to chair the recently established department of sociology and social institutions at Berkeley, sociology had already been taught in California for more than eighty years. That no department of sociology had been formed at Berkeley until 1946 speaks less to an avoidance of sociology than to the special circumstances under which the Social Gospel and other sources of the discipline reached California.

Missionary endeavor proceeded without ecumenical spirit in California. The New England-based American Home Mission Society, an alliance of Congregationalists and New School Presbyterians, had staked out California as the "Massachusetts of the Pacific,"[1] a field rich for the Puritan harvest of heathen souls and repentant sinners. When it became clear that the Gold Rush was attracting to California not only great numbers of Americans but also Europeans, Latin Americans, Australians, Pacific Islanders, and Asians, denominational disputes broke out. Several Protestant denominations sent missionaries into the Chinatowns of San Francisco and Sacramento and into the gold-mining towns. The Catholic Church sent its missionaries to tend the spiritual needs of Hispanics, Irish, and Italians. And when it became clear that the Europeans and the Chinese were competing for jobs, their respective religious leaders became spokesmen in the fierce labor conflicts that ensued.

In their struggle to gain influence over the peoples of California, the missions turned to founding educational institutions. The American Home Mission Society, through the efforts of two of its most indefatigable evangelists, Samuel H. Willey (1821–1914) and Horace Bushnell (1802–

77), attempted to establish control over California's institutions of instruction, public and private, and to entrench a Protestant orientation within the proposed university (Teggart, 1924; Ferrier, 1937, 17). Willey and Bushnell worked to have their nondenominational College of California (1855–68) become the physical, intellectual, and moral nucleus of the University of California, but they failed (Stadtman, 1970, 4–41). Opposed by their several denominational rivals—and even more significantly by a coalition of agricultural, mining, and business interests that had united with the cosmopolitan (i.e., Jewish, Catholic, Unitarian, and Freethinking) intellectual community that had settled in the San Francisco-Oakland Bay Area[2]—Willey's Congregationalist-Presbyterian alliance could not gain a single seat on the new university's board of regents when it was appointed in 1869. Willey bitterly complained that the board "turned out to include Roman Catholics, Jews, and indifferents or Skeptics—but—no minister of the Gospel (but one Unitarian) and not one of the characterizing and efficient friends of the College [of California] which had given the University its existence" (quoted in Stadtman, 1970, 36). This defeat of the Massachusetts-based Gospel movement in California was decisive for the university's development and for the future of sociology in its curriculum. Thereafter, the university's mission would be oriented around several varieties of sociodicy.

While the missionaries had lost Berkeley, they had by no means been left without influence elsewhere. At Stanford and the University of Southern California a Protestant attitude of uplift prevailed, with definite implications for academic and applied sociology. This attitude focused on the moral status of California's immigrant population. But California's racial and ethnic makeup, with large numbers of people who were neither white, Christian, European, nor American, created unique problems for Christian endeavor. The effort to extend the Gospel to California required casuistries capable of accommodating racial and cultural ecumenism, or of forging convenants excluding certain residents. Cultural ecumenism attracted the Protestant-oriented sociologists; racial exclusion appealed to the Catholic and labor oriented.

The Protestant missionaries' homiletics on the Christian covenant required the sociologists at Stanford and the University of Southern California to place a greater emphasis on the process of assimilation, a supposedly inexorable social process that would induct Asiatics, Mexicans, and other racial and cultural minorities into the American covenanted community. Assimilation became the watchword of the discipline and the single route to social salvation. Immigrants from every land, and American Indians and blacks as well, were studied, measured, and prophesied about in terms of their actual or potential assimilability. The concept, never accurately defined, gained value precisely because of its vague but powerful promise: The race problem is only temporary; America will be the redeemer nation, not only saving heathen souls from perdition but, bringing in the sheaves of a new citizenry that will eventually take its place in an inner-worldly American Christian commonwealth.

The question of assimilation was complicated by the interconnected issues of race, labor, and Americanization. Two divergent schools of thought developed, reflecting two divergent views of brotherhood and otherhood. At Stanford and the University of Southern California assimilation promised to dissolve all racial and ethnic heritages within a single moral community. At Berkeley assimiliation was subsumed under the question of labor and the desideratum of a racially organized labor hierarchy. The intellectual and social origins of these perspectives are as divergent as the moral philosophies that flow from them.

THE FAILURE OF THE ASSIMILATIONIST UTOPIA

Assimilation-oriented sociologists at the University of Southern California and Stanford promised minorities eventual deliverance from race prejudice at the same time that they reassured the WASP majority about the inevitable Americanization of the Chinese, Japanese, East Indian, Filipino, and Mexican residents in their midst. The question was not *whether* these groups would qualify for membership but when and on what terms. The Asians' work ethics, which were located not in Christian precepts but in an alleged racial covenant of clannishness, suggested to the opponents of their immigration that these peoples lacked the requisite public-spiritedness for membership in the American Christian commonwealth. The Gospelers, on the other hand, believed that these peoples could be brought into a multiracial brotherhood—when assimilation had given them the appropriate civic outlook.

The Oriental question provided the assimilationist theorists with their greatest challenge. The Protestant idea of a covenant, transformed by eastern and Chicago sociologists into a vision of monocultural America, was brought to the University of Southern California by Emory Bogardus (1882–1973), who had taken his Ph.D. at the University of Chicago in 1913, and was introduced even earlier at Stanford by Mary Coolidge (1860–1945).[3] For the first time this orientation would have to deal with the several Asian races, cultures, and religions found in California. Beginning in the 1870s, the virulent hostility of white workingmen to the Chinese—later extended to Japanese, Koreans, and East Indians—had turned on the question of their "assimilability."[4] Yet, in California, neither facts nor opinion seemed to favor the assimilation of the Chinese or Japanese.

Assimilationist theory was given a new test by the Pacific Coast Survey of Race Relations, carried out under the direction of Robert E. Park in

1926. Bogardus and Winifred Raushenbush, both of whom represented Park's point of view, were major field-workers in this project. The evidence they gathered did not support the assimilationist promise. Raushenbush found that Park's race relations cycle was not in operation in such conflict-ridden Japanese communities as Florin, near the state capital, or in San Francisco's Chinatown. Bogardus, using his social-distance scale, discovered that the Asians were still a great distance from acceptability for membership in the larger covenant.[5] Kazuo Kawai (1926), another writer in Park's race relations survey, found three "solutions," none of them assimilationist, to be the sad lot of the California-born Japanese:—isolated, unproductive ghetto life, return to Japan, or painful and usually unsuccessful struggles against American race prejudice. But Raushenbush explained negative instances away by referring to local accidents of geography or human interferences; Bogardus believed that the gaps in social distance would eventually be bridged; Park announced that the race relations cycle was irrepressible. Their faith in the redemptive qualities of assimilation brushed aside the facts produced by social research.

A study of the Japanese presence in California revealed the limits of the sociologists' assimilationist gospel. In October of 1920 Tasaku Harada, a former president of Doshisha University—a Christian institution that had been founded by a Japanese educated as a missionary at Amherst College (Davis, 1894)—surveyed 230 leading Americans, on behalf of the newly formed American-Japanese Relations Committee, on the issue of Japanese assimilation and related matters (Harada, [1922] 1971). Six of the 116 replies were from sociologists: Carver of Harvard, Giddings of Columbia, Cooley of Michigan, Ross of Wisconsin, and Small and Park of Chicago. Their answers pointed to a general sociological ambivalence about the openness of the American commonwealth to Asian people. None believed that assimilation was a likely outcome of continued immigration from Japan.[6] Positing that close relations between races that are in competition with each other can only be harmful to social order, Carver proposed that the Japanese, like the Jews of Europe, be permanently separated and occupationally segregated from white America. Giddings urged recognition of what he called "the undeniable sociological fact that a democratic republic can be maintained only if the population is on the whole homogeneous." Cooley observed that although "it is generally admitted that they [the Japanese] are personally delightful, and that they are much more popular in this regard than, say, the Jews . . . many think they are collectively dangerous . . . in large numbers . . . and would form unassimilated groups, and thus destroy the homogeneity of our population. . . . We must be guided by the facts. Much as I like the Japanese I am opposed to their immigration." Ross, still clinging to the thesis that had cost him his position at Stanford, supposed that "if immigration from

Japan be confined to very narrow proportions, and the Californians feel secure for the future, it will not be difficult to remove all discriminations against Japanese now here."

More significant, because of the theme of world brotherhood in their work, were the responses of the two Chicago sociologists. Small, champion of a Christianized American community, accused mischief makers and demogogues of stirring up anti-Japanese feeling in California, but nevertheless believed that "our cultures are so different that in the present state of racial consciousness all over the world such mechanical mixtures could not prove fortunate." Park observed that "the Japanese problem is a race problem; race problems are rooted in human nature; human nature changes to be sure, but changes very slowly." He pointed to the failure of social science to remedy the matter: "Just how this prejudice can be modified is a matter of which we know as yet too little." Finally, Park suggested that in a situation where "racial differences are as marked as they are in the case of the Japanese and the American, public sentiment opposes intermarriage. Where intermarriage does not take place assimilation is never complete and the difficulty of two races mutually accommodating themselves to one another, while maintaining each a separate racial existence, is bound to be very great" (Harada, [1922] 1971, 48–49, 35, 17, 38, 34, 38, 28, 15). America's leading Protestant sociologists could not conceive of a covenant that included the Japanese—even if they were Christians.

State officials had used the issue of unassimilability to place even greater restrictions on the Japanese. In 1920, California's Governor William D. Stephens proposed to the U.S. secretary of state that, because of their inability to assimilate, the Japanese be banned from immigrating to the United States, and that all Japanese born in America be specially registered and required to carry a certificate attesting to their nativity. He warned, "Unless the race ideals and standards are preserved here at the national gateway the conditions that will follow must soon affect the rest of the continent" (Stephens, [1923] 1978, 26). In 1922, the attorney-general of Washington, seeking to convince the U.S. Supreme Court that it was within the province of the Constitution to strip two naturalized Japanese immigrants of their American citizenship and to deny them the right to form a realty corporation in his state (Consulate of Japan, 1925, 1: 171–74), quoted directly from Park's discussion on the relationship between intermarriage and assimilation (1913, 66–83) and from the doctoral study of Park's student Jesse F. Steiner on the limits of Japanese assimilability ([1917], 1978, 180). The court, in obliging his request, recognized that an underlying issue in the assimilation of racial groups was economic as well as social exclusion from the community of the racially acceptable.

By committing themselves to the illusion of assimilation and its benefits,

Social Gospel sociologists failed to imagine that a sociological analysis of race relations might proceed from the principles contained in the Fourteenth Amendment to the Constitution, viz., that no *person* be denied the equal protections of the law be he or she native or foreign born, citizen or alien, white or colored, Occidental or Oriental, assimilated or not. Nowhere was this made clearer than when, in a prepared statement and in oral testimony before the House Committee on National Defense Migration in 1942, Jesse Steiner, the chairman of the University of Washington's sociology department, opposed the pending policy of wholesale evacuation and detention of all persons of any degree of Japanese descent residing on the West Coast. If some Japanese must be removed, Steiner said, distinctions must be drawn between the alien and the citizen, and perhaps, among the United States citizens, between those who had been educated in Japan and those who had received their schooling entirely in the United States. Steiner was arguing that proof of admissibility into the American covenant might be employed as the test for a person's enjoyment of basic civil rights. Country of origin and place of education were proposed as modifications of Constitutional guarantees. His testimony reveals a shift from an all-embracing assimilationist covenant to one contingent on geography of birth and schooling.

At Stanford University in the 1930s, Reginald W. Bell (1935) and Edward K. Strong (1970) turned the question of assimilation of Japanese on the issues of educational achievement and psychological adjustment. The race relations cycle was, in effect, qualified by recognition of a period of hardship and emotional difficulty that would impede but not halt the process of absorption. The first generation of American-born Japanese youth were the starting element of an eventual assimilation. The marginality of their status and the personal problems it would engender were incidents in the process—their suffering was the price to be paid for eventual moral regeneration and social acceptability.

By 1941, 65 percent of the Japanese living on the Pacific Coast were American citizens, born and educated in the United States. A few months after Japan's attack on Pearl Harbor, all persons of any degree of Japanese descent, numbering more than 110,000, were placed under military control and removed to specially constructed detention camps. No formal charges were ever lodged against them; no trials (except of those who openly challenged the governmental order) were ever held. Japanese-American Christians were incarcerated along with those who professed Buddhism or some other Oriental religion. Not citizenship, Americanization, or conversion to Christianity was sufficient to secure basic civil rights for the Japanese on the Pacific Coast during World War II. The American government's wholesale approach did not recognize differences in degree of social, cultural, economic, legal, or civic assimilation.

Race and color still constituted basic criteria for admission to membership in the American commonwealth.

Dorothy Swaine Thomas, then a sociologist in the Agricultural Economics Department at Berkeley, studied the demographic characteristics of the incarcerated Japanese-Americans. As a body their loyalty had been impugned by the decision to imprison them all without regard to nativity, citizenship, or patriotic attitude—all Japanese were equally suspect. Through a variety of governmental and military tests to determine their danger to America's national security, however, the internment camp administrators had devised a system of differentiating the Japanese from one another. The government's tests were designed to divide the Japanese into three groups, which Thomas and her researchers called the "spoilage"—those who were declared suspect or disloyal, who adopted pro-Japanese stances, elected to return to Japan, or, in the cases of Nisei and Kibei, renounced their American citizenship; the "salvage"—those who, having been declared to be "not disloyal" to America, elected to participate in a "selective resettlement" program in communities and cities in the Midwest or East, or who joined the American armed forces; and the "residue"—those who for various reasons, including age, infirmity, family responsibility, emotional state, or job insecurity, remained in the detention centers throughout the war (D. Thomas and Nishimoto, 1946; D. Thomas et al., 1952). The three categories were not based on mutually exclusive criteria. Although Christianized Nisei figured more numerously among the "salvage" group, and Issei and Kibei among the "spoilage," neither "spoilage," "salvage," nor "residue" distinguished completely between foreign born and native born or among Christian, Buddhist, or secular Japanese-Americans. The subterranean thesis that haunted these studies was that race was as powerful a social force along the Pacific coast as it was in the American South (see ten Broek, Barnhart, and Matson, 1954).

The West Coast variant of the American dilemma barred the Social Gospelers and assimilation-oriented Chicago, Stanford, and U.S.C. sociologists from realizing their hope for a homogeneous national community, an American Christian commonwealth. Some races were permanently, perhaps inherently, unassimilable, and could never be a part of the new secular civil covenant.

Assimilation had not been sufficient to produce the promised brotherhood of man in pre-Pearl Harbor America. After 1945 fewer and fewer assimilation studies were conducted.[7] In the next fifteen years, the significance of assimilation would gradually decline.[8] By 1980 the concept had virtually disappeared from the sociologist's vocabulary. In its place there began to emerge an image of a fractured covenant, pluralistic in spirit, that would embrace all ethnic and racial groups in America while celebrating the validity of their respective colors and creeds.[9] Americans were to live within a new national compact beyond the melting pot, dedicated to preserving America and saving the world from communism. This new international mission would, it was hoped, produce a national brotherhood united by its opposition to a foreign enemy. The Puritan covenant was to give way to a patriotic civil religion.[10]

RACIAL REGENERATION AT BERKELEY

Farming and agriculture did not develop in the same ways in California as they had in the South and the Midwest, where ideals associated with the plantation or the family farm had become institutionalized. California's farmlands had been blocked out as large tracts by the Mexicans, who incorporated the Spanish colonial hacienda system into their administration. The hacienda, comparable in many respects to the feudal manor, was a self-contained social and economic entity. Farm labor was thought of as a part of a much larger obligation of fealty to the *hacendado*. When, after 1848, the *hacendados* and the hacienda system were formally eliminated, the agricultural tracts remained intact, requiring another system of management. The Southerners who emigrated to California before and after the Civil War included former slaveowners, whose image of an agricultural society was based on the plantation system. Although the parallels between the hacienda and plantation systems are by no means exact, both have large tracts of land and cheap labor as their economic foundation. The ideal of the self-sufficient farmer, idealized in the Midwest as upholding the values and virtues of sturdy independence, equalitarianism, and individualism, did not develop in California[11] where the small-holder is more likely to describe himself as a rancher than as a family farmer.

From its beginnings the labor force in California was recruited from the Pacific basin—China, Japan, Korea, the Pacific Islands, Hawaii, and Mexico. The non-Anglo, non-Protestant character of this labor force, which the Social Gospelers at the private universities hoped to transform by assimilation, was not nearly so important to agricultural and economic sociologists at Berkeley, where the critical issue was the availability, quality, and condition of the migrant agricultural labor force. A body of racially distinct foreign migrants, neither the serfs of the hacienda nor the slaves of the plantation, would be subject to the vicissitudes of the agricultural wage scale.

The religious orientation that guided the work of the first sociologists to address the race/labor question was derived from the casuistries earlier used to justify slavery in the South, and was brought to Berkeley by its first sociologist, Joseph Le Conte, appointed professor of natural history, bot-

any, and geology in 1869. Former master of "Woodmanston," a plantation with two hundred slaves, Le Conte saw the problem of agriculture as
one of organizing racial groups to labor in a postslavery society. Like
Henry Hughes, Le Conte asserted that "slaves were not property, chat-
tels, in the sense in which other things are," and insisted, "in fact they were
never so treated in the South." Slavery was simply a system for organizing
labor power; slaveholders had merely exercised "the right claimed. . . to
[the slaves'] labor power." The postwar system required a change in social
organization from a slave system to a wage system. The market value of
slaves would now pass to the land itself, if the labor remained reliable (Le
Conte, 1892, 358). Wage labor in his argument becomes just another
form of warrantable calling. Hence, Le Conte argued in 1888 before the
California Historical Society, the South had no need to "repent" of any
"sin" of slavery because it had been a system of labor organization admirably suited to the condition of Negroes (see Bozeman, 1973, 579n). Although Le Conte confined his comments to the plantation system of the
South, they are applicable to the large-scale farm units of California. The
special organization of agriculture in California—agribusiness—is a rationalized version of the plantation system in which the slaves are replaced by migrant workers and illegal aliens. The owner of the enterprise,
unlike the plantation owner or the *hacendado*, is not responsible for the
care and feeding of the migrant worker, who leaves the farm when there
is "no more work." He is housed on the farm and may even be fed in a
central dining area, but he bears the costs of these services.

Le Conte conceived of the organization of labor in evolutionary terms,
passing from a stage of slavery into a wage system and then evolving
further into forms yet to be imagined. He proposed a historical orientation to what he insisted was "the *relative* nature of all institutions." Beyond
slavery, Le Conte perceived an unfolding of the laws of labor development that would produce even newer forms for its efficient exploitation.

> No one, I think, who has thoroughly grasped the great laws of development,
> or practiced the method of comparison, will find any difficulty in perceiving
> that free competition in labor is necessarily a transition state; that, as a perma-
> nent condition, it is necessarily a failure; and that the alternative must
> eventually be between slavery and some form of organized labor, circum-
> stances, perhaps beyond our control, determining which of these will prevail
> in different countries.

Le Conte was convinced that, as a stage in the history of labor, the system
of slavery that had existed in the southern states could be "placed on a
scientific basis which is absolutely invulnerable" to its "mere blind fanati-
cal opposers." Extending the spirit and applicability of his own thesis, he
could have argued that California's system of agribusiness exploitation of

foreign labor is suited to its age of development and equally invulnerable to criticism from those who merely sympathize with the oppressed.

It was the ingeniousness of Le Conte's formulations that made it possible for him to propose a sociology of labor that could simultaneously survive the defeat of the Confederacy, sustain the antebellum southern mystique,[12] and rationalize the subordination of the new freedmen and other agricultural laborers. His vision of the future was not fully realized in the New South, but many of his ideas, and especially his focus on the issues of education, labor, property, and social legislation, were incorporated in a new political economy of agriculture.

By 1912 a curriculum in social economics was added to Berkeley's department of economics. This program in effect supplemented the curriculum in agricultural economics, which had devoted itself to solving the problems of California agriculture, and focused on defining a new sociodicy for California's agricultural laborers. The work of the social economists pointed in two opposed directions. Those studying the urban labor force conceived of a legally constituted California covenant of white workers.[13] For those studying agriculture, the racial and cultural diversity of the labor force was treated as a social fact, not a social problem. Their perspective was not that of the Social Gospel, which Jessica Peixotto regarded as too concerned with uplift to be scientific, but of purely secular redemption—they were concerned with labor education, rural poverty, naturalization, and the economic condition and future prospects of Mexican and Asian laborers. Programs for educational uplift arose out of a desire to enhance the quality of the state's work force and improve the well-being of the worker.[14]

Recognition of the civil rights and working conditions of California's agricultural labor force transformed the race question from one whose solution depended on moral uplift, assimilation, or education to one dependent on civic identity and public policy. The worker qua worker, as a force in agricultural production, was also to be regarded as a total person. Farm laborers were released from the burden of eschatological redemption imposed on them by assimilationist sociologists. Under this dispensation, the worker must look to the state rather than God or the race relations cycle for his protection. Freed from a predestined outcome, the laborer is subject to the fateful decisions of the courts, the politicians, and the bureaucracy. The Protestant theodicy of work had been replaced by the secular sociodicy of rights.

NOTES

1. The phrase comes from the homiletic preached to the New England Society of San Francisco on December 22, 1852 by Timothy Dwight Hunt of the American Home Mission

Society: "Sons and Daughters of New England! You are the representatives of a land which is the model for every other. . . . here in our Colony. No higher ambition could urge us to noble deeds than, on the basis of the colony of Plymouth, *to make California the Massachusetts of the Pacific.*" (Quoted in Starr, 1973, 86. Emphasis in original.)

2. Despite its vast spread of territory along the Pacific Coast, California has had but one cultural and intellectual center throughout its history—the San Francisco Bay Area. From the time of Mark Twain, Bret Harte, Ambrose Bierce, and Joaquin Miller to the upsurge of the Beat poets of the 1950s and 1960s, San Francisco has been the literary center of the state. Art, music, and museums have also been there from the earliest period. The worldwide gold rush to California insured that California's entryway, San Francisco, would have a multinational population whose elites would include European Jews, Southern gentlemen, Spanish and Italian Catholics, and a mixture of freethinkers from everywhere. The fact that the Berkeley campus of the University of California was built within the orbit of this cosmopolitan elite differentiated its beginnings decisively from those of America's other universities.

3. Mary Coolidge, who had had a long association with the Social Gospel sociological tradition in the East and at the University of Chicago, took up the cause of the Chinese immigrants in California. Arguing that the Chinese were victims of unfounded racial prejudice, Coolidge pointed to their willingness to labor for the building of the country, their eagerness to learn English, their desire to escape from the pagan ways of their brethren; she asserted that a change in the hearts and minds of Caucasian Americans would lead to a recognition that the Chinese were already worthy applicants for admission to the American covenant. "It does indeed, take two to assimilate," she wrote in 1909; "and nonassimilation is the least convincing and most inconsistent of all the arguments against Chinese immigration." As Coolidge (1909, 458) conceived of the matter, the accusations against the Chinese came from "those who have not wished them to assimilate nor given them the opportunity to do so, and who do not, even now, recognize that many of them have become intelligent and patriotic Americans."

4. Labor union leaders, including Samuel Gompers, Terence Powderley, Dennis Kearney, Andrew Furuseth, and Frank Roney, fought against the Chinese worker in a struggle that, in Gompers's words, was one of "meat vs. rice" (Gompers and Guttstadt, 1902). Catholic priests shepherding Irish workmen spoke out publicly in the fight, defined by Father James Bouchard S. J. as one over "Chinaman or White Man—Which?" (see McGloin, 1949, 172–90), and insisted, in the words of Frank Pixley (1877), editor of San Francisco's aggressively nativist newspaper *The Argonaut*, that "the Chinese have no souls to save, and if they have, they are not worth the saving."

5. The concept of social distance was derived from Simmel and passed into American sociology through the teachings of Park. See Bogardus, 1926, 169–70, 208–09; 1920, 148–222; 1928; 1934.

6. It appears these American sociologists could not conceive of the positive consequences of a reverse acculturation—i.e., the decline or interpenetration of American values by those of the Orient. Such, however, was precisely the outlook on the California Asian question taken by the German sociologist Max Scheler. As Scheler conceived of the matter, a dangerous possibility of war between Japan and the United States might be averted if America were gradually to become Orientalized. That might be accomplished, he believed, if the number of marriages between white Americans and Asian—in Scheler's preference, Chinese—immigrants increased dramatically. The positive result of this biocultural mixture would be a social personality that combined the Occidental drive to master nature with the Oriental reserve, self-control, and meditation. Moreover, Scheler believed that if this rise in intermarriages were to occur at the same time that American youth revolted against Puritanism and adopted the principles of socialism and communism the resultant American cultural personality would be warmer, more generous, and more contemplative (see Staude, 1967, 234–36).

7. Opposition to the assimilation orientation in sociology had first appeared in 1913 with Horace Kallen's advocacy of cultural pluralism as the basis for democracy (1924, esp. 44–232) and was taken up by Kallen's self-designated disciple Randolph Bourne, who proposed a "trans-national America" whose preserved ethnic divisions would, he believed, act as a brake on adventurist imperialism (see Bourne, 1964; 1964a). However, throughout the first five decades of the twentieth century Kallen's and Bourne's pluralist thesis—originating out of Kallen's desire to prevent Jewishness from being dissolved in the melting pot—made little headway against the secularized Protestant covenantism that justified unreserved assimilation of all peoples. Kallen had argued that the maintenance of Jewish identity would require the defense of every minority's right to resist absorption by the covenanted commonwealth. It was not until after the failure of the promise of assimilation was openly revealed in 1942 that pluralism was rediscovered as an alternative approach.

8. Although Park had abandoned his faith in assimilation by 1937, some of his students carried the torch of Americanization for many years thereafter. Among these were analysts of Chinatowns, who perceived in their relatively closed communities an unprogressive cultural isolation and an unwarranted resistance to political, social, and economic advance. From 1920 to 1945 the University of Chicago's sociology department encouraged Chinatown studies as part of its research program in urban communities and attracted both Asian and white students—e.g., Ting C. Fan, Chin-chao Wu, Paul C. P. Siu, Helen MacGill Hughes, Roderick MacKenzie, and Clarence E. Glick—in search of an assimilationist solution to the "Oriental Question" (see Fan, 1926; Hughes, 1980–81; MacKenzie, 1928; Glick, 1980).

9. The coup de grace was given to the assimilationist orientation by the publication of *The Harvard Encyclopedia of American Ethnic Groups* (Thernstrom, 1980). With sociocultural descriptions of more than one hundred racial and ethnic groups distinguishable in American society, the contributors to the *Encyclopedia* evinced a certain perplexity and vagueness about specifying the processes whereby such a medley of peoples might become part of a cohesive society. Harold J. Abramson (1980, 150, 160) pointed out that "we have long been confronted with a major question: what happens to the groups and individuals who make up this diversity? What has happened in the past, and how can we describe what is happening in the present?" Noting that the once optimistic promise of assimilation had given way to a bewildering variety of ethnic alternatives inspiring metaphors—salad bowl, mosaic, transmuting pot, stewing pot, crucible, and symphonic orchestration—more often than understanding, Abramson lamely concluded: "There is no one single response or adaptation. The variety of styles in pluralism and assimilation suggest that ethnicity is as complex as life itself" (1980, 150, 160).

10. In the postwar era, the significance of a foreign enemy still had its effects on both the reality and the sociology of American race relations. The new enemy, however, was international communism. At first postwar sociology at Stanford was confined to a technicist study of the dynamics of small groups, an examination of consensus and conflict in the apolitical and culturally neutral arena of a laboratory-contrived human association. In more recent years, however, the older tradition of American consensus has been revived with the appointments of Alex Inkeles and Seymour Martin Lipset—experts, respectively, on Soviet and American politics and society—to its faculty. While the study of Chinese and Japanese Americans has been abandoned to the revisionists in ethnic studies, American unity and the preservation of "dynamic equilibrium" are seen as imperatives in relation to the challenge of communism.

At present sociology at Stanford continues that institution's tradition of support for a covenanted national America but substitutes the claim of a persistent national character for the religious compact and upward social mobility for assimilation. Inkeles perceives a persistent American national character that he claims has existed since colonial times and has been reaffirmed by the adaptive qualities of peoples of different color and culture in America. This national character consists in the beliefs that the United States is still "the Promised Land"; that homely virtues of persistence, initiative, self-reliance, and independence dominate thought and action; that voluntary communal activity and cooperation with neighbors, coupled with mutual trust, guide social interactions; and that efficacy, innovation, openness to new experience, hostility to authoritarianism, and equality give a sense of hopeful optimism to every undertaking. Inkeles resolves the problem of forging the American covenant by declaring it to have been in place all the time. What faith, effort, and homiletic have failed to achieve, Inkeles has accomplished by sociological fiat (see Inkeles, 1980).

Although Lipset is less optimistic about the tensile strength of the American social structure and more concerned over the persistence of gross inequalities affecting blacks, Hispanics, and women than Inkeles appears to be, he is notable for addressing the issue of the Marxist challenge to American society in terms of upward mobility rather than assimilation. He quotes with approval Werner Sombart's observation that "all Socialist Utopias come to nothing on roast beef and apple pie." Lipset believes that "classic democratic theory stemming from Aristotle suggests that free societies are most likely to be found in nations with a preponderant middle class," while "Leninism-Stalinism-Maoism have collectivized scarcity, and inequality and tyranny are necessary concomitants of such a system" (Lipset, 1980a, 25, 29, 32).

11. In fact, when the Japanese immigrants began to show a proclivity for independent farming based on the principle of the family farm, their attempts were resisted in spite of the fact that their ideology of hard work and self-sufficiency was consistent with the idealized family farmer of the Middle West.

12. By providing a comprehensive theory to justify antebellum slavery, Le Conte contributed greatly to the survival of nostalgia for the old order of prewar life in the southern states. Nostalgic ideologies of a romanticized southern agrarian culture could thus be used to sharpen the Southerner's criticism of the brutalities and human degradation of the industrial system and to affirm the truly human values to be found by working the land. That this is not an entirely idle observation is attested to by the fact that such ideologists of ruralism in the South and in the Midwest as the agrarian poets and E. A. Ross, respectively, have frequently reinforced one another's beliefs in the nobility of rural ways of life.

13. It was given thorough and painstaking analysis by Lucille Eaves, who pioneered the development of a historical sociology of labor law. At Berkeley, where she was Flood Fellow in Economics, she carried out a study of the role of California's Sinophobic workingmen's movement for effecting protective and restrictive legislation (Eaves, 1910). Although Eaves left Berkeley in 1910, the tradition of studying California's worker movements and their relation to labor legislation and the racial composition of the labor market that she had begun would continue through the 1960s in the Economics Departments at Berkeley and Los Angeles (Cross, 1935). These studies are characterized by documentation of the social, economic, and legal situation of California's workers. They show an admiration for the democratic processes and fraternal solidarity said to be demonstrated by the activities of the state's organized labor force and are sympathetic to white but not Asiatic workingmen. They thus support a limited vision of labor, one that extends only to the white laborer. Eaves's studies suggest that race serves as the dividing line between the generate and the unregenerate.

14. Among the social economists Paul S. Taylor is outstanding because he recognized that the racial and cultural diversity of California's agricultural labor force was not the pivotal issue. He did not look to assimilation as the way to solve California's agricultural labor problems. The question of the assimilability of Asians and Mexicans was not an issue because, as migrant laborers, these peoples shared the essential attributes of a common occupation. Just as a slave had been a slave and one slave had not been differentiated socially or

culturally from another, so, to Taylor and his colleagues, a worker was a worker, irrespective of race, creed, or culture.

As Taylor and Tom Vasey put it in 1936: "The use of alien workers on California farms has markedly complicated the adjustment of economic and human relations in agriculture. It produces conflicts which are at times of violent intensity. It creates problems which will require patience and firmness if they are to be solved." For these social economists the cultural diversity of the labor force was a social fact, not a social problem. In a series of studies carried out between 1928 and 1932, Taylor documented the social, economic, educational, political, naturalization, marital, and interethnic problems that affected the human rights of Mexicans in California, the Southwest, and certain parts of the Eastern and Midwestern regions (see Taylor, 1928–32). In subsequent years, working with Vasey and Kerr, Taylor reported on the socioeconomic bases of the state's rural labor unrest, documenting the violations of the workers' freedom of speech and right to organize (Taylor and Kerr, 1935; Taylor and Vasey, 1936). For Taylor and his coworkers, all laborers were human beings. As such they deserved protection of their basic human rights.

PRESBYTERIAN COMTEANISM IN CALIFORNIA

One of the great omissions in the history of American sociological thought is acknowledgement of the influence of southern Presbyterian Comteanism in the post–Civil War era. According to Josiah Royce, who was born in the new state and studied under Joseph Le Conte at Berkeley, California was peculiarly susceptible to the cavalier culture of the antebellum South. During the first decade of statehood, Royce observed, the "Northern man frequently felt commonplace, simple-minded, undignified, beside . . . this picturesque wanderer from the Southern border" and usually exaggerated the Southerner's "fluency in eloquent harangue, his vigor in invective, his ostentatious courage, his absolute confidence about all matters of morals, of politics, and of propriety, and his inscrutable union in his public discourse of sweet reasonableness with ferocious intolerance." In California, the Northerner "often followed the Southerner, and was frequently, in time, partly assimilated by the Southern civilization" (Royce, 1883, 180–81). Royce's observation reflected the dominance that southern Presbyterian deism exercised over New England Congregationalism. Nowhere was this dominance better represented than in the sociology offered at the University of California by Royce's mentor, Joseph Le Conte (1823–1901).

As a former plantation owner who had removed himself in protest from the Reconstructionist South, Joseph Le Conte came to be known as a representative of the "Chivalry" class in California—those who descended from or took as their reference group the landed gentry of the antebellum South.[1] He was a highly cultivated, erudite scholar who brought to the University of California a worldliness otherwise missing from the state at that time. The great esteem in which Le Conte was held at Berkeley not only attested to his scholarly achievements and the high regard students had for his lectures but also extended the favorable reputation he had already established in intellectual and scientific circles in the prewar South.[2]

Le Conte's project was to find ways to justify evolutionary sociology within a framework of deistic Christianity. While at Berkeley, he formulated a theoretical scheme that was as grand as that of Protestant-inspired thinkers in the East. In diametrical opposition to Lester F. Ward, who during the same period sought to eliminate God from social science, Le Conte called the Deity the "Great Architect" of all that had happened and would unfold. Le Conte considered his deism to be above the struggles of sectarian interests,[3] and he did not antagonize adherents of other Protestant denominations at the multisectarian University of California. He spent more than three decades at Berkeley reconceptualizing the world in terms of a Comtean science grounded in Christian precepts.

Throughout Le Conte's work runs a refusal to countenance a surrogate "religion of humanity" to replace sacred theodicy.[4] All science was compatible with and revealing of the knowledge and design of the "Great Architect," and in sociology in particular, and its object, human society, evolution was guided by the Creator (Le Conte, 1859). "The external world is the objectified modes, not of the mind of the observer, but of the mind of God." The world's adherence to evolutionary laws is nothing less than its subordination to the "real efficient force," which is "spirit," and the manifestation of its utter and ultimate dependence on God. Acknowledging that scientists would find it difficult to "live and work in the continual realized presence of the Infinite," Le Conte conceded that "it may, indeed, be that in our practical life and scientific work we must still continue to think of natural forces as efficient agents." But scientists should "at least remember that this attitude of mind must be regarded only as our ordinary work clothes . . . to be put aside when we return *home* to our inner higher life, religious and philosophical" (Le Conte, 1897, 301–03).

It was given to men to choose between the realms of science or philosophy. For himself, Le Conte proclaimed that "the domains of science and philosophy are not separated by hard and fast lines, they largely overlap; and it is in this borderland that I love to dwell" (Starr, 1973, 425). Somewhere in this uncharted region Le Conte hoped to find the grounds for a general evolutionary science that would be not merely compatible with religion but glorifying to God and progressive for man. He created the basis for such a science by reconciling the creationist theories of Louis Agassiz with both the evolutionary theories of Darwin and a re-spiritualized Comteanism.[5] Agassiz (1807–73), an early apostle of the "diluvial catastrophist" school, which sought to insure that Mosaic scriptural teachings would not be subverted by Lyell's "uniformitarian" geological heresies (see Gillispie, 1959, 151–52, 162–67, 175–212), announced in 1850 his conversion to a belief in "The Diversity of Origin of Human Races" in general and the Negro in particular (see Stanton, 1960, 99–109, 153–92). Although Agassiz sought to reconcile his new view with the Book of Genesis by interpreting the story of Adam as "representative" rather than literal, the otherwise admiring Le Conte would not long follow him down this heterodoxical path. Instead, Le Conte put forward a new synthesis, allowing for an incorporation of Agassiz's claim within those of Darwin and—even more significantly—harmonizing both with belief in God's great power of design and the teleological promise of Christ's ideal, the divine man (Le Conte, 1897, 275–364).

The key to Le Conte's vindication of God to science was in his teleological argument. Geology, as a temporal science (in contrast to astronomy, which is spatial) revealed in the stratification of rocks the Deity's slowly emerging plan for the development of the earth and all things that inhabit it; "in geology, history is recorded upon *tablets of stone*." But this "natural history" interpreted by science, illuminates "the divine character and mind" (Le Conte, 1858, 125, 119). The evolution of organisms and that of society were to Le Conte but manifestations of the supreme power and singular foresight of an omniscient God:

> God, foreseeing and foreknowing the end from the beginning, every possible contingency is included and provided for in the original conception. The whole idea of that infinite work of art which we call nature, is contained in the first stroke of the Great Artist's pencil and the ceaseless activity of the Deity is employed through infinite time only in the unfolding of the original conception. [1859, 104]

Le Conte undertook a synthesis of natural and social science that would be both consistent with the conservative articles of Protestant doctrine and compatible with recent discoveries in zoology and geology. The science of man and society, he insisted, was an organic science. Organic science, or morphology, searches out the evolution of *forms*, not the causal agency of *forces;* for in organic science the only causal agency is God, the First Cause. Le Conte, employing the general principles of Comte's law of development through stages to advance Agassiz's science of natural history, proclaimed that a complex variant of the "method of comparison" was the only scientific approach proper to sociology (Le Conte, 1860, 39–77).[6] This method is uniform and uniformly applicable in all organic sciences and manifests its validity in the several "series of organisms" that nature has prepared as the functional equivalents of laboratory experiments for morphologists to examine.

Le Conte's fusion of organicism and teleology permitted him to conceive of sociology as a science of both past history and future developments, and to embrace both within Christian eschatology. His sociology could look backward by following the methods of geology and produce a natural history of society; it could look forward by following the method of natural theology and predict the spiritual future of man; and it could study and contribute to the improvement of the present, synthesizing its ethical ideal with its knowledge of the laws of naturalistic development to indicate precisely how manmade modifications in the social structure would resonate with or temporarily subvert the evolutionary path. Le Conte's organic social physiology was better grounded theoretically than Talcott Parsons's later reformulation of Spencerian evolutionism.

Le Conte constructed four intersecting tendencies depicting the evolution of society. In the first, societies are conceived as social organisms arranged hierarchically in a "natural history" from the "highest" to those so "low" as to be coextensive with "barbarism." In the second, a single society is conceived as an "embryonic" organism whose growth is to be traced, as in the case of "the most civilized, from its earliest to its most mature condition," comparing "these successive stages with one another" in "the same social organism." A society in the third is viewed in relation to its position in the "geological" or evolutionary series of the several civilizations comprising "the whole human race," each civilization being perceived as if it constituted a growth phase of a single "developing organism, as *e.g.*, the Chinese, the Egyptian, the Hindoo, the Greek, the Roman and the Modern"; and in the fourth, a society is conceived as a social system in which the "social body in quiet, harmonious and healthy action, where all the social functions cooperate for the good of the whole, [stands over against] . . . the same organism in disease, fever, and delirium, in a word in various degrees and kinds of *revolution*." In the fourth case, which Le Conte termed the pathological series, he allowed for the possibility of harmonious or disharmonious social systems and equated revolution with disease. This fourfold series allowed Le Conte to assign every race, society, religion, and social order a grade of evolutionary advance. Because each series was implicated in the others, a single line was produced leading ultimately to the realization of a world civilization.

Man could participate in the evolutionary march toward a divinely determined future, but his actions might work against God's plan. One of the tasks of sociology was to discover precisely when and how man might act to further the Deity's goals. Just as the science of the biological organism had, after much effort, been so perfected that the medical art, its applied form, provided cures for human ills, so, Le Conte argued, the science of the social organism would eventually be suitably advanced for the application of a corresponding ameliorative social art. The science that would provide the corollary curative art for society was "sociology, which has already improved, and will eventually perfect, our practice of Government and industry." Like Ward, Le Conte imagined a future sociocracy; like Giddings and Ogburn, he proposed harnessing sociology to public policy.

The new science of sociology would offer explanations and suggestions for scientifically sound improvements in art and architecture (1859); the reorganization of the curriculum of public schools, colleges, and universities (1859a); and pedagogical theory appropriate for insuring general education (1861; 1888). But Le Conte regarded these as but short-run contributions; in relation to the long-range issue of the evolution of races and peoples and the formation of a single world civilization, he developed a theory of a future global social and cultural millennium.

In Le Conte's grand conception, slavery had been but the appropriate historical expression of natural developments in the social organization of the races. "Slavery," he wrote in 1892, "would certainly have come to an end, not by the external pressure of foreign sentiment, but by the internal pressure of race growth" (361). Race growth meant a regulated intermixture of races that would lead to the genetic and cultural elevation of the inferior peoples.

Southern slavery, which had rescued the Negroes from racially enervating intrabreeding in Africa, had also protected them through benevolent confinement and supervision on plantations. It would have ultimately dissolved through its own creation of a new racial order, Le Conte believed. However, the orderly progress toward its extinction had been interrupted by the arbitrary and absolutist imposition on the South of "the dogmas of universal liberty and equality, the right of self government, of free inquiry, [and] of free competition in labor" by northern abolitionists. This Enlightenment heritage of ideas was not false, Le Conte contended; but in America it had been put forward in an unscientific manner, without insertion of the qualifications that "an extensive comparison of Government of all kinds, Divine and human, and in all stages of development" (1860, 57–59) would surely have indicated.

Once slavery had been abolished by force of arms, the interrupted evolutionary process required special guidance to assist the racial development of the Negro and prevent their race's extinction. The freedmen, still children in Le Conte's evolutionary scheme, had a "quickness of memory, keenness of senses, precocity of perceptive faculties" that were clear evidence of the mental characteristics of "nearly all lower races (and indeed also of animals)" (1892, 366). Their intelligence could not compare with "the reflective . . . rational faculties which develop late, and show themselves in active life rather than in school" (367). Le Conte placed little faith in education as a solution to the race problem. An adherent of a limited Lamarckianism, he believed that only a small part of the acquisitions of any one generation was "carried over bodily into the next generation by inheritance" (366). What was required for the solution of the race problem in the South was the scientific regulation of breeding.

Le Conte proposed a policy that would elevate both blacks and marginal whites and permit their induction into a larger, ultimately world-wide covenant. Abolition had presented America with two options: either Negroes must be left to intrabreed as they would and, as an inferior group multiplying its own inferiority, contribute to their own inevitable demise; or they must interbreed with the superior Caucasians, producing hybrids whose similarly interbred offspring would then be absorbed into the higher race. As Le Conte saw it, the blond Teuton was clearly the highest of the Caucasians; other "marginal varieties" had not progressed so far. Hence he proposed a "judicious crossing" of Negroes with the lesser whites. If such a crossing could be institutionalized, he argued, the ensuing evolution might "produce a generalized type capable of indefinite progress in all directions" (1892, 374). Ultimately, civilization itself would spread to become "coextensive with human nature, with the earth surface, and with the life of humanity" (374). Le Conte's Presbyterian deism would embrace the genetic regeneration of humanity as a whole, and in this respect was far more ecumenical than the Harvard Puritans' program for eugenic redemption of American civilization. The rational application of his genetic theory would be the scientists' contribution to the fulfillment of God's universal design.

Le Conte's racial eugenics proposal was only one application of his understanding of how the process of evolution had changed since the advent of man. "In organic evolution *species* are transformed by the *environment*. In human evolution *character* is transformed by *its own ideal*. Organic evolution is by *necessary* law—human evolution is by voluntary effort, i.e., by *free* law. Organic evolution is *pushed* onward and upward from behind and below. Human evolution is *drawn* upward and forward from above and in front by the attractive force of ideals"([1897]1970, 363). In order to move the process of human evolution forward, man, especially scientific man, must harness advanced knowledge to humanity's highest ideals. To Le Conte, the highest ideal of man had already been embodied in Jesus, and "at the end the whole human race, drawn upward by this ideal, must reach the fullness of the stature of the Christ" ([1897]1970, 364). The mixture of races would be but one step toward a collective realization of that condition. Precisely because it is the voluntary and freely willed actions of men that help to remake the world, there remained the problem of evil.

Consistent with his commitment to vindicating the ways of God to organic science, Le Conte did not shrink from presenting the basis for a

scientific theodicy of good and evil. First, he discovered the positive functions of ostensible evils in the animal kingdom; in the natural disasters
that occur to man because of "heat and cold, tempest and flood, volcanoes
and earthquakes, savage beasts and still more savage men"; and in the
diseases that ravage human society. Second, and more formidable because of his doctrine of voluntarism, was his theodicy of "the most dread-
ful of all," moral evil. It was this that most challenged Le Conte's Christian
theism, for he could not acknowledge any positive aspects of sinful conduct. However, his insistence that the spiritual force that impelled human
and social evolution tended toward independence and free will compelled him to recognize that man could not have been created "a perfectly
pure, innocent, happy being, unplagued by evil and incapable of sin."
Virtue, he declared, is self-established, through choice. A being incapable
of sin "would also be incapable of virtue, would not be a moral being at all,
would not in fact be man." Sin and moral evil must be present in our lives
because "we cannot even conceive of virtue without successful conflict
with solicitations to debasement." "Essential evil," then, was something to
be controlled by striving for virtue, the Christ ideal, rather than something to be eliminated. Life becomes a permanent struggle between the
higher spiritual and lower animal parts of human nature. "For the higher
is nourished and strengthened by its connection with the more robust
lower, and the lower is purified, refined, and glorified by its connection
with the divine higher, and by this mutual action the whole plane of being
is elevated." In this evolutionary theodicy, Le Conte was able to combine a
vital Christianity with a religion of humanity.

In Le Conte's conception of the free-willed individual there is a critique
of the nescient determinism of Comtean materialism. According to Le
Conte's understanding of Comte, as society evolves further and further
along its seemingly ineluctable path "a portion of the independent life of
the individual is, as it were, given up, and goes to make up the general life
of the community, and increasing mutual dependence is the result." But,
he observed, "human society is . . . an organized body, the ultimate anatomical elements of which are individuals" (1858, 166). In its earliest stage
each individual performs all the requisite tasks necessary for existence. As
social organization advances, however, "limitation of social function or
division of labor progresses in the same proportion, until, in the most
highly organized communities, division of labor reaches its highest limit,
and the social function of each man is confined to the doing of one thing."
The price paid for this progress is "a gradual loss of personal independence" (1859, 312–13). Should the Comtean ideal prevail, such special-
ization of function with its attendant differentiation would become the
law of development. The result would be realization of "the ideal of
animal organization," in which "the individual would have no life or

significance separate from society . . . [and] the ego itself would no longer belong to the individual, but to the community" (1858, 166).

Comte's materialism contained no Christian moral guide for the future evolution of civilization. But Le Conte's advocacy of "mixture of blood, . . . universal commerce, . . . experiences of decayed civilizations, . . . [and] the highest and most vital elements of civilization, viz., the principles of Christian morality" hoped to set history in pursuit of "a broader civilization"—one in which "we may confidently expect our progress to continue indefinitely" (1880, 104) and our moral character to progress with the evolution of individual conscience. By reasserting the Christ ideal within an evolutionary theory, Le Conte resolved the Durkheimian problems that arose from the increasing division of labor, the decline of religiosity, and the onset of anomie. For Le Conte, morality in the modern world was not consigned to the collective conscience but permanently given in revealed religion. The problem of finding a secular foundation for morality led later sociologists to discard Le Conte's scientific theodicy and to replace it with proposals for civil religion or secular theodicies of revolutionary redemption.

TOWARD A UNIVERSAL GENERALIZED OTHER

Although he received his early education in the Methodist College of Belfast, Ireland, the city of his birth, Frederick J. Teggart (1870–1946) was guided less by religion than by his commitment to the values of classical humanism. His creed was that of Hesiod, the Greek poet who "set before men the first idea of human progress: the idea that a good life is attainable; that this attainment is dependent upon the thought and activity of men themselves; that the essential requisite is the actualization of the members of the community by a common regard for justice" (1947).

Whereas the American Christian social thinker placed his hope in an eventual world-wide brotherhood of man, united by a common faith and engaged in mutual acts of moral uplift, Teggart looked forward to the establishment of a universal congress of mankind, joined in the common pursuit of peace and guided by a comprehensive and usable science of history. As Teggart's student Gladys Bryson would point out (Bryson, 1932; 1932a; 1932b; 1945), American sociology—that is, the sociology that took its point of departure from Albion Small, Lester Ward, Franklin Giddings, and E. A. Ross—had taken over the spiritual objectives and selective perspectives of the eighteenth-century Scottish moral philosophers, producing a discipline that assumed a fixed human nature, a progressive teleology of human history, and an ahistorical ameliorative stance. Teggart's science of social institutions eschewed such modes of mystical idealism. In their place it sought a methodical rationalization of the trials and errors that are the basic ingredients of man's history, a practical and applied science of world peace and social justice.

Teggart believed that social scientists would never achieve an understanding, or aid others in reaching the higher ideals of civilization, if they sought man's moral salvation within the confines of the nation-state or in the relations between nation-states. National states and the warfare ideologies that supported them had become a major threat to world civilization. "Civilization is menaced by war," he observed, because "it is dominated by theories of violence and preachments of strife as the means to the establishment of a millennium" (1941). Having lived through two wars in which Germany had played the major aggressive role, Teggart pointed out that German historical thought had celebrated the rise of the war-state, and that "the theory of the War-State proclaims war and demands war as the condition of self-realization." War had become the molder of nations: "without war there would be no state. All states have come into existence through war. War will last as long as more than one state continues to exist." Modern, industrially rationalized, total war undermined the basic requisites of civilization: peace, justice, and reason.

As a first step in a secular but ethical, peace-oriented science of history, Teggart proposed that the world as a whole be the unit of study, focusing on patterns of human settlement, migration, and trade. The freedom to emigrate, the right to trade, and the unfettered commerce of ideas constituted necessary, though not sufficient, prerequisites to human advancement and the establishment of global peace. "Routes of travel . . . have had a preponderant influence upon the whole course of human development," he wrote. They facilitate "the fundamental processes through which all human advancement has taken place. First collision (though not necessarily warlike) of different cultures; then an awakening, a release from established habits and ideas; then a reestablishment of a new life upon a new level and basis" (1919). Only if the sea and land routes to areas of settlement and trade were kept open could the chances for human advancement and the possibilities of a peaceful world community be kept alive. The unrestricted movement of people, goods, and ideas had in the past contributed to the breakdown of customs, the liberation of individuals from group constraints, and the peaceful exchange of cultural products. Modern inhibitions on each of these were fast becoming frozen in nationalist foreign policies and fixed in patriotic histories.

In Teggart's view, monopolies of sea power, the restriction of immigration by national states, and the capitalist penetration and industrialization of Asia, Africa, and the islands of the Pacific threatened peace and human advancement in the twentieth century. World War I had been fought over global developments of nationalism and imperialism. These had been

given new geopolitical meaning by the researches of Sir Halford J. MacK-
inder, the geographer and strategist whose studies of the Eurasian land
mass Teggart appreciated for their transnational globalism (1919a), but
criticized for their "support of a political philosophy that appears to be
out of harmony with the most hopeful tendencies of our times" (1919a).
MacKinder's geopolitics called for building a defensive alliance of the
Atlantic powers and Germany against Russia.[7] In recognizing that "the
joint continent of Europe, Asia, and Africa is effectively, and not merely
theoretically, an island," MacKinder had, in Teggart's view, given new
scope to continentalist theories. But by presenting his materials in terms
of the vulnerability of the rimlands of Western Europe, Asia, and Africa
to invasions from the heartland area of continental drainage, MacKinder
had overemphasized current strategic issues at the expense of historical
and sociopolitical understanding. What was of world historical significance about the migrations and uprisings that had repeatedly moved
peoples out from Inner Asia to the coastal lands of the Pacific, Indian, and
Atlantic oceans and the Mediterranean was the fact that "the peoples of
the Near East and of Europe have been compelled to protect themselves
by setting up politico-military organizations." The politico-military organizations of the past and present, Teggart argued, had arisen out of
pressure from invading migrants on the local communities of settled
peoples, who had themselves been migrants or descendants of migrants
from the same area at some earlier period. This geographic factor in
human history, if properly introduced into the study of man and his
institutions, would put into perspective past and present political theories
glorifying national patriotism (1922). The national political state, having
arisen as a defensive reorganization of local communities facing an invasion of new migrants, was an obstacle to the establishment of a peaceful
world order. Policies that followed from MacKinder's thesis would only
forestall war for a time, because they would lead to future confrontations
between these enlarged geographically integrated entities. Taken alone,
geopolitical strategic and military perspectives did not contain a moral
dimension. For Teggart a just world could be achieved with an inner-
worldly ethics grounded in science.

Teggart drew his historical model of an enlightened cosmopolitan and
peaceful world from antiquity, specifically from the cultural effflores-
cence that had marked the settlements around the Mediterranean in its
classical period. The single most important development since that epoch, Teggart asserted, had been the rise of world-wide oceanic traffic
opening every continent on the globe to access from the sea. Population
movements from everywhere had produced new culture contacts and
held out the possibility of civilizational breakthroughs as great as those
that had occurred among the Ancients; in effect, the world as a whole had
become a second Mediterranean.

Teggart called attention to the fact that commercial expansion, ushered in by technological advances in navigation, had opened up new frontiers on the Atlantic and Pacific seaboards of the American continents and throughout the Asian-Pacific Basin, inviting Eurasian exploration, trade, and settlement within those hitherto unknown land masses. At first the new commerce had placed no restrictions on the traffic in goods, ideas, or people. Only later, Teggart and his student, Nicholas J. Spykman, pointed out, after mercantilism and Manchesterian free-trade liberalism had been superseded by capitalist imperialist penetration, did colonial policies become culturally destructive, global imperial rivalries introduce a new cause for war, and interrelated policies of immigration restriction and colonial exploitation provoke nativist uprisings. Capitalist imperialism, together with its concomitant political formation, the nation-state, restricted the opportunities for a free "market" in merchandise, ideas, and human beings to develop, and altered the structure of civilizational interdependence throughout the world. Recasting Teggart's conception in the language of George Herbert Mead, a world civilization would be each individual's generalized other.

THE INDIVIDUAL IN THE WORLD HISTORICAL PROCESS

Teggart looked to neither an inexorable law of historical progress nor a divine plan for human salvation. Only man could bring about social redemption. When a free commerce in goods, ideas, and peoples is allowed, he argued (1941), an intrusive potential is catalyzed for releasing a people from slavery to customs or habit. As "a result of the breakdown of customary modes of action and of thought, the individual experiences a release from the restraints and constraints to which he has been subject, and gives evidence of this release in aggressive self-assertion" (191–97), permitting the formerly traditionbound to form associations freely on the basis of self-interest. Since, however, the "overexpression of individuality is one of the marked features of all epochs of change" (197), the forms through which this individualism might express itself were many and varied. The individual, unconstrained by ties of blood, race, or custom, was the best hope of mankind. The ideology of nineteenth-century laissez-faire economics, broadened to embrace an uncontrolled international marketplace in ideas and cultures as well as goods, provided a chance for human emancipation to succeed, for new forms of human association to emerge.

History, Teggart asserted, was the account of man's trials and errors when confronted with the unknown: "The process by which man has utilized his endowment has been the same at all times, for with the first effort of thought there was inaugurated a series of experiments that has not since been interrupted" (1910). Travel, trade, and resettlement provided opportunities for frequent encounters with the unknown and for experiments to cope with it. For Teggart, humankind, confronted by the inscrutability of God, plunged into the task of making its own world.

The settlement of the New World, and especially California, was a key instance illustrating the potential for peaceful contacts and commerce of diverse civilizations. After 1492, the oceans, having assumed an importance equal to that of the ancient Mediterranean, moved peoples, cultures, and goods from Europe and Asia into the New World. California was a strategic objective of global revitalization: "Civilization, spreading out from an original focus in Eastern Asia, after traversing equal distances to the East and to the West, is drawing to a new focus on this spot" (1912).

"In contrast with the coast of California . . . the Atlantic seaboard of North America lies open to Europe. To it there was but one line of approach for an expanding western civilization, and the problem of this approach was solved once and for all by Columbus and Cabot. Henceforward the nations—Spanish, Portuguese, English, French, or Dutch—might come, for the way lay open and direct" (1912, 63). The California coast, on the other hand, presented unique problems of land and sea travel. Open to the peoples of the Pacific basin by both land and sea as well as to those who could come by sea and land from Europe, California presented a crucial historical instance of how free and unrestricted trade, migration, and settlement could result in an intercultural moral community.

Once "discovered," greater California acted like a magnet, drawing to its coastlands and interior peoples even more diverse than those who had settled the Atlantic seaboard. To California had come emigrants from Russia, Asia, Oceania, and Central and South America, as well as from Europe. Marx (Padover, 1972) had supposed that the discovery of gold in 1848 had drawn the Pacific coast into world history. However, California had been El Dorado to many of the world's peoples since the sixteenth century, Teggart pointed out. Joined to the United States by the treaty ending the war with Mexico in 1848, California still bore traces of its Spanish, Russian, English, Asiatic, and aboriginal heritages when Teggart wrote about its history sixty-four years later. California presented a challenge to civilization: would it become an arena of cultural conflict, or would its heterogenous mix of peoples and values find a means of peaceful coexistence?

The congeries of peoples that had settled the American West, especially the Pacific Coast, provided Teggart with the first of his continental case studies aimed at isolating the problems of constructing a moral community. In Teggart's view official histories were an obstacle to the creation of such a community. Official history was a record celebrating the achievements of those in authority, designating recent events as proofs of their

own group's progress. Parallel to such histories were those of the power-
less, narratives of oppression often inspired by illusions of a millennium
in which the existing structure of power would be dismantled and—in the
Christian perspective—the meek would inherit the earth, or—in the
Marxist apocalypse—the proletariat would seize the dictatorship.[8] Neither version belonged to Teggart's idea of a science of history.

"There can be no question of right or wrong, progress or decay, in
history; [rather] problems have arisen, choices have been made, adjustments have been tried; . . . their antecedents and consequents are history." Teggart offered a historical sociodicy, requiring modern man to
accept the fact that "all that can be known historically is that the present
status is a result of the adjustments attempted in the past." The challenge
was whether the historian was willing to sever his connections with "the
exponents of mystical idealism" (1923), build up a science that would
"contribute to an understanding of the processes manifested in the activities of mankind" (1916), and put that science to the service of establishing global justice.

To make his science of history universal and useful, Teggart analyzed
major world upheavals on continent-wide land masses that had changed
the course of history. Neither the wars in ancient China nor the invasions
of imperial Rome, Teggart observed, could be explained by conditions
internal to the two empires; rather, "the correspondence of wars in the
East and invasions in the West had been due to interruptions of trade"
along the vast interdependent reaches of the Eurasian continent (1939).
Teggart regarded his general approach to the study of human conflicts,
though based upon investigations of classical civilization, as applicable to
current international conflicts.

The origins of the state—of the political organization of territory—
were the starting point for any historical investigation of the sources of
man's greatest problem—war. Political organization, Teggart declared,
had arisen in the first place out of a people's departure from fundamental
attachments to traditional sodalities. Max Weber saw universalizing religions as the force behind the breakdown of kinship and clan solidarities—Teggart located this force in "naturally" induced migrations and in
the attendant development of larger political solidarities as settled peoples reorganized to resist the invasions of the uprooted. For Weber the
charisma of religious leadership and the processes of political rationalization could break traditional solidarities; for Teggart they might be broken
by the effects of migration to and warfare with established centers of
civilization. Weber had been impressed by the role of religious leadership
in European history; Teggart was impressed with the ethnic, racial, and
cultural heterogeneity of the peoples of Eurasia and the New World and
with the significance of migrations for breaking these down.

The primary difference between "primitive" and "civilized" groups,

Teggart observed, was that the former are organized and self-identified through blood relationships, while the latter achieve their sense of individual and collective definition through linkage to a given territory. The civilizing process, hence, was one of breakthrough to some kind of rational and universalistic mode of social organization, to fraternizations that incorporated the "other" into the "brotherhood" and dissolved the irrational elements of the more primitive relationships in a system of mutual calculation organized in relation to territory.

Drawing on the concepts and research of Henry Sumner Maine and Lewis Henry Morgan, Teggart regarded civilization as occurring at that moment when land replaces kinship as the basis of society and property relationships come to supersede those based on sanguinity and inheritance. Societies organized on the basis of kindred were characterized by "the unquestioned and unremitting dominance of the group over the individual," and this character, in turn, led "to the tenacious and uncompromising maintenance of customary ways and ideas" (1941, 271). Societies organized in political units, on the other hand, were open to innovation and characterized by the psychic release of individuals and collectivities from their slavery to custom and group domination. "Kingship and territorial organization," Teggart wrote, "represent simply the institutionalization of a situation which arose out of the opportunity for personal self-assertion created by the breakup of primitive organization" (273). The resultant emergence of political organization was but one instance of what can follow from bursts of released individual expression. Kingship is the first historical instance of individualism, and new bursts of individualism would lead to forms other than territorial sovereignty.

Changes in structures of domination and political organization, however, were only one instance of how trade, immigration, and settlement patterns lead to new forms of organization. An investigation of the origins of political institutions did not explain how civilization had diversified into so many cultural and institutional structures, or how the content of social life had come to have so many variations. Teggart did not regard his explanation of political institutions to be a sufficient basis for a science of history because it did not take account of the role of ideas in the development of society. A comparative social science, he argued, should focus not on institutions but on the structure of coherences that make up a person's or a group's idea system. A world integrated through trade could also become a world integrated through the free association of ideas and the debates they would evoke.

Ideas manifest themselves in varying human activities and hence are the ultimate data for social analysis. The conclusion was inescapable: "If we are to consider the content of life in addition to the exterior forms of human association, [social scientific] study . . . must concern itself with the factors and processes through which the idea systems of different groups have come to be as we find them today." He applied this perspective to his understanding of the nature of civilization: " 'Civilization' is not the product of primary emotions which man shares with animals, but of some activity which he has developed in a characteristic manner. This activity may be described as the formation and expression of ideas" (281–2).

In order to explain the impulses in men and women that lead to the expression of ideas, Teggart pointed to parallels between the beginnings of political organization and the onset of independent individual thought. The same breakdown of kindred organization that followed upon migration, collision, and conflict and produced the beginnings of political organization "tended to release the individual from the domination of the group, and to create a situation in which personal initiative and self-assertion became possible." Release from group control "opens for the individual the possibility of thinking for himself without reference to group precedent" (284–85). And the result of this cognitive liberation "reveals the fact that the most important aspect of 'release' lies, not in freeing the soldier, warrior, or berserker from the restraint of conventional modes of action, but in freeing the individual judgment from the inhibitions of conventional modes of thought" (197). Once the shackles of custom control were removed, an individual might begin to question the verities that had hitherto governed his existence and to formulate new perspectives on art, politics, religion, production, and everyday life.[9]

The free interchange of ideas among men and women left free to think for themselves was for Teggart a fundamental article of secular faith. He thus completed his own secularization of mystical thought, locating all causes in this world and assigning to the intelligence of free men the ability to change the course of history. Like other positivists before him he hoped that his work would lead to the creation of a rational world order in which a parliament of man would legislate within an international commonwealth of peace.[10] However, by locating causes in this world and thus being forced to transvalue mystical idealism into ideas, Teggart was brought back to the problem of mind—its formation, its moral character, its social functions. Teggart held up the mirror of man to himself.

TOWARD A WORLD MORAL COMMUNITY

Separating his history from both its theological and its ideological underpinnings, Teggart faced the problem of finding a replacement for them.[11] He recognized that social science had not only become the successor to the secular versions of eighteenth-century moral philosophy but had also taken upon itself the task of formulating a theory of progress. However, where other thinkers had seemed to say that science ought to validate a theory of progress, Teggart argued that the very idea of progress should become a fundamental topic for sociological investigation.

Teggart's critiques of Comte, Marx, and Darwin constitute battles to establish the high ground for a nonteleological, thoroughly disenchanted social science. Comte, considered the "outstanding figure in the effort to create a scientific study of man, or of society, in the nineteenth century," had in fact proceeded entirely by "the employment of deduction and analogy." His procedure, the "comparative method," substituted the analogy of growth for the analysis of facts. Darwin had taken over the eighteenth-century argument of Leibniz and others that "nature does not make leaps" and thus had concluded that the biological history of the earth was accomplished "by slow, gradual steps, by slight, successive transitions." The transfer of the Darwinian perspective to the scientific study of human association would only substitute the application of the pseudo-geological metaphor of "natural" change for the investigation of changes as they actually occurred in history. Teggart perceived Marx's legacy as twofold. On the one hand, it had become one of the most potent of the vastly influential ideologies that currently inspire unrest, violence, and war. At the academic level, however, it had been recognized as a philosophy and science of history, a contender for that leading position in the unification of social science that, Teggart believed, had yet to be established. He observed with apprehension how Marxism had become one of the major sources for ideas that excite "populations, classes, and individuals to acts of destructiveness." He wrote in 1941: "With the coming of the twentieth century, the fashion of thought underwent a change, and the new generation of intellectuals submitted to what they conceive to be a new type of thought by exchanging Darwinism for the teachings of Marx" (1941a, 590). Marxism was far from new in its fundamental conceptions. Its defenders, Teggart's student Margaret Hodgen pointed out in 1951, redesignated Marx "as a philosopher of the progressive or perfectibilitarian persuasion . . . [whose] aim was to state generally, theoretically, ideally, and hypothetically the historical transition of economic society through a series of normal, natural, and progressive stages from primitive communalism to modern Communism" (Hodgen, 1951, 257). In Teggart's and Hodgen's view Marx's evolutionism had not been verified by a scientific procedure and was but the latest form of secular eschatology. Through his science of history Teggart sought to achieve the practical rationalization and pacification of world order. For Max Weber rationalization was already taking place in all spheres and orders of life but with consequences unlikely to produce either peace or personal liberty. Both thinkers recognized that they lived in a post-Protestant age and both hoped to find in history an explanation of man's fate and a portent of his future in a secular world.

Teggart's preoccupation with the problem of peace linked him to such international institutions as the League of Nations and to a commitment to the values of universalism: peace on earth and good will toward men would be outcomes of a state of world organization rather than one of grace. His scientific optimism was comparable to that of other applied positivistic social scientists, but his orientation called for an unfettered symbolic interactionism among all peoples. The world as a whole, not traditional communities or the nation-state, was to become the generalized other.

NOTES

1. During the postwar era, a fierce status competition broke out in the San Francisco Bay Area, pitting the "Chivalry" gentry against the "Shovelry," the latter composed of parvenus who had made their money in mining, merchandising, and investments on the new frontier. Part of the struggle was intellectual and cultural in character and took the form of rival elements endowing art galleries and anthropological museums. One important instance is worth noting for its effect on social science at Berkeley. Phoebe Apperson Hearst, wife of George Hearst, a prominent member of the "Shovelry," endowed the university's anthropology museum and for many years paid the salaries of its first professors in that discipline out of her own pocket (see Moffat, 1981, 21–35).

2. California had passed through the prewar period of national debate over the slavery question without becoming deeply embroiled in the issue. After the war ended, as Royce would later recall, the "appointment of two prominent Southerners to chairs in the State University was in part due to the influence of a political reaction, which swept over California . . . and which gave the State for a time to the Democratic Party, despite its record as a decisively Republican State during the war." Both Le Contes had worked for the Confederate Nitre and Mining Bureau during the war and could have been subjected to searching interrogations about their political convictions and military activities by university officials. But John Le Conte, who had been superintendent of the bureau, was assured by a university regent that his role in the recently ended conflict "will never be considered by the Regents when his name comes before them." Two weeks after John had received his appointment, Joseph Le Conte joined the university's faculty (Stadtman, 1970, 51).

3. In *The Autobiography of Joseph Le Conte* (1903, 265), he reports that "So far as churches are concerned, I could never take a very *active* part in any, because it seems to me that they are all too narrow in their views. But recognizing as I do that they represent the most important of all human interests, I have always very cordially supported them all." Le Conte gave money to the Congregationalists, Episcopalians, Presbyterians, and Unitarians, and conceded "I should be glad if I could support them all. Sectarian differences are nothing to me."

4. Le Conte's criticism of Comte in this matter was severe (1860).

5. Le Conte had been tutored by Alexander H. Stephens—later vice-president of the Confederacy—before matriculating at Franklin College and completing medical studies at the College of Physicians and Surgeons in New York City. He enrolled in the natural history courses of Louis Agassiz at Harvard's Lawrence Scientific School.

6. Nominating his own mentor, Agassiz—a champion of the creationist theory of species formation against those religiously indifferent geologists who had suggested the possibility of the transmutation of species—as the successor to Comte in the development of sociology helped Le Conte to overcome his severe suspicions about the French philosopher's atheism.

7. MacKinder's thesis would later provide the geopolitical basis for the formation of the North Atlantic Treaty Organization in 1949. Then as in 1919, Germany was the defeated power of an alliance that had united the "heartland" state of Russia with most of the "rimland" states along the Atlantic seaboard. The postwar breakdown of that alliance re-opened the heartland threat to rimland states and, in accordance with the MacKinder strategy, required an alliance that would incorporate Germany as well as other former or continuing Fascist states (Italy and Spain, respectively) and states that had been neutral in the recent war (Sweden and Ireland) into a military alliance against the Soviet Union (Lyman, 1957).

8. Teggart found in the several versions of the history of Spanish California an example of these parallel histories:

> Conceivably, there are four different angles from which the history of this outlying province of Spain and Mexico might be presented. Ordinarily the historical student will be disposed to follow the activities and the development of the political power or secular government; and from this standpoint the religious will appear as almost uniformly intrusive and exasperating. On the other hand, the story may be told by the missionary, and in this case the politico-military authorities will stand out as inconsiderate, meddle-some, and overbearing. Again there is the point of view of the Mexican-Spanish settlers and their descendants, the *paisanos*, the Europeanized population engaged in the at-tempt to make California their home. . . . Lastly, one might imagine an instructive account written from the standpoint of the unfortunate Indians who, without desire or volition of their own, suddenly found themselves inextricably involved in activities the object of which they certainly could not understand. [Teggart, 1918]

9. From this observation Teggart was able to formulate a hypothesis about the condi-tions of human advance and civilizational development: Changes in the social order ensue from the collision of groups from widely different habitats and the conflicts that arise among bearers of disparate systems of ideas (1941, 290). It is remarkable how much this hypothesis accommodates to older theories of cultural change, such as that of Sumner.

10. It was perhaps because of his stress on peace that Teggart's sociology was largely ignored during the period of World War II and the ensuing Cold War; ideologies of peace and international brotherhood were not consistent with the mood of that period.

11. Especially important for Teggart in this regard was the maintenance of secular, free, public, and university libraries that could act not only as repositories of historical documents but also as places for unconstrained research. Free universities and public libraries could build up the new social science and become centers for dissemination of valuable knowledge to the public. Teggart contrasted the free public library with parish libraries, which, depen-dent on the prejudices guiding private benefaction and limited all too often to collections of homiletics in support of uplift, usually failed to serve a true intellectual and scientific goal (Teggart, 1898, 1898a, 1898b).

The perspective now known as symbolic interactionism and associated with Herbert Blumer is an adaptation of the social philosophy of George Herbert Mead and a fundamental secular reformulation of the moral philosophy of Mead's teacher, Josiah Royce. When Blumer brought Mead's conception of mind, self, and society to the department of sociology at the University of California at Berkeley, he was, in effect, bringing that perspective back to its place of origin. For Royce had developed his conceptions of self, community, loyalty, and progress out of the challenge to Puritan prescripts posed by California's frontier amorality.

In the lineage of sociopsychological thought that descends from Royce to Mead to Blumer and to Goffman there is documented a great transformation: the singular and binding covenant of the Protestant ethicists erodes in the face of the emergence of a plurality of worldly, nonbinding situational and personal ethics. In place of the community of individuals, there appears the multitude of persons, each possessed of an unanchored self and all pitted against one another and an amoral structure of pitiless institutions. It is in the sociological variant of social psychology that the worldly rejection of religion reaches its apex and, for the first time as it were, poses the problem of public philosophy in its pure, i.e., atheistic, form: What is to be the moral basis of an Enlightenment society? For Royce the answer lay in a retreat into Pauline communitarianism overlaid with Calvinist virtues; for Mead, who stripped Royce's conceptions of their religious base, a cooperative commonwealth guided by the collective will of the generalized other; for Blumer, who recognized the lingering Protestantisms in Mead's formulation of the relations between mind, self, and society, a society of conflicting interests guided

267

by the secular ethics of the public interest; for Goffman, who recognized a need to return to the elementary forms of religious life without a super-erogatory god, a sacralization of the self and a mutuality of consciously proclaimed and conscientiously employed anthropomorphoses of humanity. The setting in which each of these social psychologies developed is California, the politics and peoples of which challenged sociology like no other American arena.

Josiah Royce was born in California's Gold Rush period. The propriety, intelligence, and moral absolutes of his fiercely Puritan, English-born mother inspired her more scientifically oriented son to search for a philosophical route to religious yet positivist idealism.[1] As an undergraduate at Berkeley Royce fell under the influence of Joseph Le Conte, whose lectures and writings left an irrevocable and pervasive stamp on his own subsequent work.[2] Le Conte's southern Presbyterian deism, providing a counterpoint to Royce's Puritan outlook, found its way into the Harvard philosopher's conception of how a post-Puritan Christian character and an American religious community might be established.

Royce's central concern was to reestablish the intellectual and ethical prerequisites for a Christian community. Struck by the violent character, nefarious schemes, corrupt politics, and social disorder of life in frontier California, he attempted to develop a normative theory of character and social structure that would be faithful to the world he had observed and still consistent with Christian faith. The result was an elaborated version of Le Conte's Comtean evolutionism that looked forward to the harmonization of mind, society, and God. However, Royce's Puritanism differed from Le Conte's Christian deism in one respect: Le Conte was satisfied to vindicate the ways of God to evolutionary science (Le Conte, 1890; 1891; 1897; 1900), and he did not concern himself too much with the question of a religious community; Royce regarded the problem of the Christian community as central to his philosophical and social psychological concerns (see Royce, 1918, 75–78; McDermott, 1969, 1:34–35).

Royce employed Le Conte's conception of deistic evolution to construct an image of an ordered world: "This process of evolution will lead from disorderly to a more orderly arrangement." Adopting the attitude of a mathematical positivist, he asserted that "the philosophy of nature will show that, amid all chances [there is] some tendency to orderly cooperation" (1914). Royce combined a theory of evolution with a conception of mathematical probabilities. His probability theory projected equilibrium—that is, orderly cooperation for any given social system—while his evolutionary theory proceeded in terms of an ordered contiguous or consecutive systemic series that ultimately formed the single system of the cosmos, a system much grander in its design than that later developed by Talcott Parsons. Within this grand cosmic vision, he was still able to preserve a voluntaristic conception for the actions of an individual. The individual observer of such consecutive systemic series by his very act of observing, constitutes a major element of the process by which such series are made: there is no disjunction between the observer and the observed. To Royce, as to Le Conte, social evolution was divinely teleological: "The world is *also* there to express a perfectly determinate and absolute purpose. Its facts are incidents in a life—yes, in a life of many lives—*a rationally connected social system of beings that embody purposes in deeds*" (1901a). Anticipating the idea of the voluntaristic, functionalist social system, Royce placed the Christian covenant in evolution and inextricably connected the self with all other selves in the community.

Royce's Christian community bases its solidarity in what he called a "philosophy of loyalty." The noblest expression of the self is in its loyalty to the community. Royce's ideal community is a covenant of loyalty, ultimately a covenant of loyal Christian believers. "Royce's view of the Church," philosopher John J. McDermott reminds us, remained "that of an American Puritan." This was also true of his approach to the American community: "His analysis of living American communities," McDermott points out, "has much in common with the self-consciousness of the Puritan attempt to forge a new relationship between religious covenant and the polis" (1969, 1:41).

Royce's "philosophy of loyalty" was in effect a faith in fidelity itself. Following along the lines of Le Conte's evolutionism, he projected the eventual formation of a society whose religious ethos would be both civil and Christian (see Royce, 1916, 197–246, 349–98). His theory of loyalty was dialectical: conflicts between two equally valid group loyalties would be synthesized into a single community loyalty at a higher level. That Royce's "philosophy of loyalty" appears to be indiscriminant—as, for instance, when he praises equally the loyalty of the unionists and the secessionists in the Civil War to their respective and opposed causes—is understandable when we realize that he is employing the dialectical method that Le Conte had used, and for the same purpose—to overcome antagonisms through discovering their latent progressive function. In the case of the Civil War, the pro- and antislavery forces "actually served the one cause of the now united nation. They loyally shed their blood, North and South, that we might be free from their burden of hatred and horror." By the same token, Royce found in the many violent personal, racial, economic, and political conflicts that bloodied the first half-century of California's history "a certain idealism, often more or less unconscious," an ultimately progressive "tension between individualism and loyalty, between shrewd conservation and bold radicalism, which marks this community" (1908). Even racial antipathies—whose instinctive and psychological character Royce felt to be far more the cause of race problems than any alleged inherent inequalities—had positive and progressive functions: ultimately, they moved mankind toward a single human community. Royce provided a social theodicy that accommodated virtually all human conflicts.

The doctrine of Pauline corporatism gave Royce a basis for his own conception of a spiritual community. The parables of Jesus, Royce asserted, revealed the "two beings to whom Christian love is owed: God and the neighbor." Paul had introduced a third and more mysterious being, the "corporate entity." That "corporate entity is the Christian community," Royce declared. Paul's religious community had "a practical concreteness, a clear common sense about it." Embedded in Paul's restatement of Jesus' commandment to love thy neighbor is a new definition of inclusion in that community: "For Paul the neighbor has now become a being who is primarily the fellow-member of the Christian community." In this conception of the Christian neighbor, Royce discovered the ultimate principle of loyalty as well as the basis for a society founded on altruism and Christian brotherhood.

Royce's conception of a spiritualized community arising out of cyclical evolution that would reconstitute American society in accordance with the principles of Pauline and Puritan brotherhood ran afoul of the deepening secularization of communitarian thought. George Herbert Mead criticised Royce's conceptualization because he believed it was at odds with the current realities of self, society, and social institutions in America (see Reck, 1964, 378–83). He rejected the Le Contean principles in Royce's theory of the self—"the infinite series involved in self-representation" and the positive functions of evolving loyalty—as contrary to experience. "Causes," Mead observed, "loyalty to which unites the man to the group, so far from fusing themselves to higher causes till loyalty reaches an ultimate loyalty to loyalty [as Royce insists], remain particular and seek specific ends in practical conduct, not resolution in an attained harmony of disparate causes of infinity." Mead treated this aspect of his teacher's philosophy as "part of the escape from the crudity of American life, not an interpretation of it." Royce's "individual is American in his attitude, but he calls upon this American to realize himself as an intellectual organization of conflicting ends that is already attained in the absolute self." Mead pointed out that "there is nothing in the relation of the American to his society that provides any mechanism that even by sublimation can accomplish such a realization."

Having stripped Royce's idealism of its spiritual and metaphysical character, Mead substituted the secular sociopsychological concept of the generalized other for that of the infinite Ideal: "Royce points out that the individual reaches the self only by a process that implies still another self for its existence and thought." Such a conceptualization reversed the order of things in American life. "The American even in his religious moments did not make use of his individualism—his self-consciousness—to discover the texture of reality. . . . He did not think of himself as arising out of a society, so that by retiring into himself he could seize the nature of that society. On the contrary, the pioneer was creating communities and ceaselessly legislating changes within them." The American did not achieve self-identity from subordination to the community: "The communities came from him, not he from the community." And thus the awesome attitude toward the community that Royce expected would not arise. The American "did not hold the community in reverent respect." Mead excised the Presbyterian-Pauline Christian synthesis that Royce had constructed and returned the sociology of the self and the community to the inner-worldly pragmatism that had earlier transvalued a de-Catholicized Calvinistic Puritanism.

Mead's secularization of Royce's thought proceeds along two lines: the dissolution of community within the processes of communication and interaction, and the abolition of eschatology in the face of an open-ended history that consisted of endless actions and interactions. For the Infinite Self he substituted the self-reflective self; for Christian values, the generalized other; for the ultimate community of Pauline believers, the penultimate society of interacting selves. In Mead's conception of the world, man is truly living east of Eden: mind, self, and society are without supernatural guidance. Society without God would have to provide its own direction. The ethical, moral, and humane bases for modern societies would be given by an undefined generalized other.

Mead's conception of mind, self, and society provided the foundation for Herbert Blumer's paradigm of symbolic interaction, developed when he studied at the University of Chicago. But it was in California that the problematics of the secularized self that symbolic interaction had introduced were given their most thorough attention. Blumer moved to the University of California at Berkeley in 1951. Along with Erving Goffman, who joined the Berkeley faculty a few years later, he took up the ambiguous elements of the generalized other that had become visible in response to the diversity in California's races, ethnic groups, religious sects, social classes, and life-styles. The dissensus and pluralism of California society placed the empirical problem of how the generalized other might be formed in bold relief. A multiplicity of apparently irreconcilable definitions of the situation confronted anyone who sought a single set of values or a coordination of sentiments. No common moral tradition explained the relations of individuals to each other. California's heterogeneous beliefs and heterodox subcultures posed a fundamental problem: What kind of self, and what kind of society, could develop in this situation?

Mead's social psychology had retained a conception of the moral individual in a secular world. His conception of the generalized other as each individual's moral arbiter in the secular world allowed him to reformulate the religious ethics of a Puritan community as the civil moralities of a secular society. However, Blumer (1981) observed that while "the generalized other is the chief position from which a human participant grasps and understands the social world inside of which he has to develop his conduct," Mead gives us "no aid in tracing how people construct their 'generalized others' [nor any] techniques which would enable people and scholars alike to improve their ability to take group roles." Notwithstanding this difficulty, Blumer constructed a public philosophy around the generalized other, assuming not a covenanted harmony of interests but rather a civil ordering of conflicts.

For Blumer, labor struggles, racial strife, and other group conflicts are incidents in the evocation of the generalized other: their resolution is both cause and consequence of its existence. The characteristic feature of the self is self-interaction; however, as he points out, "self interaction has the potential of placing an individual in opposition to his associates and to his society." The problem left unanswered in Blumer's analysis is how much of this kind of conflict a society can stand and still produce individuals with a cooperative attitude and a social conscience.

Erving Goffman supplies an unexpected answer to this question. His actors do not possess a conscience, but employ the ethics and morality appropriate to a given situation; a single generalized other is no longer operative. No single relationship or set of relationships can establish a moral code for the individual or for the society as a whole. Every individual has numerous relationships and participates in many groups, each of which demands a display of conformity to its standards. But precisely because each group has or is likely to have different standards, the individual cannot develop a single, universally applicable moral judgment or ethical base: In Robert Merton's terms, the moral codes of different reference groups do not necessarily overlap. Instead, the individual presents the external signs of acquiescence to the standards of a given group, without necessarily having internalized those standards. Each of the relevant groups evaluate the performance and accepts skillful self-presentation as proof that a person does possess the qualities expected. The individual does not develop a unified self with a secure ego and a strong superego—rather, a person develops skills of personification.

Blumer could not accept the individual as merely a personification. For him, everyone had to have—indeed, as a result of the socialization process *did* have—a mechanism that is used in forming and guiding his conduct (1966). In taking it for granted that the self could form and guide its own conduct, Blumer deviated from the Puritan conception of individual freedom, which was limited to voluntaristic conformity to theologically approved codes. Goffman's deviation on this point was even more extreme. In his work the thrust is away from morally guided human interactions and toward dilemmas and problems of strategic interaction, in the microecological settings of face-to-face encounters. The self is only a presentation, a mask, behind which are other personifications and ultimately only a body.

Mead's generalized other had served as the conscience of the "inner-directed" actor, but for Goffman, if it existed at all, the generalized other was one more device pressed into the amoral service of attaining personal goals. In Goffman's sociology the process of self-rationalization, by which a conscious act of self-control and self-determination commits the individual to a given set of practices together with adherence to their attendant values, is transformed into a continuous series of not necessarily integrated self-rationalizations. Each stage in the career history of the personal biography requires new acts of self-rationalization and the presentation of new or different selves. Eliade's "archaic man" is found to be alive and well in California and perhaps the rest of America, abolishing his past, recreating his present persons, and embarking on a new future as he moves along. The processes of self-rationalization occur in accordance with the availability of real and ideal opportunities for self-realization and personal aggrandizement. Goffman depicts a society of men and women who live by an ethic of rampant opportunism.

The elevation of opportunism to a general value points to the collapse of Christia.. values as the moral foundation of American society. Thereafter salvation becomes an inner-worldly burden: the self becomes the source of its own sacrament. Individuals, thrown back upon themselves, discover that living up to the requirements of self-sacralization requires a never-ending quest for a self deified through action.

Humanness is achievable, then, only through anthropomorphosis: the social compact depends on each human's willingness to endow the other with the characteristics of a fellow human. Ultimately, Goffman asserted, the notions of individual will and personal volition—notions that have been the hallmarks of the distinction between man and beast and the basis for the claim of man's greater proximity to God—become qualities that must be *inserted* into human agents in order that the reciprocal activities of maintaining respect and establishing regard might go on. Goffman's Golden Rule is: Endow unto others the humanity you wish others to endow unto you.

By granting humanity to another, one stakes one's own claim to humanity. In Goffman's world, the only way to live is by acting on behalf of the existence and exaltation of one's own self. For those so committed, a new mundane religion is required based in a sociodicy of self-love.

Goffman's self-loving actor is always concerned with the presentation rather than the contemplation of self. Like the endlessly active Puritan who externalized his love of God by transforming the world, Goffman's actors externalize their love of themselves through endless personifications expressed in the construction and enactment of life-styles. Self and life-style are warp and woof of a single social fabric, a new civil religion (not imagined by Robert Bellah or traceable to Albion Small or Emile Durkheim) that spreads a religious canopy over alternative ways of living. Salvation is to be achieved by living life on its own terms, without regard to the constraints of the "generalized other," "public opinion," or any ideologies connected to consensus or a community covenant.

The special feature of postwar California society provided sociologists of the 1960s with many opportunities for the study of emerging secular religions of life-style. Influenced by Blumer and Goffman, these sociologists turned to the study of subcultures of everyday life. Springing up in a renewed search for cultural and personal forms that asserted the morality of individual choice, these life-styles were for California sociologists equivalents of the Skid Row, youth gangs, Gold Coast, hobo, and taxi-dancehall styles that sociologists at the University of Chicago had studied in the 1920s and 1930s. In Chicago the object of these studies had been the economic and moral salvation of what Robert Park called the "human junk" of civilization. In California their object was to chart new routes to the salvation of the self.

Sociologists at the several campuses of the University of California started from the assumption that the moral content of each life-style possessed its own validity. They were no longer concerned with the moral regeneration of disreputable people or the reform of their styles of life. Deviance, a concept central to the Protestant sociological orientation, was in effect ruled out. They did not seek to rescue the "deviant" or to show a moral preference for one life-style over another: the underlying moral orientation that has pervaded so much of American sociology is absent in their studies. This-worldly rejections of Protestant moralizing can be found, for example, in studies done at Berkeley of horse racing (Scott, 1968), "Moonies" (Lofland, 1966), conduct at bars (Cavan, 1966), drunks (Wiseman, 1970), and the mentally ill (Scheff, 1966); in studies at UCLA in ethnomethodology and in the ethnography of a real (or perhaps fraudulent or nonexistent) Yaqui *brujo* (Castaneda, 1971); at Santa Barbara and San Diego in explorations of the linguistic code of criminals (Wieder, 1974), the juridical infrastructure of juvenile justice (Cicourel, 1968), the language and performance of schoolchildren (Cicourel et al., 1974), and the dynamics of conduct at California's nude beaches (Douglas et al., 1977). Their common anthromorphosis of human dignity granted all of these people a virtual state of worldly grace.

Neither the adherents of new life-styles nor the sociologists studying them could find solace in Christian values.[3] Theirs was a search for a secular or religiously exotic substitute for self-fulfillment through vocational calling. Work, no longer appealing as the way to salvation, had lost its religious calling. In its place, the route to salvation was sought in self-love, self-realization, self-expression, or self-abnegation before non-Western gods.

In the 1950s, 1960s, and 1970s, some Americans, especially the new generation, sought refuge from bourgeois values, American wars in Korea and Vietnam, and an ever more technocentric education by turning inward. Theirs was an effort to enhance the state of each person's own soul and being. Subcultures of "surfers," "beats," and "hippies" sprang up; a variety of "Oriental" religions found ample field for proselytization. From health-food dietetics to transcendental meditation, from the pseudoscience of Scientology to the authoritarianism manqué of EST, from the physical therapy of "Rolfing" to the hydrotherapy of hot tubs, countless prepackaged and sometimes expensive self-help offerings became techniques for personal salvation. These searches for secular salvation lacked even an implicit theme of civic responsibility or social amelioration. Self-enhancing life-styles glorified the self as the new god. Calvinism's self-abasement had been replaced by self-indulgence.

The escapist movements of the 1960s and 1970s included many who sought spiritual reawakening in the hazy smoke of marijuana, the rolling waves off Hermosa Beach, poetry recitals in North Beach coffeeshops and the East Village, or the costumery of "flower children" in Haight-Ashbury or Tompkins Square. More than the death of the old God had brought this about. A considerable skepticism had developed about America's civic ideology. War, racism, poverty, and the seeming unconcern for any of these by either the professoriat or the plutocracy fractured much of the faith in both the means and the aims of public life and professional service. In fact, two revolts occurred simultaneously—one against an alleged alliance of government, industry, the military, and the institutions of higher education that had brought America to its present impasse; the other in behalf of nonrational, apolitical rebirth of consciousness outside and in repudiation of conventional values and established institutions (Irwin, 1977, 82). If there was a civil religion in America, it was suffering a legitimation crisis.

By making each person a god unto himself, salvation through self-realization and life-style reduced the size of every "religious" covenant to a single believer. However, each believer needed the mirror image of others in order to affirm the sacred truth of the faith. Groups of looking-glass selves could form secular congregations of the faithful, organized around a common life-style. But the very popularity and size of these congregations soon led to their downfall. They were invaded, subverted, and eventually all but destroyed because of the attractiveness of the counterculture values they espoused. They were defeated not only because so many others shared the dream of escape from civic responsibility but also because their ways of life provided the mass media with the raw materials for another variant of popular culture. Their salable items were incorporated into the consumer culture; their ideology co-opted by the middle classes; their "religious" exclusiveness dissolved in mass appropriation.

If society's salvation depended upon reconstituting the self by an act of self-will, then it was unlikely to be saved.[4] No public philosophy could arise out of a mass movement in behalf of egoism. The problems of the larger civil community remained, and its civic morality, whether corrupted or untarnished, could not long be ignored. Moreover, the civil community had become national in scope, its component parts mediated by mass communication. If there was a new civic morality it could be found in institutions that transcended the ethics of the local community, countercultural movements, ethnic, racial, occupational, professional, or age and sex groups. With the worldly rejections of religion, no single god is great enough to mend the fragmented covenant. Americans believing in the possibility of salvation through self-deification had now to confront the future of that illusion.

NOTES

1. At her son's request, Sarah Bayliss Royce wrote out a fine record of her experiences as a Forty-niner and of her unyielding religious and moral stance (1932).

2. After Le Conte's death, Royce wrote:

As the world goes, we have far too little chance to express what we owe to our teachers. . . . Especially is this the case when the debt that one owes to the master is of so subtle and personal a nature as the one that I owe to Professor Joseph Le Conte. . . . Now, where a range of work takes men a good way apart, spiritual indebtedness is harder to formulate; it can less easily be acknowledged by means of direct citations. . . . The sources of an inspiration cannot be formulated in notes. . . . One can only say, "The whole of my work, such as it is, is other than it could have been, if my teacher had never spoken. And whatever little good there is in that work is especially colored by his influence." In some such ways, the present writer has to express what Le Conte has always meant for him. [1901]

3. Although ethnomethodology's epistemological basis is unsettled and its language formidable and arcane, it is noteworthy that in the hands of some of its practitioners it has become something of a life-style and fad in its own right. In general the 1960s and 1970s witnessed a shift away from Blumer's symbolic interactionism and toward the southern Californian structuralism that took its cues from Garfinkel's and Goffman's increasingly convergent positions. An English sociologist, Ernest Gellner, (1979, 41–64) has noted how ecologically niched ethnomethodology has become, and, though he is ironic, Gellner is correct to point to its role in reenchanting the enervated selves of Californians.

4. As the conclusion of his essay on California (1883, 394) Royce had written:

After all, however, our lesson is an old and simple one. It is the State, the Social Order, that is divine. We are all but dust, save as this social order gives us life. When we think it our instrument, our plaything, and make our private fortunes the one object, then this social order rapidly becomes vile to us; we call it sordid, degraded, corrupt, unspiritual, and ask how we may escape from it forever. But if we turn again and serve the social order, and not merely ourselves, we soon find that what we are serving is simply our own highest spiritual destiny in bodily form. It is never truly sordid or corrupt or unspiritual; it is only we that are so when we neglect our duty.

PART VI
The Enduring Legacy of Protestantism

CHAPTER 18

Religion, State, and Civil Society in American Sociological Praxis

The problems of American sociology emanate from the dilemmas and contradictions in the relationship between God, the state, and civil society. In America's Puritan heritage there is envisioned a society composed of a voluntaristic covenant of believers, exercising mutual watchfulness over one another, acceding to legitimate civil authority but recognizing the ultimate sovereignty of God over all affairs. According to Puritan thought all men and women could become brothers and sisters within a redeemer nation. That nation would take form as a democratic commonwealth. However, in America the promise of this democratic commonwealth was threatened by new forms of worldly success and failure and new modes of social differentiation.

American sociological thinkers were the moral successors to the earlier Puritan theologians. Convinced that America was destined to be the redeemer nation for the world, these sociologists took as their project the inner-worldly perfection of American social, economic, and political institutions. Implicit in this project was the belief that a covenanted national community could be established within the boundaries of the United States.

Virtually all the American sociologists converted issues of theodicy into problems for sociodicy. Instead of vindicating the ways of God to man, they sought to justify the ways of society to its members. Hence, these sociologists searched for explanations of good and bad fortune—that is, of what appears in worldly terms to be the irrational condition that the good suffer while the evil often prosper. Just as religious believers accept theodicies that explain discrepancies in their fate with respect to death, suffering, illness, inequality, and the unequal distribution of wealth and social position, so sociologists sought to provide an understanding of these phenomena with an eye to both vindicating the ways of society to man and reforming them. In this shift the responsibility for salvation turned from prayer to praxis. Sociodicy was begun in order to prove that the Christian vision was not an illusion. The professor of sociodicy had the tasks of both the theologian and the minister.

Formulating sociodicies of race, ethnicity, nationality, labor, sex, gender, leisure, crime, deviance, health, poverty, family, education, and peace, American sociologists examined how slavery, industrialization, capitalism, urbanization, and democracy might become instrumentalities for the creation of a more perfect society. However, their "utopianism" has been "pragmatic," an attack on specific problems and the development of specific methods for problem solving. American sociologists have been much less concerned with such historical, theoretical, or ideological questions as the origins of capitalism, socialism, or democracy, economic stratification, class structure, or bureaucracy. Rather, they have envisioned their task as resolving the inequities that arise in modern society. Their perspective rested on the assumption, derived from the Enlightenment and given socio-technical expression in the works of Comte's teacher, St. Simon, that all problems are solvable by the application of reason and science. Their science of sociology sought authoritative grounds for America's moral redemption.

The transvaluation of the sacred Puritan covenant into a secular civil society required the designation of an authority that would administer inner-worldly salvation. Most American sociologists accepted the political state as that authority. Recognizing that American civil society contained diverse groupings, these sociologists encouraged the formation of a national community that would absorb (or exclude some elements of) a diversity of denominations, sects, races, and ethnic groups within a common set of American values. However, the diversity of American society posed two problems that have remained with sociology to the present day: How was the authority of the state to be utilized in the constitution and the administration of a national civil society? How were the common moral values to be transmitted to America's diverse peoples and to successive generations?

CONSTITUTING THE SECULAR COVENANT

Calvin's original interpretation of an ethnically limited covenant—God's election of Israel in which "one people is peculiarly chosen, while others are rejected" (Calvin, 1961, 5)—found painfully ambivalent expression in the sociologists' formulations of inclusion within America's redemptive social compact. Much of American sociological theory foundered on the question of the secular criteria for election or exclusion of white, red, black, yellow, and mixed-blood peoples, adherents of Catholicism, Judaism, Buddhism, and other religions, as well as atheists and agnostics. Sociologists sought an answer that would be commensurate with Protestant ideals but not necessarily with Constitutional guarantees.

Although virtually all American sociologists took it for granted that white Anglo-Saxon Protestants were members of the American covenant *ab initio*, they differed strongly over whether blacks, Asians, Indians, Jews, and southern and eastern European Catholics might be subjected to a testing period before admission to full civic participation or excluded altogether. Hughes's slavocratic social system virtually forced blacks to become less than equal members, installing them permanently as subordinate "warrantees" of the Protestant command to labor. Le Conte, convinced that Negroes could survive as a species only under the benevolent protection of slavery, proposed breeding them and the less-favored whites into a new composite race of more progressive—and therefore includable—character. Ward agonized over the racial differentiating implications of his commitment to innate intelligence as a criterion for full citizenship in the coming sociocracy. Sumner, recognizing that the compact of black subordination in slavery had been broken, regarded the uncontained violence against the freedmen in the South and the imperialist exploitation of Filipinos after 1898 as significant indicators of the failure of civilization to continue its development in America. For these early sociologists the covenant could not be resolved without first finding a solution to the race question. But they could not agree on that solution.

Hughes, Le Conte, Sumner, and Ward were not adherents of the Social Gospel. That tradition, committed to reconstituting the covenant through social science, sought to discover the inexorable social processes whereby a national community of Americans might be produced. Assimilation might blend the several cultures, ethnicities, and religions in an American melting pot. However, most sociologists insisted that assimilation was affected by a people's assimilating capacity. The sociologists' designation and measure of that capacity threatened to exclude or hold back one or several groups, and they differed among themselves over who might be capable of voluntary sociocultural submission to the American secular covenant and how long the testing time might last. The Social Gospel assimilationists, of whom Albion W. Small is a fine example, had no respect for the old world cultures, customs, and folkways of an immigrant people and did not believe that either the state or civil society had an obligation to preserve them. Democratic civil society rested on the competition of objective or political interests; creedal adherences and collective consciousness of cultural kind would have to give way to what Robert E. Park called the "coordination of sentiments" that defined assimilation. While they recognized a pluralism of interests, they would not tolerate a plurality of ethnics.

Race, however, confounded the assimilationists' hopes. Abandoning interest in creating a homogeneous national covenant, sociologists have since redefined the inclusion process to embrace a congeries of culturally and racially distinctive peoples. All could be admitted if they would bear allegiance to America's destiny in world politics. Differences in race, religion, and creed could now be social indicators of a new American secular identity.

MANAGING THE SECULAR COVENANT

The forging of an American covenant after 1850 required transposing an earlier voluntaristic submission and election to the Christian community into the secular procedures for assigning civic identity. Hughes envisioned a state-protected, benevolently despotic agrarian America, organized around a plantation slavocracy overseen by an aristocracy that would virtually dominate the whole life of the "warrantee." Le Conte put his faith in an unregulated free market economy of landowners and rural wage laborers, thereby eliminating the role of the state in the development of civic society. In contrast, Ward assigned a central role to the state—formulation of social policy would be taken away from the untrained and their elected representatives and given to the scientific expert. Recognizing that bureaucratic organization had replaced covenanted community, Sumner's state was only to guarantee equality of opportunity for all to compete within unregulated social and economic institutions. Opposed to state guarantees of equality of outcomes of that competition, Sumner believed that the Puritan covenant had been irrevocably shattered and could not be replaced by an egalitarian bureaucratic welfare state.

The sociological tradition that came out of Harvard did not focus primary attention on ministrations by the state, but developed a legitimating ideology for a leadership already in place. It looked to the individual and his incorporation within civic institutions as a means of societal self-management and moral redemption. Its theory that the individual could be fully socialized promised a psychosocial basis for civic responsibility and social order. For such Harvard thinkers as William James, Josiah Royce, Francis Greenwood Peabody, Edward Cummings, and Richard Clarke Cabot social reconstruction depended on right-mindedness and social conscience. Their orientation presumed that the problems of the American commonwealth would be solved by leading its diverse groups into acceptance of the civic covenant.

Albion W. Small, reinterpreting the moral position of the Harvard ethicists, regarded ethics as the sine qua non for the salvation of both the state and civil society. Without ethics, he believed, a rational economic utopia such as that promised by Bolshevism threatened the moral foundations of society. Sociology, standing above both religion and radicalism, was to become an ethical science of social reconstruction. Introducing this moral attitude into the Hegelian idiom, Small observed: "Conventionality is the thesis, Socialism is the antithesis, Sociology is the synthesis" (Small and Vincent, 1894, 41). Sociology would search not for a single master solution or for the solution to the problems of specific groups or classes, but for the means by which the conditions of civic life for all might be improved. The state should be so ordered as to recognize the right-minded interests of every group. Neither the proletariat nor the capitalists ought to be dominant, and revolution should not be necessary to accomplish any social end. The administration of the secular covenant would be executed according to a practical philosophy embodying the ethical principles of selfless, hard-working, Christian men of good conscience.

Writing in response to the emergence of German militaristic nationalism, Park and Teggart condemned the chauvinistic state as an immoral agency of history. In both Park's and Teggart's conception of the historical process, the world consists of numerous civil and precivil societies coming into contact, and conflict with one another and thereby generating new forms of civil association. The state is both product of and barrier to the civilizing process. Only with the withering away of the state could civil association emerge on a world-wide scale. A world association of civil societies might emerge, Teggart believed, if the knowledge of historical science were used by statesmen in behalf of international peace. For Park the obstacle to the emergence of an international civic community was the persistence of racial conflicts and solidarities. For both of these thinkers, civilization transcended the national community and the state but had yet to find its perfected expression in an international commonwealth. The state was always potentially the embodiment of nationalism, ideology, or religion—that is, of mystical idealisms that threatened civilization with their irrational propensities to world salvation through war.

The idea of a rationally ordered society within the framework of modern industrial civilization was given explicit formulation in the works of Hugo Munsterberg. He did not believe that society could depend on right-mindedness, and substituted a fetish of applied science for a faith in social conscience. Stressing scientific management, Munsterberg opposed laissez-faire economics and modified the guarantees of civil liberty. He would give scientists authority over the citizens' life and work.

A purely indigenous version of the scientifically managed society was developed by Franklin H. Giddings. Substituting consciousness of kind

for the Holy Commonwealth, he proposed a national civic ideology ultimately to be extended to all of mankind by the dissemination of democracy through imperialism. Onto the older Puritan conceptions he grafted
a positivist, scientific framework drawn from the major social and biological theories current in his lifetime. His project was addressed to creating a
secular substitute for the religious rhetoric that had ceased to play a
dominant role in America. The administration of his national state and
international empire would be executed by statistically minded magistrates who took as their charge the rational administration of mind, body,
and society—a return to the position first advanced by the father of
statistical sociology, Lambert Adolphe Jacques Quetelet (1796–1874).

However, for the modern positivists, especially the "Giddings men,"
two things have changed. First, the earlier Christian hope for a world
perfected by Social Gospel sociologists has been abandoned in favor of the
rational administration of the imperfections of the state and civil society.
Second, the instruments of research have been rationalized to such a high
degree of technical sophistication, complexity, and unintelligibility to all
but the trained expert that the methods themselves make an implicit claim
for the leadership and social guidance of society and state. This claim,
however, is only with respect to knowing how to manage social problems;
not how to solve them.

Scientifically guided state administration of civil society and social reconstruction reached its quintessential form as praxiological theory in the
works of the sociologists at the University of Wisconsin. There, at a time
when the Protestant churches no longer provided the moral framework
for civil society, Richard T. Ely sought to find another institution capable
of providing ethical guidance, moral authority, and integrative brotherhood. For Ely the only alternative was the state itself. Invested with Protestant benevolence and reconstructionist fervor, the state was to become
the church's functional equivalent, resolving the problems of the diverse
secular interests in civil society in accordance with a sacralized secular
ethic; and the university and its professors would be its vicars. The new
ecclesiastical welfare state would be exclusively Protestant, admitting to
full citizenship only those who exhibited the requisite signs of visible
saintliness, and encouraging the unregenerate to emulate them.

It was now to be the state, rather than the magistrates, that stood between God and his flock. In the Puritan communities magistrates were the
interpreters of God's will; but God's inscrutability served as an ultimate
check on their authority, lending potential instability to every mundane
authority within the Puritan community. The managerial and technocratic scientist assumed that secular leaders and their public policies already
contained their own inherent morality, and surrendered to the state the
right to decide what the good society would be. Any failure of social or

economic policy would leave the state vulnerable to the resentment and distrust of all those who felt that their God had forsaken them. Although the state of Wisconsin could not fulfill its promise during the Great Depression, the Wisconsin idea did not become a God who failed. Rather, Wisconsin negotiated a merger with the federal government, accepting the status of a subordinate denomination in the new Keynesian religion that would make the centralized welfare state God's surrogate in the economic and social guidance of a national civil society.

THE NEW FAITH IN STATE ADMINISTRATION

According to its early advocates, such as Munsterberg, Giddings, Bernard, Lundberg, and Ogburn, American positivism could be the basis for a thoroughly objective science of society. The aims of sociology would be realized when a sufficient body of knowledge had been amassed, an appropriate number of hypotheses tested, a basis for grounded prophecy established, and a method of policy evaluation perfected.

George Lundberg left the setting of societal ideals to those who would employ social scientists to work for their realization. And, he made clear, the scientist's principal employers were governments. Whereas the Puritan positivists received their societal guidance from God's word, the new positivists were guided by their secular patrons and employers, the state. The scientist must be neutral: "The only value judgment which any properly trained scientist makes about his data are judgments regarding their relevance to his problem, the weight to be assigned to each aspect, and the general interpretation to be made of the observed events" (Lundberg, 1947a, 33). Lundberg called on all social scientists "to grind out and publish systematically related and significant 'if . . . then' propositions which are demonstrably probable to a certain degree under given circumstances" (1947a, 35). According to Lundberg, they have as "their business to determine reliably the immediate and remote costs and consequences of alternative possible courses of action, and to make these known to the public" (1947a, 33). Cost accounting and prevention of societal overruns were to be the primary limitations set on social-scientific policy making.

Lundberg's positivism marked the beginning of American sociology's break from its earlier ethical and moral orientations. "Neither is it the business of the social sciences to answer . . . the question of what form of government we should have, what our treatment of other races should be, whether we should tolerate or persecute certain religious groups, whether and to what degree civil liberties should be maintained, and a multitude of other questions which agitate us" (1947a, 37–38). In this remarkable statement is contained the final step in sociology's worldly rejection of religion.

Although Lundberg's positivism was to be a resource for the state—or whatever other interests might wish to employ it—it was also to be a faith, a promise of deliverance, a new kind of secular religion to replace the older sacred belief systems that had not proved capable of saving man. Science could "save us," but who would be saved, how, and why would be determined by policy makers employing social scientific servants and counsellors. Lundberg's positivism presented sociology as one more version of a secular religion of humanity, with the task of accomplishing in this world what the Christian God would accomplish in the Kingdom of Heaven (see Salomon, 1955; 1963, 387–98). However, faith in sociology required "works." Works, in turn, required subsidy and support to enable the scientists to test the hypotheses in public policymaking. The ministers of positivism thus called for public faith in social and behavioral science— "When we give our undivided faith to science, we shall possess a faith more worthy of allegiance than many we vainly have followed in the past, and we shall also accelerate the translation of our faith into actuality" (Lundberg, 1947a, 144)—and a cordial but calculated subordination of the positivistic "church" to the managerial state, the representative and active agency of public values. First a firm commitment was required, a leap of faith: "Shall we put our faith in science or in something else? . . . This is the question which ultimately must be answered by everyone, but first by scientists themselves, by legislatures, by the Foundations, and by individuals who endow and finance research and education." And once this faith had been adopted, works in its support would, of course, be forthcoming: "Then social research institutions will make their appearance, which will rank with Massachusetts and California Institutes of Technology, Mellon Institute, the research laboratories of Bell Telephone, General Electric and General Motors, not to mention several thousand others" (1947a, 143). A good deal of Lundberg's vision has become a reality. The subsequent triumph of positivism is closely related to the fact that it had no interest in substituting itself for public policymakers and administration. Thereafter sociology turned away from a vision of the ends and towards an unstinting effort to improve the means.

In the same decade that American positivism established its claims to ethical neutrality and social utility, the members of the Vienna circle of quantitative empirical social science began to be influenced by Marxist thought. Otto Neurath was among the important group of Austrian Marxist positivists who saw no reason that predictions and controls based on careful quantitative measures and estimates might not be linked to far greater structural changes and utopian schemes of planning than were imagined by the limited-reform-oriented sociologists in America. As Neurath put it in his comment on the Russian Revolution, "For Lenin, the question, whether small, closely knit political spearheads can be formed and used successfully during a time of absolutism, was a matter of technical analysis without any emotional reference to heroism, martyrdom and the like" (1973, 382). For the Viennese positivists, ideology could lead the way to utopia by employing the techniques of social science. However, this tradition of positivism was cut short by the rise of fascism and the defeat of leftist radical ideologies in central Europe. Some of its proponents found their way to America, among them Marie Jahoda, Paul F. Lazarsfeld, and Hans Zeisel, coauthors of *Marienthal: The Sociography of an Unemployed Community* ([1933] 1971), a critical study of the effects of the Great Depression on a European community. The work of these authors resonated with that of Robert and Helen Lynd in *Middletown in Transition* (1937, 146n, 179, 201–02, 254–55, 385) and, in fact, had in common an underlying Marxist orientation. Marxist and Protestant critics of capitalism rediscovered their common roots in Comtean utopianism.

Lazarsfeld's credentials as a positivist and his youthful activities in Socialist groups at first suggested the possibility that his presence in the United States might bring a new European dissidence to American sociology. Quite the opposite was the case, however. Once in the United States, Lazarsfeld harnessed the techniques he once used to aid Socialist sociographers to the problems of marketing associations, commercial advertisers, public opinion pollsters, and election campaigns (Lazarsfeld, 1969, 270–337). From the very beginning of his career in America, he mastered the art and politics of grant and contract research. What began as the Newark Research Center expanded to the Office of Radio Research and Policies in 1938 and enlarged again to the Bureau of Applied Social Research at Columbia University after 1945. The financial arrangements to establish the latter institution, suggested in a memorandum by a committee of the Columbia University Council for Research in the Social Sciences, provided a sort of "sweetheart contract" between the bureau and business: "Emphasis will be on research and training for research. Conducting work under contracts with commercial or other organizations will not be considered inconsistent with this condition provided the research emphasis be maintained" (Lazarsfeld, 1969, 332). The identification of the bureau's work with business scotched the critical or dissenting spirit that might have developed out of the emigration of the Wiener Kreis to America. The work of the bureau established a nexus between sociology and business, especially Madison Avenue, the media, and public-opinion polling, and reinforced the practical problem orientation of American sociology.

THE END OF IDEOLOGY: A SECULAR THEODICY OF UTOPIA

Positivist sociology supports its claim of objectivity by reference to its techniques and methods and to its ability to measure attitudes and values in all human populations. Because science was not dependent for its survival on any particular kind of government, it might provide social-scientific support for any regime—fascist, communist, democratic—or serve any values—ethical, immoral, or amoral; reactionary, conservative, liberal, or radical. No values but those supporting science itself had priority. But, in need of subsidy for their ambitious projects, the followers of Bernard, Lundberg, and Ogburn turned to philanthropic foundations, business, and government for support. This opened them to the left-liberal charge of ideological servitude to conservative causes and official ideologies.

Despite their assurance that, given the opportunity, they could provide scientifically sound programs to relieve the problems of poverty (Chapin and Queen, 1937), family breakdown (Stouffer and Lazarsfeld, 1937; Bossard, 1940), racial unrest (Young, 1937), leisure among the unemployed (Lundberg, 1933, 259–64; Lundberg, Komarovsky, and McInerny, 1934; Steiner, 1937), urban blight (Ogburn, 1937; Thorndike, 1939; Queen and Thomas, 1939, 447–90), and international conflicts (Bernard and Bernard, 1933), by 1940 the positivists had not succeeded in entrenching themselves in most branches of national public policymaking or administration.[1] "Before the war there were two main places in government where sociologists as such were firmly established as essential technical personnel: in the Bureau of the Census and in the Division of Farm Population and Rural Welfare of the Bureau of Agricultural Economics" (Parsons and Barber, 1948, 247–48). With the onset of hostilities sociologists entered a large number of federal and military bureaucracies and agencies of administration. Among the most important was the Research Branch of the Information and Education Division of the War Department, whose director of research, Samuel A. Stouffer, overseeing a staff of more than forty trained social scientists, produced a voluminous study of the problems, attitudes, morale, and mustering-out procedures of the American army (Stouffer et al., 1949)—a research project that became a model for postwar mass social surveillance (Merton and Lazarsfeld, 1950). Other sociologists aided in the movement to desegregate the armed forces (Mandelbaum, 1952; Dalfiume, 1969) and in surveys measuring the effects of aerial bombardment on civilian and military morale in Germany and Japan. The Research and Analysis Branch of the Office of Strategic Services employed sociologists to interpret data gathered by secret intelligence, while the Office of War Information used the services of sociologists and anthropologists to ascertain the state of enemy morale, prepare measures for psychological warfare, and study the effective uses of propaganda. The joint efforts of the State Department and the Department of Agriculture sent teams of rural sociologists to aid farm production among America's allies in Latin America. Sociologists were among the personnel employed as administrators over the

110,000 persons of Japanese descent whom the military and, later, the civilian War Relocation Authority had arbitrarily evacuated from the West Coast and incarcerated in concentration camps (see *Final Report,* 1943; Spicer, Hansen, Luomala, Opler 1969; Myer, 1971; and Wax, 1971, 59–176). Such sociologists as Clyde Hart and Marshall Clinard were employed by the Office of Price Administration, the latter to enforce measures against black marketeering (Clinard, 1952). Lazarsfeld and Robert K. Merton became leading researchers on mass communications and civilian propaganda, working especially on the effects of radio broadcasting (Lazarsfeld and Stanton, 1941; 1944; 1949; Lazarsfeld and Kendall, 1948) and war bond campaigns (Merton et al., 1946).[2]

The great growth of sociology and of positivistic sociological research during the 1950s and 1960s was a part of America's larger social experiment in forging its own destiny. During the Cold War, universities, private foundations and government agencies willingly committed themselves to the creation of the good life in America and to extending its sway over the rest of the globe. For the first time since Comte, the sociologists' great intellectual mission seemed to be realizable. Sociology had become important as a service function within the administrative state.

The functionalists in the 1950s formulated an "anti-ideology ideology," at the same time as, and in partial consequence of, increasing government support of social scientific research and higher education. Daniel Bell's declaration of the end of ideology in the West (Bell, 1962, 393–404) was a response to the rise and fall of fascism, the rejection by many of America's radical left of Stalinism, and the apparent failure of European state socialism. In Bell's words: "For the radical intellectual who had articulated the revolutionary impulses of the past century and a half, all this has meant an end to chiliastic hopes, to millenarianism, to apocalyptic thinking—and to ideology. For ideology, which once was a road to action, has come to be a dead end" (Bell, 1962, 393). Intellectuals, Bell asserted, now shared a common view of the fundamental bases for social action and social planning. "In the Western world . . . there is today a rough consensus among intellectuals on political issues: the acceptance of a Welfare State; the desirability of decentralized power; a system of mixed economy and of political pluralism. In that sense, too, the ideological age has ended" (Bell, 1962, 402–03). For most social problems, then, an independent stance or an explicit ideological orientation were not required. Rather, social science was to harness its technical know-how to the practical programs and institutional reforms that might be realized between the poles of permanent welfare benefits, capitalist and Keynesian economic practices, and a politics of contest among a more-or-less set number of recognized competing interest groups who tacitly agreed not to violate the rules of democracy. The end of ideology was thus made ideologically consistent with pluralistic politics. It reflected an implicit acceptance of the so-ciocratic role that Ward had adumbrated, filtered, however, through the limitations on policy-making outlined by Lundberg.

The "end of ideology" meant to proclaim the bankruptcy and uselessness of Marxism as a focal point for sociological perspective. Be-cause of its association with Stalinist tyranny and—to a lesser extent—because of its intellectual insufficiency for understanding and dealing with contemporary social, economic, cultural and political issues, Marx-ism had been morally and socially discredited in Western Europe and among a great many American intellectuals, especially former Trotskyists (see Kristol, 1977, 42–43, 50–51, 54–57). By equating ideology with Marxism, some sociologists of the 1950s, who had been Trotskyists and Stalinists in their youth, hoped to identify with the expanding democratic welfare state and its growing public acceptance (see, e.g., Lipset, 1969, 143–95). Modern democracy, they supposed, would gradually absorb the underclasses—composed of racial minorities, the poor, the aged, the alien-ated—into the American mainstream while maintaining them during the interim in a state of scientifically grounded hopefulness (Steinfels, 1979; Walzer, 1979, 5–9).

To the "end of ideology" theorists, any outlook that started with a radical distrust of the inherited order of society was counterproductive to the advancement of both sociology and social amelioration. According to Edward Shils (1961, 2:1405–48), the Marxist persuasion, which he equa-ted with just such an oppositional outlook, was intellectually defective, resting upon moribund and obsolete notions of extreme utilitarianism and utopian romanticism. Moreover, Shils insisted that any alienated standpoint, such as that of Marxism, was not merely contemplative, it was manipulative as well. In place of Marxism and other oppositional so-ciologies, Shils championed a sociologism that was coextensive with the theory of action that Parsons had originated. "The failure of Marxism to satisfy, and the readiness to replace it by sociology," he wrote, "testify to an aspiration to enter into serious contact with contemporary society, and to the capacity of sociology to provide a critical self-assessment of contem-porary society." A more and more general and abstract sociology would develop. "It might well be that the more genuinely *general* and abstract the propositions of sociology become, the less they will contain a genuinely critical response to any contemporary situation." However, what re-mained of a critical stance would be encompassed within middle-range perspectives:

> The theories of the middle range will be the vehicles of the critical outlook that is essential to sociology. In its function as a critique of any contemporary society, Marxism will be replaced by middle principles and not by a general sociological theory. . . . Sociology can and almost certainly will divest itself of the quasi-Marxist, populistic, rationalistic, antiauthoritarianism and the

blindness to the nature and working of tradition that it has inherited. It will, on the whole, gain considerably thereby. It will in that event also find the idiom, just as it has already found the analytical categories, that can give expression to a closer sense of affinity with those who exercise authority. [Shils, 1961, 2:1424, 1425–26]

The affinity of sociology for political authority had already been shown, Shils believed, by the fact that "governments, political parties, military, private business, civic, and economic organizations compete with universities and. . . research institutes as employers of social scientists." (1961, 2:1435) Although this competition was more advanced in the United States, Shils observed that it was already occurring in Great Britain, France, Germany, Italy, and Poland, all countries where sociology was moderately well established. What made the new oppositionless sociology of such value was the fact that "truth is always useful to those who exercise authority, regardless of whether they wish to share that truth with those over whom their power is exercised, or whether they wish to bring about particular patterns of behavior in others, to reach their own ends." (1961, 2:1435) Even the sociological representatives of the remnants of the more critical dissenting sociology that had developed in the 1930s—an amalgam of Stalinist, Trotskyist, and ex-Trotskyist perspectives, combined after 1945 with "dissident Marxism, reclothed by Max Weber" and the neo-Freudian perspectives of Horney and Fromm— would be utilized for policy making. Not only was it possible for these critical "men of honor [to] serve . . . society and . . . those who rule it," it was very likely that they would do so since "temptations of employment . . . do bring the exponents of this kind of sociology into the service of policy." (1961, 2:1439)

"As governments incline more and more toward intervention into the economy and comprehensive economic planning, and as the welfare state progresses, a more specific knowledge of the human beings over whom authority plays appears desirable." (1961, 2:1435) The employment of sociologists by a variety of public, private, political, military, and community agencies that had expanded so much after 1945 constituted "a trend that is unlikely to be reversed." (1961, 2:1435) Their involvement in public affairs would make them advisers and contributors to policies and programs about which a benevolent state authority would and ought to exercise itself. In short, the sociologists of the 1950s and thereafter would return to what, according to Shils, had once been the role of the classical social philosopher—counselors and advisers to men of authority.

While Shils and others, such as Daniel Bell, supplied the intellectual rationale for both positivism and the policy sciences, Clark Kerr (1969, 17–18, 32, 82, 89, 96) envisioned the entire university structure as an adjunct to public policy, administration, and the welfare state. The universities became, in Kerr's felicitious phrase, "multiversities," serving a variety of extra-academic institutions, interests, and groups. The idea of progress, once an imperative of Social Gospel evangelization, gave way to the coercion of reform, in which the university was to play a central role. "Progress no longer just happens. It is forced. Individuals and agencies specialize in it." The vitality that once encouraged reading, criticizing, and applying the masters was to be buried. In its place were to be established a revised curriculum, a research arm, and a plethora of scientific institutes that would in effect extend and rationalize the Wisconsin idea to embrace the whole of the university.

As Kerr saw it, the multiversity stood at the intersection of the new division of authority in society—that between the "inner society" and the "periphery." The former is composed of the now conservative working class united with "managers and leaders, workers and white collar employees, and the independently engaged professional and agricultural and craft personnel that constitute the great productive segment of society." This inner society "is united by basic acceptance of the surrounding society and support of it, and there are no clear lines of internal cleavage." Caught below the inner society "is an 'underclass'; and standing outside of it are the 'outer-elements' of students and some intellectuals, and of the aged." The underclass, probably permanent, would constitute the source of most of America's troubles in the foreseeable future. It was the task of benevolent public administration, buttressed by a supportive and chastened body of government financed social scientists, to manage this obstreperous element in the population. Those with greatest qualifications to be managers, brokers, or spokesmen for the various interests come from the ranks of academia. The nonideological professors are best fitted to give a "disinterested" definition of public policy; humane learning was no longer to occupy an independent place in the university or in the society. Kerr's theory of the multiversity and the plural society that it served contained an all-too-easy degradation of what Robert Nisbet (1971) has called the academic dogma that knowledge should be pursued for its own sake, "as well as [a] quick and easy abrogation of the once declared jurisdictional independence of humane learning from interest group politics."[3]

PARADIGM FOR A CIVIL COVENANT

During the twenty years following World War II the positivist and functionalist perspectives converged into a paradigm embracing both abstract and concrete theory and a variety of complex applications. This comprehensive paradigm also permitted both division of labor within the discipline and professional bureaucratic control over it. Central to mainstream disciplinary growth was the development of a tripartite hierarchical division of labor and thought. At the top of this hierarchy was "pure" macrotheoretical sociology, which both Shils (1961; see also Parsons and Shils, 1951, 3–29) and C. Wright Mills (1959, 25–48)—from opposed points of view—claimed to be coextensive with general action theory and the most abstract versions of structural functionalism. Because of its general and global character, this type of theorizing promised to be neutral at both the affective and the political (ideological) levels. Macrotheoretical sociology was the domain of the purely intellectual thinker, removed from the cares and concerns of daily life and from concrete social problems. No theorist epitomized this position more than Talcott Parsons. By the mid-1960s he had not only revived interest in the global evolutionism of Herbert Spencer but also put forward his own grand evolutionary perspective on the history of the Occident (Parsons, 1966b, 1971). This evolutionary theory was not new, but instead returned sociology to architectonic histories without historical substance (Bock, 1963, 229–37; Brown and Lyman, 1978, 53–105).

Next in the hierarchy was middle-range sociology, an arena carved out and given its name by Robert K. Merton (1957: 9, 280, 328). As the name implies, middle-range sociology located itself between the abstract theories of the macrotheoretical sociologists and the myriad collections of data provided by the army of researchers who served in the ranks. However, Merton's idea of the middle range justified the linkage of positivist research to general theory by its special employment of the systems approach to social science. For Merton and other systems thinkers, all societies were social systems. As a system American society distributes rewards and punishments unevenly and even arbitrarily. Nevertheless, it functions according to a dynamic of balanced actions, patterned compensatory devices, and counterbalancing reactions. These are revealed in both manifest purposes and latent consequences, the documenting of which occupied the special attention of Merton and his disciples, who contributed new explanations for the increasing rate of juvenile delinquency, the persistence of race prejudice, the pathological and criminal reactions to a less-than-fair economic system, and the decline of altrusim in service professions. Yet, as Randall Collins (1977) has observed, Merton's sociology "detracts from the struggle for power and privilege, and tells us instead that the system distributes these things, and that if our ideals seem not to be fulfilled in reality, one should look beneath the surface to where some aspect of the great self-equilibrating system does get its way." Merton's outlook permitted a certain comfort with the dynamics of change and disruption in America. No major surgery could or should be performed on the body politic; "The height of sociological intellect is to capture the pattern and appreciate the irony." Below that height, but still within the middle range, other sociologists, working out of the Mertonian paradigm, might operate at the applied, advisorial, and policy-planning levels. There they would insure that nothing is attempted that might swing the social balance too far in one direction; that potentially harmful latent functions would be foreseen; and that the fundamental issues of stratification would be defused as problems soluble within the established law of pendular societal motion. The Mertonian orientation provided both the theoretical and praxeological circumference for two decades after 1945, a period that Collins calls "the dark ages of American sociology." And, Collins observes, Merton "helped guide sociology across those mindless and repressive years, even as he helped perpetuate the darkness."

At the bottom of Merton's disciplinary hierarchy were the sociological journeymen, drawn from the thousands of Ph.D.s educated to perform exacting measurements and trained to an incapacity for normative issues and independent theoretical perspectives. They would do the chores—surveys, field work, demographic chartings, and attitude scales—necessary for sociological intelligence and rational societal management. If such sociological technicians worked in a policy-making milieu, however, they could participate in the practical actions involved in decision making, implementation, and administration, blurring the lines between the roles of technocrat and policymaker and using the claim of disinterested scientific research as a justification for exercising influence on policy. James Coleman, a champion of "policy science," noting that the realms of scholarship and applied research are poles apart, has pointed to the potentialities for political action on the part of the policy-oriented researchers: "The disciplinary world is a world of knowledge abstracted from the world of action, but having a separate existence and a separate structure. The norms or values of the discipline favor disinterested inquiry, a search for truth, a full communication of information. The world of action tolerates secrecy, privacy, pursuit of interests, and diversity of values" (1978, 687). For Coleman—and by extension for those who accept Clark Kerr's argument for the multiversity in a competitive plural society—the policy researcher refuses to take the disciplinary pledge of disinterestedness, truth, and open inquiry and instead serves as a direct agent (employee, contractor, or consultant) of an interest group; as a clandestine or unwitting agent (employee, contractor, or consultant to a third party having a broker's or meliorist's interest in the outcome of research); or as an independent researcher seeking to maximize his own influence on social policy. In each case, however, Max Weber's admonitions in favor of science as a vocation are thrown to the winds in favor of a purposeful conflation of "science" with politics (Lyman and Vidich, 1980).

The positivistic linkup to middle range and grand theory was not accomplished by Merton alone. Although Merton's personal friendship and professional collaboration with Lazarsfeld at Columbia, and Lazarsfeld's and Stouffer's relationship with Parsons at Harvard, did much to strengthen the ties between primary data collection ("empirical research") and explanation ("theory"), Parsons, the self-proclaimed leading theorist of the postwar establishment in the discipline, still opposed the rise of Lundberg's school. Yet despite his reservations about positivism, Parsons had no quarrel with the development of all manner of statistical techniques, survey analyses, questionnaire procedures, or other mathematizations of sociology. Indeed, in 1950 he praised such improvements in techniques as *"at least* as important as that of theory" and spoke approvingly of the fact that "Cross-Cultural Survey . . . and Mr. Watson of IBM vie with each other to create more elaborate gadgets for the social scientists to play with."

While Parsons eschewed the logic of positivism but praised the technical mechanisms its perspective had spawned, Lundberg argued that there was a commonality in the intellectual basis and social outlook of both perspectives. Calling attention to the striking similarity between fellow positivist Stuart C. Dodd's sociological paraphrase of Newton's laws of motion, put forward in 1934, and Parsons's, Bales's, and Shils's theory of action, enunciated in 1953, Lundberg announced in 1964 (161–70) that, despite the strenuous objections of structural-functionalists, there was a definite and unmistakable compatibility, indeed an identity, between the approaches of positivism and functionalism.[4] Lundberg's statement was an attempt to end intradisciplinary conflicts and to proclaim his discovery of the basis for a general comprehensive paradigm, useful for theory, research, and social application and also capable of coordinating the labors of ex- or non-Marxist end-of-ideology proponents, structural functionalists, and positivists.

One effect of this attempt to coordinate sociological perspectives was simultaneously to bury Marxism and to identify it as the only alternative to the new paradigm. The purge of the left-wing professoriat, exacerbated by Wisconsin Senator Joseph McCarthy's assault on the "radical" and "homosexual" academicians at major universities, had driven some radicals underground and thus removed for a time one major ideological stance from the university. What remained of a still acceptable Marxism was reconstituted by the remnants of the non-Stalinist left as end-of-ideology social and political theory. Advocates of this perspective steadily moved into collaboration with, or at least benign neutrality toward, structural-functionalists and positivists. By 1979, a leading Marxist sociologist and a leading conservative intellectual (Bottomore and Nisbet, 1979) could jointly but still only tentatively advance as a hope for sociology what Leszek Kolakowski had predicted as the place for Marxism in the social sciences in general, namely, that "Marxism as a separate school of thought

will in time become blurred and ultimately disappear altogether. . . .
What is permanent in Marx's work will be assimilated in the natural
course of scientific development" (Kolakowski, 1969, 204).[5]

CASUISTRIES OF DYSTOPIA

The effort to unify a sociological outlook was not completed until the
mid-1960s, and even then it was not accepted by all sociologists whose
work had gone into it. By that time, however, fissures apparently too deep
to mend by ordinary methods of societal management had begun to
appear in American society. The underclasses, segments of the liberal
middle classes, and other groups marginal to societal consensus began a
criticism of society in behalf of civil rights, peace, antimilitarism, racial
and ethnic chauvinism, feminism, the aged, and—in contradiction to the
much vaunted moral consensus—the demands of organized bodies of
"deviants," such as homosexuals and transsexuals, to have their conduct
reclassified as "alternative life-styles." The systems approach had insisted
that the inherent order in American society resided in its employment of
an equilibrating mechanism whereby the excesses of the several competing and contradictory values would automatically be checked by counterreactions. Clashes in the universities and rebellions in the black ghettoes
of America's major cities suggested that the re-equilibrating mechanisms
were not at work (Lyman, 1975, 729–59). In subsequent years the promises given by policy scientists that they could resolve the problems of
school segregation (Glazer, 1975; Gross, 1977; Goldman, 1979); lead the
armies in the war on poverty (Moynihan, 1969; 1973); aid, sometimes
secretly, in the special variant of the pax Americana that prevailed in
Latin America (Horowitz, 1967); or succeed in the search for a mechanism of mind control (Schrag, 1978; Marks, 1979) were exposed as vast
exaggerations or amoral and immoral experiments.

During the four decades after 1945 the demand for middle-range and
policy science sociologists in government service, research projects, com-
merical surveys, and business organizations increased dramatically. Although sociology's program development consolidated the functionalist–
positivist paradigm and was consistent with the demands of World War
II, the Cold War, the Korean War, the Vietnam War, and the international spread of American business, this expansion eventually placed
sociology in both financial and intellectual disarray. The foci of research
proliferated to include international propaganda, military studies, housing and home finance, mental health, gerontology, juvenile delinquency,
adult crime, education, narcotics, welfare dependency, war veterans, race
relations, school desegregation, affirmative action, urban planning, industrial health and safety, model cities, community organization, public

opinion, mass communication, and the social effects of movies, medicine, death and dying, energy and environmental pollution. Each new "area" ignited short-term enthusiasm centering on "new money," recruitment, and training, and each collapsed with a new shift in budgetary allocations, leaving the "area" institutionalized in graduate schools long after program funding had dried up. For individual sociologists committed to the system, each change in budgetary allocation forced a retooling. The only constant feature of this recent history is the research methods used, which have become far more "advanced" than necessary for the simple descriptive requirements of most applied research.

The antiutopian positivism that has been characteristic of American sociology since the 1950s has not yet found solutions for America's social problems. All of the problems that the positivists promised to solve—war, poverty, racial conflict, anxiety, social and moral unrest—are still with us. In response some sociologists have called for renewed efforts, using the same techniques as before; some have become disenchanted with the welfare state and the federal bureaucracies; others have reinvigorated the old laissez-faire ideologies or sought to find solutions in a new conception of civil religion. Policymakers continue to rely on the social sciences as sources of information and policy guidance, but their present prophets are either advocates of the older New Deal economic, political, and social theories or neoconservatives, old radicals, and collectivists who became disenchanted with the left and welfare state "just in time."

Sociologists have engaged in various rationalizations of their failure. Robert A. Scott and Arnold R. Shore (1979) argue that it is sociology's academic and disciplinary outlook that has prevented it from developing truly applicable social policies; only when sociologists reorient their proposals and researches to the issues of immediate and direct concern to policy makers will they succeed in making the subject socially useful. Similarly, Charles E. Lindblom and David K. Cohen (1979) have called for a reconstruction of the policy sciences such that they will produce knowledge usable by professionals for the immediate practical solution of social problems. Nathan Glazer (1978, 1, 12) is equally radical. Arguing that professional sociologists are, or ought to be, the equal partners of policymakers, he proposes that a greater "infusion of professional perspective be added to 'disciplinary' study." Sociology and other policy sciences will thus be relieved "of . . . their own kind of airlessness, one in which concepts dance, and the life of society goes on far away as if under glass." For these thinkers, sociology is an applied science and nothing more.

James Coleman, ignoring the fact that recent policy research has not resolved any of the significant problems to which it has been applied, regards the present as sociology's most promising period and the work of the past masters as wholly irrelevant (1978, 677–703). The "rapid growth of social policy research and its increasing importance for social policy have begun in recent years to push social scientists and social philosophers toward . . . the development of a theory of purposive or directed social change," Coleman believes. Increasing the number of policy researches, adding more governmental subsidies and social scientists, strengthening the willingness of social scientists to serve whoever will employ them, and deepening the faith of policymakers and the general public in these so-cial-scientific servants will eventually have positive payoffs. "It can be expected, as the quality of social policy research expands and as its impact on social policy increases, that such theory [of purposive and directed social change] . . . will develop with some rapidity. And, because of its relation to political theory, it is likely to have an impact on the way social policy research is institutionalized in society." To such leaders in the profession, it is vital never to look back. All social-scientific roads lead to the main highway of policy research. A few wrecks or stalls on this high-way, a pile-up of vehicles at some impasse, or the sighting of bypaths and roads in other directions—or, indeed, back to the beginning for refresh-ment and advice—are to be avoided. Sociology is on the Yellow Brick Road. Ahead lies Oz and the chance to meet—or to be—the Wizard.

Some sociologists seek to resolve current problems by moving the disci-pline into an even more intimate professional association with its hitherto most generous patron, government; others hope to justify continued federal and foundation support by pointing to the virtues entailed in its failures. To them the science is worthy because it has *not* fulfilled the positivist dream of absolute prediction and total social control. Sociology has proved its virtue by *not* becoming a substitute for the democratic process, by *not* taking over the awesome powers of the Protestant God, by *not* wanting more than a service role and an advisory capacity in the American commonwealth. Nobel Prize winner Herbert Simon contrasts the limited use of the now chastened discipline with the effects of opiates: "Sociology doesn't give easy fixes, but it has given a really solid factual base to work from" (Wyman, 1982). Peter Rossi, the leading advocate of making sociology into a federally subsidized applied science, boasts: "If there was ever an idea that sociologists would rule the world and replace decision makers, then thank God we've failed" (Wyman, 1982). Rossi's invocation of the Deity as the protector of the world *from* sociology has recently been echoed by Seymour Martin Lipset (1980), who, upon dis-covering that it is quite impossible for sociologists to make accurate pre-dictions about the future of "post-industrial society," or to denote the appropriate social controls for such a society, refuses to see in these either a "counsel of despair, [or] a confession of failure or inadequacy by a social scientist." Rather, he observes, "it may be viewed as a declaration of independence, of autonomy, of insistence that people can still feel free to make their own history, that the future is not so determined that we should feel helpless about our ability to affect it." Lipset points out that "we are still far from having a Calvinist social science, from having to accept predestination." Without either God's unknowable plan for man's future or Marx's awesome but unassured revolutionary deliverance to haunt its efforts, "social science can help us, can trace relationships," and still leave the future "an uncharted sea waiting for the venturesome" (Lipset, 1980, 35).

Still another branch of the discipline hopes to vindicate sociology to government, university, and student body by arguing that it has at last reached maturity through elaboration of the structural-functional paradigm put forward by Talcott Parsons. Lewis Coser (1978, 318) calls the period of "Chicago dominance" one of "incubation." Having passed through it, "sociology . . . [can] embark on its mature career." Characteristic of sociology's immature condition, according to Coser (1976, 147), was the "Chicago reception of European sociological contributions . . . by bits and pieces." The "Chicago scholars," as Coser depicts them, "made use of one or another aspect of European work, but they did not succeed in appropriating it in a systematic manner." Why "appropriating" the European tradition "in a systematic manner" should be the test of the maturation of American sociology or of any science is never explained. Nor does Coser account for the facts that the Europeans so appropriated constitute but a select few of the large body of Continental and British sociological thinkers;[6] that most of the concepts of structural functionalism were already present and had been subjected to systematization in American sociological thought *before* Parsons systematized them (see, e.g., H. A. W[ashington], 1848; H. Hughes, 1854); and that both the statics and the dynamics of structural functionalism had been part of the Comtean-Spencerean tradition in American sociology long before Parsons wrote *The Structure of Social Action*. Instead, Parsons's systematic synthesis of the works of Durkheim, Weber, Pareto, and Marshall is assigned maturation value, and "the Harvard group, under the guidance of Parsons," is credited with having "widened the vistas of American sociologists, making them receptive to the rich heritage of the European sociological tradition." This position reflects a remarkable reconstruction and revision of both American and European thought.

Another version of the Parsons maturation thesis is put forth by Jeffrey C. Alexander (1982) in the first volume of a projected four. Entitled *Theoretical Logic in Sociology*, this work promises to reconstruct both the logic and the history of the discipline in order to restore Parsons's systems theory to healthy wholeness. According to Alexander, Parsons was "of all his generation, the only true peer of the classical tradition," and he castigates Parsons's critics for having spoken too much and too soon against the singular contributions "of a great man." "The proof of this assessment," writes Alexander, "is that in most respects the decade which followed, the 1970s, was a moribund one" (xiii–xiv). The present crisis in sociology, as Alexander sees it, is one of an unwarranted disciplinary fatigue in the face of "the trivializing effect of the ever more powerful urge for 'scientization,' . . . the flood of well-intended but too often grossly misleading critiques, . . . the false promise of imminent transformation, and . . . the death of a great man." Alexander hopes to rescue sociology by keeping the flame of Talcott Parsons brightly burning.

Coser, by proclaiming that structural functionalism is the sign of the discipline's adulthood, and Alexander, by vindicating *The Structure of Social Action*, assert that there is no further need for social theorizing. This claim links the works of Coser and Alexander with that of Nathan Glazer when he asserts that the "disciplinary" orientation—which he opposes in favor of the "professional" approach—spends too much time "studying texts, comparing texts, penetrating texts, [and] developing their implications" (Glazer, 1978).[7] If sociology has achieved all that is theoretically possible, then the profession can start planning, programming, and developing strategies for the appropriate social changes; now is the time not for more thinking, but for action.

In effect, some contemporary sociologists make the social system coextensive with contemporary American society and wish to lend their support to its management. Armored by their closed theoretical systems approach and assured of the correctness of the basic values inherent in the American democratic system, they hope that sociology can re-create the privileged position it enjoyed during the peak years of the Cold War.

The advocates of a greater professionalism and applied practice stress only one side of Puritan pragmatism: the use of social engineering to solve social problems. They overlook that part of the pragmatic tradition which descends from the Enlightenment and takes religion as an object of sociological investigation and the national state as a historical entity worthy of research and critical study.

A PUBLIC PHILOSOPHY FOR CIVIL SOCIETY

The secularizing tendencies within Protestantism itself have led sociologists to a persistent search for the bases for a civil religion. Albion W. Small postulated his as national, one that would superimpose its values on those of the several ethnic groups that made up American society. It suffered, however, from the disadvantage of excessive patriotic chauvinism. Giddings elevated the chauvinism of consciousness of kind to a legitimate national religion in its own right, even assigning to its American bearers the duty of an imperialist crusade. W. Lloyd Warner sublimated the patriotic celebrations of America's national holidays into a civil religion of military memorials and remembrance days; it found its highest expression in the necropolis, the cemetery-city of the dead where America's war casualties were given their annual honor. Neither blatant patriotism nor nationalist chauvinism have endured as civil religions in America. They were in fact transvaluations of a socially conscious Puritanism that, in the face of America's ethnic divisions and socioeconomic problems, sought consensus around the secular state, conceived as a reconstituted national covenant.

Theories of the social system represented one direction taken by secular Protestantism and its sociological representatives in their transformation of religious into state authority. The systems theory of southern Presbyterian thinkers such as Henry Hughes had not eliminated God from its conception of secular authority. For Hughes the secular authority of the slave master was legitimated by God because all authority was exercised in God's name. Northern systems theory sought to resolve the dilemma of the basis for authority when it could no longer be attributed to God and His magistrates. Congregationalists and Unitarians attempted to locate authority without reference to God and within the functioning of the system itself.

Parsons's social systems theory found a way to avoid the problem of God by dissolving authority in the harmonics of the dynamically equilibrating system itself. Society itself is made up of statuses that define rights, privileges, duties, and responsibilities, and all those who occupy these statuses have a place in the social system according to the function they perform. The maintenance of the system as a whole depends on the proper performance of roles, each individual being called upon to perform according to his abilities (but not necessarily to receive according to his needs). Authority is an attribute of all statuses and roles, but in some of them authority is the major attribute. Such authoritative roles are critical to the maintenance of the system as a whole. Authority is disembodied; executive functions belong no longer to an individual but are an attribute of an office that is itself part of a larger system of functioning roles and statuses.

The dissolution of authority into the harmonics of the system means that executives cannot be held responsible for their own acts; this secularized system of authority has no basis for morality outside of its own self-generated processes of interaction. All are moral keepers and are morally kept within a system of functionally binding interdependence.

A variant of the systems approach, exchange theory, is defined by a mechanical calculus of gain and loss. Because each exchange contains its own moral content, no moral principle is required. Systems and exchange theories "solve" the problems of authority, morality, and ethics by making the functioning of the social system into a civil religion. The wisdom of society for these theorists is contained in endless exchanges that for them embody the soul of society.

Where for Parsons and the neoutilitarian exchange theorists, such as George Homans, Peter Blau, and their followers, public morality is guided by the hidden hand of dynamic equilibrium, for some exponents of Marxist sociology it is directed by the inner-worldly ethical prophecy of historical materialism. This too becomes a civil religion as the correct handling of the contradictions among the people and the state is assigned to the Communist party, or to its bureaucratic successor, a theoretically mandated bearer of the historical conscience. This civil religion unites the individual, civil society, and the state in pursuit of a common historical purpose. One servant of this civil religion is positivistic social science, as defined by Lazarsfeld: "What has become known as Marxist sociology comes closer than any other quest of its kind to [being] the strict model for a theory" (1970, 40–42). State and civil society in Russia and America have not yet achieved perfect integration, Lazarsfeld says, because of the persistence of alienation within their respective populations. In Russia, however, the research criteria for this problem are set by the ruling party, which, as "the avant-garde of the working class," takes as its task the direction of the "economic and cultural life of the country." Having "accepted empirical social research, or, as it is often called, concrete sociology" as a way by which "concrete data on the state of the nation are provided," the party has commissioned sociological investigations that showed—in the words of two Soviet sociologists quoted by Lazarsfeld— that "in many cases the members of the collectivity, including some of the workers, have not yet become aware *(pris conscience)* of how their own fundamental interests and those of socialist society coincide." Such a lack of awareness is regarded as alienation in Soviet social thought. The individual has not yet submitted himself wholly to the precepts of the Soviet covenant, remaining, in its terms, unregenerate. His regeneration is to be accomplished with the technical assistance of the sociologists, who themselves assert that "how to suppress the alienation of man in a socialist regime can be scientifically studied through sociological inquiries." In Lazarsfeld's civil religion, the state and civil society are to be welded into an undifferentiated unity, a secular social compact devoted to the rational administration of human alienation and to following dialectical history's ineluctable path to inner-worldly salvation. As a civil religion, contemporary Soviet Marxism is characterized by both the repressiveness and the requirement of voluntary submission that marked early Puritanism. However, though its American sociological adherents do not seem to have noticed the fact, its means of securing compliance are far more severe and sweeping than those of the magistrates of early New England.

The most recent versions of a civil religion are those represented by Robert Bellah and by the neo-Marxists. In Bellah's version (1981, 10) social science itself becomes a civil religion:

> We can . . . say that in contemporary society social science has usurped the traditional position of theology. It is now social science that tells us what kind of creatures we are and what we are about on this planet. It is social science that provides us images of personal behavior and legitimations of the structures that govern us. It is to social science that the task is entrusted, so far as it is entrusted at all, of, in whatever the contemporary terms for it would be, "justifying the ways of God to man."

For Bellah, ethics, morality, and eschatology become the province of the scientific intellectual. However, in a world in which, as Bellah admits, "biblical religion has . . . been pushed to periphery," each intellectual can assert the moral superiority of his own values, and each discipline can claim to set the correct moral standards for society. These civil religions then are likely to become a cockpit of creeds.

The American neo-Marxists make their variant of sociology a prophetic civil religion. Their analyses do not focus upon injustice and inequality in order to expose the immorality of the capitalist state. Rather, they point to inherent contradictions that make the capitalist state unsuccessful in resolving its own problems of crisis management and project the solution to the Social Question onto an internationally integrated class struggle. For these thinkers civil society is only temporarily contained within national boundaries. Ultimately their vindication of society to man rests on the prophecy of the future millennium and the need to overcome those contingencies of history and experience that stand in the way of its fulfillment. These Marxists have replaced the universal brotherhood of saints with the universal comradeship of workers, the Holy Commonwealth of Puritans with a secular classless utopia. But where the Puritan divines were ethical magistrates, the neo-Marxist sociologists are "scientific" prophets. For them, "late" capitalism foreshadows the millennium.

The responses of most American sociologists to the dilemmas and contradictions of forging a secular civil society reflect the separate and sometimes conflicting strands of Protestantism and utopian Marxism. However, in the work of Erving Goffman and his followers, we find an attempt to describe a civil religion that exists without dependence on either civil society, the state, or historical inevitability. This is a civil religion of the other-directed that seeks to enhance the charisma and fend off the stigma of the presented self. In this Spinozan image, God resides in the attribution of self that each person grants to the other.

The other-directed man seeks to place responsibility for his morally questionable actions on others. Possession by the Devil is no longer a convincing explanation for moral culpability. Evil must be located either in oneself or in others: someone or something must take the blame. But in a world in which there is neither a religious ethic nor an established set of core values to guide civic or interpersonal conduct, the inscrutability of the ultimately just Calvinist God has been replaced by the inaccessibility of the morally responsible agent. Society becomes a species of communicative conduct in which each member presents what he hopes are efficacious excuses or justifications for acts called into question. All of life is reduced to self-interest and self-promotion; the voracious ego governs the relations of the one with the other. Goffman's observations represent a critical end-point in the analysis of the moral structure of the civil community. The generalized other has disappeared.

Goffman's sociology is a recognition of the anguishing dilemmas that man faces in a world without God, without theodicy, without eschatology. The normlessness of that world drives people to seek distraction in risky ventures, strategic ploys, manipulations of relations in public, game frameworks, and adventures—that is, unusual activities carried out in times and places separately carved from their routine world. But, just as for Simmel (1968), the worldly revolutionaries who seek to emancipate *life* permanently from its own *forms* are doomed to discover the impossibility of their task as they see their own emancipatory acts converted into still other constraining forms; so also contemporary religious escapes from the paradoxes of self and dilemmas of conscience prove, only more distressingly, that there is no exit from the burdens and acceptance of responsibility for the world.

The transvaluation of theodicy into sociodicy has coincided with a general and pervasive secularization and rationalization taking place throughout the Occident. Yet the original problems of theodicy remain. Men and women still seek to create meaningful lives for themselves; they attempt to comprehend the natural and social inequities, injustices, and misfortunes that cry out for explanation. American sociology as the successor to Protestant theology is compelled to assume the burden of providing a sociodicy. Though it inherited the world after industrialization and immigration had deprived Puritanism of its effectiveness as theodicy, it has not yet recognized that a sociodicy carries with itself a burden of ethics that transcends the philosophy of administration.

The philosophy of social order that is described in positivism, functionalism, and exchange theory takes the hapless individual as a given. The alienation of the individual from God, the state, and the other is left to personal resolution. The forms which these resolutions take constitute the paradigms of deviance, a separate subdivision of sociology. Perfecting the management of the administrative state may go on without concern for the soul—or, in many cases, the body—of the individual. The central instrument for achieving perfectibility is left to the administrative bureaucracy, which has yet to develop or be guided by a public philosophy.[8]

The problem of public philosophy is implicit in the work of Herbert Blumer. Blumer searched for the institutions, and the processes defining their interaction, that would shape a public morality, and thought he had found them in power and conflict relationships and in public opinion. He conceived of civil society as an arena of interests with the state acting as a referee among them. A party to no contracts itself, except to that which legitimates its authority, the state ensures that every contract between groups and interests is carried out according to the overriding public interest. But in Blumer's democratic conception, the state is also a creature of all these groups and interests. By incorporating but standing above all interests the state serves the generalized interest of society itself. It thus becomes the agency of the generalized other, embodying public morality and implementing public good.

Sociologists working within secular frameworks have not permitted their worldly rejection of religion to forget the humanity of the person. They have developed a number of independent approaches to the self, the community, mass communications, race relations, the nature of the state, history, and international relations. Associated with such heterodox sociologists as William Graham Sumner, John Cummings, Frederick J. Teggart, Robert E. Park, Herbert Blumer, Erving Goffman, and their intellectual descendants, most of these approaches eschew a teleology, whether of an eschatological or irreligious kind. Whereas the positivists and the functionalists have exchanged the promised utopia of a world-wide Christian community for the bloodless entelechy of a society-centered dynamic equilibrium, the heterodox sociologists speak of an open-ended world, of existential phenomena, of the contingencies of history, and of the individual located somewhere between freedom and determinism. From these heterodoxies flow the intellectual visions of a sociodicy yet to be developed for a modern industrial society.

NOTES

1. During the 1930s sociology suffered a crisis much like that of the 1980s. Unemployment was so high that F. Stuart Chapin suggested a restriction on the granting of Ph.D.s, a proposal seen by Ellsworth Faris as one more attempt by the positivists to reduce the number of their Chicago School rivals (see the exchange between Chapin and Faris, 1934, 506–12). The Committee on Opportunities for Trained Sociologists, formed by the American Sociological Society in 1934, recommended two years later that sociological training and field experience become qualifications for federal and state civil-service positions; that graduate study be reformulated as technical training for work in public administration; that sociology claim a place in state planning commissions, that a publicity chairman be appointed to give the discipline's accomplishments greater public exposure; that non-Ph.D.s should no longer be hired for teaching positions, and in general that sociology be expanded into those university centers that had thus far resisted it (Rhodes, 1980, 4). Other proposals favored swelling classroom enrollments by attracting social-welfare majors, embarking more seriously on a "quest for applicable sociology," developing the discipline "along such lines that its bearing

on various practical human needs and problems shall be more evident than seems to have been the case heretofore," on rewriting the textbooks so that sociology's "important, ultimately practical bearings on problems of citizenship, problems of personal conduct, and on the problems encountered in various occupations" would be highlighted (House, [1936] 1970, 427–28). Ultimately, none of these proposals proved effective. Sociology, like the nation as a whole, was rescued from the Depression by World War II.

2. However, as Parsons and Barber observed, "As compared with the lawyers, the economists, and the psychologists, sociologists as a professional group were not in a favorable position to make a major contribution to the war." Parsons and Barber attribute sociology's unfavorable position to the discipline's failure at that time to have carved out "a clearly recognized sphere of technical competence" (see Parsons and Barber, 1948, 247).

3. Nisbet states the point directly and without qualification:

I firmly believe that direct grants from government and foundation to individual members of university faculties, or to small company-like groups of faculty members, for the purpose of creating institutes, centers, bureaus, and other essentially capitalistic enterprises within the academic community to be the single most powerful agent of change that we can find in the university's long history. For the first time in Western history, professors and scholars were thrust into the unwonted position of entrepreneurs in incessant search for new sources of capital, of new revenue, and, taking the word in its larger sense, of profits. Whereas for centuries the forces of commerce, trade, and industrialization outside the university had registered little if any impact upon the academic community beyond perhaps a certain tightening of forces within, the new capitalism, *academic capitalism*, is a force that arose within the university and that has had as its most eager supporters the members of the professoriat. [Nisbet, 1971, 72–73]

4. Among the issues that had separated Lundberg from other positivists and functionalists were his attitude toward government funding of research and his opposition to America's entry into World War II. The functionalists, together with a significant coterie of non-Stalinist Marxists, supported the New Deal and the war and later enlisted in the Cold War. Lundberg, however, demanded federal subsidies for an ideologically neutral sociology. In 1947 he savaged the Senate for refusing to include the social sciences in the newly established National Science Foundation (see Lundberg, 1947), rebuked his colleagues for succumbing to Marxist perspectives and other "unscientific" orientations (1947; 1945) and later repudiated the alleged obstacles to the professional advancement and public recognition of social science (1950a). The functionalists took a different tack. They incorporated the techniques employed by those positivists and behaviorists who had supported America's efforts in the war—e.g., Stouffer and Lazarsfeld—but denounced "operationalism" for building theory from the wrong end. "In its commitment to particular methodological tools and to puzzle-solving activity," Henrika Kuklick (1973, 16) recently observed, "operationalism constituted no less a paradigm than functionalism, but because it did not focus on current sociological preoccupations the profession as a whole agreed that it was *not theoretical but methodological.*" But Lundberg's paradigm certainly did focus on the major preoccupations of sociology. The trouble was not with its focus but with its point of view and with Lundberg's political attitudes, particularly his opposition to the war.

5. In fact something else seems to have occurred. A resurgence of Marxism in a variety of forms currently captures the attention and imagination of a considerable portion of this generation's sociologists. Marxism's premature burial in the 1950s and the transubstantiation of its scientific spirit into the body of the new mainstream paradigm in the 1960s and 1970s have given this newly resuscitated perspective something of the status of that which is raised miraculously from the dead. The revived Marxism is treated by some of its adherents as an orthodoxy and identified as truth by those who wish to oppose other orthodoxies (see

Flacks, 1982). Its academic advocates often engage in exegetical work and contribute to the critical analysis of Western institutions from a strict sectarian point of view.

6. One notes Parsons's omission of Simmel, Dilthey, Rickert, Schmoller, the Scottish Moralists, the Spanish Catholic sociologists, the Cameralists, etc.

7. The position taken by Glazer in 1981 is similar to that put forward by Lundberg in 1945. Lundberg was convinced that sociology's acceptance as an equal to the natural sciences was being held back by its commitment to its classical European tradition: "The formulations of Marx, Spencer, Weber, Pareto, and others have too frequently been accepted as gospel by sociologists, who have accordingly supposed it to be their primary function to expound these texts." He proposed that sociologists instead turn to formulating a "new type of sociological theory [that] is *definitely designed to be tested and capable of being tested* by methods accredited to other sciences." Lundberg accurately foresaw the shift that would take place: "I predict that in the proximate future most sociologists will turn away from this [classical] type of 'sociological theory' to the type of theory construction followed in the other natural sciences" (1945, 504).

8. As an organizational form, bureaucracy rests upon and creates a great distance between those who administer and those who are the administered, between those who plan and those who are planned for, between those who produce and those who consume, between entertainment impresarios and audiences, between political party and voter. Because of their position at the top of a hierarchy administrators need information about the institutions over which they are the managers. Sociologists have filled this administrative need by inventing new techniques for conducting mass surveys of public opinion, voter and consumer preferences, audience reactions and the specific behavior of various age, status, economic and sexual groups. They have also created complex tools for measuring organizational behavior, and counting populations including their growth and decline by age, sex, race, religion, urban area and region. Certainly Comte, not to mention St. Simon, Marx, Giddings, Ogburn, and Lundberg, would be impressed by the formidable array of technology now available for sociological research.

These newly invented research technologies have been diffused throughout American universities and the research bureaus of government, business, and advertising. The spread of these research methods coincided with the growth of bureaucracy at all levels of society. As a result, the technologies of empirical social research have begun to be integrated into the day-to-day operation of virtually all spheres of life. Modern sociology has thus joined the administrative apparatus of modern public and private bureaucracies adding new dimensions to the problem of alienation, and becoming part of the secular system of societal management.

BIBLIOGRAPHY

Aaron, Daniel. 1977. *Writers on the Left*. New York: Oxford University Press.

Abrams, M. H. 1973. *Natural Supernaturalism: Tradition and Revolution in Romantic Literature*. New York: W. W. Norton.

Abrams, Philip. 1968. *The Origins of British Sociology, 1834–1914: An Essay with Selected Papers*. Chicago: University of Chicago Press.

Abramson, Harold J. 1980. "Assimilation and Pluralism." In *Harvard Encyclopedia of American Ethnic Groups*, edited by Stephan Thernstrom. Cambridge, Mass.: Belknap Press of Harvard University Press.

Adorno, T. W., Else Frenkel-Brunswick, Daniel J. Levinson, and R. Nevitt Sanford. 1950. *The Authoritarian Personality*. New York: Harper & Row.

Agassiz, Louis. 1850. "The Diversity of Origin of Human Races." *Christian Examiner* 49.

Ahlstrom, Sydney E. 1972. *A Religious History of the American People*. New Haven: Yale University Press.

Alexander, Jeffrey C. 1982. *Theoretical Logic in Sociology*. Vol. 1, *Positivism, Presuppositions, and Current Controversies*. Berkeley: University of California Press.

Alihan, Milla A. 1938. *Social Ecology*. New York: Columbia University Press.

Allen, Gay Wilson. 1967. *William James: A Biography*. London: Rupert Hart-Davis.

Allport, Gordon W. 1966. "Prejudice and the Individual." In *The American Negro Reference Book*, edited by John P. Davis. Englewood Cliffs, N.J.: Prentice-Hall.

———. 1966a. "William James and the Behavioral Sciences." *Journal of the History of the Behavioral Sciences* 2.

Amory, Cleveland. 1957. *The Proper Bostonians*. New York: E. P. Dutton.

Andrews, Charles M. 1973. *Our Earliest Colonial Settlements*. Ithaca, N.Y.: Cornell University Press.

Andrews, Stephen Pearl. 1975. "Love, Marriage and the Condition of Woman." In *Love, Marriage and Divorce, and the Sovereignty of the Individual: A Discussion Between Henry James, Horace Greeley and Stephen Pearl Andrews*, edited by Charles Shively. Weston, Mass.: M & S Press.

Angell, R. [1928]1980. *The Campus: A Study of Contemporary Undergraduate Life in the American University*. New York: D. Appleton, 1928; New York: Arno Press, 1980.

Arato, Andrew, and Paul Breines. 1979. *The Young Lukacs and the Origins of Western Marxism*. New York: Seabury Press.

Archibald, Katherine. 1949. "The Concept of Social Hierarchy in the Writings of St. Thomas Aquinas." *Historian* 12.

Arendt, Hannah. 1958. *The Origins of Totalitarianism*. 2d ed. New York: Meridian Books.

———. 1974. *Rahel Varnhagen: The Life of a Jewish Woman*. Revised ed. Translated by Richard Winston and Clara Winston. New York: Harcourt, Brace, Jovanovich.

Aron, Raymond. 1955. *The Century of Total War*. Boston: Beacon Press.

Ashley, William James. 1893. "On the Study of Economic History." *Quarterly Journal of Economics* 7.

_____. 1907. "The Present Position of Political Economy." *Economic Journal* 17.

Bacon, Francis. 1939. "The Great Instauration." In *The English Philosophers From Bacon to Mill*, edited by E. A. Burtt. New York: Modern Library.

Baker, Paul J. 1973. "The Life Histories of W. I. Thomas and Robert E. Park." *American Journal of Sociology* 79.

Baker, Ray Stannard. [1908]1964. *Following the Color Line: American Negro Citizenship in the Progressive Era*. New York: Harper Torchbooks.

Baldwin, James Mark. 1906. "The History of Psychology." In Rogers, ed., *Congress of Arts and Science*.

Baltzell, E. Digby. 1979. *Puritan Boston and Quaker Philadelphia: Two Protestant Ethics and the Spirit of Class Authority and Leadership*. New York: Free Press.

Bannister, Robert C. 1979. *Social Darwinism: Science and Myth in Anglo-American Social Thought*. Philadelphia: Temple University Press.

Barber, Bernard. 1970. "L. J. Henderson: An Introduction." In *L. J. Henderson on the Social System: Selected Writings*. Chicago: University of Chicago Press.

Barnes, Clifford W. 1893. "Stages in the Theological Development of Martin Luther." M.A. thesis, University of Chicago.

Barnes, Harry Elmer. 1927. "James Harvey Robinson." In H. W. Odum, ed., *American Masters of Social Science*.

_____. 1948. "The General Character of American Sociology." In Barnes, ed., *Introduction to the History of Sociology*.

_____. 1948a. "William Graham Sumner: Spencerianism in American Dress." In Barnes, ed., *Introduction to the History of Sociology*.

_____. 1968. *S.v.* "Bernard, L. L." In *International Encyclopedia of the Social Sciences*, edited by David L. Sills. New York: Macmillan, Free Press.

_____, ed. 1925. *The History and Prospects of the Social Sciences*. New York: Alfred A. Knopf.

_____, ed. 1948. *An Introduction to the History of Sociology*. Chicago: University of Chicago Press.

_____, ed. [1953]1969. *Perpetual War for Perpetual Peace: A Critical Examination of the Foreign Policy of Franklin Delano Roosevelt and Its Aftermath*. New York: Caxton, 1953; New York: Greenwood Press, 1969.

Barrett, Paul H., ed. 1980. *Metaphysics, Materialism and the Evolution of Mind: Early Writings of Charles Darwin*. Chicago: University of Chicago Press.

Becker, Ernest. 1971. *The Lost Science of Man*. New York: George Braziller.

Bell, Daniel. 1962. "The End of Ideology in the West: An Epilogue." In *The End of Ideology: On the Exhaustion of Political Ideas in the Fifties*. Revised ed. New York: Collier Books.

_____. 1973. *The Coming of Post-Industrial Society*. New York: Basic Books.

Bell, Reginald W. [1935]1978. *Public School Education of Second-Generation Japanese in California*. Stanford: Stanford University Press, 1935; New York: Arno Press, 1978.

Bellah, Robert. 1981. "The Power of Religion in the Contemporary Society." Pt. 2, *Biblical Religion and the Ideology of the Modern World*. Office of University and

Young Adult Ministries, General Board of Global Ministries—National Division.

Bendix, Reinhard. 1951. *Social Science and the Distrust of Reason.* University of California Publications in Sociology and Social Institutions, no. 1. Berkeley: University of California Press.

Bendix, Reinhard, and Seymour Martin Lipset, eds. 1966. *Class, Status, and Power: Social Stratification in Comparative Perspective.* 3d ed. New York: Free Press.

Bensman, Joseph, and Arthur J. Vidich. 1971. *The New American Society: The Revolution of the Middle Class.* Chicago: Quadrangle Press.

_____. 1976. "The Crisis of Capitalism and the Failure of Nerve." *Sociological Quarterly* 46.

Bernard, Jessie. 1949. "Reply to Lundberg's Comments." *American Sociological Review* 14.

_____. 1973. "My Four Revolutions: An Autobiographical History of the ASA." *American Journal of Sociology* 78.

Bernard, L. L. 1911. *The Transition to an Objective Standard of Social Control.* Chicago: University of Chicago Press.

_____. 1913. "The Higher Criticism of Karl Marx." *Forum* 49.

_____. 1916. "War and the Democratic State." *American Journal of Sociology* 22.

_____. 1917. "A Theory of Rural Attitudes." *American Journal of Sociology* 22.

_____. 1919. "The Objective Viewpoint in Sociology." *American Journal of Sociology* 25.

_____. 1920. "The Education of the Rural Ministry." *Schools and Society* 11.

_____. 1922. "Religion and Theology." *Monist* 32.

_____. 1922a. "The Conditions of Social Progress." *American Journal of Sociology* 28.

_____. 1923. "Invention and Social Progress." *American Journal of Sociology* 29.

_____. 1923a. "Neuro-Psychic Technique." *Psychological Review* 30.

_____. [1924]1979. *Instinct: A Study in Social Psychology.* New York: Henry Holt, 1924; New York: Arno Press, 1979.

_____. 1925. "Scientific Method and Social Progress." *American Journal of Sociology* 31.

_____. 1926. *Introduction to Social Psychology.* New York: Henry Holt.

_____. 1926a. "The Interdependence of Factors Basic to the Evolution of Culture." *American Journal of Sociology* 32.

_____. 1927. "Hereditary and Environmental Factors in Human Behavior." *Monist* 37.

_____. 1927a. "Sociology in Argentina." *American Journal of Sociology* 33.

_____. 1927b. "The Psychological Foundations of Society." In Davis and Barnes, *Introduction to Sociology.*

_____. 1928. "The Development of Methods in Sociology." *Monist* 38.

_____. 1928a. "Why South Americans Fear Us." *North American Review* 226.

_____. 1929. "Mind—Its Emergence as a Mechanism of Adjustment." In *Modern Scientific Knowledge of Man and Society,* edited by Fredrick A. Cleveland. New York: Ronald Press.

_____. 1931. "An Interpretation of Sociological Research." *American Journal of Sociology* 37.

_____. 1931a. "Attitudes and the Redirection of Behavior." In K. Young, *Social Attitudes*.

_____. 1932. "Sociological Research and the Exceptional Man." *Papers and Proceedings of the American Sociological Society*, no. 27.

_____. 1936. "The Conflict between Primary Group Attitudes and Derivative Group Ideals in Modern Society." *American Journal of Sociology* 41.

_____. 1936a. "Henry Hughes, First American Sociologist." *Social Forces* 15.

_____. 1937. "The Historic Pattern of Sociology in the South." *Social Forces* 16.

_____. 1939. *Social Control in Its Sociological Aspects*. New York: Macmillan.

_____. 1940. "The Method of Generalization for Social Control." *American Sociological Review* 5.

_____. 1942. *An Introduction to Sociology: A Naturalistic Account of Man's Adjustment to His World*. New York: Thomas Y. Crowell.

_____. 1942a. "Recent Discussions Regarding Social Psychology." *American Journal of Sociology* 47.

_____. 1944. *War and Its Causes*. New York: Henry Holt.

Bernard, L. L. and Jessie. 1928. "The Negro in Relation to Other Races in Latin America." *Annals of the American Academy of Political and Social Science*, no. 140.

_____. 1933. *Sociology and the Study of International Relations*. Washington University Studies, n.s., Social and Philosophical Sciences, no. 4. St. Louis: Washington University.

_____. [1943]1965. *Origins of American Sociology: The Social Science Movement in the United States*. New York: Thomas Y. Crowell, 1943; New York: Russell & Russell, 1965.

Bernstein, Barton U. 1963. "Francis Greenwood Peabody: Conservative Social Reformer." *New England Quarterly* 36.

Berry, B. 1965. *Race and Ethnic Relations*. 3d ed. Boston: Houghton-Mifflin.

Bierstedt, Robert. 1981. *American Sociological Theory: A Critical History*. New York: Academic Press.

Bigelow, Karl Worth. 1925. "Economics." In Barnes, *History and Prospects of the Social Sciences*.

Bliss, William D. P., and Rudolph M. Binder, eds. 1908. *The New Encyclopedia of Social Reform*. 4th ed. New York: Funk & Wagnalls.

Bloom, Harold. 1973. *The Anxiety of Influence: A Theory of Poetry*. New York: Oxford University Press.

Blumer, Herbert George. 1928. "Method in Social Psychology." Ph.D. diss., University of Chicago.

_____. 1933. *Movies and Conduct*. New York: Macmillan.

_____. 1935. "Moulding of Mass Behavior through the Motion Picture." *Publication of the American Sociological Society*, no. 29.

_____. 1939. "The Nature of Race Prejudice." *Social Process in Hawaii* 5.

_____. [1939]1979. *Critiques of Research in the Social Sciences: An Appraisal of Thomas and Znaniecki's "The Polish Peasant in Europe and America."* New York: Social Science Research Council, 1939; New Brunswick, N.J.: Transaction Books, 1979.

_____. 1940. "The Problem of the Concept in Social Psychology." *American Journal of Sociology* 45.

————. 1947. "Sociological Theory in Industrial Relations." *American Sociological Review* 12.

————. 1951. "Paternalism in Industry." *Social Process in Hawaii* 15.

————. 1953. "Psychological Import of the Human Group." In *Group Relations at the Crossroads,* edited by Muzafer Sherif and M. D. Wilson. New York: Harper & Brothers.

————. 1954. "Social Structure and Power Conflict." In *Industrial Conflict,* edited by Arthur Kornhauser, Robert Dubin, and Arthur M. Ross. New York: McGraw-Hill.

————. 1954a. "What Is Wrong with Social Theory?" *American Sociological Review* 19.

————. [1955]1973. "Reflections on Theory of Race Relations." In *Race Relations in World Perspective: Papers Read at the Conference on Race Relations in World Perspective, Honolulu, 1954,* edited by Andrew W. Lind. Honolulu: University of Hawaii Press, 1955; Westport, Conn.: Greenwood Press, 1973.

————. 1956. "Social Science and the Desegregation Process." *Annals of the American Academy of Political and Social Science,* no. 204.

————. 1956a. "Sociological Analysis and the 'Variable'." *American Sociological Review* 22.

————. 1958. "Race Relations as a Sense of Group Position." *Pacific Sociological Review* 1. Reprinted in *Race Relations: Problems and Theory—Essays in Honor of Robert E. Park,* edited by Jitsuichi Masuoka and Preston Valien. Chapel Hill: University of North Carolina Press, 1961.

————. 1958a. *The Rationale of Labor–Management Relations.* Rio Piedras, Puerto Rico: Labor Relations Institute, University of Puerto Rico.

————. 1958b. "Research on Race Relations: The United States of America." *International Social Science Bulletin* 10.

————. 1959. "Suggestions for the Study of Mass-Media Effects." In *American Voting Behavior,* edited by E. Burdick and A. J. Brodbeck. Glencoe, Ill.: Free Press.

————. 1960. "Early Industrialization and the Laboring Class." *Sociological Quarterly* 1.

————. 1964. "Industrialization and the Traditional Order." *Sociology and Social Research* 48.

————. 1965. "Industrialisation and Race Relations." In *Industrialisation and Race Relations: A Symposium,* edited by Guy Hunter. London: Oxford University Press.

————. 1965a. "The Future of the Color Line." In *The South in Continuity and Change,* edited by John C. Mckinney and Edgar T. Thompson. Durham, N.C.: Duke University Press.

————. 1966. "Sociological Implications of the Thought of George Herbert Mead." *American Journal of Sociology* 71.

————. 1966a. "The Idea of Social Development." *Studies in Comparative International Developments.* St. Louis: Social Science Institute, Washington University.

————. 1967. "Threats from Agency-Determined Research: The Case of Camelot." In *The Rise and Fall of Project Camelot: Studies in the Relationship between Social*

Science and Practical Politics, edited by Irving L. Horowitz. Cambridge, Mass.: MIT Press.

———. 1968. *S.v.* "Fashion." In *International Encyclopedia of the Social Sciences,* edited by David L. Sills. New York: Macmillan and the Free Press.

———. 1969. "Fashion: From Class Differentiation to Collective Selection." *Sociological Quarterly* 10.

———. 1969a. "The Methodological Position of Symbolic Interactionism." In his *Symbolic Interactionism: Perspective and Method.* Englewood Cliffs, N.J.: Prentice-Hall.

———. 1969–70. "Industrialization and Problems of Social Disorder." In *Studies in Comparative International Development.* Beverly Hills, Calif.: Sage Publications.

———. 1972. "Action vs. Interaction: A Review of Relations in Public: Microstudies of the Public Order by Erving Goffman." *Transaction: Social Science and Modern Society* 9.

———. 1977. "Comments on Lewis' 'The Classic American Pragmatists as Forerunners to Symbolic Interactionism'." *Sociological Quarterly* 18.

———. 1981. "George Herbert Mead." In *The Future of the Sociological Classics,* edited by Buford Rhea. London: George Allen & Unwin.

Blumer, Herbert, and Troy Duster. 1980. "Theories of Race and Social Action." In *Sociological Theories: Race and Colonialism.* Paris: UNESCO.

Blumer, Herbert, and Philip M. Hauser. 1933. *Movies, Delinquency, and Crime.* New York: Macmillan.

Bock, Kenneth E. 1948. "The Comparative Method." Ph.D. diss., University of California, Berkeley.

———. 1955. "The Study of War in American Sociology." *Sociologus* 5.

———. 1963. "Evolution, Function, and Change." *American Sociological Review* 28.

———. 1966. "The Comparative Method of Anthropology." *Comparative Studies in Society and History* 8.

———. 1980. *Human Nature and History: A Response to Sociobiology.* New York: Columbia University Press.

Bogardus, Emory S. 1920. *Essentials of Americanization.* Revised ed. Los Angeles: University of Southern California Press.

———. 1926. "Social Distance: A Measuring Stick." *Survey Graphic* 56.

———. 1928. *Immigration and Race Attitudes.* Boston: D. C. Heath.

———. 1934. *The Mexican in the United States.* University of Southern California School of Research Studies, no. 5, Social Science Series, no. 8. Los Angeles: University of Southern California Press.

———. [1940]1960. *The Development of Social Thought.* New York: David McKay, 1940, 1960.

———, ed. 1933. *Social Problems and Social Processes: Selected Papers from the Proceedings of the American Sociological Society, 1932.* Chicago: University of Chicago Press.

Bossard, James H. S., ed. [1940]1974. "Children in a Depression Decade." *Annals of the American Academy of Political and Social Science,* no. 212, 1940; New York: Arno Press, 1974.

Bottomore, Tom, and Robert Nisbet. 1978. "Introduction" to *History of Sociological Analysis.*

Bottomore, Tom, and Robert Nisbet, eds. 1978. *A History of Sociological Analysis.* New York: Basic Books.

Bourne, Randolph. 1964. "Trans-National America." In *War and the Intellectuals,* edited by Carl Resek. New York: Harper Torchbooks.

———. 1964a. "The Jew and Trans-National America." In *War and the Intellectuals,* edited by Carl Resek. New York: Harper Torchbooks.

Bozeman, Theodore Dwight. 1973. "Joseph Le Conte: Organic Science and a 'Sociology for the South'." *Journal of Southern History* 39.

Brackett, Jeffrey R. 1913. "Francis Greenwood Peabody." *Survey* 30.

Breen, J. H. 1980. *Puritans and Adventurers: Change and Persistence in Early America.* New York: Oxford University Press.

Broehl, Wayne G., Jr. 1968. *The Molly Maguires.* Cambridge, Mass.: Vintage/ Chelsea House.

Brown, E. Richard. 1979. *Rockefeller Medicine Men: Medicine and Capitalism in America.* Berkeley: University of California Press.

Brown, Lawrence Guy. [1933]1969. *Immigration: Cultural Conflicts and Social Adjustments.* New York: Longmans Green, 1933; New York: Arno Press, 1969.

Brown, Richard Harvey, and Stanford M. Lyman, eds. 1978. *Structure, Consciousness and History.* Cambridge, England: Cambridge University Press.

Bruder, Victor W. 1912. "The Relation of Religion to the 'On-Going' of the Social Process." M.A. thesis., University of Chicago.

Bryson, Gladys. 1932. "The Emergence of the Social Sciences from Moral Philosophy." *International Journal of Ethics* 42.

———. 1932a. "Sociology Considered as Moral Philosophy." *Sociological Review* 24.

———. 1932b. "The Comparable Interests of the Old Moral Philosophy and the Modern Social Sciences." *Social Forces* 11.

———. 1939. "Some Eighteenth Century Conceptions of Society." *Sociological Review* 33.

———. [1945]1968. *Man and Society: The Scottish Inquiry of the Eighteenth Century.* Princeton: Princeton University Press, 1945; New York: Augustus M. Kelley.

Buck, Paul, ed. 1965. *Social Sciences at Harvard, 1860–1920: From Inculcation to the Open Mind.* Cambridge, Mass.: Harvard University Press.

Buckhout, Robert. 1975. "Eyewitness Testimony." *Jurimetrics Journal* 15.

Burgess, Ernest W., ed. [1926]1968. *The Urban Community: Selected Papers from the Proceedings of the American Sociological Society, 1925.* New York: Greenwood Press.

Burgess, Ernest W., and Donald Bogue, eds. 1964. *Contributions to Urban Sociology.* Chicago: University of Chicago Press.

Burnham, James. 1941. *The Managerial Revolution.* New York: John Day.

Busch, Francis X. 1962. *Prisoners at the Bar: An Account of the Trials of the William Haywood Case, the Sacco-Vanzetti Case, the Loeb-Leopold Case, the Bruno Hauptman Case.* Toronto: New American Library of Canada-Signet Books.

Cahnman, Werner J. 1978. "Robert Park at Fisk." *Journal of the History of the Behavioral Sciences* 14.

Calvin, John. 1961. *Institutes: Institutes of the Christian Religion,* edited by John T. McNeil, translated by Ford L. Battles. Philadelphia: Westminster Press.

Carey, James T. 1975. *Sociology and Public Affairs: The Chicago School.* Beverly Hills: Sage Publications.

Carter, Paul A. 1971. *The Decline and Revival of the Social Gospel.* Revised ed. Hamden, Conn.: Archon Books.

Carver, Thomas Nixon. 1893. "The Place of Abstinence in the Theory of Interest." *Quarterly Journal of Economics* 8.

———. 1894. "The Theory of Wages Adjusted to Recent Theories of Value." *Quarterly Journal of Economics* 8.

———. 1905. *Sociology and Social Progress: A Handbook for Students of Sociology.* Boston: Ginn.

———. [1935]1974. *The Essential Factors of Social Evolution.* Cambridge, Mass.: Harvard University Press, 1935; New York: Arno Press, 1974.

Cash, W. J. [1941]1960. *The Mind of the South.* New York: Vintage Books.

Castaneda, Carlos. 1971. *The Teachings of Don Juan: A Yaqui Way of Knowledge.* Berkeley: University of California Press.

Cavan, Sherri. 1966. *Liquor License: An Ethnography of Bar Behavior.* Chicago: Aldine.

Cayton, Horace R., and Anne O. Lively. 1955. *The Chinese in the United States and the Chinese Christian Churches.* New York: National Council of the Churches of Christ in the United States of America.

Chambers, Clarke A. 1971. *Paul U. Kellogg and the Survey: Voices for Social Welfare and Social Justice.* Minneapolis: University of Minnesota Press.

Chapin, F. Stuart. 1928. "A New Definition of Social Institutions." *Social Forces* 6.

———. 1934. "The Present State of the Profession." *American Journal of Sociology* 39.

———. 1935. *Contemporary American Institutions.* New York: Harper & Brothers.

———. 1935a. "Some Results of Quantitative Analysis of the Institutional Patterns of Churches." *Social Forces* 13.

———. 1950. "Sociometric Stars as Isolates." *American Journal of Sociology* 56.

Chapin, F. Stuart, and Stuart A. Queen. [1937]1972. *Research Memorandum on Social Work in the Depression.* New York: Social Science Research Council, 1937; Arno Press, 1972.

Chorover, Stephan L. 1980. *From Genesis to Genocide: The Meaning of Human Nature and the Power of Behavior Control.* Cambridge, Mass.: MIT Press.

Chugerman, Samuel. 1939. *Lester F. Ward, the American Aristotle: A Summary and Interpretation of His Sociology.* Durham, N.C.: Duke University Press.

Church, Robert L. 1965. "The Economists Study Society: Sociology at Harvard, 1891–1902." In Paul Buck, ed., *Social Sciences at Harvard, 1860–1920.* Cambridge, Mass.: Harvard University Press.

Cicourel, Aaron V. 1968. *The Social Organization of Juvenile Justice.* New York: John Wiley & Sons.

———, et al. 1974. *Language Use and School Performance.* New York: Academic Press.

Clark, Terry Nichols. 1973. *Prophets and Patrons: The French University and the Emergence of the Social Sciences.* Cambridge, Harvard University Press.

Clinard, Marshall. 1952. *The Black Market.* New York: Holt, Rinehart, & Winston.

Clow, Frederick R. 1919. "Cooley's Doctrine of Primary Groups." *American Journal of Sociology* 25.

Cohen, Morris Raphael. 1950. *Reflections of a Wondering Jew.* Boston: Beacon Press.

Cohen, Steven R. 1981. "Reconciling Industrial Conflict and Democracy: The Pittsburgh Survey and the Growth of Social Research in the United States." Ph.D. diss., Columbia University.

Cole, Stephen. 1975. "The Growth of Scientific Knowledge: Theories of Deviance as a Case Study." In Coser, *Idea of Social Structure.*

Coleman, James. 1978. "Sociological Analysis and Social Policy." In Bottomore and Nisbet, eds., *History of Sociological Analysis.*

Collier, Peter, and David Horowitz. 1976. *The Rockefellers: An American Dynasty.* New York: Hòlt, Rinehart, & Winston.

Collins, Randall. 1977. Review symposium on Coser, *Idea of Social Structure. Contemporary Sociology* 6.

Commons, John R. 1920. *Races and Immigration in America.* New ed. New York: Macmillan.

Comte, Auguste. [1822]1969, 1975. "Plan of the Scientific Operations Necessary for Reorganizing Society." In both Rieff, ed., *On Intellectuals: Theoretical Studies,* and Lenzer, ed., *Auguste Comte and Positivism.*

———. 1975. "The Fundamental Theory of the Great Being—Whence a Conspectus of the Religion of the Race and Its Existence in the Normal State." In Lenzer, ed., *Auguste Comte and Positivism.*

———. 1975. "Characteristics of the Positive Method in Its Application to Social Phenomena." In Lenzer, ed., *Auguste Comte and Positivism.*

Condit, Ira M. 1900. *The Chinaman as We See Him and Fifty Years of Work for Him.* Chicago: Fleming H. Revell.

Consulate General of Japan. [1925]1978. *Documental History of Law Cases Affecting Japanese in the United States, 1916–1924.* San Francisco: Consulate General of Japan, 1925; New York: Arno Press, 1978.

Cooley, Charles Horton. 1927. *Life and the Student.* New York: Alfred A. Knopf.

———. 1956. *Social Organization and Human Nature and the Social Order.* Glencoe, Ill.: Free Press.

———. [1918]1966. *Social Process.* New York: Scribner, 1918; Carbondale: Southern Illinois University Press, 1966.

———. [1930]1969. *Sociological Theory and Social Research: Selected Papers,* edited by Robert Cooley Angell. New York: Henry Holt, 1930. Augustus M. Kelley.

Coolidge, Mary. 1909. *Chinese Immigration.* New York: Henry Holt.

Cory, Herbert Ellsworth. 1919. *The Intellectuals and the Wage Workers: A Study in Educational Psychoanalysis.* New York: The Sunwise Turn.

———. 1941. *The Emancipation of a Freethinker.* Milwaukee: Bruce.

Coser, Lewis A. 1976. "Sociological Theory from the Chicago Dominance to 1965." In *Annual Review of Sociology,* edited by Alex Inkeles, James Coleman, and Neil Smelser. Palo Alto, Calif.: Annual Reviews.

———. 1978. "American Trends." In Bottomore and Nisbet, eds., *History of Sociological Analysis.*

Coser, Lewis, ed. 1975. *The Idea of Social Structure: Papers in Honor of Robert K. Merton*. New York: Harcourt, Brace, Jovanovich.

Coser, Lewis A., and Robert Nisbet. 1975. "Merton and the Contemporary Mind: An Affectionate Dialogue." In Coser, *Idea of Social Structure*.

Cotton, John. 1956. "Christian Calling." In Miller, *American Puritans*.

Cross, Ira B. [1935]1966. *History of the Labor Movement in California*. Berkeley: University of California Publications in Economics, no. 14. New York: Johnson Reprint Corp.

Culin, R. Stewart. 1903. "America the Cradle of Asia." *Proceedings of the American Association for the Advancement of Science* 52.

Cullen, Michael J. 1975. *The Statistical Movement in Early Victorian England: The Foundations of Empirical Social Research*. New York: Barnes & Noble.

Cummings, E. E. 1953. *six nonlectures*. Cambridge, Mass.: Harvard University Press.

Cummings, Edward. 1887. "Action under the Labor Arbitration Acts." *Quarterly Journal of Economics* 1.

———. 1889. "The English Trades-Unions." *Quarterly Journal of Economics* 3.

———. 1890a. "Social Economy at the Paris Exposition." *Quarterly Journal of Economics* 4.

———. 1890b. "Cooperative Production in France and England." *Quarterly Journal of Economics* 4.

———. 1892. "University Settlements." *Quarterly Journal of Economics* 6.

———. 1893. "Report of the Connecticut Labor Bureau." *Quarterly Journal of Economics* 7.

———. 1895. "Industrial Arbitration in the United States." *Quarterly Journal of Economics* 9.

———. 1897. "Cooperative Stores in the United States." *Quarterly Journal of Economics* 11.

———. 1897a. "Charity and Progress." *Quarterly Journal of Economics* 12.

———. 1899. "A Collectivist Philosophy of Trade Unionism." *Quarterly Journal of Economics* 13.

Cummings, John. 1900. "Ethnic Factors and the Movement of Population." *Quarterly Journal of Economics* 14.

Cummings, Joseph. 1887. "Capitalists and Laborers." *Proceedings of the 35th Meeting of the American Association for the Advancement of Science*. Salem, 1887. Quoted in Hopkins, *Rise of the Social Gospel*.

Currie, Ian. 1978. *You Cannot Die: The Incredible Findings of a Century of Research on Death*. New York: Methuen.

Curti, Merle, and Vernon Carstensen. 1949. *The University of Wisconsin: A History, 1848–1925*. Madison: University of Wisconsin Press.

Cutler, James Elbert. [1905]1969. *Lynch-Law: An Investigation into the History of Lynching in the United States*. Montclair, N.J.: Patterson Smith.

Dalfiume, Richard M. 1969. *Desegregation of the U.S. Armed Forces: Fighting on Two Fronts, 1939–1953*. Columbia: University of Missouri Press.

Daniel, Cletus E. 1981. *Bitter Harvest: A History of California Farmworkers, 1870–1941*. Ithaca: Cornell University Press.

Darwin, Charles. [1859] n.d.a. *The Origins of Species by Means of Natural Selection or the Preservation of Favored Races in the Struggle for Life*. New York: Modern Library.

———. [1867] n.d. *The Descent of Man and Selection in Relation to Sex*. New York: Modern Library.

Davie, M. 1939. "The Pattern of Urban Growth." In *Studies in the Science of Society*, edited by George P. Murdock. New Haven: Yale University Press.

Davis, J. D. 1894. *A Sketch of the Life of Rev. Joseph Hardy Neesima, LLD, President of Doshisha University*. New York: Fleming H. Revell.

Davis, Jerome. 1927. "Sociology Applied to Social Problems." In Davis and Barnes, eds., *Introduction to Sociology*.

Davis, Jerome, and Harry Elmer Barnes, eds. 1927. *An Introduction to Sociology: A Behavioristic Study of American Society*. Boston: D. C. Heath.

Davis, Lawrence B. 1973. *Immigrants, Baptists, and the Protestant Mind in America*. Urbana: University of Illinois Press.

Dawson, Jerry F. 1966. *Friedrich Schleiermacher: The Evolution of a Nationalist*. Austin: University of Texas Press.

De Grazia, Alfred, Rollo Handy, E. C. Harwood, and Paul Kurtz, eds. 1968. *The Behavioral Sciences: Essays in Honor of George A. Lundberg*. Great Barrington, Mass.: Behavioral Research Council.

De Mille, Richard. 1976. *Castaneda's Journey: The Power and the Allegory*. Santa Barbara: Capra Press.

———. 1980. *The Don Juan Papers: Further Castaneda Controversies*. Santa Barbara: Ross Erikson.

Dewey, John. 1973. *Lectures in China, 1919–1920*, edited and translated by Robert W. Clopton and Tsuin-chen Ou. Honolulu: University Press of Hawaii.

Dibble, Vernon K. 1975. *The Legacy of Albion Small*. Chicago: University of Chicago Press.

Diner, Steven J. 1975. "Department and Discipline: The Department of Sociology at the University of Chicago, 1892–1920." *Minerva* 13.

———. 1980. *A City and Its Universities: Public Policy in Chicago, 1892–1919*. Chapel Hill: University of North Carolina Press.

Dodd, William E. 1918. "The Social Philosophy of the Old South." *American Journal of Sociology* 23.

Dollard, John. 1957. *Caste and Class in a Southern Town*. Garden City, N.Y.: Doubleday Anchor Books.

Donald, David Herbert. 1978. *Liberty and Union: The Crisis of Popular Government, 1830–1890*. Boston: Little, Brown.

Dorfman, Joseph. 1934. *Thorstein Veblen and His America*. New York: Viking Press.

Dorn, Jacob H. 1967. *Washington Gladden: Prophet of the Social Gospel*. Columbus: Ohio State University Press.

Douglas, Jack, et al. 1977. *The Nude Beach*. Beverly Hills: Sage Publications.

Doyle, Bertram. [1937]1971. *The Etiquette of Race Relations: A Study of Social Control*. Chicago: University of Chicago Press. 1937; New York: Schocken Books, 1971.

Du Bois, Ellen Carol, ed. 1981. *Elizabeth Cady Stanton/Susan B. Anthony: Correspondence, Writings, Speeches*. New York: Schocken Books.

Du Bois, W. E. B. [1899]1967. *The Philadelphia Negro: A Social Study*. Philadelphia:

Publications of the University of Pennsylvania. Series in Political Economy and Public Law. 1899; New York: Benjamin Blom, 1967.

――――. [1940]1968. *Dusk of Dawn: An Essay toward an Autobiography of a Race Concept.* New York: Harcourt, Brace, and World, 1940; New York: Schocken Books, 1968.

――――. 1968. *The Autobiography of W. E. B. Du Bois: A Soliloquy on Viewing My Life from the Last Decade of Its First Century.* New York: International Publishers.

――――. [1901]1969. *The Black North in 1901: A Social Study.* A Series of Articles Originally Appearing in the *New York Times.* November–December, 1901. New York: Arno Press and the *New York Times.*

――――. 1973–78. *The Correspondence of W. E. B. Du Bois,* edited by Herbert Aptheker. Vol. 1, *1877–1934;* vol. 2, *1934–1944;* vol. 3, *1944–1963.* Amherst: University of Massachusetts Press.

――――. 1980. *Prayers for Dark People,* edited by Herbert Aptheker. Amherst: University of Massachusetts Press.

Dunbar, Charles Franklin. 1886. "The Reaction in Political Economy." *Quarterly Journal of Economics,* 1.

――――. 1891. "The Academic Study of Political Economy." *Quarterly Journal of Economics* 5.

Duncan, H. G., and W. L. 1937. "Henry Hughes, Sociologist of the Old South." *Sociology and Social Research* 21.

Duncan, Hugh Dalziel. 1964. *The Rise of Chicago as a Literary Center from 1885 to 1920: A Sociological Essay in American Culture.* Totowa, N.J.: Bedminster Press.

――――. 1965. *Culture and Democracy: The Struggle for Form in Society and Architecture in Chicago and the Middle West during the Life and Times of Louis H. Sullivan.* Totowa, N.J.: Bedminster Press.

Duncan, Otis Dudley, ed. 1964. *William F. Ogburn on Culture and Social Change.* Chicago: University of Chicago Press.

Dykhuizen, George. 1978. *The Life and Mind of John Dewey,* edited by Jo Anne Boydston. Carbondale: Southern Illinois University Press.

Dynes, Russell R. 1974. "Sociology as a Religious Movement: Thoughts on Its Institutionalization in the United States." *American Sociologist* 9.

Eaves, Lucille. [1910]1966. *A History of California Labor Legislation with an Introductory Sketch of the San Francisco Labor Movement.* University of California Publications in Economics, no. 2. Berkeley: University of California, 1910; New York: Johnson Reprint Corp., 1966.

Eldridge, J. E. T., ed. 1971. *Max Weber: The Interpretation of Social Reality.* New York: Charles Scribner's Sons.

Ellwood, Charles A. [1910]1919. *Sociology and Modern Social Problems.* New ed. New York: American Book Co.

――――. 1911. "Marx's 'Economic Determinism' in the Light of Modern Psychology." *American Journal of Sociology* 17.

Ely, Richard T. [1886]1969. *The Labor Movement in America.* New York: Thomas Y. Crowell, 1886; New York: Arno Press and the *New York Times,* 1969.

Etzioni, Amitai. 1959. "The Ghetto—A Reevaluation." *Social Forces* 37.

Evan, William M. 1962. *Law and Sociology: Exploratory Essays.* New York: Free Press of Glencoe.

Everett, John Rutherford. 1946. *Religion in Economics: A Study of John Bates Clark, Richard T. Ely and Simon N. Patten.* Morningside Heights, N.Y.: King's Crown Press.

Fan, Ting C. [1926]1974. *Chinese Residents in Chicago.* Ph.D. diss., University of Chicago, 1926; San Francisco: R&E Research Associates, 1974.

Faris, Ellsworth. 1934. "Too Many Ph.D.'s?" *American Journal of Sociology* 39.

———. 1937. "If I Were a Jew." In his *Nature of Human Nature.* New York: McGraw-Hill.

Faris, Robert E. Lee. 1967. *Chicago Sociology, 1920–1932.* San Francisco: Chandler.

Faulkner, Harold U. [1931]1971. *The Quest for Social Justice, 1898–1914.* New York: Macmillan, 1931. Chicago: Quadrangle, 1971.

Ferrier, William Warren. n.d. *Origin and Development of the University of California.* Berkeley: Sather Gate Book Shop.

———. 1937. *Ninety Years of Education in California, 1846–1936.* Berkeley: Sather Gate Book Shop.

Final Report: Japanese Evacuation from the West Coast, 1942. 1943. Washington, D.C.: United States Government Printing Office.

Fisher, Jacob. 1980. *The Response of Social Work to the Depression.* Cambridge, Mass.: Schenkman.

Fitzhugh, George. 1854. *Sociology for the South,* Richmond, Va.: A. Morris. Reprinted in Wish, ed. 1960. *Ante-Bellum.*

Flacks, Richard. 1982. "Marxism and Sociology." In *The Left Academy: Marxist Scholarship on American Campuses,* edited by Bertell Ollman and Edward Vernoff. New York: McGraw-Hill.

Fletcher, Ronald. 1971. *The Making of Sociology: A Study of Sociological Theory.* Vol. 1, *Beginnings and Foundations.* New York: Charles Scribner's Sons.

Foner, Eric. 1980. *Politics and Ideology in the Age of the Civil War.* New York: Oxford University Press.

Foner, Philip S. 1965. *History of the Labor Movement in the United States.* Vol. 4, *The Industrial Workers of the World, 1905–1917.* New York: International Publishers.

———. 1977. *The Great Labor Uprising of 1877.* New York: Monod Press.

———, ed. 1955. *The Life and Writings of Frederick Douglass.* Vol. 4, *Reconstruction and After.* New York: International Publishers.

———. 1969. *The Autobiographies of the Haymarket Martyrs.* New York: Humanities Press.

Ford, James. 1930. "Social Ethics." In Morison, *Development of Harvard University . . . 1869–1929.*

Forman, Henry James. 1933. *Our Movies Made Children.* New York: Macmillan.

Frazier, E. Franklin. 1957. *Black Bourgeoisie: The Rise of a New Middle Class in the United States.* Glencoe, Ill.: Free Press.

———. 1957a. *Race and Culture Contacts in the Modern World.* Boston: Beacon Press.

———. 1961. "Racial Problems in World Study." In Masuoka and Valien, *Race Relations.*

Fuhrman, Ellsworth R. 1980. *The Sociology of Knowledge in America, 1883–1915.* Charlottesville: University Press of Virginia.

Fuller, Varden. 1940. "The Supply of Agricultural Labor as a Factor in the Evaluation of Farm Organization in California." Ph.D. diss., University of California at Berkeley.

Galbraith, John Kenneth. 1958. *The New Industrial State.* Boston: Houghton Mifflin.

Galilei, Galileo. 1610. *The Assayer.* Quoted in Morris Kline, *Mathematics: The Loss of Certainty.* New York: Oxford University Press, 1980.

Gans, Herbert J., Nathan Glazer, Joseph Gusfield, and Christopher Jencks, eds. 1979. *On the Making of Americans: Essays in Honor of David Riesman.* Philadelphia: University of Pennsylvania Press.

Garfinkel, Harold. 1967. "Some Rules of Correct Decisions That Jurors Respect." In his *Studies in Ethnomethodology.* Englewood Cliffs, N.J.: Prentice Hall.

Gay, Peter. 1970. "Voltaire's Anti-Semitism." In his *Party of Humanity: Essays in the French Enlightenment.* New York: W. W. Norton.

Gella, Aleksander, ed. 1976. *The Intelligentsia and the Intellectuals: Theory, Method and Case Study.* Beverly Hills: Sage Publications.

Gellner, Ernest. 1979. *Spectacles & Predicaments: Essays in Social Theory.* New York: Cambridge University Press.

Genovese, Eugene. 1969. *The World the Slaveholders Made: Two Essays in Interpretation.* New York: Pantheon Press.

George, Katherine, and Charles George. 1955. "Roman Catholic Sainthood and Social Status: A Statistical and Analytical Study." *Journal of Religion* 25.

_____. 1958. "Protestantism and Capitalism in Pre-Revolutionary England." *Church History* 27.

Gerth, Hans H. 1962. "The Retreat from Ideology as a Prerequisite for American Trade-Unions." *La premiere internationale* 2.

Gerth, Hans H., ed. and trans. 1958. *The First International: Minutes of the Hague Congress in 1872 with Related Documents.* Madison: University of Wisconsin Press.

Gerth, Hans H., and C. Wright Mills, eds. 1946. *From Max Weber: Essays in Sociology.* New York: Oxford University Press.

Gibson, Otis. [1877]1978. *The Chinese in America.* Cincinnati: Hitchcock & Walden, 1877; New York: Arno Press, 1978.

Giddings, Franklin Henry. 1893. "The Ethics of Social Progress." In *Philanthropy and Social Progress: Seven Essays Delivered before the School of Applied Ethics at Plymouth, Mass., during the Session of 1892.* New York: Thomas Y. Crowell.

_____. [1896]1970. *The Principles of Sociology.* New York: Johnson Reprint Corp., 1970.

_____. [1900]1972. *Democracy and Empire: With Studies on Their Psychological, Economic, and Moral Foundations.* Freeport, N.Y.: Books for Library's Press, 1972.

_____. [1900]1972. "The Gospel of Non-Resistance." In his *Democracy and Empire.*

_____. [1900]1972. "The Ethical Motive." In his *Democracy and Empire.*

_____. [1900]1972. "The Psychology of Society." In his *Democracy and Empire.*

_____. [1906]1974. "Concepts and Methods of Sociology." In Rogers, *Congress of Arts and Science.*

_____. [1924]1974. *The Scientific Study of Human Society.* Chapel Hill: University of North Carolina Press, 1924; New York: Arno Press, 1974.

Gillin, John L. 1931. "Recent Sociological Trends." *Sociology and Social Research* 15.

————. 1937. "The Personality of Edward Alsworth Ross." *American Journal of Sociology* 42.

Gillispie, Charles Coulston. 1959. *Genesis and Geology: A Study in the Relations of Scientific Thought, Natural Theology, and Social Opinion in Great Britain, 1790–1850.* New York: Harper Torchbooks.

Glacken, Clarence J. 1956. "Changing Ideas of the Habitable World." In *Man's Role in Changing the Face of the Earth,* edited by William L. Thomas, Jr. Chicago: University of Chicago Press.

————. 1960. "Count Buffon on Cultural Changes of the Physical Environment." *Annals of the Association of American Geographers* 50.

————. 1965. Introduction to John Kirtland Wright, *The Geographical Lore of the Time of the Crusades.* New York: Dover.

————. 1966. "Reflections on the Man–Nature Theme as a Subject for Study." In *Future Environments of North America,* edited by F. Fraser Darling and John P. Milton. Garden City, N.Y.: Natural History Press.

————. 1967. *Traces on the Rhodian Shore: Nature and Culture in Western Thought from Ancient Times to the End of the Eighteenth Century.* Berkeley: University of California Press.

————. 1970. "Man against Nature: An Outmoded Concept." In *The Environmental Crisis: Man's Struggle To Live With Himself.* Edited by Harold W. Helfrich, Jr. New Haven: Yale University Press.

Gladden, Washington. [1886]1976. *Applied Christianity: Moral Aspects of Social Questions.* Boston: Houghton Mifflin, 1886; New York: Arno Press, 1976.

————. 1905. "Mr. Rockefeller and the American Board." *Outlook* 79.

————. 1911. *The Labor Question.* Boston: Pilgrim Press.

Glazer, Nathan. 1975. *Affirmative Discrimination: Ethnic Inequality and Public Policy.* New York: Basic Books.

————. 1978. "The Disciplinary and the Professional in Graduate School Education in the Social Sciences." Address presented to the Conference on the Philosophy and the Future of Graduate Studies, University of Michigan, 1978. Reported in "Glazer: Graduate Training Needs Professional Perspective." *Footnotes* 6.

Gleason, Philip. 1980. *S.v.* "American Identity and Americanization." In *The Harvard Encyclopedia of American Ethnic Groups,* edited by Stephan Thernstrom. Cambridge, Mass.: Belknap Press of Harvard University Press.

Glick, Clarence E. 1980. *Sojourners and Settlers: Chinese Migrants in Hawaii,* Honolulu: Hawaii Chinese History Center and the University Press of Hawaii.

Goddard, Arthur, ed. 1968. *Harry Elmer Barnes, Learned Crusader: The New History in Action.* Colorado Springs: Ralph Myles.

Goist, Park Dixon. 1971. "City and 'Community': The Urban Theory of Robert Park." *American Quarterly* 23.

Goldman, Alan H. 1979. *Justice and Reverse Discrimination.* Princeton, N.J.: Princeton University Press.

Goldmann, Jack Benjamin. 1971. *A History of Pioneer Jews in California, 1849–1870.* San Francisco: R&E Research Associates.

Gompers, Samuel. 1925. *Seventy Years of Life and Labor: An Autobiography.* New York: E. P. Dutton.

Gompers, Samuel, and Herman Guttstadt. 1902. "Meat vs. Rice: American Man-hood against Asiatic Coolieism—Which Shall Survive?" Pamphlet printed by the American Federation of Labor, 1902. United States Senate Document 137. Washington, D.C.: U.S. Government Printing Office, 1902.

Goodman, Cary. 1979. *Choosing Sides: Playground and Street Life on the Lower East Side*. New York: Schocken Books.

Gorelick, Sherry. 1981. *City College and the Jewish Poor: Education in New York, 1880–1924*. New Brunswick, N.J.: Rutgers University Press.

Goren, Arthur A., ed. 1982. *Dissenter in Zion: From the Writings of Judah L. Magnes*. Cambridge, Mass.: Harvard University Press.

Gossett, Thomas F. 1963. *Race: The History of an Idea in America*. Dallas: Southern Methodist University Press.

Gouldner, Alvin W. 1954. *Patterns of Industrial Bureaucracy*. Glencoe, Ill.: Free Press.

———. 1965. *Wildcat Strike: A Study in Worker–Management Relations*. New York: Harper Torchbooks.

———. 1970. *The Coming Crisis of Western Sociology*. New York: Basic Books.

———. 1973. *For Sociology: Renewal and Critique in Sociology Today*. New York: Basic Books.

———. 1975. "Sociology and the Everyday Life." In Coser, *Idea of Social Structure*.

Grathoff, Richard, ed. 1978. *The Theory of Social Action: The Correspondence of Alfred Schutz and Talcott Parsons*. Bloomington: Indiana University Press.

Griffith, Ernest S. 1974. *A History of American City Government: The Progressive Years and Their Aftermath, 1900–1920*. New York: Praeger.

Gross, Barry R., ed. 1977. *Reverse Discrimination*. Buffalo: Prometheus Books.

Guess, Malcolm. 1930. "Henry Hughes, Sociologist, 1829–1862." M.A. diss., University of Mississippi.

Hale, Matthew, Jr. 1980. *Human Science and Social Order: Hugo Munsterberg and the Origins of Applied Psychology*. Philadelphia: Temple University Press.

Harada, Tasaku. [1922]1971. *The Japanese Problem in California*. San Francisco: privately printed, 1922; R&E Research Associates, 1971.

Hawke, David Freeman. 1980. *John D.: The Founding Father of the Rockefellers*. New York: Harper & Row.

Hawkins, Richmond Laurin. [1936]1966. *Auguste Comte and the United States (1816–1853)*. Cambridge, Mass.: Harvard University Press, 1936; New York: Kraus Reprint Corp., 1966.

Heizer, Robert F., and Alan F. Almquist. 1971. *The Other Californians: Prejudice and Discrimination under Spain, Mexico, and the United States to 1920*. Berkeley: University of California Press.

Herbst, Jurgen. 1959. "From Moral Philosophy to Sociology: Albion Woodbury Small." *Harvard Educational Review* 29.

———. 1961. "Francis Greenwood Peabody: Harvard's Theologian of the Social Gospel." *Harvard Theological Review* 54.

Hermann, Janet Sharp. 1981. *The Pursuit of a Dream*. New York: Oxford University Press.

Herreshoff, David. 1967. *The Origins of American Marxism: From the Transcendentalists to DeLeon*. New York: Pathfinder Press.

Heyl, John D., and Barbara S. Heyl. 1976. "The Sumner–Porter Controversy at Yale: Pre-Paradigmatic Sociology and Institutional Crisis." *Sociological Inquiry* 46.

Hill, Herbert. 1967. "The Racial Practices of Organized Labor—the Age of Gompers and After." In Arthur M. Ross and Herbert Hill, eds., *Employment, Race, and Poverty.* New York: Harcourt, Brace and World.

―――. 1973. "Anti-Oriental Agitation and the Rise of Working-Class Racism." *Society* 10.

―――. 1981. "Comments on Manning Marable, 'Toward a Black Politics: Beyond the Race-Class Dilemma'." *Nation* 232.

Hill, Mozell C. 1953. "Some Early Notes of Robert E. Park." *Phylon: Atlanta Journal of Race and Culture* 14.

Hiller, Ernest T. [1928]1969. *The Strike: A Study in Collective Action.* Chicago: University of Chicago Press, 1928; New York: Arno Press, 1969.

Hinkle, Roscoe C., Jr., and Gisela J. Hinkle. 1954. *The Development of Modern Sociology.* New York: Random House.

Hodgen, Margaret T. 1939. "Domesday Water Mills." *Antiquity* 13.

―――. 1942. "Geographical Diffusion as a Criterion of Age." *American Anthropologist* 44.

―――. 1942a. "Fairs of Elizabethan England." *Economic Geography* 18.

―――. 1945. "Glass and Paper: An Historical Study of Acculturation." *Southwestern Journal of Anthropology* 1.

―――. 1950. "Similarities and Dated Distributions." *American Anthropologist* 52.

―――. 1951. "Karl Marx and the Social Scientists." *Scientific Monthly* 72.

―――. 1952. *Change and History: A Study of the Dated Distributions of Technological Innovations in England.* Viking Fund Publications in Anthropology, no. 18. New York: Wenner-Gren Foundation for Anthropological Research.

―――. 1971. *The Department of Social Institutions, 1919–1946.* Pasadena: n.p.

―――. 1974. *Anthropology, History and Cultural Change.* Viking Fund Publications in Anthropology, no. 52. Wenner-Gren Foundation for Anthropological Research. Tucson: University of Arizona Press.

Hodges, Donald C. 1981. *The Bureaucratization of Socialism.* Amherst: University of Massachusetts Press.

Hofstadter, Richard. 1955. *Social Darwinism in American Thought.* Revised ed. Boston: Beacon Press.

Hofstadter, Richard, and Walter P. Metzger. 1955. *The Development of Academic Freedom in the United States.* New York: Columbia University Press.

Hollinger, David A. 1975. *Morris R. Cohen and the Scientific Ideal.* Cambridge, Mass.: MIT Press.

Holmes, George Frederick. 1849. "On the Importance of the Social Sciences in the Present Day." *Southern Literary Messenger* 15.

―――. 1852. "Faith and Science—Comte's Positive Philosophy." *Methodist Quarterly Review* 34, 4th ser., 4.

―――. 1856. "Relation of the Old and the New Worlds." *De Bow's Review* 20.

―――. 1857. "Theory of Political Individualism." *De Bow's Review* 22.

Homans, George. 1950. *The Human Group.* New York: Harcourt, Brace.

———. 1955. "The Sociologist's Contribution to Management in the Future." *Manager* 33. Reprinted in Homans, *Sentiments and Activities*.

———. 1962. *Sentiments and Activities: Essays in Social Science.* New York: Free Press of Glencoe.

Hopkins, Charles Howard. 1940. *The Rise of the Social Gospel in American Protestantism, 1865–1915.* New Haven: Yale University Press.

Horowitz, Irving Louis, ed. 1967. *The Rise and Fall of Project Camelot: Studies in the Relationship between Social Science and Practical Politics.* Cambridge, Mass.: MIT Press.

———. 1969. *Sociological Self-Images: A Collective Portrait.* Beverly Hills: Sage Publications.

Hourwich, Isaac A. [1912]1969. *Immigration and Labor: The Economic Aspects of European Immigration to the United States.* New York: G. P. Putnam's Sons, 1912; New York: Arno Press, 1969.

House, Floyd Nelson. [1936]1970. *The Development of Sociology.* Westport, Conn.: Greenwood Press.

Howard, George Elliott. [1904]1964. *A History of Matrimonial Institutions Chiefly in England and the United States with an Introductory Analysis of the Literature and Theories of Primitive Marriage and the Family.* Chicago: University of Chicago Press, 1904; New York: Humanities Press, 1964.

Howe, Julia Ward. [1899]1969. *Reminiscences, 1819–1899.* New York: New American Library.

Hoxie, R. Gordon. 1955. *A History of the Faculty of Political Science, Columbia University.* New York: Columbia University Press.

Hughes, Everett, and Helen MacGill Hughes. 1952. *Where Peoples Meet: Racial and Ethnic Frontiers.* Glencoe, Ill.: Free Press.

Hughes, Helen MacGill. 1940. *News and the Human Interest Story.* Chicago: University of Chicago Press.

———. 1980–81. "On Becoming a Sociologist," *Journal of the History of Sociology: An International Review* 3.

Hughes, Henry. 1848–53. *The Diary of Henry Hughes of Port Gibson, Mississippi, January 1, 1848–May 1, 1853.* Microfilm typescript of the original Henry Hughes Papers, Mississippi State Archives, Jackson, Mississippi.

———. [1854]1968. *A Treatise on Sociology, Theoretical and Practical.* Philadelphia: Lippincott, Grambo, 1854; New York: Greenwood Press, 1968.

———. 1858. "State Liberties, or the Right to African Contract Labor." *De Bow's Review* 25.

———. 1859. *A Report on the African Apprentice System, Read at the Southern Commercial Convention, Vicksburg, Mississippi, May 10, 1859.* Vicksburg, Miss.: n.p.

Huntington, James. 1893. "Philanthropy—Its Success and Failure." In *Philanthropy and Social Progress: Seven Essays.* New York: Thomas Y. Crowell.

I'll Take My Stand: The South and the Agrarian Tradition, by Twelve Southerners. [1930]1962. New York: Harper Torchbooks.

Inglis, Brian. 1973. *Roger Casement.* New York: Harcourt, Brace, Jovanovich.

Inkeles, Alex. 1980. "Continuity and Change in the American National Character." In Lipset, *Third Century.*

Iovtchouk, M., and L. Kogan. 1966. "Changement dans le vie spirituelle des ouvries en URSS." In *La Sociologie en URSS, Rapports des membres de la delegation sovietique au vie Congres International de Sociologie*. Moscow: n.p., 1966. Quoted in Lazarsfeld, *Main Trends in Sociology*.

Irwin, John. 1977. *Scenes*. Beverly Hills: Sage Publications.

Isaac, Jules. 1964. *The Teaching of Contempt: Christian Roots of Anti-Semitism*, translated by Helen Weaver. New York: Holt, Rinehart, & Winston.

Jaeger, Gertrude, and Philip Selznick. 1964. "A Normative Theory of Culture." *American Sociological Review* 29.

Jahoda, Marie, Paul F. Lazarsfeld, and Hans Zeisel. [1933]1971. *Marienthal: The Sociography of an Unemployed Community*, translated by the authors and John Reginall and Thomas Elsaesser. Chicago: Aldine-Atherton, 1971.

James, William. 1890. "Psychology at Harvard University." *American Journal of Psychology* 3.

———. [1890]1950. *Principles of Psychology*. New York: Dover.

———. 1899. *Human Immortality: Two Supposed Objections to the Doctrine*. 2d ed. Boston: Houghton Mifflin.

———. 1899a. *Talks to Teachers on Psychology and to Students on Some of Life's Ideals*. New York: Henry Holt.

———. [1899]1968. "On a Certain Blindness in Human Beings." In *Writings*.

———. 1968. *The Writings of William James: A Comprehensive Edition*, edited by John J. McDermott. New York: Modern Library.

Jandy, Edward C. [1942]1969. *Charles Horton Cooley: His Life and His Social Theory*. New York: Octagon Books.

Janowitz, Morris. 1966. Introduction to *W. I. Thomas: On Social Organization and Social Personality*. Chicago: University of Chicago Press.

Jay, Martin. 1980. "The Jews and the Frankfurt School." *New German Critique* 19.

Jencks, Christopher. 1979. "The Social Basis of Unselfishness." In Gans et al., *On the Making of Americans*.

Jocher, Katharine, Guy B. Johnson, George L. Simpson, Rupert B. Vance, eds. 1964. *Folk, Region, and Society: Selected Papers of Howard W. Odum*. Chapel Hill: University of North Carolina.

Johnson, Allen, and Dumas Malone, eds. 1930. *Dictionary of American Biography*. New York: Charles Scribner's Sons.

Johnson, Alvin. [1952]1960. *Pioneer's Progress: An Autobiography*. Lincoln: University of Nebraska Press.

Johnson, Charles S. [1943]1970. *Background to Patterns of Negro Segregation*. New York: Thomas Y. Crowell.

Johnson, Guy Benton, and Guion Griffis Johnson. 1980. *Research in Service to Society: The First Fifty Years of the Institute for Research in Social Science at the University of North Carolina*. Chapel Hill: University of North Carolina Press.

Jones, Ronald. [1942]1978. "Testimony of the Oregon State Senator from Brooks, Oregon in the House of Representatives." In *National Defense Hearings before the Select Committee Investigating National Defense Migration: Representatives of the 77th Congress, Second Session, pts. 29, 30 and 31*. Washington, D.C.: U.S. Government Printing Office, 1942; New York: Arno Press, 1978.

Jowett, Garth. 1976. *Film: The Democratic Art*. Boston: Little, Brown.

Kallen, Horace Meyer. 1914. *William James and Henri Bergson: A Study in Contrasting Theories of Life*. Chicago: University of Chicago Press.

———. [1924]1974. *Culture and Democracy: Studies in the Group Psychology of the American Peoples*. New York: Boni & Liveright, 1924; New York: Arno Press, 1974.

Kaplan, Sydney. 1955. "Taussig, James and Peabody: A 'Harvard School' in 1900?" *American Quarterly* 7.

Kawai, Kazuo. 1926. "Three Roads, and None Easy." *Survey Graphic* 56.

Keenan, Barry. 1977. *The Dewey Experiment in China: Educational Reform and Political Power in the Early Republic*. Harvard East Asian Monographs, no. 81. Cambridge, Mass.: Harvard University Press.

Keller, Albert Galloway, and Maurice R. Davie, eds. 1969. *Essays of William Graham Sumner*. Hamden, Conn.: Archon Press.

Keller, Phyllis. 1979. *States of Belonging: German-American Intellectuals and the First World War*. Cambridge, Mass.: Harvard University Press.

Kellogg, Paul U. 1908. "The Pittsburgh Survey of the National Publication Committee of *Charities and the Commons*." *Charities and the Commons* 19 (1908).

Kerr, Clark. 1969. *Marshall, Marx and Modern Times: The Multi-Dimensional Society*. Cambridge, Mass.: Harvard University Press.

Kett, Joseph F. 1977. *Rites of Passage: Adolescence in America, 1790 to the Present*. New York: Basic Books/Harper Colophon.

King, Henry Churchill, et al., eds. 1908. *Education and National Character*. Chicago: Religious Educational Association.

Kline, Morris. 1980. *Mathematics: The Loss of Certainty*. New York: Oxford University Press.

Knight, Frank H. [1940]1974. "Quantification: The Quest for Precision." In Wirth, *Eleven Twenty-Six*. Chicago: University of Chicago Press, 1940.

Knudten, Richard D. 1968. *The Systematic Thought of Washington Gladden*. New York: Humanities Press.

Kolakowski, Lezek. 1969. *Marxism and Beyond*. London: Pall Mall Press.

Konrád, George, and Ivan Szelényi. 1979. *The Intellectuals on the Road to Class Power: A Sociological Study of the Role of the Intelligentsia in Socialism*, translated by Andrew Arato and Richard E. Allen. New York: Harcourt, Brace, Jovanovich.

Kraditor, Aileen. 1981. *The Radical Persuasion, 1890–1917: Aspects of the Intellectual History and the Historiography of Three American Radical Organizations*. Baton Rouge: Louisiana State University Press.

Kristol, Irving J. 1977. "Memoirs of a Trotskyist." *New York Times Magazine* (23 January, 1977).

Kuklick, Henrika. 1973. "A 'Scientific Revolution': Sociological Theory in the United States, 1930–1945." *Sociological Inquiry* 43.

Kuklik, Bruce. 1977. *The Rise of American Philosophy: Cambridge, Massachusetts, 1860–1930*. New Haven: Yale University Press.

Larsen, Otto N. 1968. "Lundberg's Encounters with Sociology and Vice Versa." In de Grazia et al., *Behavioral Sciences*.

Lasswell, Harold. 1968. "The Garrison State." In *War: Studies from Psychology, Sociology, Anthropology,* edited by Leon Bramson and George W. Goethals. Revised ed. New York: Basic Books.

Lazarsfeld, Paul. 1969. "An Episode in the History of Social Research: A Memoir." In *The Intellectual Migration: Europe and America, 1930–1960,* edited by Donald Fleming and Bernard Bailyn. Cambridge, Mass.: Belknap Press of Harvard University Press.

———. 1970. *Main Trends of Research in the Social and Human Sciences,* pt. 1. The Hague: Mouton/UNESCO.

———. 1973. *Main Trends in Sociology.* New York: Harper Torchbooks.

Lazarsfeld, Paul, and Patricia L. Kendall. [1948]1979. *Radio Listening in America: The People Look at Radio—Again.* New York: Prentice-Hall, 1948; New York: Arno Press, 1979.

Lazarsfeld, Paul, and Frank N. Stanton, eds. [1941]1979. *Radio Research, 1941.* New York: Duell, Sloan & Pearce, 1941; New York: Arno Press, 1979.

———. [1944]1979. *Radio Research, 1942.* New York: Duell, Sloan & Pearce, 1944; New York: Arno Press, 1979.

———. [1949]1979. *Communications Research, 1948–1949.* New York: Harper & Brothers, 1949; New York: Arno Press, 1979.

Lazarsfeld, Paul, William H. Sewell, and Harold Wilensky. 1967. Introduction to their *Uses of Sociology.* New York: Basic Books.

Le Bon, Gustave. [1896]1952. *The Crowd.* London: Ernest Benn, 1952.

———. [1913]1980. *The French Revolution and the Psychology of Revolution.* New Brunswick, N.J.: Transaction Books.

———. [1924]1974. *The Psychology of Peoples.* New York: G. E. Stechert, 1924; New York: Arno Press, 1974.

Le Conte, Joseph. 1858. "Lectures on Coal." *Smithsonian Institution Annual Report, 1857.* Washington, D.C.: Government Printing Office.

———. 1859. "Morphology and Its Connection with Fine Art." *Southern Presbyterian Review* 12.

———. 1859a. "The Principles of a Liberal Education." *Southern Presbyterian Review* 12.

———. 1860. "The Relation of Organic Science to Sociology." *Southern Presbyterian Review* 13.

———. 1861. "Natural History as a Branch of School Education; and the School, the College, and the University, in Relation to One Another and to Active Life." *Southern Presbyterian Review* 14.

———. 1878. "Man's Place in Nature." *Princeton Review* 2.

———. 1880. "The Effect of Mixture of Races on Human Progress." *Berkeley Quarterly: A Journal of Social Science* 1.

———. 1888. "Sense-Training and Hand-Training in the Public Schools." *Pacific Educational Journal* 3.

———. 1890. "The Natural Grounds of Belief in a Personal Immortality." *Andover Review: A Religious and Theological Monthly* 14.

———. 1891. "The Relation of the Church to Modern Scientific Thought." *Andover Review: A Religious and Theological Monthly* 16.

―――. [1892]1969. *The Race Problem in the South.* New York: D. Appleton, 1892; Miami: Mnemosyne, 1969.

―――. 1897. "The Relation of Biology to Philosophy." *Arena* 17.

―――. [1897]1970. *Evolution: Its Nature, Its Evidences, and Its Relation to Religious Thought.* 2d ed. New York: D. Appleton, 1897; New York: Kraus Reprint Corp., 1970.

―――. 1900. "A Note on the Religious Significance of Science." *Monist* 10.

―――. 1903. *The Autobiography of Joseph Le Conte.* Edited by William Dallam Armes. New York: D. Appleton.

Lee, Rose Hum. 1960. *The Chinese in the United States of America.* Hong Kong: Hong Kong University Press.

―――. 1978. *The Growth and Decline of Chinese Communities in the Rocky Mountain Region.* New York: Arno Press.

Lenzer, Gertrud, ed. 1975. *Auguste Comte and Positivism: The Essential Writings.* New York: Harper Torchbooks.

Lewis, J. David, and Richard L. Smith. 1980. *American Sociology and Pragmatism: Mead, Chicago Sociology, and Symbolic Interaction.* Chicago: University of Chicago Press.

Lichtenberger, James P. 1909. *Divorce: A Study in Social Causation.* New York: McGraw-Hill.

Lieberson, Stanley. 1980. *A Piece of the Pie: Blacks and White Immigrants since 1880.* Berkeley: University of California Press.

Lindblom, Charles E., and David K. Cohen. 1979. *Usable Knowledge: Social Science and Social Problem Solving.* New Haven: Yale University Press.

Lindsay, Samuel McCune. [1899]1967. Introduction to DuBois, *Philadelphia Negro.*

Lipset, Seymour Martin. 1950. *Agrarian Socialism: The Cooperative Commonwealth Federation in Saskatchewan—A Study in Political Sociology.* Berkeley: University of California Press.

―――. 1955. "The Department of Sociology." In Hoxie, *History of . . . Political Science, Columbia University.*

―――. 1960. *Political Man: The Social Bases of Politics.* Garden City, N.Y.: Doubleday.

―――. 1963. *The First New Nation: The United States in Historical and Comparative Perspective.* New York: Basic Books.

―――. 1969. "Socialism and Sociology." In Horowitz, ed., *Sociological Self-Images.*

―――. 1980. ed., *The Third Century: America as a Post–Industrial Society.* Chicago: University of Chicago Press.

Lipset, Seymour Martin, and Asoke Basu. 1976. "The Roles of the Intellectual and Political Roles." In Gella, ed., *The Intelligentsia and the Intellectuals.*

Lipset, Seymour Martin, Martin Trow, and James Coleman. 1956. *Union Democracy: The Internal Politics of the International Typographical Union.* Glencoe, Ill.: Free Press.

Lofland, John. 1966. *Doomsday Cult: A Study of Conversion, Proselytization, and Maintenance of Faith.* Englewood Cliffs, N.J.: Prentice-Hall.

Loomis, A. S. [1942]1978. "Testimony." In *National Defense Hearings before the*

Select Committee Investigating National Defense Migration: Representatives of the 77th Congress, Second Session, pts. 29, 30 and 31. Washington, D.C.: U.S. Government Printing Office, 1942; New York: Arno Press, 1978.

Lotchin, Roger W. 1974. *San Francisco 1846–1856: From Hamlet to City.* New York: Oxford University Press.

Louis, William Roger, and Jean Stengers, eds. 1968. *E. D. Morel's History of the Congo Reform Movement.* Oxford: Clarendon Press.

Lubove, Roy. 1965. *The Professional Altruist: The Emergence of Social Work as a Career, 1880–1930.* Cambridge, Mass.: Harvard University Press.

Lumb, Ruby Lee. 1908. "The First Three Years of Paul's Career as a Christian." M.A. thesis, University of Chicago.

Lundberg, George A. 1926. "Sex Differences on Social Questions." *School and Society* 23.

———. 1927. "The Demographic and Economic Basis of Political Radicalism and Conservatism." *American Journal of Sociology* 32.

———. 1930. "Public Opinion from a Behavioristic Viewpoint." *American Journal of Sociology* 36.

———. 1931. "The Interests of Members of the American Sociological Society, 1930." *American Journal of Sociology* 37.

———. 1933. "Training for Leisure." *Recreation* 27.

———. 1943. "What to Do with the Humanities." *Harper's Magazine* 182.

———. 1944. "Scientists in Wartime." *Scientific Monthly* 58.

———. 1944a. "Sociologists and the Peace." *American Sociological Review* 9.

———. 1945. "The Proximate Future of American Sociology: The Growth of Scientific Method." *American Journal of Sociology* 50.

———. 1945a. "Can Science Save Us?" *Harper's Magazine* 191.

———. 1947. "The Senate Ponders Social Science." *Scientific Monthly* 64.

———. 1947a. "Sociology versus Dialectical Immaterialism." *American Journal of Sociology* 53.

———. [1947]1961. *Can Science Save U?* 2d ed. New York: David McKay.

———. 1948. "Some Views on Semantics in International Relations." *American Perspective* 2.

———. 1950. "Conflicting Concepts of National Interest." *American Perspective* 4.

———. 1950a. "Alleged Obstacles to Social Science." *Scientific Monthly* 70.

———. 1952. "Inter-Ethnic Relations in a High-School Population." *American Journal of Sociology* 58.

———. [1953]1969. "American Foreign Policy in Light of National Interest at the Mid-Century." In Barnes, ed., *Perpetual War for Perpetual Peace.*

———. 1964. *Foundations of Sociology.* New York: David McKay.

———. 1968. "Prefatory Foreword." In Goddard, *Harry Elmer Barnes.*

Lundberg, George A., Mirra Komarovsky, and Mary Alice McInerny. [1934] 1969. *Leisure: A Suburban Study.* New York: Agathon Press.

Lyman, Stanford M. 1957. "The Impact of Germany on the North Atlantic Treaty Organization." M.A. thesis, University of California at Berkeley.

———. 1961. "The Structure of Chinese Society in Nineteenth Century America." Ph.D. diss., University of California at Berkeley.

————. 1961–62. "Overseas Chinese in America and Indonesia." *Pacific Affairs* 34.

————. 1962. *The Oriental in North America*. Radio lecture series, Canadian Broadcasting Company. Vancouver: University of British Columbia Extension.

————. 1970. *The Asian in the West*. Social Science and Humanities Publication no. 4, Western Studies Center, Desert Research Institute. Reno: University of Nevada System.

————. 1972. *The Black American in Sociological Thought: A Failure of Perspective*. New York: G. P. Putnam's Sons.

————. 1974. *Chinese Americans*. New York: Random House.

————. 1975. "Legitimacy and Consensus in Lipset's America; From Washington to Watergate." *Social Research* 42.

————. 1977. *The Asian in North America*. Santa Barbara: American Bibliographic Center-Clio Press.

————. 1977a. "The Significance of Asians in American Society." In his *Asian in North America*.

————. 1978. *The Seven Deadly Sins: Society and Evil*. New York: St. Martin's Press.

————. 1978a. "The Acceptance, Rejection and Reconstruction of Histories: On Some Controversies in the Study of Social and Cultural Change." In Brown and Lyman, *Structure, Consciousness and History*.

————. 1979. "Stewart Culin and the Debate over Trans-Pacific Migration." *Journal for the Theory of Social Behavior* 9.

————. 1980. "The Earliest American Chinatown Studies and a Hypothesis about Pre-Columbian Migration." Paper presented to the National Conference on Chinese American Studies, San Francisco, October 1980.

————. 1982. "The Rise and Decline of the Functionalist Positivist Paradigm: A Chapter in the History of American Sociology." *Hyoron Shakaikagaku* [Social Science Review] *of Doshisha University* 30.

————. 1982a. "Interactionism and the Study of Race Relations at the Macrosociological Level: The Contribution of Herbert Blumer." Paper presented at the Tenth World Congress of Sociology, Mexico City, August 1982.

————. 1982b. "De la ciudad a la sociologia urbana." I cursos de Verano en San Sebastian, San Sebastian, Spain, August 1982.

————. 1983. "Neglected Pioneers of Civilizational Analysis: R. Stewart Culin and Frank Hamilton Cushing." *Social Research* 50.

Lyman, Stanford M., and Arthur J. Vidich. 1980. "Prodigious Fathers, Prodigal Sons." *Qualitative Sociology* 2.

Lynd, Robert S. [1939]1964. *Knowledge for What: The Place of Social Science in American Culture*. New York: Grove Press.

Lynd, Robert S., and Helen Merrell Lynd. 1937. *Middletown in Transition: A Study in Cultural Conflicts*. New York: Harcourt, Brace.

MacIver, R. M. 1931. "Is Sociology a Natural Science?" *Proceedings and Papers of the American Sociological Society* 25.

MacKenzie, Norman, and Jeanne MacKenzie. 1977. *The Fabians*. New York: Simon & Schuster.

MacKenzie, Roderick. 1928. *Oriental Exclusion: The Effect of American Immigration*

Laws, Regulations, and Judicial Decisions upon the Chinese and Japanese on the Pacific Coast. Chicago: University of Chicago Press.

Maitland, Frederic. 1936. "The Body Politic." In his *Selected Essays,* edited by H. D. Hazeltine et al. Cambridge, England: Cambridge University Press.

Mandelbaum, David G. 1952. *Soldier Groups and Negro Soldiers.* Berkeley: University of California Press.

Mann, Arthur. 1954. *Yankee Reformers in the Urban Age.* New York: Harper Torchbooks.

Mannheim, Karl. 1953. *Ideology and Utopia: An Introduction to the Sociology of Knowledge,* translated by Louis Wirth and Edward Shils. New York: Harcourt, Brace.

Marks, John. 1979. *The Search for the "Manchurian Candidate": The CIA and Mind Control.* New York: New York Times/Quadrangle.

Martindale, Don. 1976. *The Romance of a Profession: A Case Study in the Sociology of Sociology.* Social Science Series no. 3. St. Paul: Wildflower.

Martineau, Harriet. [1837]1962. *Society in America.* Edited by Seymour Martin Lipsett. Garden City, New York: Doubleday Anchor.

Martineau, Harriet, ed. and trans. 1875. *The Positive Philosophy of Auguste Comte.* 2d ed. London: Trubner.

Marx, Karl. 1972. *Early Texts,* edited and translated by David McLellan. Oxford: Basil Blackwell.

——. 1972a. "The Global Consequences of the Discovery of Gold in California." In *Karl Marx, on America and the Civil War,* edited and translated by Saul K. Padover. New York: McGraw-Hill.

Masuoka, Jitsuichi, and Preston Valien, eds. 1961. *Race Relations: Problems and Theory—Essays in Honor of Robert E. Park.* Chapel Hill: University of North Carolina Press.

Matson, Floyd W. 1964. *The Broken Image: Man, Science and Society.* New York: George Braziller.

Matthews, Fred H. 1973. "Robert Park, Congo Reform and Tuskegee: The Molding of a Race Relations Expert, 1905–1913." *Canadian Journal of History* 8.

Matza, David. 1966. "The Disreputable Poor." In Bendix and Lipset, eds., *Class, Status and Power.*

May, Henry F. [1959]1979. *The End of American Innocence: A Study of the First Years of Our Own Time, 1912–1917.* New York: Alfred A. Knopf, 1959; Oxford University Press, 1979.

McClymer, John F. 1980. *War and Welfare: Social Engineering in America, 1890– 1925.* Westport, Conn.: Greenwood Press.

McDermott, John J. 1969. "The American Context." In Royce, *Basic Writings.*

McEntire, Davis. 1952. *The Labor Force in California: A Study of Trends in Labor Force, Employment and Occupations in California, 1900–1950.* Berkeley: University of California Press.

McGloin, John Bernard. 1949. *Eloquent Indian: The Life of James Bouchard, California Jesuit.* Stanford: Stanford University Press.

McKelvey, Blake. 1963. *The Urbanization of America, 1860–1915.* New Brunswick, N.J.: Rutgers University Press.

McKinney, John C., and Edgar T. Thompson, eds. 1965. *The South in Continuity and Change.* Durham: Duke University Press.

McKittrick, Eric L., ed. 1963. *Slavery Defended: The Views of the Old South.* Englewood Cliffs: Prentice-Hall-Spectrum.

McLoughlin, William G. 1978. *Revivals, Awakenings, and Reform: A Essay on Religion and Social Change in America, 1607–1977.* Chicago: University of Chicago Press.

McWilliams, Carey. 1939. *Factories in the Fields: The Story of Migratory Farm Labor in California.* Boston: Little, Brown.

———. 1979. *The Education of Carey McWilliams.* New York: Simon & Schuster.

Mead, George Herbert. 1930. "Cooley's Contribution to American Social Thought." *American Journal of Sociology* 35.

———. 1964. *George Herbert Mead: Selected Writings,* edited by Andrew J. Reck. Indianapolis: Bobbs-Merrill.

Mead, Sidney E. 1977. *The Old Religion in the Brave New World: Reflections on the Relationship between Christendom and the Republic.* Berkeley: University of California Press.

Mears, Eliot Grinnel. [1928]1974. *Resident Orientals on the American Pacific Coast: Their Legal and Economic Status.* Chicago: University of Chicago Press, 1928; New York: Arno Press, 1974.

Merriam, Charles E. [1925]1970. *New Aspects of Politics.* 3rd ed. Chicago: University of Chicago Press.

Merton, Robert K. 1936. "Puritanism, Pietism, and Science." *Sociological Review* 28.

———. 1957. *Social Theory and Social Structure.* Revised ed. Glencoe, Ill.: Free Press.

———. 1968. *Social Theory and Social Structure.* Enlarged ed. New York: Free Press.

Merton, Robert K., and Paul Lazarsfeld, eds. 1950. *Continuities in Social Research: Studies in the Scope and Method of "The American Soldier."* Glencoe, Ill.: Free Press.

Merton, Robert K., L. Broom, and L. S. Cottrell, Jr., eds. 1959. *Sociology Today: Problems and Prospects.* New York: Basic Books.

Merton, Robert K., Marjorie Fiske, and Alberta Curtiss. 1946. *Mass Persuasion.* New York: Harper and Brothers.

Metzker, Isaac, ed. 1971. *A Bintel Brief: Sixty Years of Letters from the Lower East Side to the Jewish Daily Forward.* New York: Ballantine Books.

Mill, John Stuart. 1971. *A Logical Critique of Sociology,* edited by Ronald Fletcher. London: Michael Joseph.

Miller, David L. 1973. *George Herbert Mead: Self, Language and the World.* Austin: University of Texas Press.

Miller, Perry. 1956. *The American Puritans: Their Prose and Poetry.* Garden City, New York: Doubleday Anchor Books.

Mills, C. Wright. 1959. *The Sociological Imagination.* New York: Oxford University Press.

———. 1964. *Sociology and Pragmatism: The Higher Learning in America,* edited by Irving Louis Horowitz. New York: Oxford University Press.

Mills, Theodore M. 1967. *The Sociology of Small Groups.* Englewood Cliffs, N.J.: Prentice Hall.

Moffat, Frances. 1981. *Dancing on the Brink of the World: The Rise and Fall of San Francisco Society.* New York: G. P. Putnam's Sons.

Moodie, T. Dunbar. 1975. *The Rise of Afrikanerdom: Power, Apartheid, and the Afrikaner Civil Religion.* Berkeley: University of California Press.

Morgan, Edmund S. 1976. "The Puritan Ethic and the American Revolution." In his *Challenge of the American Revolution.* New York: W. W. Norton.

Morgan, J. Graham. 1966. "Sociology in America: A Study of Its Institutional Development until 1930." Ph.D. diss., Balliol College, Oxford University.

———. 1980. "Women in American Sociology in the 19th Century." *Journal of the History of Sociology: An International Review* 2.

Morison, Samuel Eliot. 1930. *The Development of Harvard University since the Inauguration of President Eliot, 1869–1929.* Cambridge, Mass.: Harvard University Press.

———. 1936. *Three Centuries of Harvard.* Cambridge, Mass.: Harvard University Press.

———. 1958. *Builders of the Bay Colony.* Boston: Houghton Mifflin.

Morton, Frederic. 1980. *A Nervous Splendor: Vienna, 1888/1889.* Harmondsworth, England: Penguin Books.

Moynihan, Daniel Patrick. 1969. *Maximum Feasible Misunderstanding: Community Action in the War on Poverty.* New York: Free Press.

———. 1973. *The Politics of Guaranteed Income: The Nixon Administration and the Family Assistance Plan.* New York: Vintage Books.

Munsterberg, Hugo. 1893. "The New Psychology, and Harvard's Equipment for Teaching It." *Harvard Graduates' Magazine* 1.

———. 1895. "The New Psychology." In *The Old Psychology and the New,* edited by Larkin Dunton. Boston: New England Publishing Co.

———. [1901]1971. *American Traits: From the Point of View of a German.* Port Washington, N.Y.: Kennikat Press.

———. 1907. *The Americans,* translated by Edwin B. Holt. New York: McClure, Phillips.

———. 1907a. Letter to the editor. *Nation* 85. Quoted in Hale, *Human Science and Social Order.*

———. 1908. *On the Witness Stand: Essays on Psychology and Crime.* New York: McClure.

———. 1913. *Psychology and Industrial Efficiency.* New York: Houghton Mifflin.

———. 1914. *Psychology and Social Sanity.* New York: Doubleday, Page.

———. 1914a. *Psychology: General and Applied.* New York: D. Appleton.

———. 1915. *The War and America.* New York: D. Appleton.

———. [1916]1970. *The Film—A Psychological Study: The Silent Photoplay in 1916.* New York: D. Appleton, 1916; New York: Dover, 1970.

———. 1980. "How Men Differ." Unpublished manuscript. Quoted in Hale, *Human Science and Social Order.*

———. 1980a. "Experiments on Harry Orchard." Unpublished manuscript. Quoted in Hale, *Human Science and Social Order.*

Murray, Stephen. 1980. "Resistance to Sociology at Berkeley." *Journal of the History of Sociology: An International Review* 2.

Myer, Dillon S. 1971. *Uprooted Americans: The Japanese Americans and the War Relocation Authority during World War II.* Tucson: University of Arizona Press.

Neill, Stephen. 1964. *A History of Christian Missions.* Harmondsworth, England: Penguin Books.

Neurath, Otto. 1973. *Empiricism and Sociology,* edited by Marie Neurath and Robert S. Cohen. Boston: D. Reidel.

Nisbet, Robert A. [1940]1980. *The Social Group in French Thought.* Ph.D. diss., University of California, 1940; New York: Arno Books, 1980.

———. 1953. *The Quest for Community: A Study in the Ethics of Order and Freedom.* New York: Oxford University Press.

———. 1966. *The Sociological Tradition.* New York: Basic Books.

———. 1968. *Tradition and Revolt: Historical and Sociological Essays.* New York: Random House.

———. 1969. *Social Change and History: Aspects of the Western Theory of Development.* New York: Oxford University Press.

———. 1970. *The Social Bond.* New York: Alfred A. Knopf.

———. 1971. *The Degradation of Academic Dogma: The University in America, 1945–1970.* New York: Basic Books.

———. 1973. *The Social Philosophers: Community and Conflict in Western Thought.* New York: Thomas Y. Crowell.

———. 1980. *History of the Idea of Progress.* New York: Basic Books.

———. 1982. *Prejudices: A Philosophical Dictionary.* Cambridge, Mass.: Harvard University Press.

Nonet, Philippe, and Philip Selznick. 1978. *Law and Society in Transition: Toward Responsive Law.* New York: Colophon Books.

North, Cecil C. 1908. "The Influence of Modern Social Relations upon Ethical Concepts." Ph.D. diss., University of Chicago.

Oberschall, Anthony. 1965. *Empirical Social Research in Germany, 1848–1914.* New York: Basic Books.

Odum, Howard. [1929]1946. *American Social Problems: An Introduction to the Study of People and Their Dilemmas.* New York: Henry Holt.

———. [1951]1969. *American Sociology: The Story of Sociology in the United States through 1950.* New York: Greenwood.

Odum, Howard, ed. 1927. *American Masters of Social Science: An Approach to the Study of the Social Sciences through a Neglected Field of Biography.* New York: Henry Holt.

Ogburn, William Fielding. [1912]1968. *Progress and Uniformity in Child-Labor Legislation: A Study in Statistical Measurement.* Studies in History, Economics, and Public Law, Faculty of Political Science of Columbia University, no. 48(2). New York: Columbia University Press, 1912; New York: AMS Press, 1968.

———. [1922]1966. *Social Change with Respect to Cultural and Original Nature.* New York: Dell-Delta.

———. [1927]1974. "Sociology and Statistics." In Ogburn and Goldenweiser, *Social Sciences.*

———. 1928. "Responsibility of the Social Sciences." *American Journal of Sociology* 34.

———. 1930. "The Folk-Ways of a Scientific Sociology." *Scientific Monthly* 30.

———. 1934. "Limitations of Statistics." *American Journal of Sociology* 40.

———. [1937]1974. *Social Characteristics of Cities: A Basis for Interpretations of the Role of the City in American Life.* Chicago: International City Managers' Association, 1937; New York: Arno Press, 1974.

Ogburn, William Fielding, and Alexander Goldenweiser. [1927]1974. *The Social Sciences and Their Interrelations.* Boston: Houghton-Mifflin, 1927; New York: Arno Press, 1974.

Ollman, Bertell, and Edward Vernoff, eds. 1982. *The Left Academy: Marxist Scholarship on American Campuses.* New York: McGraw-Hill.

O'Neill, William L. 1966. "Divorce and the Professionalization of the Social Scientist." *Journal of the History of the Behavioral Sciences* 2.

Orleans, Peter. 1966. "Robert Park and Social Area Analysis: A Convergence of Traditions in Urban Sociology." *Urban Affairs Quarterly* 1.

Oster, George F., and Edward O. Wilson. 1978. *Caste and Ecology in the Social Insects.* Princeton: Princeton University Press, 1978.

Otlet, Paul. 1932. "Sur la constitution de la sociologie mondiale." *Annales de l'Institut international de sociologie (Sociologie de la guerre et de la faix)* 16. Quoted in L. L. Bernard, *Social Control in Its Sociological Aspects.*

Padover, Saul K., ed. and trans. 1972. *Karl Marx, on America and the Civil War.* New York: McGraw-Hill.

———. 1973. *Karl Marx on the First International.* New York: McGraw-Hill.

Page, Charles H. 1969. *Class and American Sociology: From Ward to Ross.* New York: Schocken Books.

———. 1982. *Fifty Years of the Sociological Enterprise: A Lucky Journey.* Amherst: University of Massachusetts Press.

Pajus, Jean. [1937]1971. *The Real Japanese California.* Berkeley: James J. Gillick, 1937; San Francisco: R&E Research Associates, 1971.

Park, Robert E. 1900. "The German Army: The Most Perfect Military Organization in the World." *Munsey's Magazine* 24.

———. 1904. *Masse und Publikum: Eine methodologische und soziologische Untersuchung.* Bern: Lack & Grunau.

———. 1905. "A City of Racial Peace." *World To-Day* 9.

———. 1906. "A King in Business: Leopold II of Belgium, Autocrat of the Congo and International Broker." *Everybody's Magazine* 15.

———. 1906a. "The Terrible Story of the Congo." *Everybody's Magazine* 15.

———. 1908. "Agricultural Extension among the Negroes." *World To-Day* 15.

———. 1913. "Racial Assimilation in Secondary Groups with Particular Reference to the Negro." *Publications of the American Sociological Society* 8.

———. 1919. "The Conflict and Fusion of Cultures, with Special Reference to the Negro." *Journal of Negro History* 4.

———. [1922]1971. *The Immigrant Press and Its Control.* Montclair, N.J.: Patterson Smith.

———. 1924. Foreword. In Maurice T. Price, *Christian Missions and Oriental Civilizations: A Study in Cultural Contact.* Shanghai: privately printed.

———. [1925]1967. "The City: Suggestions for the Investigation of Human Behavior in the Urban Environment." In Park et al., *The City.*

———. 1926. "Our Racial Frontier on the Pacific." *Survey Graphic* 56.

_____. [1928]1969. Introduction to Hiller, *The Strike.*

_____. 1930. *S.v.* "Assimilation, social." In Seligman and Johnson, *Encyclopaedia of the Social Sciences.*

_____. 1931. Review of Werner Sombart, *Die drei Nationaloekonomien.* Munich and Leipzig, Verlag von Duncker & Humblot, 1930. In *American Journal of Sociology* 36.

_____. 1933. "William Graham Sumner's Conception of Society: An Interpretation." *Chinese Social and Political Science Review* 17.

_____. 1936. "Human Ecology." *American Journal of Sociology* 42.

_____. 1938. "Reflections on Communication and Culture." *American Journal of Sociology* 44.

_____. 1939. "The Nature of Race Relations." In E. T. Thompson, *Race Relations and the Race Problem.*

_____. 1950–55. *Collected Papers of Robert Ezra Park.* 3 volumes: 1. *Race and Culture;* 2. *Human Communities;* 3. *Society: Collective Behavior, News and Opinion, Sociology and Modern Society.* Edited by Everett Cherrington Hughes, Charles S. Johnson, Jitsuichi Masuoka, Robert Redfield, and Louis Wirth. Glencoe, Ill.: Free Press.

_____. 1950. "An Autobiographical Note." In his *Race and Culture.* Vol. 1 of his *Collected Papers.*

_____. 1950a. "The Race Relations Cycle in Hawaii." In his *Race and Culture.* Vol. 1 of his *Collected Papers.*

_____. 1972. *The Crowd and the Public and Other Essays,* edited by Henry Elsner, Jr., translated by Charlotte Elsner. Chicago: University of Chicago Press, 1972. Originally published as *Masse und Publikum.*

Park, Robert E., Ernest W. Burgess, and Roderick D. McKenzie. [1925]1967. *The City.* Chicago: University of Chicago Press.

Parker, Carleton Hubbell. [1920]1972. "Report on the Wheatland Hop Fields' Riot." Appendix to his *Casual Laborer and Other Essays.* Seattle: University of Washington Press.

Parkes, James. 1969. *Anti-Semitism.* Chicago: Quadrangle Books.

Parsons, Frank. 1908. "The Vocational Bureau." *Arena* 40. Quoted in Hale, *Human Science and Social Order.*

Parsons, Talcott. 1936. "Introduction: On Certain Sociological Elements in Professor Taussig's Thought." In *Explorations in Economics: Notes and Essays Contributed in Honor of F. W. Taussig.* New York: McGraw-Hill.

_____. [1937]1949. *The Structure of Social Action: A Study in Social Theory with Special Reference to a Group of Recent European Writers.* New York: McGraw-Hill, 1937; Glencoe, Ill.: Free Press, 1949.

_____. [1940]1965. "The Motivation of Economic Activities." *Canadian Journal of Economics and Political Science* 6 (1940). Reprinted in *Readings in Economic Sociology,* edited by Neil J. Smelser. Englewood Cliffs, N.J.: Prentice-Hall.

_____. 1944. "The Theoretical Development of the Sociology of Religion: A Chapter in the History of Modern Social Science." *Journal of the History of Ideas* 5.

_____. 1950. "The Prospects of Sociological Theory." *American Sociological Review* 15.

_____. 1951. *The Social System.* Glencoe, Ill.: Free Press.

_____. 1966. "Full Citizenship for the Negro American? A Sociological Problem?" In Parsons and Clark, eds., *The Negro American.*

_____. 1966a. "Introduction: Why 'Freedom Now', Not Yesterday?" In Parsons and Clark, eds., *The Negro American.*

_____. 1966b. *Societies: Evolutionary and Comparative Perspectives.* Englewood Cliffs, N.J.: Prentice-Hall.

_____. 1971. *The System of Modern Societies.* Englewood Cliffs, N.J.: Prentice-Hall.

_____. 1977. *The Evolution of Societies,* edited by Jackson Toby. Englewood Cliffs, N.J.: Prentice-Hall.

_____. 1977a. "On Building Social System Theory: A Personal History." In his *Social Systems and the Evolution of Action Theory.*

_____. 1977b. *Social Systems and the Evolution of Action Theory.* New York: Free Press.

_____. 1979. "The Symbolic Environment of Modern Economics." *Social Research* 46.

Parsons, Talcott, and Bernard Barber. 1948. "Sociology, 1941–1946." *American Journal of Sociology* 53.

Parsons, Talcott, and Kenneth Clark, eds. 1966. *The Negro American.* Boston: Houghton Mifflin.

Parsons, Talcott, and Edward A. Shils, eds. [1951]1962. *Towards a General Theory of Action.* New York: Harper Torchbooks.

Parsons, Talcott, E. Shils, K. D. Naegele, and J. R. Pitts, eds. 1961. *Theories of Society: Foundations of Modern Sociological Theory.* New York: Free Press of Glencoe.

Peabody, Francis Greenwood. 1886. "Social Reforms as Subjects of University Study." *Independent* 38 (14 January, 1886). Quoted in Hopkins, *Rise of the Social Gospel.*

_____. 1901. "The Religion of a College Student." *Forum* 31.

_____. 1908. "The Universities and the Social Conscience." In King et al., eds., *Education and National Character.*

Pear, Robert. 1980. "As Use of Polygraph Grows, Suspects and Lawyers Sweat." *New York Times* (13 July, 1980).

Perlman, Selig. [1922]1950. *The History of Trade Unionism in the United States.* New York: Augustus M. Kelley.

Perry, Louis B., and Richard S. Perry. 1963. *A History of the Los Angeles Labor Movement, 1911–1941.* Berkeley: University of California Press.

Persons, Stow. 1968. "The Cyclical Theory of History." In Strout, *Intellectual History in America.* Vol. 1, *Contemporary Essays on Puritanism, The Enlightenment, and Romanticism.*

Peterson, George E. 1964. *The New England College in the Age of the University.* Amherst: Amherst College Press.

Philpott, Thomas Lee. 1978. *The Slum and the Ghetto: Neighborhood Deterioration and Middle Class Reform, Chicago, 1880–1930.* New York: Oxford University Press.

Phizacklea, Annie, and Robert Miles. 1980. *Labour and Racism.* London: Routledge & Kegan Paul.

Pixley, Frank M. [1877]1978. "Testimony." In *Report of the Joint Special Committee to Investigate Chinese Immigration,* U.S. Senate, 44th Congress, 2d Session. Report no. 689. Washington, D.C.: Government Printing Office, 1877; New York: Arno Press, 1978.

Potts, David B. 1962. "The Prospect Union: A Conservative Quest for Social Justice." *New England Quarterly* 35.

––––––. 1965. "Social Ethics at Harvard, 1881–1931: A Study of Academic Activism." In Buck, *Social Sciences at Harvard, 1860–1920.*

Proceedings of the Asiatic Exclusion League, 1907–1913. 1977. New York: Arno Press.

Queen, Stuart A., and Lewis Francis Thomas. 1939. *The City: A Study of Urbanism in the United States.* New York: McGraw-Hill.

Raphelson, Alfred C. 1967. "Lincoln Steffens at the Leipzig Psychological Institute, 1890–1891." *Journal of the History of Behavioral Sciences* 3.

Ratner, Sidney. [1953]1969. Preface to his edition of *Vision and Action: Essays in Honor of Horace M. Kallen on his Seventieth Birthday.* Port Washington, N.Y.: Kennikat Press.

Ratzenhofer, G. [1905]1974. *Wesen und Zweck der Politik (1893).* Quoted in Albion W. Small. *General Sociology.*

Rauschenbusch, Walter. [1907]1964. *Christianity and the Social Crisis,* edited by Robert D. Cross. New York: Harper Torchbooks.

Raushenbush, Winifred. 1926. "Their Place in the Sun." *Survey Graphic* 56.

––––––. 1979. *Robert E. Park, Biography of a Sociologist.* Durham, N.C.: Duke University Press.

Recent Social Trends in the United States: Report of the President's Research Committee on Social Trends. 1933. New York: McGraw-Hill.

Reck, Andrew J., ed. 1964. *George Herbert Mead: Selected Writings.* Indianapolis: Bobbs-Merrill.

Redfield, Robert. 1960. *The Little Community.* Chicago: University of Chicago Press.

Reep, Samuel. 1911. "Social Policy of Chicago Churches." Ph.D. diss., University of Chicago.

Reiss, Albert J., Jr., ed. 1968. *Cooley and Sociological Analysis.* Ann Arbor: University of Michigan Press.

Rhea, Buford, ed. 1981. *The Future of the Sociological Classics.* London: George Allen & Unwin.

Rhodes, Lawrence J. 1980. "Seventy-fifth Anniversary: Society Experienced Major Social Change in Turbulent '30s." *Footnotes* 8.

Rieff, Philip, ed. 1969. *On Intellectuals: Theoretical Studies, Case Studies.* Garden City, N.Y.: Doubleday.

Riesman, David. 1964. *Abundance for What? and Other Essays.* Garden City, N.Y.: Doubleday.

Riesman, David, Nathan Glazer, and Reuel Denney. 1953. *The Lonely Crowd: A Study of the Changing American Character.* Garden City, N.Y.: Doubleday-Anchor.

Ripley, William Z. 1900. "Ethnic Theories and Movements of Population: A Rejoinder." *Quarterly Journal of Economics* 14.

Roethlisberger, F. J., William J. Dickson, and Harold Wright. [1939]1966. *Management and the Worker: An Account of a Research Program Conducted by the Western*

Electric Company, Hawthorne Works, Chicago. Cambridge, Mass.: Harvard University Press.

Rogers, Howard J., ed. [1906]1974. *Congress of Arts and Science, Universal Exposition, St. Louis, 1904: Selected Papers.* Boston: Houghton Mifflin, 1906; New York: Arno Press, 1974.

Rose, Arnold M. 1948. "Anti-Semitism's Root in City Hatred." *Commentary* 6.

———, ed. 1953. *Race Prejudice and Discrimination: Readings in Intergroup Relations in the United States.* New York: Alfred A. Knopf.

Rosenbaum, Fred. 1976. *Free to Choose: The Making of a Jewish Community in the American West: The Jews of Oakland, California from the Gold Rush to the Present Day.* Berkeley: Judah L. Magnes Memorial Museum.

Rosenblith, Walter A. [1950]1967. Afterword. In Norbert Wiener, *The Human Use of Human Beings: Cybernetics and Society.* New York: Avon Books.

Ross, Edward Alsworth. [1901]1969. *Social Control: A Survey of the Foundations of Order.* Cleveland: Press of Case Western Reserve University.

———. [1907]1973. *Sin and Society: An Analysis of Latter-Day Iniquity.* New York: Harper Torchbooks.

———. 1911. *The Changing Chinese: The Conflict of Oriental and Western Cultures in China.* New York: Century.

———. 1912. *Changing America: Studies in Contemporary Society.* New York: Century.

———. [1912]1974. *Social Psychology: An Outline and Source Book.* New York: Macmillan, 1912; New York: Arno Press, 1974.

———. 1914. *The Old World and the New: The Significance of the Past and Present Immigration to the American People.* New York: Century.

———. 1920. *The Principles of Sociology.* New York: Century.

———. 1920a. "Individuation." *American Journal of Sociology* 25.

———. [1922]1970. *The Social Trend.* Freeport, N.Y.: Books for Libraries Press.

———. [1927]1977. *Standing Room Only?* New York: Century, 1927; New York: Arno Press, 1977.

———. 1936. *Seventy Years of It: An Autobiography.* New York: D. Appleton Century.

———. 1937. "Freedom in the Modern World." *American Journal of Sociology* 42.

———. 1940. *New-Age Sociology.* New York: Appleton-Century-Crofts.

———. 1945. "Fifty Years of Sociology in the United States." *American Journal of Sociology* 50.

Royce, Josiah. [1883]1948. *California, From the Conquest in 1846 to the Second Vigilance Committee in San Francisco: A Study of American Character.* New York: Alfred A. Knopf.

———. 1901. "Joseph Le Conte." *International Monthly* 4.

———. 1901a. "The Linkage of Facts." *The World and the Individual.* New York: Macmillan.

———. 1908. "The Pacific Coast. A Psychological Study of the Relations of Climate and Civilization." In his *Race Questions, Provincialism, and Other American Problems.* New York: Macmillan.

————. 1914. "The Mechanical, The Historical, and the Statistical." *Science*, n.s. 29.

————. 1916. *The Philosophy of Loyalty*. New York: Macmillan.

————. [1918]1968. *The Problem of Christianity*. Chicago: University of Chicago Press.

————. 1969. *Basic Writings of Josiah Royce*, edited by John J. McDermott. Chicago: University of Chicago Press.

————. 1969a. "Words of Professor Royce at the Walton Hotel at Philadelphia, December 29, 1915." In Royce, *Basic Writings*.

Royce, Sarah. [1932]1977. *A Frontier Lady: Recollections of the Gold Rush and Early California*, edited by Ralph Henry Gabriel. Lincoln: University of Nebraska Press.

Ruml, Beardsley. [1940]1974. "Social Science Research in Retrospect and Prospect." In Wirth, *Eleven Twenty-Six*.

Salomon, Albert. 1955. *The Tyranny of Progress: Reflections on the Origins of Sociology*. New York: Noonday Press.

————. 1963. *In Praise of Enlightenment: Essays in the History of Ideas*. Cleveland: Meridian Books.

Salomon, Gottfried. 1934. *S.v.* "Ratzenhofer, Gustav (1842–1904)." In Seligman and Johnson, *Encyclopaedia of the Social Sciences*.

Saxton, Alexander. 1971. *The Indispensable Enemy: Labor and the Anti-Chinese Movement in California*. Berkeley: University of California Press.

Scheff, Tom. 1966. *Being Mentally Ill: A Sociological Theory*. Chicago: Aldine Press.

Schleiermacher, Friedrich. 1958. *On Religion: Speeches to Its Cultural Despisers*, translated by John Oman. New York: Harper Torchbooks.

Schmid, Robert. 1948. "Gustav Ratzenhofer: Sociological Positivism and the Theory of Social Interests." In Barnes, ed. *Introduction to the History of Sociology*.

Schneider, Joseph. 1950. "Primitive Warfare: A Methodological Note." *American Sociological Review* 15.

————. 1952. "On the Beginnings of Warfare." *Social Forces* 31.

Schneider, Louis. 1975. "Ironic Perspective and Sociological Thought." In Coser, *Idea of Social Structure*.

Schrag, Peter. 1978. *Mind Control*. New York: Delta-Dell.

Schutz, Alfred. 1966. *Collected Papers*. Vol. 3, *Studies in Phenomenological Philosophy*, edited by I. Schutz. The Hague: Martinus Nijhoff.

Schwendinger, Herman, and Julia R. Schwendinger. 1974. *The Sociologists of the Chair: A Radical Analysis of the Formative Years of North American Sociology, 1883–1922*. New York: Basic Books.

Scott, Marvin B. 1968. *The Racing Game*. Chicago: Aldine.

Scott, Marvin B., and Stanford M. Lyman. 1970. *The Revolt of the Students*. Columbus: Charles Merrill.

Scott, Robert A., and Arnold R. Shore. 1979. *Why Sociology Does Not Apply: A Study of the Use of Sociology in Public Policy*. New York: Elsevier North Holland.

Seager, Robert, II. 1959. "Some Denominational Reactions to Chinese Immigration to California, 1856–1892." *Pacific Historical Review* 28.

Seligman, Ben B. 1971. *Main Currents in Modern Economics*. Vol. 1, *The Revolt against Formalism*. Chicago: Quadrangle Books.

Seligman, Edwin R., and Alvin Johnson, eds. 1930. *Encyclopaedia of the Social Sciences.* New York: Macmillan.

Selznick, Philip. 1944. "Revolution Sacred and Profane." *Enquiry: A Journal of Independent Radical Thought* 2.

————. 1952. *The Organizational Weapon: A Study of Bolshevik Strategy and Tactics.* New York: McGraw-Hill.

————. 1953. *TVA and the Grass Roots: A Study in the Sociology of Formal Organization.* Berkeley: University of California Press.

————. 1957. *Leadership in Administration: A Sociological Interpretation.* Evanston, Ill.: Row, Peterson.

————. "The Sociology of Law." In Merton, Broom, and Cottrell, Jr., eds., 1959.

Selznick, Philip, Philippe Nonet, and Howard M. Vollmer. 1969. *Law, Society, and Industrial Justice.* New York: Russell Sage Foundation.

Senate Subcommittee of the Committee on Education and Labor. "Documentary History of the Strike of the Cotton Pickers of California, 1933." U.S. Congress, hearings on S. res. 266, *Violations of Free Speech and Rights of Labor*, pt. 54, exhibit 8764.

Shibutani, Tamotsu. 1966. *Improvised News: A Sociological Study of Rumor.* Indianapolis: Bobbs-Merrill.

————. 1980. *The Derelicts of Company K.* Berkeley: University of California Press.

Shibutani, Tamotsu, and Kian Moon Kwan. 1965. *Ethnic Stratification: A Comparative Approach.* New York: Macmillan.

Shils, Edward. 1961. "The Calling of Sociology." In Parsons et al., *Theories of Society.*

————. 1980. "Tradition, Ecology and Institution in the History of Sociology." In his *Calling of Sociology and Other Essays in the Pursuit of Learning.* Chicago: University of Chicago Press.

Shively, Charles, ed. 1975. *Love, Marriage, and Divorce, and the Sovereignty of the Individual: A Discussion between Henry James, Horace Greeley, and Stephen Pearl Andrews, and a Hitherto Unpublished Manuscript, Love, Marriage, and the Condition of Women by Stephen Pearl Andrews.* Weston, Mass.: M&S Press.

Sibley, Elbridge. 1974. *Social Science Research Council: The First Fifty Years.* New York: Social Science Research Council.

Simmel, Georg. 1900. "A Chapter in the Philosophy of Value," translated by Albion W. Small. *American Journal of Sociology* 5.

————. 1968. "On the Concept and Tragedy of Culture." In his *Conflict in Modern Culture and Other Essays*, translated by K. Peter Etzkorn. New York: Teachers College Press.

————. 1978. *The Philosophy of Money*, translated by Tom Bottomore and David Frisby. London: Routledge & Kegan Paul.

Simons, Sarah . 1901. "Social Assimilation." *American Journal of Sociology* 6.

————. 1901a. "Social Assimilation." *American Journal of Sociology* 7.

————. 1901b. "Social Assimilation," *American Journal of Sociology* 7.

————. 1901c. "Social Assimilation." *American Journal of Sociology* 7.

————. 1902. "Social Assimilation." *American Journal of Sociology* 7.

Simpson, George E., and J. Milton Yinger. 1959. "The Sociology of Race and Ethnic Relations." In Merton et al., *Sociology Today.*

Siu, Paul C. P. 1964. "The Isolation of the Chinese Laundryman." In Burgess and Bogue, *Contributions to Urban Sociology*.

Small, Albion W. 1895. "The Era of Sociology." *American Journal of Sociology* 1.

————. 1895a. "Private Business is a Public Trust." *American Journal of Sociology* 1.

————. 1895b. "The State and Semi-Public Corporations." *American Journal of Sociology* 1.

————. [1933, 1935, 1936, 1937]. "The Letters of Albion W. Small to Lester F. Ward. I–IV." (1890–1910) *Social Forces* 12 (1933); 13 (1935); 15 (1936); 15 (1937).

————. 1896. Review of Giddings, *Principles of Sociology*. *American Journal of Sociology* 2.

————. 1897. Review of Giddings, *Theory of Socialization*. *American Journal of Sociology* 3.

————. 1897a. "The Meaning of the Social Movement." *American Journal of Sociology* 3.

————. [1905]1974. *General Sociology: An Exposition of the Main Developments in Sociological Theory from Spencer to Ratzenhofer*. Chicago: University of Chicago Press, 1905; New York: Arno Press, 1974.

————. [1910]1971. *The Meaning of the Social Sciences*. Chicago: University of Chicago Press, 1910; New York: Johnson Reprint Corp., 1971.

————. 1912. "Socialism in the Light of Social Science." *American Journal of Sociology* 17.

————. 1914. "The Social Gradations of Capital," *American Journal of Sociology* 19.

————. 1915. "What is Americanism?" *American Journal of Sociology* 20.

————. 1915a. "What is Americanism? Supplement." *American Journal of Sociology* 20.

————. 1915b. "The Bonds of Nationality." *American Journal of Sociology* 20.

————. 1916. "Fifty Years of Sociology in the United States (1865–1915)." *American Journal of Sociology* 21.

————. 1919. "The Church and Class Conflicts: An Open Letter to the Laymen's Committee on Interchurch Survey." *American Journal of Sociology* 24.

————. 1919a. "Some Structural Material for the Idea 'Democracy'." *American Journal of Sociology* 25.

————. 1920. "Christianity and Industry." *American Journal of Sociology* 25.

————. 1925. "The Sociology of Profits." *American Journal of Sociology* 30.

Small, Albion W., and George E. Vincent. [1894]1971. *An Introduction to the Study of Society*. New York: American Book Co., 1894; Dubuque, Iowa: Brown Reprints, 1971.

Smith, Mark C. 1979–80. "Robert Lynd and Consumerism in the 1930s." *The Journal of the History of Sociology: An International Review* 2.

Snizek, William, Ellsworth R. Fuhrman, and Michael K. Miller, eds. 1979. *Contemporary Issues in Theory and Research: A Metasociological Perspective*. Westport, Conn.: Greenwood Press.

Solomon, Barbara Miller. 1956. *Ancestors and Immigrants: A Changing New England Tradition*. New York: John Wiley & Sons.

Sorokin, Pitirim A. 1936. "Is Accurate Social Planning Possible?" *American Sociological Review* 1.

Sowell, Thomas. 1981. *Ethnic America: A History.* New York: Basic Books.

Speer, William. 1870. *The Oldest and the Newest Empire: China and the United States.* Hartford: S. S. Scranton.

Spicer, Edward H., Asael T. Hansen, Katherine Luomala, and Marvin K. Opler. 1969. *Impounded People: Japanese-Americans in the Relocation Centers.* Tucson: University of Arizona Press.

Spiegelberg, H. 1969. *The Phenomenological Movement: An Historical Introduction.* 2d ed. The Hague: Martinus Nijoff.

Spykman, Nicholas J. 1942. *America's Strategy in World Politics: The United States and the Balance of Power.* New York: Harcourt Brace.

Stadtman, Verne A. 1970. *The University of California, 1868–1969.* New York: McGraw-Hill.

Stanton, William. 1960. *The Leopard's Spots: Scientific Attitudes toward Race in America, 1815–1859.* Chicago: University of Chicago Press.

Starr, Kevin. 1973. *Americans and the California Dream, 1850–1915.* New York: Oxford University Press.

Staude, John Raphael. 1967. *Max Scheler, 1874–1928: An Intellectual Portrait.* New York: Free Press.

Stein, Walter J. 1973. *California and the Dust Bowl Migration.* Westport, Conn.: Greenwood Press.

Steinberg, Stephen. 1981. *The Ethnic Myth: Race, Ethnicity and Class in America.* New York: Atheneum Press.

Steiner, Jesse F. [1937]1972. *Research Memorandum on Recreation in the Depression.* New York: Social Science Research Council, 1937; New York: Arno Press, 1972.

———. [1917]1978. *The Japanese Invasion: A Study in the Psychology of Inter-Racial Contacts.* Chicago: A. C. McClurg, 1917; New York: Arno Press, 1978.

Steinfels, Peter. 1979. *The Neo-Conservatives: The Men Who are Changing America's Politics.* New York: Simon & Schuster.

Stephens, William D. [1923]1978. Quoted in *Report of the Honorable Roland S. Morris on Japanese Immigration and Alleged Discrimination against Japanese Residents in the United States.* Washington, D.C.: Government Printing Office, 1923; New York: Arno Press, 1978.

Stern, Bernhard J. 1932. "Giddings, Ward, and Small: An Interchange of Correspondence." *Social Forces* 10.

———. ed., 1935. *Young Ward's Diary: A Human & Eager Record of the Years Between 1860 and 1870 as they Were Lived in the Vicinity of the Little Town of Towanda, Pennsylvania; in the Field as a Rank and File Soldier in the Union Army; and Later in the Nation's Capital, by Lester Ward, Who Became the First Great Sociologist the Country Produced.* New York: G. P. Putnam's Sons, 1935.

———, ed. 1933–37. "The Letters of Albion W. Small to Lester F. Ward, I–IV." *Social Forces,* XII (December, 1933); XIII (March, 1935), XV (December, 1936); XV (March, 1937).

———, ed. 1938–1949. "The Ward–Ross Correspondence. I–IV, 1906–1912." *American Sociological Review* 3 (1938); 11 (1946); 12 (1947); 13 (1948); 14 (1949).

Stern, Madeline B. 1968. *The Pantarch: A Biography of Stephen Pearl Andrews.* Austin: University of Texas Press.

Stern, Sheldon M. 1965. "William James and the New Psychology at Harvard." In Buck, *Social Sciences at Harvard*.

Stimson, Grace Heilman. 1955. *Rise of the Labor Movement in Los Angeles*. Berkeley: University of California Press.

Stouffer, Samuel A. 1980. *An Experimental Comparison of Statistical and Case History Research Methods on Attitude Research*. New York: Arno Press.

Stouffer, Samuel A., and Paul F. Lazarsfeld. [1937]1972. *Research Memorandum on the Family in the Depression*. New York: Social Science Research Council, 1937; New York: Arno Press, 1972.

Stouffer, Samuel A., E. A. Suchman, L. C. DeVinney, S. A. Star, and R. M. Williams, Jr. [1949]1974. *Studies in Social Psychology in World War II*. Vol. 1, *The American Soldier: Adjustment during Army Life*. Princeton: Princeton University Press, 1947; New York: Arno Press, 1974.

Strodtbeck, Fred L. 1962. "Social Process, the Law and Jury Functioning." In Evan, *Law and Sociology*.

Strong, Edward K. 1970. *The Second-Generation Japanese Problem*. New York: Arno Press.

Strout, Cushing, ed. 1968. *Intellectual History in America*. Vol. 1, *Contemporary Essays on Puritanism, The Enlightenment, and Romanticism*. New York: Harper & Row.

Summerscales, William. 1970. *Affirmation and Dissent: Columbia's Response to the Crisis of World War I*. New York: Teacher's College Press.

Sumner, William Graham. [1879]1969. "The Influence of Commercial Crises on Opinions about Economic Doctrines." An Address before the Free Trade Club. New York City. May 15. Reprinted in his *Essays*. 2:44–66.

———. 1883. *What Social Classes Owe to Each Other*. New York: Harper & Brothers.

———. [1887]1969. "State Interference." *North American Review* 145 (August). Reprinted in his *Essays*. 2:136–49.

———. [1888]1969. "Democracy and Plutocracy." *Independent* (15 November). Reprinted in his *Essays*. 2:213–19.

———. 1889. "The Conflict of Plutocracy and Democracy." *Independent* (10 January). Reprinted in his *Essays*. 2:226–30.

———. 1890. *Andrew Jackson as a Public Man: What He Was, What Chances He Had, and What He Did With Them*. Boston: Houghton Mifflin.

———. [1890]1969. "What the 'Social Question' Is." *Independent*, (20 November), Reprinted in his *Essays*. 1:435–41.

———. [1899]1969. "The Conquest of the United States by Spain." Reprinted in his *Essays*. 2:266–303.

———. [1906]1940. *Folkways: A Study of the Sociological Importance of Usages, Manners, Customs, Mores, and Morals*. Boston: Ginn.

———. [1933]1969. "The Bequests of the Nineteenth Century to the Twentieth." *Yale Review* 22. Reprinted in his *Essays*. 1:208–35.

———. 1969. *Essays of William Graham Sumner*. Edited by Albert G. Keller and Maurice R. Davie, Hamden, Conn.: Archon Press.

Sutton, Francis X. 1982. "Rationality, Development, and Scholarship." *Social Science Research Council Items* 36.

Szasz, Ferenc. 1981. "The American Quest for Religious Certainty, 1880–1915."

In *The American Self: Myth, Ideology, and Popular Culture,* edited by Sam B. Girgus. Albuquerque: University of New Mexico Press.

Takahashi, Jere. 1982. "Japanese American Responses to Race Relations: The Formation of Nisei Perspectives." *Amerasia Journal* 9.

Takaki, Ronald T. 1971. *A Pro-Slavery Crusade: The Agitation to Re-Open the African Slave Trade.* New York: Free Press.

———. 1979. *Iron Cages: Race and Culture in Nineteenth-Century America.* New York: Alfred A. Knopf.

Tarde, G. [1899]1974. *Social Laws: An Outline of Sociology,* translated by Howard C. Warren. New York: Macmillan, 1899; New York: Arno Press, 1974.

Taussig, Frank William. 1888. "A Suggested Rearrangement of Economic Study." *Quarterly Journal of Economics* 2.

———. 1906. "The Love of Wealth and the Public Service." *Publications of the American Economic Association,* 3d ser., 7.

———. 1930. "Economics, 1871–1929." In Morison, *Development of Harvard University . . . 1869–1929.*

Taylor, Graham. [1930]1976. *Pioneering on Social Frontiers.* Chicago: University of Chicago Press, 1930; New York: Arno Press, 1976.

Taylor, Paul S. [1928–32]1970. *Mexican Labor in the United States.* University of California Publications in Economics, nos. 6–7, 1928–32; New York: Arno Press, 1970.

Taylor, Paul S., and Clark Kerr. 1935. "Uprisings on the Farms." *Survey Graphic* 24.

Taylor, Paul S., and Tom Vasey. 1936. "Historical Background of California Farm Labor." *Rural Sociology* 1.

Taylor, William R. 1930. *Cavalier and Yankee: The Old South and American National Character.* Garden City, N.Y.: Doubleday-Anchor.

Teggart, Frederick J. 1898. "The First Advocate of Free Public Libraries." *Nation* 67.

———. 1898a. "Franklin and Torrey." *Nation* 67.

———. 1898b. "The Destruction of the Alexandrian Library." *Nation* 67.

———. 1910. "The Circumstance or the Substance of History." *American Historical Review* 15.

———. 1912. "The Approaches to California." *Southwestern Historical Quarterly* 16.

———. 1916. *Prolegomena to History: The Relation of History to Literature, Philosophy, and Science.* Berkeley: University of California Press.

———. 1918. Review of Zephyrin Engelhardt, *Missions and Missionaries of California* (vols. 3–4: *Upper California,* pts. 2–3, and index to vols. 2–4). *American Historical Review* 23.

———. 1919. "Human Geography, An Opportunity for the University," *The Journal of Geography* 18.

———. 1919a. "Geography as an Aid to Statecraft: An Appreciation of Mac-Kinder's 'Democratic Ideals and Reality,'" *Geographical Review* 8.

———. 1922. "Clio." *University of California Chronicle* 24.

———. 1923. Review of Benedetto Croce, *History: Its Theory and Practice. American Historical Review* 28.

———. 1929. "Notes on 'Timeless' Sociology." *Social Forces* 7.

———. 1939. *Rome and China: A Study of Correlations in Historical Events*. Berkeley: University of California Press.

———. 1941. *The Theory and Processes of History*. Berkeley: University of California Press.

———. 1941a. "War and Civilization in the Future." *American Journal of Sociology*, 46.

———. 1942. "Causation in Historical Events." *Journal of the History of Ideas* 3.

———. 1947. "The Argument of Hesiod's *Works and Days*." *Journal of the History of Ideas* 8.

———, ed. [1924]1971. *Around the Horn to the Sandwich Islands and California, 1845–1850: Being a Personal Record Kept by Chester S. Lyman*. Freeport, N.Y.: Books for Libraries Press.

ten Broek, Jacobus, Edward N. Barnhart, and Floyd W. Matson. 1954. *Prejudice, War, and the Constitution*. Berkeley: University of California Press.

Tenney, Alvan A. 1910. "Some Recent Advances in Sociology." *Political Science Quarterly* 120.

Thernstrom, Stephan, ed. 1980. *Harvard Encyclopedia of American Ethnic Groups*. Cambridge: The Belknap Press, Harvard University Press.

Thomas, Dorothy Swaine, and Richard Nishimoto. 1946. *The Spoilage*. Vol. 1 of *Japanese-American Evacuation and Resettlement*. Berkeley: University of California Press.

Thomas, Dorothy Swaine, Charles Kikuchi, and James Sakoda. 1952. *The Salvage*. Vol. 2 of *Japanese-American Evacuation and Resettlement*. Berkeley: University of California Press.

Thomas, W. I. 1904. "The Psychology of Race Prejudice." *American Journal of Sociology* 9.

———. 1906[1974]. "The Province of Social Psychology." In Rogers, *Congress of Arts and Science*.

———. 1907. "The Significance of the Orient for the Occident." *Publications of the American Sociological Society: Papers and Proceedings* 2.

———. [1907]1974. *Sex and Society: Studies in the Social Psychology of Sex*. Chicago: University of Chicago Press, 1907; New York: Arno Press, 1974.

———. 1973. "Life History." In Baker, "Life Histories of . . . Thomas and . . . Park."

Thomas, W. I., and Florian Znaniecki. [1918–20]1958. *The Polish Peasant in Europe and America*. New York: Dover.

Thompson, Edgar T., ed. 1939. *Race Relations and the Race Problem*. Durham, N.C.: University of North Carolina Press.

Thompson, L. L. 1978. "Brief for Respondent" [in the case *Takuji Yamashita and Charles Hio Kono, Petitioners*, vs. *Grant Hinkle, as Secretary of the State of Washington*, United States Supreme Court, case no. 16567]. In Consulate of Japan, *Documental History of Law Cases Affecting Japanese in the United States, 1916–1924*. New York: Arno Press.

Thorndike, Edward L. [1939]1976. *Your City*. New York: Harcourt, Brace, 1939; New York: Arno Press, 1976.

Thwing, Charles F. 1893. "Harvard and Yale in the West." *Harvard Graduates' Magazine* 1.

———. [1911]1970. "The American Family." *Hibbert Journal* (1911); reprinted as chap. 2 of his *American Society: Interpretations of Educational and Other Forces.* Freeport, N.Y.: Books for Libraries Press.

Townsend, L. T. 1876. *The Chinese Problem.* Boston: Lee & Shepard.

Toynbee, Arnold. 1954. *A Study of History.* New York: Oxford University Press.

Trattner, Walter I. 1979. *From Poor Law to Welfare State: A History of Social Welfare in America.* 2d ed. New York: Free Press.

Troeltsch, Ernst. 1960. *The Social Teachings of the Christian Churches.* New York: Harper Torchbooks.

Trotter, Wilfred. 1916. *Instincts of the Herd in Peace and War.* London: Ernest Benn.

United States Department of the Interior, War Liquidation Unit, formerly War Relocation Authority. n.d. *People in Motion: The Postwar Adjustment of the Evacuated Japanese Americans.* Washington, D.C.: United States Government Printing Office.

Veblen, Thorstein. [1899]1973. *The Theory of the Leisure Class.* Boston: Houghton-Mifflin.

———. 1917. *An Inquiry into the Nature of Peace and the Terms of Its Perpetuation.* New York: Viking Press.

———. [1921]1965. *The Engineers and the Price System.* New York: Viking Press, 1921; New York: Augustus M. Kelley, 1965.

Vidich, Arthur J. 1980. "Inflation and Social Structure: The United States in an Epoch of Declining Abundance." *Social Problems* 27.

———. 1981. *The Political Consequences of Colonial Administration.* New York: Arno Press.

———. 1982. "Estado Actual de la Sociologia Norteamericano." *Fourth Colombian National Congress of Sociology.* Cali, Colombia, August 1982.

———. 1982. "The Moral, Economic and Political Status of Labor in American Society." *Social Research* 49.

Vidich, Arthur J., and Stanford M. Lyman. 1983. "Secular Evangelism at the University of Wisconsin." *Social Research* 50.

Vidich, Arthur J., Stanford M. Lyman, and Jeffrey C. Goldfarb. 1981. "Sociology and Society: Disciplinary Tensions and Professional Compromises." *Social Research* 48.

Viertel, John, translator. 1972. *Aspects of Sociology.* Boston: Beacon Press.

Wade, Louise C. 1964. *Graham Taylor, Pioneer for Social Justice, 1851–1938.* Chicago: University of Chicago Press.

Walzer, Michael. 1979. "Nervous Liberals." *New York Review of Books* (11 October).

Ward, Lester F. [1860–70]1935. *Young Ward's Diary: A Human and Eager Record of the Years between 1860 and 1870 as They Were Lived in the Vicinity of the Little Town of Towanda, Pennsylvania; in the Field as a Rank and File Soldier in the Union Army; and Later in the Nation's Capital, by Lester Ward, Who Became the First Great Sociologist the Country Produced.* Edited by Bernhard J. Stern. New York: C. P. Putnam's Sons.

———. [1933–37]. "The Letters of Albion W. Small to Lester F. Ward (1890–

1910). I–IV," edited by Bernhard J. Stern. *Social Forces* 12 (1933); 13 (1935); 15 (1936); 15 (1937).

———. [1883]1968. *Dynamic Sociology, or Applied Social Science as Based upon Statistical Sociology and the Less Complex Sciences.* New York: D. Appleton, 1883; New York: Johnson Reprint Corp., 1968.

———. [1892]1906. *The Psychic Factors of Civilization.* 2d ed. Boston: Ginn.

———. 1894. "A Monist Theory of Mind." *Monist* 4.

———. 1902. "Contemporary Sociology." *American Journal of Sociology* 7.

———. [1903, 1907]1970. *Pure Sociology: A Treatise on the Origin and Spontaneous Development of Society.* 2d ed. New York: Macmillan, 1903, 1907; New York: Augustus M. Kelley, 1970.

———. 1906. *Applied Sociology: A Treatise on the Conscious Improvement of Society by Society.* Boston: Ginn.

———. 1938–49. "The Ward–Ross Correspondence. I–IV," edited by Bernhard J. Stern. (1891–1912) *American Sociological Review* 3 (1938); 11 (1946); 12 (1947); 13 (1948); 14 (1949).

Washington, Booker T. 1903. Introduction to H. F. Kletzing and W. H. Crogman, *Progress of a Race, or the Remarkable Advancement of the Afro-American from the Bondage of Slavery, Ignorance and Poverty to the Freedom of Citizenship, Intelligence, Affluence, Honor and Trust.* Atlanta: J. L. Nichols.

———. 1915. "Inferior and Superior Races." *North American Review* 201.

W[ashington], H[enry] A[ugustine]. 1848. "The Social System of Virginia." *Southern Literary Messenger* 14.

Watson, J. B. 1913. "Psychology as a Behaviorist Views It." *Psychological Review* 20. Quoted in Robert I. Watson, *The Great Psychologists,* 3d ed. Philadelphia: J. B. Lippincott, 1973.

———. [1924]1970. *Behaviorism.* New York: W. W. Norton.

Wax, Rosalie H. 1971. "Fieldwork in the Japanese American Relocation Centers, 1943–1945." In her *Doing Fieldwork: Warnings and Advice.* Chicago: University of Chicago Press.

Weber, Marianne. 1975. *Max Weber: A Biography,* translated and edited by Harry Zohn. New York: John Wiley & Sons.

Weber, Max. 1930. *The Protestant Ethic and the Spirit of Capitalism,* translated by Talcott Parsons. New York: Charles Scribner's Sons.

———. 1946. "The Protestant Sects and the Spirit of Capitalism." In *From Max Weber: Essays in Sociology,* edited and translated by H. H. Gerth and C. Wright Mills. New York: Oxford University Press.

———. 1952. *Ancient Judaism,* edited and translated by Hans H. Gerth and Don Martindale. Glencoe, Ill.: Free Press.

———. 1971. "A Research Strategy for the Study of Occupational Careers and Mobility Patterns," translated by D. Hytch. In Eldridge, *Max Weber.*

———. 1975. *Roscher and Knies: The Logical Problems of Historical Economics,* translated by Guy Oakes. New York: Free Press.

Weimann, Jeanne Madeline. 1981. *The Fair Women.* Chicago: Academy Chicago.

Weinberg, Julius. 1972. *Edward Alsworth Ross and the Sociology of Progressivism.* Madison: State Historical Society of Wisconsin.

White, Ronald C., Jr., and C. Howard Hopkins. 1976. *The Social Gospel: Religion and Reform in Changing America*. Philadelphia: Temple University Press.

Whyte, William Foote. [1943]1964. *Street Corner Society: The Social Structure of an Italian Slum*. Chicago: University of Chicago Press.

Wiebe, Robert H. 1962. *Businessmen and Reform: A Study of the Progressive Movement*. Cambridge, Mass.: Harvard University Press.

Wieder, D. L. 1974. *Language and Social Reality: The Case of Telling the Convict Code*. The Hague: Mouton.

Wiener, Norbert. [1950]1967. *The Human Use of Human Beings*. New York: Avon Books.

Wiley, Norbert. 1979. "The Rise and Fall of Dominating Theories in American Sociology." In Snizek et al., *Contemporary Issues in Theory and Research*.

Williams, William Appleman. 1980. *Empire as a Way of Life: An Essay on the Causes and Character of America's Present Predicament along with a Few Thoughts about an Alternative*. New York: Oxford University Press.

Wilson, E. O. 1979. *On Human Nature*. New York: Bantam Books.

————. 1980. *Sociobiology*. Abridged ed. Cambridge, Mass.: Belknap Press of Harvard University Press.

Wilson, William J. 1978. *The Declining Significance of Race*. Chicago: University of Chicago Press.

Wirth, Louis. [1928]1956. *The Ghetto*. Chicago: University of Chicago Press, Phoenix Books.

————. [1940]1974. *Eleven Twenty-Six: A Decade of Social Science Research*. Chicago: University of Chicago Press, 1940; New York: Arno Press, 1974.

Wiseman, Jacqueline P. 1970. *Stations of the Lost: The Treatment of Skid Row Alcoholics*. Englewood Cliffs, N.J.: Prentice-Hall.

Wish, Harvey. 1941. "George Frederick Holmes and the Genesis of American Sociology." *American Journal of Sociology* 46.

————. 1941a. "Stephen Pearl Andrews, American Pioneer Sociologist." *Social Forces* 19.

————. [1943]1962. *George Fitzhugh, Propagandist of the Old South*. Baton Rouge: Louisiana State University Press. 1943; Gloucester, Mass.: Peter Smith.

————, ed. 1960. *Ante-Bellum: Writings of George Fitzhugh and Hinton Rowan Helper on Slavery*. New York: Capricorn Books.

Wofford, Harris. 1980. *Of Kennedys and Kings: Making Sense of the Sixties*. New York: Farrar, Straus, & Giroux.

Wohl, R. Richard. 1969. "The 'Country Boy' Myth and Its Place in American Urban Culture: The Nineteenth-Century Contribution." Edited by Moses Rischin. *Perspectives in American History* 3.

Woods, Robert A. 1893. "The University Settlement Idea." In *Philanthropy and Social Progress: Seven Essays Delivered before the School of Applied Ethics at Plymouth, Mass. during the Session of 1892*. New York: Thomas Y. Crowell.

Wright, Gwendolyn. 1980. *Moralism and the Model Home: Domestic Architecture and Cultural Conflict in Chicago, 1873–1913*. Chicago: University of Chicago Press.

Wyman, Anne C. 1982. "Does Sociology Do Anybody Any Good?" *San Francisco Sunday Examiner and Chronicle* (17 January 1982).

Young, Donald R. [1921]1975. Introduction to the "republished edition" of W. I. Thomas, Robert E. Park, and Herbert A. Miller. *Old World Traits Transplanted.* Montclair, N.J.: Patterson Smith.

———. [1937]1972. *Research Memorandum on Minority Peoples in the Depression.* New York: Social Science Research Council, 1937; New York: Arno Press, 1972.

Young, Kimball. 1935. "Review of the Payne Fund Studies." *American Journal of Sociology* 40.

———, ed. 1931. *Social Attitudes.* New York: Henry Holt.

Zarchin, Michael M. 1964. *Glimpses of Jewish Life in San Francisco.* 2d revised ed. Oakland: Judah L. Magnes Memorial Museum.

Index

Aaron, Daniel: revolt against Puritanism, 2

Achievement: and concept of economic motivation, 83

Action: Mead's theory, 271

Action theory: Comteanism in, 83; positivism in, 297

Adorno, Theodor W.: and attitudinal surveys, 210

Advertising: and behaviorism, 97

Agassiz, Louis: creationist theory of, 250–51, 265n5, 266n6

Alexander, Jeffrey C.: and the restoration of systems theory, 301–02

Alienation: problems in resolving, 306; and sociology, 309n8

Allen, Joseph Henry: and Comteanism in America, 3

Altruism: trend toward, 73; decline of, 295

America: pre-Civil War, 1; changes in social structure after *1865*, 2; political chaos in, 42; as a social system, 295

American Civil War: and crumbling values, 37

American Comteanism: and Protestant intellectuals, 3; in *1855*, 16. *See also* Comteanism

American Economic Association: and statistical social science, 140; founded by Ely, 154

American Federation of Labor: anti-Asiatic policies of, 156, 245n4

American Home Mission Society: in California, 235

American Journal of Sociology: 174; and Christian sociology, 181; and "era of sociology," 182

American Museum of Natural History, 181

American Society for Christian Sociology: Christianization of social science, 154

American Sociological Review: and quantitative sociology, 174

American Sociological Society: and statistical redemption, 138; and coordination of social science, 140; and Bernard's anti-eastern sentiments, 173; Lundberg's presidency, 176; Vincent's presidency, 180

American Statistical Association: and statistical social science, 138, 140

Andrews, Stephen Pearl: American Comtean, 16–17; radicalism of, 165n8

Androcracy: defined, 30

Angell, Robert Cooley: social psychology of, 164n1

Anglo-Saxons: myth of superiority, 117; civic participation of, 283. *See also* Assimilation; Race Relations

Anthropology: major problems in, at Harvard, 57. *See also* Ethnography

Anthropomorphism: in Goffman's social psychology, 273–74; and worldly grace, 274

Anthroposociology: in Hughes' sociology, 15; and sociobiology, 86n13

Anti-Semitism: in Carver's sociology, 81; at Harvard, 86n10; in Ross' sociology, 158, 164n2, 165n5; of Lundberg, 176

Applied psychology: in Ward's view, 22

Aptitudes: faith in, 92–94

Art: and intellect, 24

Aryans: in Ward's sociology, 29

Asceticism: Christian indifference to nature, 21; in Puritanism, 108. *See also* Calvinism; Protestantism; Puritanism

Ashley, William James: economics and sociology of, 70

Asiatics: exclusion of, 156, 158, 162; racism against, 164n4–65; in assimilation theory, 236–41, 247n14; and social distance scale, 238; and civic participation, 283. *See also* Assimilation; Race Relations; *and specific ethnic groups*

Assimilation: and social karyokinesis, 28–30; and full social membership, 98–99; and "Kultur" concept, 100n5, 100n6, 189; and anti-assimilation, 158; and consensus, 189; of American blacks, 192–93; Park's theory of, 205–06, 213, 246n8; Blumer's repudiation of, 209–13; Parsons's concept of inclusion, 213; and California Protestantism, 236–37; failure of utopia, 237–42; studies of Chinese in America, 237, 238, 245n3, 246n8, 246n10; studies of Japanese in America,

Quakers: in Sumner's sociology, 38
Quetelet, Lambert Adolphe Jacques: father of statistical sociology, 286

Race: as a central theme in social science, 17; Comte on, 17n1; and inequality, 24, 27–30; and social evolution, 27; and intelligence, 27, 253; and utopia, 29–30; Ward's concept of world race, 30; and philosophy of lynching, 35n3; and eugenics, 80, 254, 283; as predestined, 157; and community, 203; dialectic with class, 205–06; and class struggle, 206; and stratification, 210–11; and industrialization, 213–15; designification of, 214; and religion, 235–37; and human nature, 239; regeneration of, 242–44
Race relations: sociology of, 28; and assimilation theory, 28–29, 195–93, 209, 237–41, 245n3, 246n8, 283, 284; between blacks and whites, to Sumner, 48n4; Carver's typology of, 81–82; racism against Asiatics, 156, 164n4; exclusion of Asiatics from secular covenant, 162; and capitalism, 202; moral foundation for, 202–05; and Moravian Church, 204; and Protestantism, 204; the uncovenanted community, 209–13; not solved by eschatology, 210; and domination, 211; and politics, 211; and public opinion, 211; and civil rights, 212; rationalization of, 213–15; situational studies of, 230n6; types of prejudice, 230n7; studies of Chinese in America, 237–38, 246n8, 246n10; studies of Japanese in America, 237–41, 246n10; cycle of, 238; and social distance scale, 238; anti-Chinese sentiments, 245n4; problems as instinctive, 269–70; and social conflict, 285. *See also* Asiatics; Assimilation; Ethnicity; Eugenics; Inequality; Race; Races; *and individual theorists and ethnic groups*
Races: non-white and suffering, 25; amalgamation of, 27; extermination of, 164n4, 177n1. *See also* Race; Race Relations
Rape: Ward's philosophy of, 35n3; as justification for lynching, 48n4
Rationalism: and pragmatism, 67; and natural science, 74. *See also* Rationality; Rationalization

Rationality: and American social problems, 4; and casuistry, 11; of the state, 12; in Ward's sociology, 20–21; in charity, 85n3; and social order, 105–06, 285; in consciousness, 109; and social engineering, 121; equated with quantitative research, 126; and reformist movement, 128; and human nature, 136; absence of in crowds, 224; and fortune, 281–82. *See also* Rationalism; Rationalization
Rationalization: of morals, 56; in economic theory, 77; of election, 77; of Puritanism, 77; of social research, 126–27, 134–48; of philanthropy, 132–33; and stewardship, 137; of sociology, 137, 163, 286; of medicine, 143; of the Prussian army, 199; and race relations, 213–15; of methodology, 256–57; and industry, 257–58; political, 261; in Weber's theory, 264–65; of the self, 273; of state and civil society, 286; of sociology's failures, 299; as a general trend, 306–07. *See also* Rationalism; Rationality
Ratzenhofer, Gustav: assimilation theory of, 100n5; interest-conflict theory of, 183–84, 189–90
Raushenbush, Winifred: and assimilation theory, 238
Reason: in world civilization, 257. *See also* Rationalism; Rationality; Rationalization
Recreation: utility of, to Ogburn, 136
Redemption: in social theory, 70
Redfield, Robert: as a sociologist, 207n7
Reference group: theory of, 110, 272
Reform: moral, through social policy, 129–31
Reformation: and individualism, 111
Reformism: and Protestantism, 151. *See also* Meliorism
Regionalism: and race relations, 212
Religion: and American social science, 17; as an obstacle to progress, 20; Ward's confrontation with, 20–23; to disappear as a social constraint, 21; formalization of, 22; secularization of, 68; distinguished from theology, 168; and race, 204, 235–37. *See also* Calvinism; Protestantism; Puritanism; Rationalization; Secularization
Reverie: Blumer's concept of, 228–29
Revivalism: nineteenth century, 60–61; and the Sunday School Movement, 63;